_f_P

How Hollywood Learned

to Stop Worrying and

Love the Summer

BLOCKBUSTER

TOM SHONE

FREE PRESS
New York London Toronto Sydney

*f*P

FREE PRESS
A Division of Simon & Schuster, Inc.
1230 Avenue of the Americas
New York, NY 10020

For information about special discounts for bulk purchases,
please contact Simon & Schuster Special Sales at
1-800-456-6798 or business@simonandschuster.com

Book design by Ellen R. Sasahara

Manufactured in the United States of America

1   3   5   7   9   10   8   6   4   2

Library of Congress Cataloging-in-Publication Data
Shone, Tom, 1967–
Blockbuster : How Hollywood learned to stop worrying and love the summer /
Tom Shone.
p. cm.
Includes bibliographical references and index.
1. Motion pictures—United States. 2. Motion picture industry—United States—
Finance. I. Title: Blockbuster. II. Title: How Hollywood learned to stop worrying
and love the summer. III. Title.

PN1993.5.U6S4927 2004
791.43'0973—dc22   2004057679

ISBN 0-7432-3568-1

FOR GENEVIEVE

CONTENTS

Introduction   THE BOYS OF SUMMER   1

ACT I: 1975–1983
WAKING GIANTS

Chapter 1   PANIC ON THE 4TH OF JULY   23

Chapter 2   EMPIRE STATE EXPRESS   44

Chapter 3   HALLOWEEN FOR GROWN-UPS   65

Chapter 4   THE EDUCATION OF ELLEN RIPLEY   82

Chapter 5   FIRST ACTION HERO   102

Chapter 6   MORNING IN AMERICA   122

ACT II: 1984–1993
COMETH THE TITANS

Chapter 7   TIME TRAVELERS INC.   141

Chapter 8   RIPLEY REDUX   161

Chapter 9   WAR ZONES, HIGH CONCEPTS   174

Chapter 10   THE LONG DARK NIGHT   185

Chapter 11   EXTINCTION   199

Chapter 12   PLANET HOLLYWOOD   215

ACT III: 1994–2004

DECLINE AND FALL

Chapter 13 OOPS, APOCALYPSE!   233

Chapter 14 STARING INTO THE ABYSS   249

Chapter 15 DOES SIZE MATTER?   264

Chapter 16 THE EMPIRE STRIKES BACK   278

Chapter 17 UN-AMERICAN ACTIVITIES   293

Conclusion RETURN OF THE KINGS   307

Acknowledgments   315

Sources   317

Bibliography   322

Picture Credits   326

Index   327

"All Rome today is at the circus. The public has long since cast off its cares; the people that once bestowed commands, consulships, legions, and all else, now meddles no more and craves just two things: bread and games."

—Juvenal, *Satires* no. 10, second century A.D.

"Everyone's gone to the movies."

—Steely Dan, *Katy Lied*, 1975 A.D.

INTRODUCTION

THE BOYS OF SUMMER

When he was five, Steven Spielberg was taken by his father to see *The Greatest Show on Earth,* Cecil B. DeMille's movie about the circus—except he didn't hear his father say the word "movie," only the word "circus." He'd never seen a movie before, but he knew what to expect from a circus: elephants, lions, ringmaster, clowns . . . After a wait in line for an hour and a half, they entered the theater, and he laid eyes on the row upon row of chairs, all folded up, in front of a blank screen, "nothing but a flat piece of white cardboard, a canvas, and I look at the canvas and suddenly a movie comes on and it's *The Greatest Show on Earth.*" He thought it the Worst Swindle in Town, couldn't believe his father had done this to him. "'Gee, that's not fair,' he thought, 'I wanted to see three-dimensional characters and all this was was flat shadows, flat surfaces.' I was disappointed by everything after that. I didn't trust anybody. . . . I never felt life was good enough so I had to embellish it."

The embellishments took many forms, each requiring the sort of improvisational skills known only to those growing up in suburban Cincinnati in the fifties. There was the time he rigged his mother's pressure cooker to explode, splattering the kitchen with food, or the time he tossed one of her cherry pies to the ceiling and watched as all the pie filling glooped to the floor. He was fascinated by anything that had the texture of blood—cherries, ketchup—which he could then use

1

to smear over the walls or the heads of his sister's dolls. He was a scrawny kid—crew cut, ears out to here, like the kid on the cover of *Mad* magazine—and ravenously curious, endlessly bombarding his father with questions relating to fire engines and things blowing up. Teachers worried about him; he seemed to go in such fits and starts, always starting one thing, then, getting bored, moving on to the next. "I didn't know what the hell he was," said his mother later. "Steven wasn't exactly cuddly. What he was was scary."

It was when the family moved from Cincinnati to Phoenix that the boy's experiments in pandemonium kicked up a notch. The landscape itself promised so much: on the one hand a suburban sprawl of lawns, backyards, and sprinklers, and edging it, the Arizona desert with its scorpions and Gila monsters. The perfect place to lock yourself in the upstairs bathroom, until the Phoenix fire brigade were summoned—great red trucks tearing up and down the quiet suburban streets, much to the admiration of his neighbor's children. "I thought it was really neat," said one, "seeing the fire department coming through the windows and everything." By this time Spielberg had rediscovered the movie theater, and made the secondary, but equally important discovery that they needn't be just for watching movies. If they had balcony seats, for instance, they were also a perfect place from which to projectile-vomit a mixture of peas, cream cheese, and milk, as Spielberg did on the audience who had come to see Irwin Allen's *The Lost World* in 1960.

The only thing that seemed to induce anything like calm in the boy was TV. He would soak up as many episodes of *The Twilight Zone* and *Science Fiction Theater* as he could, and when his parents tried to limit his intake, he would sneak down at night and stick his eye right up to the snow on the RCA nineteen-inch screen, seeking ghostly communion with the black-and-white images that flickered past. "I was this far away from the TV set and there would always be some out-of-the-way channel, some far-off channel that was getting its signal through the station that wasn't broadcasting and there would be ghosts and images of some broadcasting station five hundred miles away."

Seven hundred miles away, in Modesto, California, the young George Lucas was tuned into much the same wavelength—a pixilated blur of

Adventure Theater, Flash Gordon serials, and Crusader Rabbit cartoons—except this time, the TV was to be found around at his neighbor's house. This was the mid-fifties and TVs had only just reached Modesto, a strangely disoriented sort of place, sitting in the middle of the flattest California landscape, like a Midwestern town that had blown too far west. Come 6:00 p.m. and off the boy would scoot to his neighbor's house to watch whatever was on. When Lucas was ten, his parents bought their own TV set and saw their son practically disappear into it. It was large and rotatable, which meant he could watch it from any angle in the living room. "Movies had extremely little effect on me when I was growing up," he would say later. "I hardly ever went, and when I did it was to meet girls. Television had a much larger effect."

He was a tiny kid. At age six he weighed only thirty-five pounds—a peanut. Fretful and anxious, he had a midlife crisis when he was eight—"What is God?" he wondered. "But more than that, what is reality? What is this?"—and was never very enthusiastic about the answers. But he loved TV, comics—had a collection of over six hundred—and building models. Not just puny little model planes, either, but complete ersatz environments fashioned from old dollhouses and cardboard boxes, using milk cartons for sofas and lipstick tubes for lamps. Unlike Spielberg, Lucas was a finisher—always seeing every task through to its meticulous conclusion. He built a haunted house that he then charged the local kids to come see; and when some new phone lines were laid, he took the giant wooden spool the technicians had left behind and converted it into a miniature roller-coaster ride for his model cars. "That was my whole life," he said. "I lived, ate, breathed cars. That was everything to me." He decided he was going to be a racing driver, performing victory laps for the roaring crowds at Le Mans, Monte Carlo, and Indianapolis, and when he was fifteen, his parents bought him his first real car, a tiny Fiat Bianchina with a two-cylinder engine—"a sewing machine motor" he complained. "It was a dumb little car. What could I do with that?" He found, though, that he could take curves much better than the bigger cars, and soon you couldn't tear him away from the go-kart track behind the foreign car garage on Main Street. "We'd be going like a bat out of hell," said one friend. "George could really drive. He was really good at that."

❑ ❑ ❑

When the Chicago White Sox won the American League pennant in
the fall of 1959—their first title in forty years—the city fathers were so
excited they switched on all the air-raid sirens, and Robert Zemeckis,
then aged seven, sat back and drank in the whole crazy spectacle: "My
parents and all their friends rushing out onto the street, wondering
what was happening. It was surreal; everyone was standing around,
convinced that we'd been invaded from Mars." In the late fifties, Richard
Daley was mayor of Chicago, then a termite hill of political corruption
and the perfect place for a naturally suspicious kid like Zemeckis to
sharpen his cynicism. He noticed that when it snowed, the local alder-
man always got his drive plowed first on the street. Everything seemed
like a ruse to him, a stunt, a trick—or else just a straight kick in the
head, neither good nor bad, just volatile, wild: ain't that something?

You could always track him down in a movie theater: he was the
wiseacre who sat in the front row, going, "That guy's not really dead,"
or "That looks fake." He saw *Death in Venice,* which he thought "one of
the most boring movies ever made." But when he saw Gene Hackman
get shot in the head in *Bonnie and Clyde,* it had a blistering effect on
him. He thought, "The director is doing something to me. How did he
do that to me?" He always wanted to know how things were done. The
films he loved best were movies like *The Blob* and *13 Ghosts,* movies
which gave you a shock through your seat, or you watched through
3-D glasses: such gimmicks seemed more honest to him, somehow,
more up-front about cinema's innate powers of trickery. He watched
The Tingler, and loved it when Vincent Price announced "The Tingler
is in the theater," only to have the house lights in the cinema go dead.
"And the screen we're watching goes completely black, and we all start
screaming. . . . It was absolutely great."

Growing up in Chippewa, Canada, with Niagara Falls thundering
away in the distance, James Cameron used to lull himself to sleep by
waging imaginary galactic wars. The only problem was, the special
effects sucked and the score wasn't up to scratch: "I remember lying in
bed at night and listening to awful music while choreographing epic

space battles in my head. I was imagining both the battle itself on a huge screen and ways to film it. This was frustrating given the lack of technical knowledge I had at this point."

There being a shortage of people Cameron could fire, aged ten, he had to content himself with watching other people's movies and giving them a dressing down instead. He was "the archetypal small-town movie fan," spending his lunch money on movies on the weekend and living off Twinkies during the week. He caught one of the *Godzilla*s and thought it the worst film he'd ever seen, then Kubrick's *2001: A Space Odyssey,* which was a bit more like it. It made him dizzy—"I just couldn't figure out how he did all that stuff." Like Lucas, he was a comics reader—learning how to draw by copying the Marvel drafts-men of *Spider-Man, X-Men, The Hulk*—and a model builder, once sending some mice over the edge of the falls in a small submersible made from old mayonnaise jars, an Erector Set, and a paint bucket. And like Spielberg, he was a dedicated enemy of the public peace, building catapults that launched rockets at the neighbors' front lawns, and, most famously, a hot-air balloon out of an old dry-cleaning bag and some candles that flew right down the street. "It actually got to the point where the local fire department got called out to chase it," remembered his brother Mike. "We ended up making it into the papers because people thought it was a UFO."

The idea that you should look for clues to the identity of tomorrow's box office titans by checking in the records of your local fire brigade hasn't really caught on in Hollywood, but maybe it should, for apart from Spielberg's and Cameron's skirmish with their local fire trucks, there was little else to suggest that this generation would go on to direct the great landmarks in the next twenty-five years of cinema. Their first contact with the medium was entirely lacking the sort of hushed reverence one expects of one's auteurs, instead marked by dis-appointment and impatience: the movies seemed like just so many flat shadows, flickering on cardboard. They longed for something more visceral, more athletic, something capable of punching through the screen, through the fourth wall, and raising the public alarms outside the theater: films with all the excitement of firetrucks hurtling down your street. For the most part, they got their kicks elsewhere, in comics and on TV, wherever they could find them. There was no "popular culture" as we know it today. That phrase, with its charge of punkish, publicly endorsed glamour, was decades off. It was just "junk" or "trash" and to track it down required patience, dedication, and cunning, like being an enthusiast of postwar Hungarian cinema today. You had to go around to your neighbor's house, like Lucas, or sneak down at night after your parents had gone to bed, like Spielberg, and if that failed, then there was nothing else for it, you simply had to gather together your mayonnaise jars and telephone cable spools, and build your own thrills yourself. They were the boys who built pop culture in their backyards.

Both Zemeckis and Cameron, coming of age just a few years later, had things slightly easier, with Zemeckis soaking up the horror films of William Castle, then in his prime with *The Tingler* and *House on Haunted Hill;* while Cameron availed himself of the portfolio of characters loosed by Marvel Comics in the early sixties—the Fantastic Four, the X-Men, Spider-Man—but even so, it was slim pickings. "The seventies were the last decade where movies were being made by people who didn't grow up on television," says Bob Gale, Zemeckis's writing partner on the *Back to the Future* movies. "Now my daughter is fourteen years old and she watches *Friends* and *I Love Lucy* and everything in between, *Laverne and Shirley,* all these different eras are coexisting in her brain, which is very different from the experience of my generation, which was deep, structured, rigid: once a show was off the air it was off the air. If a movie was out of release that was it, you didn't see it again. I remember, they would bring back *The Godfather* and Bob and I would go see it every night because we didn't know the next chance we'd get."

Bob Gale's daughter has things easy, you have to say. The dedicated thrill-seeker, these days, doesn't have to be that dedicated, and doesn't have to do that much seeking. What with their *Terminator* DVDs and their *Back to the Future* reruns, their *Indiana Jones* box sets and their *Star Wars* toys, their *Alien* video games and their tickets to the nearest *Jurassic Park* theme park, they're sitting pretty. The backyard is in their front room. They can download, plug in, rent, buy, surf, and sample thrills that are just hanging there, ready for the taking. Nestled within a spaghetti junction of wires and cords, leads and cables, they are treated like the consumer kings they most assuredly are—the target of a billion-dollar entertainment industry that hops at their feet, desperate to catch their eye. Should they unplug themselves and saunter on down to the movie theater, a rotation of summer blockbusters will process past; if their heart is softened by partisanship or pity, they can keep tabs on the fates of these movies by tracking their grosses online; but ultimately, the fate of these behemoths will be decided by them, much in the way that the fate of the gladiators lay at the feet of the crowd at the Colosseum, where, in the words of historian Jerome Carcopino, the caesars "exhausted their ingenuity to provide the public with more festivals than any people, in any country, at any time, has ever seen."

The caesars never lived to see the blockbuster movie season in America—one long canyon run, stretching between Memorial Day and Labor Day, into which the studios set loose one $150 million behemoth after another, in the dim hopes of finding public favor. Just as it was in Rome, the second-most-popular spectator sport is not watching these spectacles, but watching the crowds who have come to watch the spectacles, and ruing the imminent decline of the West. "Such sights are for the young," sighed Pliny the Elder. "These and similar things prevent anything memorable or serious being done in Rome," agreed Cicero. So, too, with today's blockbuster demolition derby, whose ever-increasing intensity shakes our more moralistic critics to their furthermost fillings. "The place where 'magic' is supposed to occur has seemed a lifeless pit of torn velour, garish anonymity, and spilled Pepsi," film critic David Thomson has written. "The medium has sunk beyond anything we dreamed, leaving us stranded, a race of dreamers." Writing on the centenary of cinema in 1998, Susan Sontag added her voice to Thomson's jeremiad: "Cinema's hundred years seem to have the shape of a life cycle: an inevitable birth, the steady accumulation of glories, and the onset, in the last decade, of an ignominious, irreversible decline." So go the cries of our modern-day Juvenals: *all Rome is at the circus, such sights are for the young, nothing but bread and games.*

The industry's boosters, on the other hand, point to the ever faster blur of broken records—*The Lost World* beats *Jurassic Park*, *Men in Black* beats *The Lost World*, *Spider-Man* beats *Men in Black*, *The Matrix*

Reloaded beats *Spider-Man*—and certainly, if you look at the list of all-time box office blockbusters, you'll find the block crammed to busting with movies released from the last five years or so. Cameron's *Titanic* leads from the front, prowline proudly jutting forward, closely followed by Lucas's *The Phantom Menace* and Spielberg's *Jurassic Park*. In the top fifty, a staggering twenty films are from the last four years, another twenty-three from the nineties, leaving only seven places for an entire century of cinema to fight over. The eighties get a showing of four films, the seventies three, but as for anything released before *The Exorcist* in 1973, well, I don't know how to tell you this but sit down and pour yourself a stiff drink. Everything else is gone, the fifties vanished, the forties a rumor, the Golden Age of Hollywood, *kerplooey*. Tomorrow may be another day, but for this list, it's yesterday that's having a few problems.

In fact, it's the list that has a problem, and it's a big one: it takes no account of inflation—a dangerous thing to do with box office records, which are nothing if not the love child of rapacious inflation and an impressionable dollar. Adjust the list to today's ticket prices and it's a very different story, with *Titanic* dropping 5 places to 6th position, *The Phantom Menace* plummeting 16 places to 19th, *Jurassic Park* 12 places to 17th, *Forrest Gump* 6 places to 22nd—and they're the lucky ones. Of films from the last fifteen years, only a couple more survive, *Spider-Man* clinging on by his sticky fingertips at 35, and *Return of the King* just avoiding the fiery Pit of Mordor at 47. All the rest—all the sound and fury of *Independence Day* and *Twister,* the bluster and bombast of *Armageddon* and *Pearl Harbor*—are wiped from the map. It's their turn to be history. It's like Czechoslovakia after the Velvet Revolution, all the communist hard-liners on the run while the dissidents return in weary triumph. A big welcome back, if you please, for James Bond (*Thunderball, Goldfinger*), and for Walt Disney (*Snow White, 101 Dalmatians, Fantasia, The Jungle Book, Sleeping Beauty, Bambi, Pinocchio*). A big hand, too, for *Butch Cassidy and the Sundance Kid,* and that other dynamic duo, *Mary Poppins* and *Ben-Hur.* The fifties now sweep back with seven films, as do the sixties. The forties are now represented by four films; hell, there's even a film from the thirties in there. Only one, mind you, but what a strike, in at number one again, after all these years: *Gone With the Wind.* Even bigger news, though, is the massive comeback staged by the seventies, now represented by a dozen films—including *Airport, Jaws, The Towering Inferno, Love Story, The Sting, Star Wars, Grease,* and *The Godfather.* Who would have thought it? After all this time: the seventies turned out to be the golden age of the blockbuster, the era in which the ziggurat that is popular cinema reached its gleaming zenith.

This is not the story we have been told. The story we have been told—in book after book, and in article after article—has it that the seventies, far from being the golden age of the blockbuster, were the golden age of the American art house, cut down in its prime when the age of the blockbuster dawned at the end of it. In the early seventies, we weren't supposed to be queuing up to watch über-schlock like *Love Story* and *Airport,* we were supposed to be huddling in respectfully small numbers around films like *The Last Movie* and *The Last Picture Show* and wondering if their titles would come true when studio squares caught on and busted us. We weren't supposed to be forging such mass megahits as *The Exorcist* and *The Sting,* we were supposed to be comparing notes on whether Robert Altman or Arthur Penn had more artfully disabused us of our expectations as a mass audience, and as for *Jaws* and *Star Wars,* they weren't supposed to emerge from a crowded field of a dozen other blockbusters, they were supposed to rear up and bite everyone on the ass from out of nowhere. This certainly is the story we were told by Peter Biskind in his book *Easy Riders, Raging Bulls,* which ends with the great auteurs of the seventies numb with shock at their Judas-like betrayal by Lucas in 1977. "*Star Wars* was in, Spielberg was in. We were finished," Martin Scorsese told Biskind. "*Star Wars* swept all the chips off the table," complained William Friedkin. "What happened was like when McDonald's got a foothold, the taste for good food just disappeared . . . everything has gone back toward a big sucking hole."

This is, if you like, the "Magic Bullet" theory of modern film history: the conviction, shared by almost everyone—but particularly those, like Friedkin, who had a film opening the same week as *Star Wars*—that all it took was a single shot from Lucas's laser cannons to bring down the Camelot that was American film in the seventies. In which case, Biskind's book was the era's Warren Report, a prodigious body of research marshaled toward the end of straightforward frame-up. It certainly didn't feel like the death of cinema at the time—*A Star Is Born* felt far worse—and as for being dragged into a big sucking hole, well yes, but in a good way. I was ten when *Star Wars* came out. It first appeared on my radar in the form of some publicity stills, which appeared in a British comic called *2000 A.D.*, and which caused me to adopt a posture closely modeled on that of a pointer dog who has just caught wind of his first pheasant—a position I held until my parents caved in and took me up to London to see the thing. That I remember. Of the film itself, I remember nothing—I must have been in some sort of shock—but I do remember the second time I saw it, and the third and fourth time—that was when I watched two screenings, back to back, using one ticket, shrinking down into my seat and hoping the ushers didn't see me—and by the eighth or ninth time, I had the film pretty well etched onto the back of my skull, and could replay it at will, on my walks to and from school; which is just as well because by then the forces of grown-up cinemagoing had gathered, staged their countercoup, and forced the local cinema manager to put something else on. It was back to orangutans and CB radios.

This story is not uncommon, as a quick glance at the vast fan literature that surrounds *Star Wars* will tell you. In his essay in the collection *A Galaxy Not So Far Away,* novelist Jonathan Lethem reveals that he saw the film twenty-one times that summer and only stopped at twenty-one because the number seemed "safely ridiculous and extreme . . . yet stopping at only twenty seemed too mechanically round. Adding one more felt plausibly arbitrary, more realistic." You begin to see what Friedkin's *Sorcerer* or any other of the other films released that year were up against, if fans called it a day at twenty-one simply in the interests of psychological *realism*. So if anyone killed the American film industry, let's be clear about this: it was me and Lethem, and the millions of other kids just like us, who gathered together in the summer of 1977, seized our chance, and staged a coup d'etat of our local movie theaters, thus launching Hollywood, in Biskind's words, on its course toward "infantilizing the audience . . . overwhelming him and her with sound and spectacle, obliterating irony, aesthetic self-consciousness, and critical reflection." Believe me, this took some work. Those suckers don't go down overnight. The toy manufacturers Kenner had, for example, been caught napping. Instead of Luke Skywalker action figures, all you could buy was a voucher that promised you Luke Skywalker action figures in the not-too-distant future. This didn't matter, though, because I set about merchandising the film on my own: I made a Jawa costume out of an old sack, a nylon stocking, and some LEGO car headlights; I made a Luke Skywalker costume out of a judo tunic—I actually enrolled in a judo class and turned up for lesson one, solely in order to get my hands on the kit—and I built little dioramas for the action figures, when they arrived, consisting of a cardboard box filled with some sand that a friend's mother had brought back inside a tourist knickknack from Tunisia, which of course was where *Star Wars* had been filmed.

Whatever else this tells you—don't let your son's friends loose on your tourist knickknacks—it shows you that the merchandising of *Star Wars* was not part of some Machiavellian bid to turn movies into toys: *Star Wars* was going to get turned into a toy by me and my friends whether it liked it or not. It was what you did with *Star Wars:* you turned it into a toy, so you could keep playing with the movie in your head, as Lucas had played with it in his head, in the years before he got to make it, sat in boring, flat Modesto while he dreamed up ways of escape. That was how *Star Wars* felt, too, arriving in our backyards like the droids do in Luke's—as a clarion call to adventure, an invitation to another, impossibly glamorous universe where movies like *Star Wars* happened all the time.

Which is, of course, roughly what happened. Was there any better time to be young and thrill-hungry and going to the movies? The years that followed were all rather glorious. I suspect that in time, the generation who came of age in the early blockbuster era will come to be regarded with much the same hushed respect that attends those who caught the Beatles when they were seventeen. What a grand piece of historical luck it was to be in your early teens when *Raiders of the Lost Ark* came out—when Spielberg and Lucas were in their prime and the very act of going to the movies seemed to come with its own brassily rousing John Williams score. Later on, we would learn to cuss and curse the infantilization of the American film industry, just like everyone else, but back then we were too busy infantilizing it to notice. We sat there like dauphin princes, while an entire industry devoted the best minds of a generation—the best directors, the best writers—to the task of making movies that stood a slim chance of finding our favor. Is there a more exquisite piece of narrative clockwork in modern cinema than *Back to the Future?* They spent *three years* writing it—and here it was laid beneath the feet of squalling fourteen-year-olds, like a Fabergé football, or a filigree-silver chewing gum wrapper—24-karat popcorn. As for *The Terminator,* opinion is still divided on its exact contribution to the cause of World Cinema, but one thing is clear: anyone who thinks that but for the example of Lucas and Spielberg, James Cameron would have hung fire and called it a day—like the wallflower we know him to be—is dreaming. If *Star Wars* and *Jaws* hadn't done it, then *The Terminator* would have, and if *The Terminator* hadn't, then *Top Gun* or *Die Hard,* and if not them, then we had plenty more where those came from. It was going to happen. We were too many.

"Steven and I come from the visceral generation," said Lucas in 1997, when *Star Wars* was rereleased, "one of the things we tapped into—not just Steven and I, but our whole sixties generation—is that we don't come from an intellectual generation. We enjoyed the emotional highs we got from movies and realized that you could crank up the adrenaline to a level way beyond what people were doing." If Spielberg and Lucas did jump-start a revolution, it is one that has long since passed its makers. As much separates *Jaws* and *Star Wars* from today's blockbusters as once separated them from *The Sound of Music.* It's doubtful, in fact, whether either film would get released in today's filmmaking climate. "*Star Wars* would get pounded today. Some executive would get to the point where Darth Vader is revealed as Luke's father and he would say, 'Give me a break'" said Willard Huyck, co-writer of *The Empire Strikes Back,* in 1997. The rerelease of *Jaws* prompted similar thoughts from its makers. Says Richard Zanuck, its producer, "Steven and I have talked a couple of times recently about had we had the ability to do a CGI shark, we probably wouldn't have made as good a picture. It would have been too perfect and we would have used it too much. The fact is we intended to show the shark in the first scene with the girl. We didn't have it, so in a weird way because we didn't have the tools we had a better picture. We had to invent things to keep the shark alive."

"Times have changed," says Spielberg now. "It's like when the first 747s landed at Los Angeles International Airport, everybody thought flying through the sky was the greatest marvel they had ever seen—floating through the air, seemingly in slow motion. Today we never even look at 747s. They're a dime a dozen, and it's that way with the blockbuster. If there was one blockbuster every three years, it meant a lot more than when you have a blockbuster every three weeks. Everybody tends to go for the bleachers when they're hitting, everyone wants to be Sammy Sosa now, or McGwire, when they're batting and there's nothing wrong with that. It's just that audiences are starting to accept movies, some of which aren't really very good. It's the job of each of these studios to market these movies as the must-see movie of the year, so they go after blockbuster status by creating a grand illusion. Now sometimes they've got a real engine behind that grand illusion, meaning the movie is damned good and the audience will say they got their money's worth. Other times the audience comes on the promise of seeing something they've never seen before and it becomes just another sci-fi action yarn, and they feel disappointed, but it doesn't stop them coming back next week to see if the next studio can keep the same promise."

To some, this will call to mind the scene in *Indiana Jones and the Last Crusade* in which Indy, having plummeted over the cliff on the back of a tank, reappears behind his grieving father to wonder what the fuss is all about. But then one of the curious things about the idea that we are all plunging to our doom on the back of the blockbuster is not how many people think this about Hollywood, but how many people in *Hollywood* think this about Hollywood, which should be more than enough to make you suspicious. It is by far the most parroted opinion in Los Angeles. Everywhere you go you will meet filmmakers who will cheerfully opine that there are way too many comic book adaptations/sequels/merchandising cash-ins, before turning back to their mixing desks to put the finishing touches to *Daredevil II: Double Dare,* or whatever else it is they are working on, before busting the ceiling again with yet another record-breaking blockbuster, which everyone goes to see and then forgets about in a week. One of the more perplexing things about today's annual blockbuster binge, in fact, is that it has become very hard to determine which films are genuinely popular and which are not—which is to say, films we would actively seek out, as opposed to merely sit through. Oftentimes, all we have to do is check that a movie is as bad as everyone says it is, in enough numbers, and—*poof!*—we've accidentally launched another block-buster film franchise on an unsuspecting world. The heat generated by these things seems to have bent the light by which we see them, the very nature of popularity itself taking on a miragelike shimmer, and through the haze has risen an entirely new half-breed of film, neither a hit nor a flop, neither popular nor unpopular but just *there,* hanging in the sky like an untethered blimp or derelict space station: semipopular culture, or kind-of popular culture—a culture of semisatiation, geared to the satisfaction of the mildly curious with the not-quite-boring: Curiosity Culture.

This is, needless to say, a very serious development, both for those who revere the art of popular filmmaking, but also for those who hate it—those who think every chord struck in the public's breast rings false. For when the battle between the hard-core Biskindites and teenage thrill-junkies has raged and worn itself out, that was the one thing everyone could always point to, the one thing popular culture always had going for it: it was at least popular. That was part of the thrill of watching it, reacting to it as an audience; it was what allowed academics to study it, panhandling it for signs of the popular will; it was what gave independent movies something to be independent from, and Peter Biskind something to vent his righteous anger over, and go home muttering about lowest-common-denominator film-making. If only! One of the more disconcerting aspects of today's blockbuster industry is that the aforementioned pandering has no time or space to take place: the traffic on these things is just too fast. That world-famous Lowest Common Denominator doesn't even get a chance to kick in. (Did anyone ever work out, by the way, what denom-ination it turned out to be? Pounds, dollars, or yen? I'm keen to know before the market gives out.) All Biskind and the critics can do, in such a landscape, is point to a film we are all curious about and harrumph about lowest-common-denominator interest levels, and then proceed to endorse films about which nobody is the least bit curious, films as uninteresting, from the outset, as possible. It certainly explains a lot of what passed for independent cinema in the nineties, but it doesn't get you very far with the blockbuster.

We're going to have a tough time explaining it all to our children as we look back over the box office records of the last years of the twentieth century.

"So that was the big hit of 1998," they will say, curling up on our knee, pointing to *Godzilla*.

"Well, no, actually everyone hated it."

"But it did $376 million! Look, it was number three that year. It must have been great. And look at that one, *Pearl Harbor* . . . $450 million. That one was number five. I'm number five in my math class."

"Yes, well, your math class is kind of different. Hollywood does its math in its own special way . . ."

"How come?"

"Well . . . You see there are these things called marketing budgets and opening weekends and in the nineties they sort of ganged up and what happened was we all wanted to see what all the fuss was about and by the time we'd realized—"

"Hey, look at these! *Wild Wild West* . . . $217 million . . . *Waterworld* . . . $255 million. And *Last Action Hero,* that took in $121 million all over the world! A lot of people in a lot of different countries sure loved those movies."

"Well, no, actually they were seen as catastrophic flops and globally reviled."

"I don't understand."

(Feebly): "Um . . ."

"Daddy?"

"Yes hon?"

"Tell us again what it was like when you went to see movies you *liked* . . ."

This book, then, is for them: a book about the movies we really liked back in the time when liking them was relatively simple; a book that tells the story of how, after a decade of disconnect, American movies suddenly found themselves plugged into the popular will once again, and how the power surge sent Hollywood flying, before frying the nerve endings and brain cells of all concerned—the story of how popular culture suddenly became very popular indeed, before the popularity went to its head and it turned into the global class clown. This story doesn't end with Spielberg and Lucas, it begins with them, and what a great beginning it was, for few films begin with as little fanfare as this anymore. It was preceded by just thirty seconds of credits—in later films, the director in question would hone it down still further, not wishing to distract the audience with thoughts of this or that actor, and how big his or her paycheck was—instead plunging us straight into the water, while it was still warm.

> EXT. BEACH—NIGHT: It is a pleasant, moonlit, windless night in mid-June. We see a long straight stretch of white beach. Behind the low dunes are the dark shapes of large expensive houses.

> EXT. CHRISSIE IN THE WATER: Her expression freezes . . . She reaches underwater to touch her leg. Whatever she feels makes her open her mouth to scream, but she is slammed again, hard, whipped into an arc of about eight feet, up and down, submerging her down to her open mouth, choking off any scream she might try to make . . .

TOP 50 ALL-TIME BOX OFFICE BLOCKBUSTERS
(Unadjusted for inflation)

1.	*Titanic*	Paramount	$1,845.0	(1997)
2.	*The Lord of the Rings: The Return of the King*	New Line	$1,118.9	(2003)
3.	*Harry Potter and the Sorcerer's Stone*	WB	$976.5	(2001)
4.	*The Lord of the Rings: The Two Towers*	New Line	$926.3	(2002)
5.	*Stars Wars: Episode I— The Phantom Menace*	Fox	$924.5	(1999)
6.	*Jurassic Park*	Universal	$914.7	(1993)
7.	*Harry Potter and the Chamber of Secrets*	WB	$876.7	(2002)
8.	*The Lord of the Rings: The Fellowship of the Ring*	New Line	$871.4	(2001)
9.	*Finding Nemo*	Disney	$864.6	(2003)

10. *Shrek 2*	Dreamworks	$829.4	(2004)
11. *Spider-Man*	Sony	$821.7	(2002)
12. *Independence Day*	Fox	$817.0	(1996)
13. *E.T. the Extra-Terrestrial*	Universal	$792.9	(1982)
14. *The Lion King*	Disney	$783.8	(1994)
15. *Star Wars*	Fox	$775.4	(1977)
16. *Harry Potter and the Prisoner of Azkaban*	WB	$751.9	(2004)
17. *The Matrix Reloaded*	WB	$738.6	(2003)
18. *Spider-Man 2*	Sony	$713.5	(2004)
19. *Forrest Gump*	Paramount	$677.4	(1994)
20. *The Sixth Sense*	Disney	$672.8	(1999)
21. *Pirates of the Caribbean: The Curse of the Black Pearl*	Disney	$653.9	(2003)
22. *Star Wars: Episode II— Attack of the Clones*	Fox	$649.5	(2002)
23. *The Lost World: Jurassic Park*	Universal	$618.6	(1997)
24. *The Passion of the Christ*	Newmarket	$609.5	(2004)
25. *Men in Black*	Sony	$589.4	(1997)
26. *Armageddon*	Disney	$553.7	(1998)
27. *Mission: Impossible 2*	Paramount	$545.4	(2000)
28. *The Day After Tomorrow*	Fox	$538.7	(2004)
29. *The Empire Strikes Back*	Fox	$538.4	(1980)
30. *Monsters, Inc.*	Disney	$525.4	(2001)
31. *Terminator 2: Judgment Day*	TriStar	$519.8	(1991)
32. *Ghost*	Paramount	$517.6	(1990)
33. *Aladdin*	Disney	$504.1	(1992)
34. *Twister*	WB	$495.9	(1996)
35. *Troy*	WB	$490.8	(2004)
36. *Toy Story 2*	Disney	$485.0	(1999)
37. *Bruce Almighty*	Universal	$484.6	(2003)
38. *Saving Private Ryan*	Dreamworks	$481.8	(1998)
39. *Shrek*	Dreamworks	$478.5	(2001)
40. *Home Alone*	Fox	$477.6	(1990)
41. *Return of the Jedi*	Fox	$475.1	(1983)
42. *Indiana Jones and the Last Crusade*	Paramount	$474.2	(1989)

43.	*Jaws*	Universal	$470.7	(1975)
44.	*Pretty Woman*	Disney	$463.4	(1990)
45.	*The Matrix*	WB	$460.4	(1999)
46.	*Gladiator*	Dreamworks	$457.6	(2000)
47.	*The Last Samurai*	WB	$456.8	(2003)
48	*Mission: Impossible*	Paramount	$456.5	(1996)
49.	*Ocean's Eleven*	WB	$450.7	(2001)
50.	*Pearl Harbor*	Disney	$449.2	(2001)

TOP 50 ALL-TIME BOX OFFICE BLOCKBUSTERS

(Adjusted for inflation)

1.	*Gone With the Wind*	MGM	$1,218,328,752	(1939)
2.	*Star Wars*	Fox	$1,074,061,157	(1977)
3.	*The Sound of Music*	Fox	$858,764,718	(1965)
4.	*E.T. the Extra-Terrestrial*	Universal	$855,381,641	(1982)
5.	*The Ten Commandments*	Paramount	$789,930,000	(1956)
6.	*Titanic*	Paramount	$779,086,619	(1997)
7.	*Jaws*	Universal	$772,315,273	(1975)
8.	*Doctor Zhivago*	MGM	$748,536,797	(1965)
9.	*The Exorcist*	WB	$666,729,078	(1973)
10.	*Snow White and the Seven Dwarfs*	Disney	$657,270,000	(1937)
11.	*101 Dalmatians*	Disney	$602,501,023	(1961)
12.	*The Empire Strikes Back*	Fox	$591,573,955	(1980)
13.	*Ben-Hur*	MGM	$590,940,000	(1959)
14.	*Return of the Jedi*	Fox	$567,178,243	(1983)
15.	*The Sting*	Universal	$537,531,427	(1973)
16.	*Raiders of the Lost Ark*	Paramount	$531,495,386	(1981)
17.	*Jurassic Park*	Universal	$520,077,229	(1993)
18.	*The Graduate*	Avco	$515,995,503	(1967)
19.	*Star Wars: Episode I— The Phantom Menace*	Fox	$511,705,203	(1999)
20.	*Fantasia*	Disney	$500,752,174	(1940)
21.	*The Godfather*	Paramount	$475,903,072	(1972)
22.	*Forrest Gump*	Paramount	$475,611,919	(1994)

23.	*Mary Poppins*	Disney	$471,436,364	(1964)
24.	*The Lion King*	Disney	$466,708,371	(1994)
25.	*Grease*	Paramount	$463,838,169	(1978)
26.	*Thunderball*	UA	$451,044,000	(1965)
27.	*The Jungle Book*	Disney	$444,289,879	(1967)
28.	*Sleeping Beauty*	Disney	$438,236,618	(1959)
29.	*Ghostbusters*	Columbia	$426,552,256	(1984)
30.	*Butch Cassidy and the Sundance Kid*	Fox	$425,463,862	(1969)
31.	*Bambi*	Disney	$424,566,310	(1942)
32.	*Independence Day*	Fox	$422,471,535	(1996)
33.	*Love Story*	Paramount	$422,088,813	(1970)
34.	*Beverly Hills Cop*	Paramount	$421,311,216	(1984)
35.	*Spider-Man*	Sony	$418,993,019	(2002)
36.	*Home Alone*	Fox	$407,361,771	(1990)
37.	*Pinocchio*	Disney	$406,442,101	(1940)
38.	*Cleopatra*	Fox	$405,116,278	(1963)
39.	*Goldfinger*	UA	$399,789,000	(1964)
40.	*Airport*	Universal	$398,651,040	(1970)
41.	*American Graffiti*	Universal	$396,257,142	(1973)
42.	*The Robe*	Fox	$394,690,910	(1953)
43.	*Around the World in 80 Days*	UA	$389,630,769	(1956)
44.	*Blazing Saddles*	WB	$381,261,907	(1974)
45.	*Batman*	WB	$379,616,347	(1989)
46.	*The Bells of St. Mary's*	RKO	$378,352,941	(1945)
47.	*The Lord of the Rings: The Return of the King*	New Line	$376,142,702	(2003)
48.	*The Towering Inferno*	Fox	$370,095,239	(1974)
49.	*National Lampoon's Animal House*	Universal	$364,892,308	(1978)
50.	*The Passion of the Christ*	Newmarket	$362,198,530	(2004)

Grosses as of February 29, 2004, adjusted to the estimated 2003 average ticket price of $6.03.

© Box-Office Mojo.

ACT I
1975–1983

WAKING GIANTS

CHAPTER 1

PANIC ON THE 4TH OF JULY

"We entered the bicentennial year having survived
some of the bitterest times in our brief history. We longed
for something to draw us together again."
—America's Bicentennial Report, 1976

"She was the first . . ."
—*Jaws* poster, 1975

The final cut of Steven Spielberg's *Jaws* was unveiled to the world on the night of March 28, 1975, at the Lakewood Theater, in Long Beach, California.

It wasn't the first screening of the film; a rough cut had already been tested in Dallas—as far away from salt water as possible, to see how the movie would play in the mainland. "There was a driving rain," remembers producer Richard Zanuck, "and we were concerned that nobody would show up. In those days we didn't use recruited audiences. We used regular audiences. Somebody from publicity would tell a local disc jockey to drop a rumor once or twice during the day." A nervous Spielberg hovered at the back by the door, biting his nails and watching the audience, having taken a Valium to calm himself. His producers, David Brown and Richard Zanuck, had fortified themselves with a couple of stiff drinks. About twenty minutes into the film, one audience member got up and started walking out, and Spielberg thought to himself: "Oh My God, I went over-the-top with that blood." The guy then ran to the bathroom, where he promptly threw up before returning to his seat. That's when Spielberg knew he had a hit. "The audience was screaming and the popcorn was flying in the air," he remembers. "I thought someone had hired 650 clackers, and had paid them a lot of money to scream at all the appropriate moments and laugh at all the appropriate moments." Afterward, Spielberg, Zanuck, and Brown rushed back to their hotel suite, to read the test cards excitedly to one another, drinking champagne until four in the morning. Brown remembers "one card which said, 'This is a great movie, now don't fuck it up.'"

Naturally, Spielberg wanted to improve it. The Dallas screening had shown that the picture had one big scream—when the shark comes at Roy Scheider while he is chumming at the back of the boat, at the eighty-minute mark. Zanuck and Brown had been delighted. "David and I grabbed each other's arms, and just clutched each other," says Zanuck. "It was at that moment that we knew we had a giant hit. They bought it! They bought that dummy shark!" Spielberg, though, wanted more—for there to be two big screams in the movie. He asked his editor, Verna Fields, if he could borrow her swimming pool, clouded it up with Carnation Milk, shot a scene where a head swings out of a sunken boat, and cut it into the movie, just in time for the preview in Long Beach.

"Everything played even bigger than it had in Dallas," remembers Zanuck. "People were ripping out the seats. The place went crazy." In the gap between the two screenings something fundamental had changed, and not just the movie. What had happened at the screening in Dallas—all the raw shock and relief—was now, in Long Beach, taking on something of the nature of a science, hastily improvised and impromptu, but a science nonetheless, as the film's makers set about calibrating the mysterious alchemy that seemed to have sprung up between *Jaws* and its audience. "Nobody knew that Roy Scheider saying 'We're going to need a bigger boat' was going to get an enormous laugh," said editor Verna Fields. "It didn't read that way in the script. It didn't sound that way in the dailies, and I don't think as we ran it any of us ever thought of it in terms of a huge laugh. But we had to go back and try to raise the volume; otherwise, nobody would ever get to hear

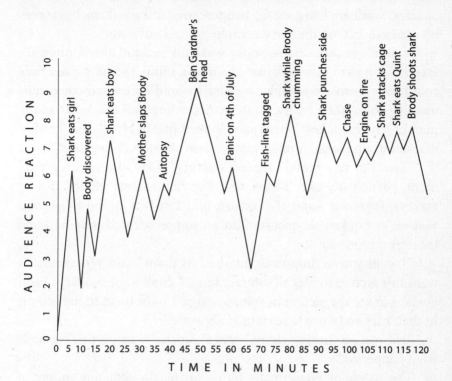

that line thoroughly because the audience is still mumbling from the shock of seeing the shark come out of the water."

Second time around, in Long Beach, Fields taped the audience response to check they could hear the line. They could. The tapes also revealed that Spielberg had gotten what he wanted: one scream at eighty minutes, when the shark lunges at Roy Scheider chumming, and another at fifty minutes, when the head pops out of the boat (see graph). He had his two screams—and yet, as he noted wistfully, "with the audience now so distrustful of me because of that end-of-the-first-act fright, the scream that had previously gone off the Richter scale in Dallas was only half as intense in Lakewood. The audience was put on such defensive behavior because of the first surprise; they were looking for something to pop out from that moment on. When the shark came out of the water, it wasn't as dynamic as it was in Dallas. But I left it like that, yeah. And we got two screams." The comment contains a rather telling diagnosis of the problems to which the blockbuster would be heir—all its inflationary drives, gratuitous escalations, Pyrrhic redundancies. Spielberg had gone for two screams, and got them, but somehow they didn't top the one scream he started out with.

It didn't matter: the response was still so loud that Universal's executives had to pile back into the men's room, the only place they could hear themselves think, in order to hold an excited emergency meeting about their release strategy. According to Zanuck, the chairman of Universal, Lew Wasserman, looked first at Hy Martin, head of marketing, and asked him: "Hy, how many theaters do we have?"

"Lew, I'm very proud," replied Martin. "There's been such excitement, particularly after Dallas, that I've had to beat off the theater owners. Everyone wants the picture, and I'm very proud to tell you that we've booked the picture into an unprecedented nine hundred theaters on June 20."

"I want you to drop three hundred of them," said Wasserman. "I want this picture to play all summer long. I don't want people in Palm Springs to see the picture in Palm Springs. I want them to have to get in their cars and drive to see it in Hollywood."

"He was so fucking clever," says Zanuck, "because that's exactly what happened."

The nicety of Wasserman's ploy—artificially reducing supply in order to create demand—would soon get lost in the crush. *Jaws* would soon be credited, and blamed, with having pioneered the trick of opening a film "wide," which is to say, in as many theaters as you possibly could. Traditionally, this was a tool of the exploitation industry— you opened a film in as many theaters as possible before word of mouth could kill it—but starting with *The Godfather* in 1972, it had become a way for studios to announce their faith in a movie's blockbuster ambitions. The same with the use of heavy TV advertising, also credited to *Jaws,* but also a revolution that had been waiting to happen: when Warner Brothers used TV spots to promote a rerelease of *Billy Jack* in 1971, and were rewarded with box-office of over $30 million, *Variety* called it "a revolutionary new tactic." Universal devoted $700,000 to promoting *Jaws*—the largest such expenditure in the studio's history. Eight months before the film opened, Zanuck, Brown, and author Peter Benchley began appearing on TV and radio talk shows. Three days before the opening, they unleashed a massive national advertising blitz, centering on the image of the shark's mouth pointing vertically up at a swimming girl. "One thing that David Brown and I insisted on," says Zanuck, "was that that symbol be carried on the hardcovers and the softcover [of the book] and the ads for the film and the movie poster so there was consistency. People on beaches—wherever they were—were seeing that symbol. We didn't have to say 'Jaws' to let people know what it was."

Jaws opened on June 20 in 409 theaters, and in its first three days had grossed $7,061,573. Spielberg's secretary walked into his office and handed him the figures on a slip of paper, saying, "Here's the opening figures," and Spielberg just stared at the number. "Then I kept waiting for the next weekend to drop off and it didn't, it went up and it went up and it went up, and Universal kept taking ads of the shark on the front page of Variety. The Godfather was the film to beat in those days, at about $86 million in theater rentals—and then we started to do, like, $130 million in rentals." Within a few weeks Jaws had beaten The Godfather's $86 million, and The Exorcist's $89 million, to become the first film to break the $100 million mark—Hollywood's sound barrier, the one nobody said could be beat. One evening that summer, Spielberg pulled into a Los Angeles ice cream parlor, Baskin-Robbins 31 Flavors on Melrose. "There was a line when I walked in, and they were all talking about Jaws. They were saying 'God, it is the most frightening film I ever saw. I've seen it six times.' It was just like the whole 31 Flavors was talking about it. I got my ice cream cone, pistachio, that's my favorite kind, and I got back into my car and I drove home. I turned on the TV set, and there was this story about the Jaws phenomenon on network news. And I realized—the whole country is watching this! That was the first time that it really hit me that it was a phenomenon. I thought this is what a hit feels like."

What manner of beast was Jaws? A "hit"? A "phenomenon"? Nobody knew what to call it. In the mid-seventies, The Wall Street Journal had alerted readers to a new age of "spectaculars," while Variety opted for "super-blockbuster," and The New York Times, in 1978, plumped for "super-grosser." Michael Eisner, then head of Paramount, attempted a definition: "The super-grossers are things that become cultural phenomena. There is no way that you can work out on paper what a cultural phenomenon should be." Forget working out on paper what they should be: what were you to *call* the damn things? Hollywood was about to embark on a lexical inflation game that was the equal of its economic one, resulting in today's bewildering array of terms—blockbuster, event movie, franchise film, tent pole picture. Even the term "blockbuster" has been subject to a strange sideways drift: once a purely economic term, with no generic preference, it was conferred solely by a movie's box office returns—and, by default, the audience. Thus *The Sound of Music* was a blockbuster and *Fiddler on the Roof* and *Kramer vs. Kramer.* Today, it has—to paraphrase Julie Andrews—become the name a movie calls itself, before it is even out of the gate. Thus *Variety* will speak today of a blockbuster "failing" at the box office—which would have caused endless confusion to someone from 1975: a film was either a riotous success, in which case it was a blockbuster, or else it wasn't. Now, it signifies a type of movie: not quite a genre, but almost; often science fiction but not necessarily; something to do with action movies although not always. Most definitely not *Kramer vs. Kramer,* though. Wherever in the movie universe films about the pains of recently divorced New Yorkers come from, the post-*Jaws* summer blockbuster sits in the opposite corner, burping on bathers.

To the postwar generation, things were much simpler. If someone asked them what a blockbuster was they simply pointed to *Gone With the Wind*—the very definition of a blockbuster, if only because for several decades it was the only one they had. Occupying an unparalleled hold on the number one spot from 1939 to 1972—almost forty years—*Gone With the Wind* was the Hoover of blockbuster movies, both brand leader and one-movie monopoly, sucking up the competition on all sides. "The business of *Gone With the Wind* was not just steady, it was an economy unto itself," writes David Thomson in his biography of producer David Selznick. Selznick had ambitions for *Gone With the Wind* from the word go: he used the casting call to find his Scarlett O'Hara as a nationwide publicity gimmick; and once he had secured his participants, everyone in the production—Selznick, director Victor Fleming, Vivien Leigh, Clark Gable—took up their positions for what amounted to a four-way group snarling session that lasted almost a year. "It was a case of utter chaos. They burned themselves, and out of the ashes rose this Phoenix of a picture," said Marcella Rabwin, Selznick's assistant at RKO. "I have never known so much hatred. The whole atmosphere was so acrid. Leigh hated Fleming, with a passion. Fleming hated her. He called her the vilest names. Clark Gable hated David." As the picture neared completion, Selznick knew what he had on his hands and wrote to Metro's head of marketing, invoking D. W. Griffith's *Birth of a Nation,* and saying, "The picture is turning out so brilliantly that its handling will have to be on a scale and of a type never before tried in the picture business."

By far the most interesting thing about *Gone With the Wind,* though, at least to today's eyes, is what happened after its release: which is to say precisely nothing. Nobody started manufacturing Rhett Butler dolls. Nobody tried to copy it, or make it happen again; it didn't spawn a sequel, let alone an entire industry. Selznick tried to follow it up with *Duel in the Sun,* a film for which he pioneered an interesting new trick of opening the film wide—as wide as he could, in thirty-eight theaters. "If the public's 'want to see' for a forthcoming picture samples higher than the reaction of the test audience's," noted one critic, "you sell your picture in a hurry before the curious have a chance to get wise." But the tactic—which would turn out to be one of the mainstays of today's blockbuster industry—failed, along with the picture. It was back to *Gone With the Wind,* whose reign at the top was further boosted by reissues in 1947, 1954, 1961, 1967, 1989, and 1998. The American people had spoken: they had their blockbuster, and occasionally they would take it out of its display case to have another look at it, but then they would pop it back in again, with a satisfied sigh. The first serious competition it faced came from Cecil B. DeMille's remake of his own film, *The Ten Commandments,* which took up a close second position in 1956; while the arrival of *Ben-Hur* in 1959 made it a three-chariot race, and from 1960 to 1965 those three films took up a neat triangular stranglehold at the top of the box office charts, until Julie Andrews vaulted up the mountainside and joined them in 1965 with *The Sound of Music.* Box office statisticians, you can't help but feel, had an easy life back then. Sat atop the pyramid, their feet up, occasionally glancing down to see what dim jockeying they could see down below but basically filing the same report, every year, like the BBC's royal reporters: *yep, still there.*

The reason they had life so easy was that the habit of going to the movies was dying. When *Gone With the Wind* was released, a full 46 percent of the American population went to the movies every week, as a matter of course—not to see this movie or that movie, but simply to go to the movies, to see what was playing—but this habit had been slowly eroded by television and the population exodus away from the big city centers toward the suburbs. If you wanted to strike terror into an average movie executive's heart in the fifties and sixties, all you had to do was give him a rough précis of Steven Spielberg's childhood: the vision of a suburban mall-rat, glued to the television, was pretty much his worst nightmare realized. "Today people go to see a movie; they no longer go to the movies," observed one distraught movie executive in 1967. The question was: what sort of movie would get them out of the house? Throughout the fifties and sixties, the studios kept up a steady stream of biblical epics and DeMillean spectaculars, on the logic that whatever TV did, Hollywood had to do the opposite—if TV was fast, dumb, and morally nonnutrient, the movies would be long, slow, and good for you—but it hadn't really done anything other than make for bloated money losers like *Cleopatra* and *The Robe.* They weren't TV, but they weren't much else, besides not being TV, sometimes for hours at a time, and audiences soon learned to stay away. Flush with the success of *The Sound of Music,* Fox had tried its hand at a series of spectacular musicals—*Hello, Dolly!, Paint Your Wagon, Doctor Dolittle* —only to see them fail, too, pushing the studio to the brink of insolvency. By 1971, both attendance levels and profits had reached an all-time low, leaving many of the studios plunged deep in red ink, desperately seeking new management—like MGM, Warner Brothers, United Artists—or else, like Universal and Columbia, teetering on the edge of liquidation. The studio system was close to collapse.

Then you hit the seventies, and all hell breaks loose. The box office statistician is groggily awoken, his slumber ruined forever. In the course of the first half of the decade, there are a series of new number ones, each breaking the others' records—first *Love Story,* in 1970, and then, in 1972, *The Godfather,* whose producer, Robert Evans, told *Time* magazine, "The making of blockbusters is the newest art-form of the 20th-century." The future was clear: the studios could draw audiences out of their homes by packaging movies as gala "events"—often adapted from a best-selling book, like *The Godfather,* and presented with a flourish by the studio ("Paramount is proud to present . . ."). The blockbuster as it emerged in the early seventies was a decidedly high-end, no-expense-spared, red-carpet affair; even 1970's *Airport*— the first of the disaster flicks, and the model for all the flame-grilled blimps that followed—received no fewer than ten Oscar nominations. The idea that these things might be simply fast and thrilling—rather than weighed down with prize-winning intent, like marrows—hadn't really occurred to anyone. The penny finally drops at the very end of *Airport,* when disaster finally deigns to strike, or rather, when disaster threatens to strike before being narrowly averted by Captain Dean Martin, thus leaving *Airport* just what it says it is, a film about an airport: two hours of air traffic control, weather reports, and marital discord, as Martin and his crew chew their way through their leaky marriages and furtive infidelities. The seventies were the Decade of Divorce—the era when the topic emerged from the bedroom and into the spotlit glare of public debate—but it is still disorienting to find the disaster flick, of all things, at the vanguard of that debate.

By the time of *Airport '77* the producers had learned their lesson, crashing the plane after just forty minutes, but for the most part, watching these early blockbusters now is a little like watching a time-lapse image of man trying to invent fire: a false trail of half-strikes, yelps, and scraped knuckles, as producers attempted to wow us with the seriousness of their dramatic credentials, while their sense of fun sat, shriveled and unnoticed, in the corner. It was a straight knockout victory for theme over thrills. In Irwin Allen's *The Poseidon Adventure* ("Hell. Upside Down"), priest Gene Hackman leads a tough-minded investigation into the value of Faith in a Godless universe, when all audiences had bought tickets for was a tough-minded investigation of the value of foot ladders in an upturned boat. Allen was the king of this middlebrow marshland, valiantly attempting to represent every tier of society in his films, from janitor to president, on the basis that if you wanted half the Western world to attend your film, you simply cast the other half. By the time of *The Towering Inferno,* in 1974, however, audiences had worked out the basic math of these pictures for them-selves: the number of A-list stars alive at the end of the picture equaled the number of A-list stars alive at the beginning of the picture, minus one for realism, or in the cause of noble self-sacrifice.

So what was so different about *Jaws?* In one sense, nothing at all. "This is Universal's extraordinary motion picture version of Peter Benchley's best-selling novel . . ." intoned the trailers, with the sort of silver-platter flourish that now seems as quaint as three-color disco lights: they thought Benchley was the attraction? The *book?* Benchley's novel was that most curious of seventies artifacts: the misanthropic best-seller, full of such loathing for the common herd, you wonder why on earth the common herd bothered with the thing: "They had no body odor," notes police chief Brody of the bathers he watches over. "When they sweated, the girls smelled faintly of perfume; the boys smelled simply clean. None of which is to say that they were either stu-pid or evil." Peter Benchley, step forward and accept the 1975 People's Friend Award! Spielberg cut out the sourpuss posturings and gave the part of Brody to Roy Scheider, telling him, "I don't want to feel that you could ever kill that shark." Charlton Heston had wanted the part, but as Spielberg's screenwriter Carl Gottleib pointed out, Heston had just saved a jetliner in *Airport 1975* and he was going to save Los Ange-les in *Earthquake,* so "it just didn't seem right for him to be wasting his time with a little New England community." The blockbuster would eventually become synonymous with the effortless accomplishments of singular superheroes, but *Jaws,* from the outset, was an exercise in dramatic downsizing, attuned to the scruffy, low-slung heroism of or-dinary men, engaging in pitched battle with just a single shark, which kills only four people in the entire movie—and not at a single stroke, like an earthquake, but in four separate courses, from soup to nuts. It was, in other words, a repeat offender, in whom Spielberg had found a perfect reflection of his own restlessly kinetic instincts as a director. When the *Orca* is going at full throttle to catch up with the shark, Richard Dreyfuss's admiring headshake of disbelief is entirely genuine: *"Fast fish!"*

He should know. Dreyfuss's reaction times—the flash flood grins that light up his face, the octave-vaulting scat of his line readings—are the second fastest thing in the movie, and from the moment Dreyfuss set foot in *Jaws,* he told audiences all they needed to know about how different a movie this was going to be. He steps onto the jetty, while all the bounty hunters are heading out in their overcrowded boats to hunt the shark, laughs that Daffy Duck–on–helium laugh of his, and says to no one in particular, "They're all going to die!"—a prognostication of doom sung in the happiest of singsong lilts. And there you have *Jaws,* a film buoyed up by more high spirits than any movie about killer sharks ought by rights to be. Barreling along beneath cloudless skies that are a perfect match for its director's temperament, *Jaws* picked up its audience, wiped them out, and deposited them on the sidewalk, two hours later, exhausted but delighted. What stays with you, even today, are less the movie's big shock moments than the crowning gags, light as air, with which Spielberg gilds his action—Dreyfuss crushing his Styrofoam cup, in response to Quint crushing his beer can, or Brody's son copying his finger-steepling at the dinner table, both moments silent, as all the best moments in Spielberg are, and both arising from the enforced improv session that arose while he and his crew waited for his shark to work. You simply didn't get this sort of thing from *The Poseidon Adventure*: no ironic machismo moments involving Styrofoam cups, no tenderly observed finger-steepling at the dinner table. This didn't feel like a disaster movie. It felt like a day at the beach.

To get anything resembling such fillets of improvised characterization, you normally had to watch something far more boring—some chamber piece about marital disintegration by John Cassavetes, say— and yet here were such things, popping up in a movie starring a scary rubber shark. It was nothing short of revolutionary: you could have finger-steepling and scary rubber sharks *in the same movie.* This seemed like important information. Why had no one told us this before? Spielberg had completely upended the pyramid of American film, ridding the blockbuster of its rather desperate bids for "prestige" while also visiting on it the sort of filigree dramatic technique normally associated with films much further up the brow. The effect on audiences was properly electric, for now we knew, and we would never go back, willingly, to the old system of cinematic apartheid that had existed before, dictating that popular movies must be dumb, and highbrow films boring. Spielberg had upped the game for everyone. Now, there would be very little excuse for the sort of middlebrow ponder-ings we had accepted in the name of popular entertainment up until this point, and at the other end of the spectrum, even art films would have to have a very good excuse not to try and entertain us just that little bit more. An entertainment revolution was underway.

It seems worth pointing out: the art of popular cinema was about to get, at a rough estimate, a bazillion times better. The era in which dedicated thrill junkies had to make do with *Rollerball* and *Death Race 2000* and *The Hindenberg* and *Rollercoaster* and *Meteor* was about to give way to the era of *Alien* and *Indiana Jones* and *Superman* and *Die Hard*. Yes, Martin Scorsese would find it harder to find the money to make his movies, and yes, it was goodbye to films featuring hippies and bikes, and yes, a lot of studio suits were about to get very rich and buy themselves obnoxiously fast Ferraris, and dope would make way for cocaine, granted. But the art of popular cinema—the art perfected a generation before by the likes of Selznick, Howard Hawks, and Alfred Hitchcock—that tradition was about to get a huge boost in the arm from the release of *Jaws*. Hawks found most moviemaking in the seventies abysmal; asked what he thought of *The Night They Raided Minsky's* and *The Boys in the Band*, "lousy" was Hawks's reply. "Make a good chase. Make one better than anyone's ever done." The result was *The French Connection*. What Hitchcock thought of the seventies is sadly not on record, but it is not too hard to imagine him recoiling, slack-jawed in horror, from the narrative desert of *Zabriskie Point*, and alighting with something like relief on the polished narrative clockwork of a film like *Back to the Future* or *The Terminator*.

None of this was immediate, of course. The next decade would still find time for expensive crud like *The Wiz, Honky Tonk Freeway,* and *Raise the Titanic,* whose title never ceases to amaze: they were going to *undo* all the good work done by that iceberg and then shout about it in the title? An anti-disaster movie! Excitement in reverse! That's the sort of thing you want to keep quiet about, surely. Eventually, though, people would catch on and popular entertainment would raise its game. Even leaving aside the obvious examples, we'd get *An Officer and a Gentleman, Tootsie, Ghostbusters, Beverly Hills Cop, Big*—not movies that would change the way anyone looks at the world, perhaps, but solid, four-square hits whose breezy sense of fun would have been, if not inconceivable without the gale of high spirits that blew through cinemas with *Jaws,* then certainly harder to pull off if Spielberg had chosen to make *Lucky Lady* instead, and it had been *Nashville* or *At Long Last Love* that had made $100 million that year. "*Jaws* changed the business forever," writes Peter Biskind. "As costs mounted, the willingness to take risks diminished proportionately. Moreover, *Jaws* whet corporate appetites for big profits quickly, which is to say, studios wanted every film to be *Jaws.*" Still, it could have been worse. It could have been *The Stepford Wives.* If you're going to remodel the entire industry on a single movie, *Jaws* is, on balance, a pretty good movie to pick: it is fast and funny and tender and oblique and exciting in an intriguingly non-macho way, although most critics at the time, needless to say, didn't see it like that. "A coarse-grained and exploitative work which depends on excess for its impact," wrote the *Los Angeles Times.* "You feel like a rat being given shock treatment," said *The Village Voice.* "A mind-numbing repast for sense-sated gluttons," intoned the critic of *Commentary.* It's not too hard to understand their dismay. The upper registers of the box office had, until 1975, remained completely free of great whites, man-eating or otherwise, for close on a century; the top ten had been a matter of biblical mountains, parting seas, the rise and fall of Rome, all supplanting one another with the speed of a glacier; and suddenly here was this rubber shark, devouring all before it. The response had to be a fake—an instance of moviemaking voodoo, mass hysteria. "Its symptoms are saucered eyes, blanched faces, and a certain tingle anxiety about going near the water," wrote *Newsweek* of "*Jaws*mania," with the tone of concerned doctors at a 1964 Beatles concert. Elsewhere, the cynicism took on a more seventies, Watergate-era tinge. "Audiences who think they made *Jaws* a success are pitifully naive about the mass media," wrote Stephen Farber in a *New York Times* article entitled "*Jaws* and *Bug*: The Only Difference Is the Hype," a theme later continued by Michael Pye and Linda Myles in their book, *The Movie Brats,* which claimed *Jaws* effected "the transformation of film into event through clever manipulation of the media." For of course, all manipulation of the media is "clever" manipulation of the media, particularly if you happen to work in the media, for what other sort would get past your finely tuned radar?

What is most striking about "*Jaws*mania" today, however, is what a grassroots operation it was, driven not by the studio but by private profiteers, pirates, or just entrepreneurs with a single goofy idea. A *Jaws* discotheque opened in the Hamptons, complete with a wooden shark; a Georgia fisherman started selling shark jawbones for $50; a New York ice cream stand renamed its staple flavors sharklate, finilla, and jawberry; a Silver Spring specialty dealer began selling strap-on Styrofoam shark fins, for anyone who wanted to start a mass panic in the privacy of their own beach. Meanwhile, up and down the coast towns of America, hotels reported a spate of canceled bookings, as people caught wind of the sudden rise in reported shark attacks: which is to say, commercial interests lost actual money because of the release of *Jaws*. So much for synergy. In fact, the official Universal merchandising was minimal—T-shirts, beach towels, posters—and when Spielberg proposed a chocolate shark, he was turned down—the first and last time in the career of Steven Spielberg that he would be refused a merchandising opportunity by a studio.

"It was a chocolate shark with cherry juice filling, so when you bite the shark, blood comes out, but edible blood," says Spielberg now. "That's where my head was at in 1975. My first experience with merchandising, based on a phenomenal blockbuster, came with Disney's Davy Crockett when I was a kid. I went out and my mom bought me a coonskin cap and a plastic flintlock rifle resembling Davy Crockett's rifle, Old Betsy, and a little plastic powder horn, ostensibly to load the powder into your flintlock. So I was no stranger to being caught up in a national craze. Sometimes it's about a film, sometimes it's about a hula hoop, or a Slip 'n Slide by Wham-O. It doesn't necessarily have to be the film media that creates a national rush to be part of a phenomenon, and God willing you won't be left out of it. It's a great way for kids who aren't popular to be momentarily popular, to be in support of a new national pastime. In the early days when I was making *Jaws*, I looked upon all this as something we had no control over. The blockbuster was created not by the film director or the studio's marketing machine. The blockbuster originally was made by the general public."

"*Jaws* opened up a vein in the public consciousness," says David Brown. "Movies used to be a solitary experience. You sat in the dark, alone, no matter how many people surrounded you. But with *Jaws* people started to talk back to the screen and applaud shadows. On a screen that couldn't hear them. The whole notion of applauding a movie would have been ludicrous in the twenties and thirties. . . . Zanuck and I could walk by a theater and know what reel was playing by the sounds that came out. That was a new experience. Audience participation. The new word is interactive I guess." It marked a crucial advance on the decade's previous blockbusters. Say what you like about *Love Story* but it was not really an audience participation film, unless you counted the synchronized smooching going on in the back row; nor was *The Godfather,* which was essentially a study in collective isolation; you watched it alone, no matter how full the cinema was, and you left the theater eyeing your fellow moviegoers with new unease, uncertain whether you would care to share a theater with them again. But *Jaws* united its audience in common cause—a shared unwillingness to be served up as lunch—and you came out delivering high-fives to the three hundred or so new best friends you'd just narrowly avoided death with. And then you came back the next day to narrowly avoid it again. For here was the second major defining mark of the summer blockbuster: you watched it again, and not in the spirit of sepia-tinted nostalgia with which audiences ambled along to see *Gone With the Wind* a decade after its release, but in a time frame condensed by the sheer viscerality of the experience: you watched *Jaws* again for the same reason that people head back into a thrill ride, or keep doing bungee jumps. Thanks to these repeat viewings, *Jaws* stayed around all summer, becoming in turn the thing millions of Americans most remember about that summer—a multi-million-dollar madeleine. A Colt 45 Malt Liquor commercial offered the first of many *Jaws* parodies; Bob Hope quipped that he was too scared to take a bath: "My rubber duck was circling me"; while political cartoonists seized on the shark as representing—variously—taxes, unemployment, inflation, male chauvinism, Ronald Reagan, and the Hawaii Media Responsibility Commission. That's what America did in the summer of 1975: it watched *Jaws.*

"One of the wonderful things about *Jaws* was that the cultural impact was greater than you could make today," says Sidney Sheinberg, Spielberg's mentor at Universal. "Nowadays, the release of movies most resembles a television show: the whole idea is, get all this money, get all the people you can to see it the first weekend. I'm not sure you could make that sort of cultural impact with today's blockbusters, which everyone sees so quickly and which then disappear from consciousness. Compared to the impact you could make when it sits there all summer, and more and more people are seeing it, and it's feeding on itself, as *Jaws* did." If you went back to the film, in fact, as many were doing that summer, you noticed that it told two stories, only one of which happens to be about a giant shark. The shark eats the girl, then the boy; but then look what happens: the town reacts as if school was out. It erupts into a boomtown of petty profiteering and casual lawlessness; kids start scrawling graffiti on billboards; bounty hunters head out to sea in a big crazy flotilla, shooting guns into the water; and Spielberg is on fire—hopped-up on the whole crazy spectacle, just as he was by the flotilla of cars in *Sugarland Express,* and the media circus that trailed his outlaw couple. Spielberg's fascination with the echo-chamber of the mass media receives further amplification in *Jaws;* for the bounty hunters come back with a shark that does get their picture in the paper, and the next thing you know, the story has gone national. The national networks arrive, and are soon crawling all over the beach with their cameras, just in time to catch the next shark attack, which turns out to be a hoax: two small boys, wearing a wooden fin, who are pulled, dripping, from the water. If you want a trenchant analysis of *Jaws*mania, in other words, your best bet has always been to check out *Jaws* itself. It's all there, up on the screen—the hysteria bleeding into hoopla, the hoopla into hype, and the hype into hoax.

"We need summer dollars," pleads the mayor, anxious to play down the threat. "We depend on the summer crowds for our very lives. You yell 'shark' and we got a panic on our hands on the 4th of July." Which is when Dreyfuss delivers his great speech. "What we are dealing with here is a perfect engine, an eating machine. It's really a miracle of evolution. All this machine does is swim, eat, and make little sharks." For those who care to see it, there was an allegory there for what was about to happen to Hollywood: "Panic on the 4th of July" would, henceforth, be the motto pinned up on the door of every marketing executive, while a "perfect engine" for making more sharks the dream of every producer. The first July 4th movie was also a prescient allegory for all the other July 4th movies to come. It's one of the reasons why *Jaws*mania, with its nod to Beatlemania, was always a bit of a misnomer, unless *Newsweek* meant mid-period Beatles, around the time of *Sgt. Pepper,* when Paul McCartney fabricated an ersatz supergroup to deflect and channel back into the ether some of the Beatles' own fame: *Jaws* is of exactly the same order of self-conscious pop craft. The object of national hysteria, national hysteria was also its subject, its object, its very method. When audiences honked their horns at drive-ins, or strapped on their fake shark fins, they weren't buying into the hype; they were buying into the movie, which contained its own hype within it, like an echo waiting to be born in the summer haze that hovers above Spielberg's island.

"Inside the movie, it's a national media event," says the director. "I know. And I was the last to have predicted that that was what was going to happen with the film's release. I had no idea. All of us, including Richard Dreyfuss, who never believed this film would float, we were phoning each other reporting these experiences we were having in all these previews wondering what went right, because for nine months of principal photography, everything went wrong, and we could not believe that some chord was about to be struck. Lew Wasserman was showing the movie in fire stations and barns—anyplace they could put up a projector. I actually thought Lew had lost his mind when he told me he was going to go out in almost five hundred theaters. That hadn't been done by any Universal film before. Today, art films are released in 409 theaters, and *Jaws* certainly was not an art film. I never took that story so seriously as to think I was making Melville. I wasn't."

Jaws's breezy divestment of all the usual guarantees of blockbuster "prestige" caused no end of crossed wires come Oscar time, with nominations for the film and its editing, but not its director. "I didn't get it! I wasn't nominated," complained Spielberg at the time, having made the mistake of inviting a camera crew to watch his reaction to the award announcements. "This is what is called commercial backlash. When a film makes a lot of money, people resent it. Everybody loves a winner, but nobody loves a winner." Here, then, was *Jaws*'s final contribution to the newly emergent art of the summer blockbuster: whatever happens, and unlike their predecessors, they do not win Oscars. *Jaws*'s failure to win anything but technical awards—1975 was the year of *One Flew Over the Cuckoo's Nest*—would be echoed by *Star Wars*'s loss to *Annie Hall* in 1977, by *Raiders of the Lost Ark*'s to *Ordinary People* in 1981, and *E.T.*'s to *Gandhi* in 1982, as fine a series of upper-cut injustices as can be imagined, *Ordinary People* and *Gandhi* having long since ascended to the ranks of the Great Unwatched in the sky, while *Raiders* and *E.T.* have turned into much-loved classics that the Academy should have been falling over itself to reward. Their prejudice against blockbusters would prove hard to shift—not until *Forrest Gump* in 1994 would any film that made over $100 million win a Best Picture statuette, thus opening up the corridor for *Titanic* in 1998— although money is only half the story. Certainly in the case of *E.T.* versus *Gandhi,* the Academy was faced with a clear choice between two leathery, twinkly gurus: one selling peace, love, and understanding, the other selling peace, love, understanding, and Reese's Pieces. But the real key to understanding the Academy Awards is the state of pure aesthetic terror in which the voting takes place: for 346 days of the year, the assorted members of the Academy—actors, producers, directors— devote every breath of their living being to the task of putting bodies into seats, and then, on just one day of the year, they are suddenly ambushed by the question, "Yes, but is it Art?" It's understandably terrifying. So what happens is that they don't vote for the best film, they vote for the film that most fully reassures them that they are not voting for the wrong film. Historical films are more reassuring than fantasy films (you're saying none of this stuff *happened?*), films that make a decent amount of money are more reassuring than films that make truckloads of money (that could be the clammy embrace of Mammon, or possibly the mass delusion of crowds, or both), and films that get turned into bumper stickers, like *Jaws,* are less reassuring than films that make a principled stand against the tyranny of the majority, like *One Flew Over the Cuckoo's Nest.*

The effect of *Jaws*'s Oscar snub on Spielberg himself was divisive, opening a fault line that would run right down the next decade of his career, as he hankered for a respectability that never quite arrived and sought popular success that he then distrusted. It wasn't long before he was talking down *Jaws* to anyone who would listen, in an Uncle Tom–like ingestion of the standard critical line on the film. "*Jaws* is almost like I'm directing the audience with a cattle prod, it was the simplest movie I had ever seen in my life," he told one reporter. "It was just the essential moving, working parts of suspense and terror." And, a little later: "No movie had ever grossed $100 million in the U.S. and Canada. On its way to making what it eventually made, $400 million around the world, it was regarded by everyone as a kind of carnival freak. They said it must have been the heat of that summer that gave the shark legs, that took him inland so far, gobbling up the country like little Pacmen. So I began believing it was some kind of freak, and agreeing when people said it could never happen again. What vindicated me was when *Star Wars* came out and became the second film to gross $100 million." Note that careful notation of rank—"the second film to gross $100 million." It's accurate, but *Star Wars* also took half as much again as *Jaws;* raking in $193 million after six months. Spielberg now had company. He also had a rival.

TIME LINE

1970

1. *Love Story* (Paramount) $48,700,000
2. *Airport* (Universal) $45,200,000
3. *M*A*S*H* (Fox) $36,700,000
4. *Patton* (Fox) $28,100,000
5. *In Search of Noah's Ark* (Sunn) $23,800,000
6. *Woodstock* (WB) $16,400,000
7. *Ryan's Daughter* (MGM) $14,600,000
8. *Tora! Tora! Tora!* (Fox) $14,500,000
9. *The Aristocats* (Disney) $11,500,000
10. *Joe* (Cannon/MGM) $9,500,000

1971

1. *Fiddler on the Roof* (United Artists) $38,200,000
2. *Billy Jack* (WB) $32,500,000
3. *The French Connection* (Fox) $26,300,000
4. *The Summer of '42* (WB) $20,500,000

5. *Deep Throat* (Damiano) $20,000,000
6. *Diamonds Are Forever* (United Artists) $19,800,000
7. *Dirty Harry* (WB) $18,100,000
8. *A Clockwork Orange* (WB) $17,500,000
9. *Little Big Man* (National General) $17,000,000
10. *The Last Picture Show* (Columbia) $14,100,000

1972

1. *The Godfather* (Paramount) $86,300,000
2. *The Poseidon Adventure* (Fox) $42,100,000
3. *What's Up, Doc?* (WB) $28,500,000
4. *Deliverance* (WB) $22,600,000
5. *Jeremiah Johnson* (WB) $21,900,000
6. *Cabaret* (Allied Artists/ABC) $20,200,000
7. *The Getaway* (National General/WB) $18,400,000
8. *Lady Sings the Blues* (Paramount) $11,000,000
9. *Sounder* (Fox) $9,500,000
10. *Pete 'n' Tillie* (Universal) $8,500,000

1973

1. *The Exorcist* (WB) $89,300,000
2. *The Sting* (Universal) $78,200,000
3. *American Graffiti* (WB) $55,300,000
4. *The Way We Were* (Columbia) $25,800,000
5. *Papillon* (Allied Artists) $22,500,000
6. *Magnum Force* (WB) $20,100,000
7. *Robin Hood* (Disney) $17,200,000
8. *Last Tango in Paris* (United Artists) $16,700,000
9. *Paper Moon* (Paramount) $16,600,000
10. *Live and Let Die* (United Artists) $16,000,000

1974

1. *The Towering Inferno* (Fox) $48,800,000
2. *Blazing Saddles* (WB) $47,800,000
3. *Earthquake* (Universal) $35,900,000
4. *The Trial of Billy Jack* (WB) $31,100,000
5. *Benji* (Mulberry) $30,800,000

6. *The Godfather: Part II* (Paramount) $30,700,000
7. *Young Frankenstein* (Fox) $30,100,000
8. *Airport 1975* (Universal) $25,300,000
9. *The Longest Yard* (Paramount) $23,000,000
10. *That's Entertainment!* (MGM) $19,100,000

1975

1. *Jaws* (Universal) $129,500,000
2. *One Flew Over the Cuckoo's Nest* (United Artists) $60,000,000
3. *The Rocky Horror Picture Show* (Fox) $35,000,000
4. *Shampoo* (Columbia) $24,500,000
5. *Dog Day Afternoon* (WB) $22,500,000
6. *Return of the Pink Panther* (United Artists) $22,100,000
7. *Grizzly Adams* (Sunn) $21,900,000
8. *Three Days of the Condor* (Paramount) $21,500,000
9. *Funny Lady* (Columbia) $19,300,000
10. *The Other Side of the Mountain* (Universal) $58,853,106

*Figures show U.S. domestic gross

CHAPTER 2

EMPIRE STATE EXPRESS

"What a piece of junk!"

"She'll make point five beyond the speed of light. She may not look like much, but she's got it where it counts, kid."

—Luke Skywalker and Han Solo, *Star Wars*, 1977

Twentieth Century Fox knew they had a hit on their hands. If *2001: A Space Odyssey* had shown that science fiction was back in vogue again, then this film promised to take it to the next level: a pacey sci-fi action-adventure, using state-of-the-art special effects, set against a stunning backdrop of sun-parched deserts and velvety deep space. This was as sure a thing as sure things got. Having carefully watched Universal's handling of *Jaws*, Fox knew exactly what to do. They put all their marketing muscle behind the film, picked a prime release date—June 21—booked it into as many theaters as they could muster, and then sat back and waited.

So much for *Damnation Alley*, Roger Zelazny's post-apocalyptic road movie of 1977, which despite a hopeful, last-minute title change to *Survival Alley*, promptly went the way of pre-apocalyptic civilization and disappeared in a puff of smoke. *Star Wars*, on the other hand, had a tough time getting into any moviehouses at all. Fox's market research had come up with conclusive proof that anything with "star" or "war" in its title was death at the box office, so Lucas and his mentor at Fox, Alan Ladd, Jr., were given Memorial Day as their release date, "a dead date, the deadest date in the history of movies," says Ladd. Kids were still in school, and kids were thought to be the movie's only chance of success. Ladd had to blackmail distributors into booking *Star Wars* by promising them *The Other Side of Midnight,* Fox's other main release that summer—"blockbooking," as it was known, and which had been illegal since the fifties. "Most people only booked *Star Wars* because they had to," he says, sheepishly. "We didn't give them a choice. As illegal as it was, that's the way the distribution game was played." Even so, no theater in the suburb of Hollywood agreed to show the film, and Mann's Chinese Theatre only did so at the last minute, because Fox's *Sorcerer* wasn't finished in time. *Star Wars* was, as *Newsweek* would report, "undoubtedly the sleeper of the year."

"They didn't know what it was, just had no idea what it was," says Lucas. "It took me two years to get that thing off the ground and the only reason it got off the ground was that Alan liked *American Graffiti* and said, 'I don't understand this movie, I don't get it at all, but I think you're a talented guy and I want you to make this movie.' It started out as a $3 million low-budget science fiction film. And even when Laddie read the script he said, 'I still don't know what this movie is, but I'm going to let you make it.' When the budget got up to $10 million they were getting very frightened. Nobody expected it to be a blockbuster." Hollywood would not be Hollywood if it didn't devote all its energies, every now and again, to the cause of making huge, vibrant Day-Glo mistakes, but everyone's inability to recognize the rough beast that was *Star Wars,* slouching its way toward the box office, feels right somehow—or at least eerily true to the sneaky rhythm of bona fide revolutions, which always seem to roll out in staggered fashion, following first a charismatic leader into the field—a Danton, a Trotsky, a Spielberg—while a quieter tactician—a Robespierre, a Lenin, a Lucas—brings up the rear. (And both then pave the way for a third figure: a Napoleon, a Stalin, a Cameron, the men who would be king of the world.) If Spielberg's battle had been fought on the open seas, beneath the glare of an openly mutinous crew, Lucas's took place behind the closed doors of Industrial Light & Magic's facility at Van Nuys, on the outskirts of L.A., where Lucas was struggling to pull his special effects into shape.

When production on the film had first been announced, it had acted as a homing beacon for a whole generation of model makers, sculptors, and sci-fi enthusiasts—who heard the call, like a dog whistle, and emerged, the geeks from the woodwork, to work at ILM. "It seemed like the college art and design department but with money," says Lorne Peterson, who headed up the model workshop. They called it the "country club" because of its lack of a dress code—with everyone in shorts, T-shirts, flip-flops—or time clock. "Friday nights, the transition between work and play was pretty smooth," says Peterson. "You'd work late, 7:00, 7:30 and then the girlfriends and boyfriends would show up. You had a big open space, a good sound system, no neighbors." It was the summer of Stevie Wonder's *Songs in the Key of Life,* and Fleetwood Mac's *Rumours*—which blasted out on four-foot-high speakers, while technicians played flute in the parking lot, or hammered away on an old abandoned piano. Van Nuys had turned into something of an Animal House for sci-fi geeks. One time, remembers Peterson, they devised a makeshift Slip 'n Slide from an old airplane escape chute and a hose to cool off at lunchtime, "and at that moment [producer] Gary Kurtz arrived back from England with a couple of studio heads to check up on us. They pulled up in a large dark limo. They made it about one length into the parking lot, saw us, and then backed into reverse and left."

"It was a great embarrassment to me personally," says Ladd, whose boss at Fox, CEO Dennis Stanfill, was vehemently opposed to the film. When Stanfill had taken control of Fox in the early seventies, the company had been close to collapse, posting losses of $1.3 million, thanks to what Stanfill called "*The Sound of Music–Hello, Dolly!* syndrome"—the big musicals that had almost sunk the company in the late sixties. Like many executives in Hollywood he had forsworn expensive blockbusters, and every time the budget of *Star Wars* came up for review before the board, he tried to shut down production. "One of my toughest problems was trying to explain to people within the company that it was groundbreaking," says Ladd. "I had huge arguments with Dennis, who was appalled with what was happening with the effects budget. The chief financial officer kept coming to me every week saying, 'We've got to close down this ILM. He's bleeding us dry. They don't know what they're doing. They're all messed up.' The studio were screaming at me: 'Where are the effects, where are the effects?'" The system that Lucas's effects technicians were trying to perfect—"motion control"—was a computer-guided camera that rotated, swiveled, tracked, and dollied in exactly repeatable sequences, making it possible to layer up action sequences in which everything—foreground, background, the camera—was moving at the same time. It would liberate the camera, allowing the dizzying rushes of speed for which *Star Wars* became famous, but it was slow work. "It would take us forever to set something up," says Ken Ralston, who was on X-wing duty, "and all we'd shot was eighteen frames of an X-wing going *weee!* And we'd be, 'Wow. I don't know. It's awfully quick isn't it?' Now it seems slow, because things have speeded up so much."

Lucas's speed-freak instincts went back to his teenage years, when, in his souped-up Fiat Bianchina, he had raced with his friends across the mud flats around Modesto—the only experience to blast through Lucas's formidable boredom reflexes: "The engine, the noise, being able to peel rubber through all four gears with three shifts, the speed," he remembered. "It was the thrill of doing something really well. When you drift around a corner and come up at just the right time, and shift down—there's something special about it. It's like running a really good race. You're all there, and everything is working." And there you have *Star Wars.* There have been numerous attempts to plumb for depths in Lucas's space epic—Jungian readings, Taoist decodings, and perilous descents into its mythical deep structure, most notably by Joseph Campbell, whose investigation of mythological archetypes, *The Hero with a Thousand Faces,* provides a blueprint for almost every scene in the film: the hero's call to adventure, the refusal of that call, the arrival of the supernatural aid, the crossing of the first threshold, and so on. "Until Campbell told us what *Star Wars* meant, started talking about collective memory and cross-cultural shared history," said composer John Williams, "we regarded it as a Saturday morning space movie." There are good reasons to be suspicious of this—most of Campbell's mythic archetypes turn out, on closer inspection, to be merely clichés in a caveman costume—but foremost is the fact that if you were ten, or thereabouts, when you saw the film, the mythic archetype into which *Star Wars* most forcefully plugged was the one about driving really, really fast with a bunch of new friends: *you're all there, and everything is working.*

Lucas didn't happen upon his distillation of this feeling overnight.

Before he made his space epic about driving really, really fast with a bunch of new friends, he made a movie set in Wisconsin about driving really, really fast with a bunch of old friends, *American Graffiti*. Before that, he made a film simply about driving fast: *1.42:08*, his USC student film about a race car lapping the track. And before that, he made his film about just driving: *Herbie*, in which Lucas's camera went cruising around town, catching the passing street life in its gleaming hood and polished fender, and not to be confused with the *The Love Bug* Herbie of the 1968 Disney hit.

People were always a weak point. Anyone who read the first draft of *Star Wars* thought it pure gobbledygook. "I couldn't figure out what the hell it was about," said cinematographer Haskell Wexler, who turned down the chance to work on the film. "I told George, you have to get some humanity into this thing." Originally titled *The Star Wars*, Lucas's first draft began, "The Story of Mace Windu: a revered Jedi-Bendu of Ophuchi who was related to Usby CJ Thape, Padawaan learner to the famed Jedi . . ." Over the course of two years, it went through four different drafts, each written with a No. 2 pencil in Lucas's tiny, tidy handwriting on green- and blue-lined paper. Lucas would pack each draft in a briefcase, together with some clean underwear, and fly to Los Angeles to show his work to his screenwriter friends, Gloria Katz and Bill Huyck. They would say something like "this character doesn't work," Lucas would nod, go "uh-huh" and fly back home to San Francisco to rework it. Mace Windu was replaced by Kane Starkiller, and Kane Starkiller by Luke Skywalker. Originally an elderly general, Luke would become a teenager, then a farmboy. As Luke's role grew, Princess Leia receded. Two workmen named C-3PO and R2-D2 became robots. Obi Wan and Darth Vader started as one character, then bifurcated. Han Solo was a huge green-skinned monster with gills and no nose, then became burly and bearded, before finally becoming a "tough James Dean–style pilot, a cowboy in a spaceship."

To anyone familiar with the digital technology that Lucas would later introduce to moviegoers in the movie *Willow*, these transformations are weirdly familiar: the script was morphing. At least, all the elements that were traditionally thought of as making up cinema—characters, actors, story line—were morphing. When it came to dialogue Lucas could be comically vague (BUREAUCRATS: "It's restricted. You'll have to wait . . . etc." KANE: "Get out of my way, boy, before I grind you into the surface . . . etc."). But as much as the characters continued their cellular subdivision and regrouping, the world they inhabited remained pretty much the same: a world of gleaming chrome and desert sands, cloud cities and moon-sized battle stations, land-speeders and light-sabers—the latter making "a low buzzing sound" and "electric snapping and popping" sound when they clashed. The sights and sounds of this world are registered with pointillist precision. Lucas may not have known what he wanted bureaucrats to say, but he knew what color explosion their Death Star would make.

"I'd wanted to make it much bigger than it was," says Lucas, "much more out there in terms of creatures and aliens, and the environments and all that stuff and I had to really restrict my imagination to a very very thin line that I could make work. . . . I was forced constantly to write something very, very small; even though *Star Wars* seems very big, it was an illusion, it's technically very small: I was always going 'I wanna do this, oh I can't do that.'" The actual shoot of the movie—at Elstree studios in London—had been, for Lucas, an exercise in systematic frustration. "George would sit on the edge of his bed every morning—he had these terrible foot infections," said Gloria Katz. "We would sit with him, try to convince him not to kill himself. He was so disappointed he couldn't get anything he wanted, the crew was making fun of him. The cameraman was surly, would say, 'Bring the dawg in, put light on the dawg,' talking about Chewbacca. George kept saying, 'I just can't take this,' and we kept saying, 'Come on, George, you can do it, you can get up, you can get to the set.' He was really in a very fragile state. The final insult was the English crew voted the last day of the movie whether they were going to do overtime. They voted no."

When Lucas returned, he was convinced that he'd shot a $10 million trailer. "I only got 30 percent, I only got 30 percent," he told people. When he checked in at Industrial Light & Magic, to see what progress they had made, he was appalled to find that they'd spent over half of their $2 million budget and only had three shots to show for it. After a screaming match with his effects supervisor, John Dykstra, he flew back to San Francisco, and by the time he was picked up by his wife, Marcia, he'd developed severe chest pains. They drove straight to Marin General Hospital, where he was diagnosed with hypertension and exhaustion and kept overnight. "It wasn't funny, he was wrecked," said Bill Huyck. "People have gallows humor about films, but George had jumped off the gallows."

In March of 1977, Lucas was ready to show the film to a group of his friends at his house in San Anselmo. Steven Spielberg, Brian De Palma, and screenwriters Willard Huyck and Gloria Katz were joined by Alan Ladd, to see how Fox's $10 million had shaped up on screen. It was a disaster. "We watch the movie," recalled Huyck, "and the crawl went on forever, there was tons of backstory, and then we're in this spaceship, and then here's Darth Vader. Part of the problem was that almost none of the effects had been finished, and in their place George had inserted World War II dogfight footage, so one second you're with the wookie in the escape ship and the next you're in *The Bridges at Toko-Ri*. It was like, George what is going on?" At the end of the movie, everyone sat back aghast. Marcia started crying, whispering, "It's the *At Long Last Love* of science fiction. It's awful." Katz shushed her, "Laddie's watching, Just look cheery."

Ladd hated Harrison Ford's performance—thought it was too camp—and resolved to ask Lucas to fix it in the editing, but for the moment he said nothing and simply left. Everyone else headed out to a Chinese restaurant; as soon as they sat down Lucas asked them, "All right, whaddya guys really think?" De Palma plowed into it: "It's gibberish," he said. "The first act, where are we? Who are these fuzzy guys? Who are these guys dressed up like the Tin Man from Oz? What kind of movie are you making here? You've left the audience out. You've vaporized the audience."

"Brian wouldn't let up," said Katz. "He was out of control. He was like a crazed dog." Everyone else offered Lucas their condolences, which was somehow worse; but he kept eating his dinner, nodding his head, taking it all in. Only Spielberg thought *Star Wars* would make any money. "That movie is going to make $100 million," he said. "And I'll tell you why. It has a marvelous innocence and naïveté to it, which is George, and people will love it."

But of course the screening was a disaster, as it had to be. Trying to watch *Star Wars* without its effects must have been like trying to infer the dimensions of a piece of sculpture by smell alone. One of the ironies of *Star Wars*'s success was that it would bring heightened attention to bear on films in the weeks just prior to their release—as the studios anxiously tested films before audiences—while at the same time rendering that process more nonsensical than it had ever been: thanks to Lucas's effects revolution, at no other time in Hollywood history would films less resemble their final finished state than in those few weeks prior to release. *Star Wars* wasn't evolving in traditional cinematic space; it was evolving elsewhere, in hyperspace, if you like—emerging in some hitherto uncharted relationship between the editing and the effects and the music, all brought into optimal conjunction only once, and only at the very last minute. Nobody knew what they had, not even the people working on it—particularly the people working on it. "You gotta realize that George is the visionary," says Ken Ralston. Even at the premiere, "they still didn't know what this movie was going to be. We sat there at the Academy Theater and I felt like I was blasted into my seat. It was like, 'That's great: who did this? Oh *we* did it, I don't believe it.' It was all in George's head, how it was going to come together . . . we were just shocked."

In the last few weeks before release, ILM was working seven days a week, three shifts, around the clock, in order to get their effects finished in time, while Lucas hunkered down in the editing room with his wife, Marcia. "He was miserable," recalled Carrie Fisher. "He was staying up eighteen and twenty hours a night, trying to make it perfect—they were literally pulling the film from his hands. He kept saying, 'Never again, I'm never going to do this again.'"

Star Wars opened on May 25 and broke the house records in all thirty-five of its theaters. Ladd rang up Lucas, incandescent with excitement. "It's amazing, there are lines around the block, I've never seen anything like it."

"Look, all science fiction films open big on the first weekend," replied Lucas. "Everything has done that." In a deliberate show of diffidence, Lucas flew to Hawaii, as he had done the week *American Graffiti* opened, and was joined there by Ladd and his wife. Ladd had begun to compile the box office figures in a book. "I had a book that thick of every theater," he remembers. "By this time it had expanded to a few more theaters, it's broken all the houses' records, *Jaws*'s and everything else, and I go,

'George, do you want to look at the figures,' and he went 'no no,' but every time I looked over he was sneaking a look at the book."

One night they were driving back from dinner, and they saw a queue for *Star Wars* snaking around the block. Lucas suggested they go in and sneak a peek at the audience. "It was a madhouse in there, screaming and shouting, amazing," says Ladd. "So we were driving back to the hotel and George is in a terrible dark mood. And I said, George, what's your problem? Isn't this fantastic, lines around the block, this great emotional response?' And he goes, 'This shot isn't right, that shot isn't right . . .' He's just made history and he's tearing the movie to shreds, trashing it like crazy. Finally Marcia just went 'Oh, shut up, George.'"

In the summer of 1977, the sci-fi fanzine *Starlog* ran a feature on the making of *Star Wars* and then didn't stop for a decade. In the years to come, they ran articles on the film's scenery painters, interviews with the actor who played Darth Vader's right-hand man, and with Mark Hamill's stand-in ("Randy here is a stand-in for Fett. Glenn you can guess by his height. Darla, being the only girl, you can figure out"). By 1983, they had gotten around to printing the floor plans of Aunt Beru's kitchen, and in 1985—eight years after the film's release—they finally laid their hands on that ever-elusive interview with the actor who played Luke's right-hand man, Wedge—a character who had ended up on the cutting room floor. To say that *Star Wars* inspired a loyalty bordering on the religious is understating it: when fans died, their obituaries would often say, simply, "He was a *Star Wars* fan." Peter Suschitzky, Lucas's cinematographer on *The Empire Strikes Back,* tells a story about the time he took his kids, then aged ten and four, to visit the set of the film, only to find that when they regaled their friends with the story the next day at school, they weren't believed, "not because it seemed too cool, but because they didn't think of the *Star Wars* movie as ever having been made by human hand. It was simply *there,* like the Bible." For a generation of fans, 1977 would forever be a sort of cinematic year zero: the year movies proper began.

It certainly bears an almost comic lack of resemblance to every other movie released in 1977—it's the Martian at the back of the yearbook photo. Unlike the other films that year, it didn't feature Burt Reynolds, or CB radios, or eighteen-wheeler trucks, or banjos, or any other of the dust-kicking accoutrements of the Kentucky Fried movies that were tearing up and down America's back roads at the time. What it had instead were hammerheaded aliens and high-speed dogfights, light-sabers and land-speeders, twin suns and detonating moons, all strung together by a director who seemingly couldn't wait to get from one end of his freshly summoned universe to the other. Everywhere you looked in *Star Wars* you saw marvels, and everywhere you looked you found characters who treated those marvels with the disdain you or I might reserve for an egg whisk. Up to this point sci-fi movies had been populated with types who acted as if they were as unfamiliar with the technology around them as was the audience, but when Han Solo tosses a blaster to Luke, he doesn't have to say what it does, or where the safety catch is—Luke simply catches it in midair, like one of those L-Dopa patients in *Awakenings,* and starts blasting. Even better is the moment when they first board the *Millennium Falcon* to flee the Imperial guards, start her up, and she stalls. Nobody had ever had a spaceship that *stalled* in a sci-fi film before.

To properly understand why this might have caused the hearts of the world's youth to skip a collective beat, you have to realize that to the average ten-year-old, there was only one thing that could possibly be cooler than the thought of owning your own spaceship. And that was the thought of owning your own spaceship for such a length of time that it had broken down on you repeatedly, falling into exactly the same state of fond, familiar decrepitude into which people let their cars sink. "What a piece of junk!" exclaims Luke. "She may not look like much," replies Han Solo, "but she's got it where it counts, kid!"—an exchange of dialogue that provides such a neat encapsulation of critical opinion on the film that you wonder why critics in 1977 didn't simply put their feet up and leave the film to itself. For junk is everywhere in *Star Wars*. It fills its characters' garages and homes, their spaceships and speeders. One race of creatures trades exclusively in junk: when R2-D2 and C-3PO land on Tatooine, they fall into the hands of Jawas, small feral creatures who drive around the planet in a big mobile rag-and-bone shop for robots, stopping every now and again to hold a garage sale, which is how Luke comes to buy the droids—as junk. The *Star Wars* universe, in other words, seems to run on roughly the same principle as a New York thrift store, only with less in the way of woolly hats. The only piece of new technology on display is, of course, the Death Star, which disposes of its junk in a big garbage masher, and into which Luke and his merry band naturally fall, like seeking like. That the Empire are the only people in the universe who haven't yet heard of recycling is enough to mark them out as the bad guys. The good guys don't buy off the peg; they tinker and solder, retrofit and weld. They are to be found in their garages, souping up their land-speeders, or up to their necks in the wiring of the *Millennium Falcon*. As Han Solo says proudly, "I made a few modifications to her myself."

Everything points back, in other words, to Lucas's most formative experience—souping up his Fiat Bianchina in his garage—and forward toward his defining aesthetic as a filmmaker. For *Star Wars*, as many critics have pointed out, is itself junk—quite literally so. It is made up from the spare parts of other movies—offcuts of western, snippets of swashbuckler, and scraps of dialogue well past their sell-by date. "You can type this shit, George, but you sure as hell can't say it," complained Harrison Ford—the only real actor in there, who further embarrassed proceedings by giving the only real performance, in which his disdain for the goings-on is palpable: the sequels would fight hard to keep him and Luke separated, as if sensing that Luke's ascent up the Jedi pole would never withstand Ford's powers of sarcasm. But then *Star Wars* was never really about good acting, any more than the Road Runner cartoons were about the detailed delineation of beaks. Good acting would have completely ruined it. A film that avoids close-ups like an introvert avoiding eye contact at a party, it is a movie consumed with motion blur and escape velocity, forward thrust and back blast. That's all the Force was, really, once you had stripped it of some of the more mystical mumbo-jumbo in which Lucas wrapped it: that feeling you get when you're driving so fast and well that you feel you've merged with your car, no longer really conscious of the decisions that you're making, but thinking through the car's fenders and chassis. If you've ever gone into the Zone while playing a video game, it's much the same feeling. *Star Wars* is junk but it is fast junk. It's got it where it counts.

To American audiences in 1977, it was cultural catnip. "The moment you saw that warship coming overhead, the audience just burst into applause," remembers Alan Ladd. "Something I'd never seen in a theater before, in all the previews I had been to. It brought tears to my eyes, I had to get up and walk out of the theater and around the block to get ahold of myself." The film "showed people it was all right to become totally involved in a movie again; to yell and scream and applaud and really roll with it," and it met them halfway just as *Jaws* had done, ending with a ceremony in which its heroes turned to face the camera to riotous applause—a sort of cinematic high-five, across the fourth wall, between the movie and its audience. In San Francisco, the manager of the Coronet on Geary Boulevard reported scenes that looked like outtakes from the film's alien cantina scene: "I've never seen anything like it. We're getting all kinds. Old people, young people, children, Hare Krishna groups. They bring cards to play in line. We have checker players, we have chess players. People with paints and sequins on their faces. Fruit eaters like I've never seen before. People loaded on grass and LSD. At least one guy's been here every day." People even queued up to watch the people queuing up. "It's become a family amusement to watch the people in the lines," said one Washington, D.C., resident. "It's really changing the neighborhood," complained another. "We used to have quiet streets and now there are just people walking up and down the neighborhood from six until midnight."

America is not, by nature, a queuing nation—preferring, in 1977, to leave that sort of thing to the Russians—but the queues for *Star Wars* marked the high point of that venerable tradition, soon to be eliminated by the smooth-running efficiency of the multiplex: the cinema queue, in all its pushy, pullulating, rowdy, ragged glory. Only a few months earlier, in *Annie Hall*, Woody Allen had exacted retribution on a noisy fellow queue member by ushering on Marshall McLuhan to silence him, but that was a queue for *The Sorrow and the Pity*, a film to be received in an air of suitably churchlike calm, not a blockbuster like *Jaws* and *Star Wars*, the queues for which, it is safe to say, were probably the only form of benign mass congregation America had seen in a decade, outside of a sports stadium. To most Americans in the mid-seventies, the sight of more Americans meant one of two things: 1) anti-Vietnam demonstrations, or 2) queues for gas. The 1976 Bicentennial celebrations in Boston, meanwhile, had proved a decided dud—denounced as a "Buy-Centennial" by those protesting its three-hundred-plus corporate sponsors, while protesters dumped packages marked "Gulf Oil" and "Exxon" into the harbor, and hauled a Nixon effigy about the bay. When official reenactors cried "Down with King George!" the shout came back: "Down with King Richard!" An official report into the incident concluded, "We entered the Bicentennial year having survived some of the bitterest times in our brief history. We cried out for something to draw us together again." It was quite a conundrum: how could the nation celebrate its youth as a scrappy rebel republic, when all around it sat all the signs—Vietnam, Exxon, Nixon—that it had transformed into the very empire it once opposed?

Star Wars was your answer. It was virtual patriotism—flag waving without any of the embarrassment that then clung to overly public display of the Stars and Stripes. It was pomp without the circumstance—a chance for the country's pent-up triumphalism to play out in the harmless vacuum of space, where audiences could cheer on the scrappy rebels once again, boo the evil empire, and generally have themselves a ball. Strangely enough, Hollywood has never made a definitive movie about the American War of Independence; the Civil War gave it *Gone With the Wind,* but the war that founded the actual country itself has proved a curious blind spot for Hollywood. Partly, it's because the story is so well propagated, in classrooms up and down the country, that it has lifted off into the level of myth—it's just part of the woodwork of American culture, part of the narrative DNA of Hollywood, and of every movie in which a little guy takes on the big guy and wins. *Star Wars* may be as close to a direct and head-on distillation of this founding myth as Hollywood has ever come. Lucas hadn't just given America a hit film. He had given the nation something of its youth, and at a time when it was feeling, if not its age, then certainly a little middle-aged spread. One of the great things, in fact, about the early blockbusters of Lucas and Spielberg is just how much of America they give you. Critics normally like to say that about films like *The Deer Hunter,* or *All the President's Men,* films by more politicized directors who faced up, four-square, to the problems enmeshing the country at the time. *Star Wars,* on the other hand, is "just" escapism, although there is nothing more revealing than an escape route—the velocity and trajectory with which fantasy finds its headway into a nation's dream life, and in *Star Wars,* you got to see the nation's dream life laid bare: "Pomp and parade, shows, games, sports, guns, bells, bonfires, and illuminations, from one end of the continent to the other from this time forward, forever more" was how President John Adams recommended Americans celebrate the first July 4th, in 1776. Over the years Americans would improvise their own summer season activities, all as blissfully meaningless as the next, from letting off fireworks to hurling themselves over the edge of Niagara Falls in a barrel. As of 1977, American citizens had a new meaningless activity to add to the list, one with all the luminosity of fireworks and none of the bruises of barrel navigation: they went to the movies.

To be precise: they went to see the latest blockbusters. Even more so than the movies, they may be the quintessential American form, for many countries have film industries, but only America makes blockbusters. France once tried to turn a much loved comic strip, *Astérix and Obélix,* into a fully functioning film franchise and the results were not pretty. And while America has its own art house and independent movie traditions, noble and thriving, something about the gentle give-and-take of hundreds of millions of dollars seems to lubricate a certain level of creativity in American movies. Blockbusters have thus quickly ascended to the pantheon of products—like McDonald's, Coca-Cola, and MTV—that are both revered and reviled the world over as the embodiment of Americanness Incarnate, if only for the simple reason that they share with their parent nation two of its defining attributes *as* a nation: its size and its speed—its girth and the gearbox required to cross it. The size, Hollywood already had covered—overwhelming scale was what distinguished and ultimately doomed the old DeMillean spectaculars—but it was the missing element, speed, that Lucas supplied in 1977, summoning a note that was both unmistakably American—a "jaunty, wise-ass, fast, very modern, sort of a teenaged thing, a polished chrome kind of feel" as screenwriter Lawrence Kasdan put it—and wholly exportable at the same time. It took Russia by storm, where as one diplomat put it, "R2-D2, whatever he speaks, it isn't English." In Britain, audiences could politely ignore the fact that the Empire sounded British and concentrate instead on the fact that they looked German. In Germany, the reverse. In Italy, critics found the film an allegory for communism, while in France, critics denounced it as "crypto-fascist": the Death Star resembled nothing so much as Albert Speer's models for Berlin, they pointed out; and even the rebel ceremony at the end was clearly modeled on the 1933 Nuremberg rally. It was the opening salvo in what would amount to an all-out war between the French and the blockbuster, which would reach a bloody climax in 1993—when half of France ground to a halt to watch *Jurassic Park,* and the other half denounced the first half for succumbing to American "cultural imperialism." It is worth remembering, perhaps, that French film critics, perhaps understandably, tend to see crypto-fascism in a lot more places than film critics from other countries, and that it is the Speer-like immensity of the Death Star that leads to its downfall, rendering it penetrable by the smaller X-wings, nippy maneuverability winning the day, just as it did in *Jaws.* Besides which, the politics of *Star Wars* is probably best wrapped up using that old rule of cinema, the one that states that no film starring Harrison Ford will ever cause you or your friends to submit to totalitarian dictatorship.

But this rule—call it Dr. Jones's First Theorum—was a new rule in 1977, and yet to be rigorously tested, so the French can't be blamed for not having heard of it. Amongst American critics, *Star Wars* got a great reception, much better than *Jaws,* for it was less ostensibly sensationalistic, with a more obvious scroll of movie history hanging over it. In *Time,* Jay Cocks called it "a remarkable confection; a subliminal history of the movies, wrapped in a riveting tale of suspense and adventure, ornamented with some of the most ingenious special effects ever contrived for film." Its rerelease, in 1997, was however, a different matter, which left Lucas's reputation resting just a few notches above that of Mephistopheles. Three things happened in quick succession to secure a quick conviction. First, the centenary of cinema, in 1996, which gave everyone their victim. Second came the rerelease of *Star Wars,* which gave everyone their suspect. Third and finally, we had the publication in 1998 of *Easy Riders, Raging Bulls,* which supplied judge, jury, and executioner in the form of film historian Peter Biskind. The book was a rousing bohemian rhapsody to the so-called movie brats like Martin Scorsese, Francis Ford Coppola, and Arthur Penn, who under cover of the studios' confusion following their near collapse in the early seventies, marched straight out of film school and snuck under the gates of the citadel to make such movies as *Mean Streets, Chinatown, The Godfather, Bonnie and Clyde*—films high on equal amounts French New Wave, auteur theory, and pot, which played fast and loose with genre, merrily splintered their time schemes, let loose as many moral ambiguities as you could shake a stick at on the way to endings as unhappy as any in Christendom. Lucas and Spielberg, on the other hand, are found guilty of returning "the 70s audience, grown sophisticated on a diet of European and New Hollywood films, to the simplicities of the pre-60s Golden Age of movies" and—worse—not taking anywhere near enough drugs.

They can't help but come across as dweeby outsiders, standing out from Biskind's bacchanalian frieze like priests at the Playboy Mansion, although one of the curious things about Biskind's in crowd is how even those on the inside of it don't seem to belong there. It's an inherent problem, I guess, with a group photograph of a bunch of mavericks—they're always wandering off out of frame. Despite snapshots of Coppola and Scorsese in their Castro-beard phase, they both make for rather unconvincing hippies. Nor is it too hard to look at Biskind's countercultural canon and sense audiences rewarding whatever Old Hollywood virtues they could find beneath these movies' scuffed New Hollywood exterior. What made *The French Connection* a hit: its air of 6:00 a.m. scuzziness or its fender-bending car chase? And what were *Bonnie and Clyde, The Godfather,* and *The Exorcist* if not high-end retoolings of old pulp genres, just like *Jaws* and *Star Wars?* Biskind begins to realize this, and so the purges begin: Coppola and Friedkin are fine until they achieve success, at which point they are kicked off his team for being advance-guard Reaganites; then it's out with Peter Bogdanovich for being too "classical" in his storytelling. If you further subtract Scorsese and Altman—whose talent survived the killing fields of 1977—who exactly were the true auteurist casualties of the blockbuster era? Basically, if you spend your movie-watching life according to Biskind's fierce ideological strictures, you're going to be spending an awful amount of time in the company of Dennis Hopper. A wild and crazy guy, but still.

"Dennis believed, and this was a revelation after we found it out, because he cut for months under this misapprehension—that once you made a cut you couldn't put anything back," said one of Hopper's collaborators on *Easy Rider.* "It was absolutely stunning. He was the worst editor that's ever been." Or as Biskind prefers, Hopper "liberated *Easy Rider* from the prettifying aesthetic of technical excellence," which is one way of putting it. Another might be that *Easy Rider* was as meretri-

cious a bit of youth exploitation as any of the blockbuster era, and that
its true legacy was the bunch of B-grade biker movies and Summer of
Love cash-ins, all wholly liberated from technical excellence, which followed: *Getting Straight, The Revolutionary, The Strawberry Statement*
("where a boy . . . and a girl . . . meet . . . and touch . . . and BLOW THEIR
MINDS"). Watching a film like *The Trip*—a dry run for *Easy Rider* written by Jack Nicholson, starring Hopper and Peter Fonda, and featuring,
if memory serves, a joint-smoking scene shot from the point of view of
the joint—it's not too hard to see why so many of the nation's youth
were so eager to clamber aboard the *Millennium Falcon* in 1977. They
didn't want a trip; they wanted a ride.

Biskind isn't alone in misreading the success of *Easy Rider*. So too,
did everybody—out-of-the-park left-field hits always leave a trail of confusion and disarray in their wake—but what if what audiences were responding to was not the film's politics but the anything-goes summer
breeze that swept them into theaters? What if the thing that made *Easy
Rider* a hit was that single shot of Peter Fonda, complete with Captain
America helmet, blazing a trail down the highway to the sound of Step-
penwolf? Subtract the politics and pot and wouldn't you end up with a
movie a little like *Star Wars?* "A cinema of moments, of images, of sensory stimuli increasingly divorced from story" in Biskind's words. "The
movies leapt ahead—through hyperspace if you will—to the 80s and
90s, the era of non-narrative music videos, and VCRs, which allowed
users to view film in a non-narrative way, surfing the action beats with
fast forward." That's some leap. You wonder what it looked like on acid.
As a roll call of the bogeymen that critics see bedeviling contemporary
cinema, it can scarcely be bettered—action beats, VCRs, MTV . . . One
can almost see the poor moviegoer, twitching and spasming in their seat,
as their overstimulated lobes receive their instructions from the blockbuster power grid. "The eye and mind are both bewildered by the too
sudden and too frequent shifts of scene," wrote William Eaton in an article for *American Magazine* entitled "A New Epoch in the Movies."
"There is a terrible sense of rush and hurry and flying about, which is in-
tensified by the twitching film and generally whang-bang music," and
who, with the laser bolts of 1977 still ringing in their ears, could disagree?

There's only one problem: Eaton wrote this in 1914. The new-
fangled epoch in question wasn't the blockbuster era, but the silent era,

Hollywood's most boisterous boom time, when the studios plowed what money they had into luring kids into the newly built nickelodeons to watch delicately shaded character studies of speeding locomotive trains, such as *Empire State Express* (1897)—a film that, most critics agree, not only boasts one of the coolest titles in recorded history, but that blasted audience members right out of their socks: "Two ladies in one of the boxes on the left-hand of the horseshoe, which is just where the flyer vanishes from view, screamed and nearly fainted as it came apparently rushing upon them," ran one newspaper's account. "They recovered in time to laugh at their needless excitement." The Force, one guesses, was with them. This is the problem with death-of-film arguments like Biskind's; they have an uncanny ability to resemble accounts of the birth of film, when the best minds of a generation fathered a squalling brat of a medium, hopelessly addicted to sensation and show, and never happier than when frying the nerves of its audience. Biskind's "cinema of moments, of images, of sensory stimuli increasingly divorced from story" is a pretty good description of the very first films, for all silent movies were, by definition, action movies, and many were straightforward thrill rides, unadorned by such fripperies as plot, or characters, or stars. They were made fast, and sold by brand name ("Every day a Biograph feature"), playing out in nickelodeons whose viewing conditions weren't too far from the modern-day multiplex, to an audience comprised mostly of immigrants and teenagers. "The backbone of today's business is the attendance of young people from seventeen to twenty-three years of age," Harold Corey sniffed in *Everybody's Magazine* in 1919. "At 23 other interests develop."

By then, plots had arrived, but only just. According to the *Brooklyn Eagle* in 1906, the modern-day audience "must have something happening every minute, allowing for no padding with word-painting, following climax after climax." Anyone who thinks *Star Wars* invented breakneck pacing need only check out the early chase flicks of D. W. Griffith, which still leave the projector reels spinning, even today. For *The Lonedale Operator*, Griffith mounted his camera on the front of a speeding train; and for *The Girl and Her Trust* had it placed onboard a car that was racing alongside a racing train, with another car in hot pursuit. How often the modern-day blockbuster, from *Raiders of the Lost Ark* to *The Terminator*, would dust off the same chase movie mechanics first pioneered by Griffith, although then as now, it left many critics nursing cricked necks. In the *New York Times* in 1915, Alexander Woollcott wrote, "It is easy to predict that the cut-back, and similar evidences of restlessness, will fade gradually from the screens, to be used only on special occasions." It didn't of course, the restlessness spread further, and movies got faster still, slowed only by Griffith's discovery, in 1915 with *The Birth of a Nation,* of another of cinema's constituent dimensions: scale. Upon its release in 1915, the film's camera operator, Karl Brown, noted that "Bigger and better, bigger and better became the constantly chanted watchword of the year. Soon the two words became one. Bigger meant better, and a sort of giganticism overwhelmed the world, especially the world of motion pictures."

All in all, it hadn't taken long—just under twenty-five years—for the cinema to discover speed, for speed to give way to size, size to spectacle, hype to hoopla, and "unprecedented splendour of pageantry . . . combined with grotesque incoherence of design and utter fatuity of thought," as the *Times* called Griffith's *Intolerance*—the first of the megaflops, as perhaps any film in which the characters pay prolonged tribute to the goddess Ishtar was, perhaps, always destined to be. To anyone who has sat through the last twenty-five years of American film, in fact, the first twenty-five years offer a strangely familiar landscape, a land of speed freaks and hucksters, teenage kicks and sensation merchants, all running to familiar rhythms and following much the same course. All the keys to the blockbuster era are to be found here, in the silent era. "The first newspaper coverage of motion pictures presented them as a technological phenomenon ('Edison's marvel'), then as a social problem ('nickel madness'), and ultimately as an economic statistic ('the nation's fourth largest industry')," writes Richard Koszarski in *An Evening's Entertainment.* The blockbuster era would follow much the same course, from the explosive special effects of *Star Wars* (technological phenomenon), to the worries over *Batman*'s hype (social problem), to the hysteria surrounding the budget of *Titanic* (economic statistic). There is even, around the twenty-year mark, a huge technological revolution, forged in the flurry of fresh dollars: the invention of sound in 1927 and the mainstream arrival of CGI, computer-generated imaging, in 1991.

"*Star Wars* is basically a silent film, was designed to be a silent film," says Lucas. "In terms of people's aesthetics, especially critics: they complained bitterly when sound came in, that the medium had been destroyed, but the concept of cinema started as a vaudeville show. It started as a magic act. They took the magician off the bill, put up this sheet and they ran this magic thing, where you could see things you couldn't see. They say summer is now dominated by films that are aimed toward kids. Well, kids are the audience. It's a market-driven medium and it always has been. If anything, the irony of that whole hypothesis that was put forward—which was completely ludicrous—that Steven and I changed Hollywood, or changed cinema, changed the movies, when in reality, what people don't realize is that there's an ecology of the marketplace, which is half of the money that is made in the grosses of a movie goes to the theater owners. The other half goes to the distributors. The theater owners made so much money on *The Godfather* and *Jaws* and *Star Wars* that they built the multiplex and it allowed the distributors to come into being like Miramax and all these other low-budget small distributors, who could start making money because they could get on the screens, and that's the secret of this whole business. If you can't get on the screens you can't get shown and the more screens you have the more chance you have. That's what really changed. When *Star Wars* came out there was no independent film industry. Now there's a huge independent film industry. That was the result of those films."

It all depends on what you mean by "cinema," as they say, although one of the weirder things about this comment is that the critical traffic only goes one way: critics get to excoriate *Jaws* and *Star Wars* for failing to live up to the exalted standards set by *Apocalypse Now* or *The Godfather,* but nobody ever says of *Five Easy Pieces,* "great, as good a chamber piece on the disintegration of the American family as could be imagined, but it could have done with an aerial dogfight or two." Nobody ever gets to come out of *Nashville,* going "Wonderful, a classic really, but I could have done with more in the way of killer sharks." We're all too scared of being kicked out of film class. Well, now we know better: if it's historical precedent you're after, it doesn't get much better than the origin of the medium. In one sense, Spielberg and Lucas didn't betray cinema at all: they plugged it back into the grid, returning the medium to its roots as a carnival sideshow, a magic act, one big special effect, punching through the fourth wall—the screams that greeted *Jaws* in the theater floating back to the screams that first greeted *Empire State Express,* whose speed-freak instincts whip and blur into those of *Star Wars.* They also set the industry on exactly the same course followed by the silent era, the "death of cinema" also a kind of rebirth, all its vices and virtues borne out in excelsis, playing out in much the same fashion and over exactly the same period of time, from pulse-quickening boom to arterial-fattened bust in the space of a single generation.

TIME LINE

1976

1. *Rocky* (United Artists) $56,500,000
2. *A Star Is Born* (WB) $37,100,000
3. *King Kong* (Paramount) $36,900,000
4. *All the President's Men* (WB) $31,000,000
5. *Silver Streak* (Fox) $30,000,000
6. *The Omen* (Fox) $28,500,000
7. *The Bad News Bears* (Paramount) $24,300,000
8. *The Enforcer* (WB) $24,100,000
9. *Midway* (Universal) $21,600,000
10. *Silent Movie* (Fox) $21,200,000

1977

1. *Star Wars* (Fox) $193,800,000
2. *Close Encounters of the Third Kind* (Columbia) $81,800,000
3. *Saturday Night Fever* (Paramount) $74,100,000
4. *Smokey and the Bandit* (Universal) $59,000,000
5. *The Goodbye Girl* (MGM) $41,900,000
6. *Oh, God!* (WB) $31,500,000
7. *The Deep* (Columbia) $31,200,000
8. *The Rescuers* (Disney) $30,100,000
9. *The Spy Who Loved Me* (United Artists) $24,300,000
10. *Semi-Tough* (United Artists) $22,900,000

*Figures show U.S. domestic gross.

CHAPTER 3

HALLOWEEN FOR GROWN-UPS

"I refuse to send off to another world,
as the first example of earth's intelligence, a man
who wants to go and set up a McDonald's franchise."
—Paul Schrader

"That's exactly the guy I want to send!"
—Steven Spielberg

The cash from *Star Wars* was like water from a flailing hose—if you were standing nearby, you got wet. No film had ever made anything like that much money before; all the means of scooping it up and siphoning it off that the studios would later develop simply weren't in place yet. A giddy Lucas gave away 25 percent of his share in points, each worth $300,000, to Alec Guinness, Harrison Ford, Mark Hamill, Carrie Fisher, John Williams, and Spielberg, as the film's box office receipts climbed from $100 million, after just three months, to $193 million by the end of the year. During those first three months, Fox was making $1.2 million a day from the movie, sending its shares rocketing from $6 to $25 per share. At the end of the year it posted earnings of $50.8 million for 1977, a 47.4 percent increase over 1976. It was, said CEO Dennis Stanfill, "five years' growth in one," and it continued to carry the company for the next few years, provided Fox with 85 percent of its earnings in 1978, and 62 percent of its earnings in 1979. Blockbusters, it was now clear, didn't just get studios out of a pinch; they bankrolled them for many years to come.

The merchandising was its own micro-economy. When Fox had struck its deal with Lucas, back in 1975, they had suggested they pay him only $100,000 to direct, plus 40 percent of the profits—a figure which they fully expected to rise, as negotiations went on. Instead, Lucas agreed, if they would cede him the merchandising and sequel rights to the film. "Fox's head of business thought he'd died and gone to heaven," says Ladd. "Merchandising? What was that worth?" By August 25 the novelization sold over two million, the two-disc sound-track had sold out, and toy-maker Kenner, totally swamped by demand for *Star Wars* figures, was putting out "Early Bird Certificate Packages"—a box with illustrations of the figures on the lid, some decals, and a mail-in form entitling the purchaser to figures once Kenner made them. By 1981, the assorted merchandising would have generated $1 billion—over five times more than the actual movie. "Everyone talks about how brilliant I was to get the licensing, and the sequels and everything," says Lucas. "All I wanted to do was, I had three movies, because my movie got too big and I cut it in three different pieces. My only interest was to make sure I got those three movies made. I was of the mind-set all filmmakers are, which was that I got one done, and it's not going to be a success and nobody's going to want to do it, so I got the rights so I could control it, and I wanted to get the licensing because I wanted to make posters and T-shirts and promote the film. It wasn't until a year after the movie was out that we started to deal with toys, and all those other things, so that whole idea that all this was product-driven is nonsense."

For Alan Ladd, *Star Wars*'s success marked a thrilling vindication over chairman Stanfill, who grudgingly called himself "bemused, gratified, and perplexed" by the film's success. "It may simply be that people see the picture, love it, and want to own a piece of it. On the other hand, it could also be that the market has been rather dull of late, and that's why we've been given the play." It didn't make any sense to him. Here was the studio resuscitated by the very thing—blockbusters—that had gotten it into difficulty in the first place, and certainly in 1977 there were plenty of the older breed of blockbuster wheezing into cinemas: Warner Bros. *Exorcist II: The Heretic* (costing $11 million), United Artists *A Bridge Too Far* ($24 million), Paramount and Universal's *Sorcerer* ($18 million), and Fox's *The Other Side of Midnight* ($9 million). Those looking for signs of the Brave New World of cinema that had just dawned, on the other hand, had to try their luck with *Rollercoaster, Airport '77,* or else *The Deep, The Pack,* and all the other *Jaws* ripoffs that swam into moviehouses that summer. If you slit the belly of the summer of 1977—much as Richard Dreyfuss slit the belly of the shark in *Jaws*—out flooded a slew of flotsam and jetsam, great chunks of undigested Spielberg, reconverted back into his constituent B-movie enzymes. The studios may have wanted every movie to be *Jaws,* but they didn't have much luck. As *Jaws 2* proved, they couldn't even make a *Jaws* movie that was like *Jaws.*

Quickest off the mark was producer Dino De Laurentiis, a five-foot-six, cigarillo-chomping Neapolitan whose three-pronged assault on *Jaws*'s box office included *The White Buffalo,* starring Charles Bronson and a large, marauding shagpile rug, *Orca,* starring Richard Harris and a large vengeful killer whale—it was *Death Wish* for fish—and, the year before, *King Kong,* a remake of the 1933 classic. "No one cry when *Jaws* die," proclaimed De Laurentiis, "but when the monkey die, people gonna cry. Intellectuals gonna love *Kong;* even film buffs who love the first *Kong* gonna love ours. Why? Because I give them no crap. I no spend two, three million to do quick business. I spend 24 million on my *Kong.* I give them quality. I got here a great love story, a great adventure. And she rated PG, for everybody."

Would that the film had had an ounce of that Barnum-like gusto. It is resolutely anti-Barnum, making over the original as a whey-faced ecological fable, pitting paleontologist Jeff Bridges against evil oil magnate Charles Grodin, who gazes on Kong and envisions a series of advertisements modeled on Exxon's "Put a Tiger in Your Tank" campaign. "You're an environmental rapist," yells Bridges, "the kids will burn every one of your gas stations from Maine to California!" The film's principled stand against the ravages of commerce came backed up by a series of tasteful promotional tie-ins with Jim Beam whiskey, 7-Eleven, and Schrafft candy. It would be one of the more resounding ironies of the blockbuster age, that movies so driven by the lure of money would be so shamefaced about the making of it. The likes of DeMille and Griffith used to be proud of their profligacy—Griffith actually rounded *up* the budget of *Intolerance* by a few thousand, in order to suggest to the public how seriously he took his duties as a big spender—but their modern antecedents would show rather less backbone, with *Waterworld* devoting every breath in its $200 million body to warn us of the danger of wasting the world's resources, while *Jurassic Park* would take a similarly firm stand against the evils of the theme park industry. Back in 1977, you could almost hear the click of the De Laurentiis brain: if multi-million-dollar denuncifications of the evils of corporate commerce were what the kids wanted, then multi-million-dollar denunciations of the evils of corporate commerce were what they would get.

By far the most lucrative of the *Jaws* cash-ins was *The Deep*—the brainchild of Peter Guber, a young entertainment lawyer who had scaled Columbia's executive ladder with a speed attributable, in part, to astonishing reserves of loquaciousness. Guber's big watchword was "the Big Mo"—the Big Momentum. The risks of making blockbusters was so off-putting to studios, he had noticed, that they weren't really in the business of making movies at all; they were in the business of coming up with sound reasons *not* to make them. Any project therefore needed, in order to get a green light, the Big Mo—the magic momentum necessary to steamroll it through the gridlocked studio decision-making process. "The Big Mo isn't something. It's everything," says Guber. "Not making the picture, let alone making it great. You don't get to make the picture until you get someone to say okay. And to do that you had to create a support base within the company that allowed the senior management to take the necessary risk. The way we did it in *The Deep* was by getting Peter Benchley's first book after *Jaws*. We got Robert Shaw, who just did *Jaws*. We got the big star who had just come out of TV: Nick Nolte. We had the hot Jacqueline Bisset. So even though the picture was expensive, it had so much momentum that the management didn't have to say yes. They had to say no. And that's hard when something's got momentum."

Armed with a marketing budget of $3 million, Guber personally supervised every aspect of the movie's PR, inviting journalists down to witness the underwater shoot, which he further documented in a book called *Inside The Deep,* in which he hammered up every glitch into a *Jaws*-style fiasco: "We have a long way to go, and we're running horrendously behind schedule, but the excitement is overwhelming . . . in spite of frequent panic attacks, I am really up to my ears in the making of a major motion picture." He came up with a vertical poster design that echoed *Jaws*'s; released a theme song, "Down Deep Inside" by Donna Summer on transparent blue vinyl; even concocted a rum cocktail called The Deep ("It should be served in a tall glass, simulating the tall, vertical ad look of *The Deep*"), and orchestrated a $1.3 million TV advertising campaign that would—by his calculations—expose every potential audience member to fifteen images of the movie before its release on June 17, a date so chosen because, as he told the *New York Times,* "the maids and the blue collars and much of the industry get paid twice a month. They put their checks in the bank on the 15th, have them clear by the 16th, and they're ready to spend by the 17th."

Someone had been paying attention in the summer of 1975. "*Jaws* changed the navigational stakes for financiers, producers, and distributors," says Guber. "The upper limits of what a movie could do changed not just incrementally, but exponentially. It showed that a film could capture the widest possible audience almost from the outset, with a very wide, deep platform release, as opposed to a platform release, where the most financial reward could be captured in the early weeks of a release, when the return to the distributor was at its highest. You brought in a lot of money very fast, at the beginning." For anyone expecting *Jaws, The Deep* was the most transcendent of let-downs—boasting, by way of underwater killers, only a supporting role for a rather morose-looking eel—but before news of that eel could leak out, the film had grossed more than $8 million in three days, and by the end of the year had taken over $30 million. Such cunning would pay off even more handsomely, a decade later, with a film that, in 1980, existed only in the form of a single-spaced, nine-page memo, presented to Guber by the writer Michael Uslan: "No longer portrayed as a pot-bellied caped clown, *Batman* has again become a vigilante who stalks criminals in the shadow of night."

"*Batman* was a nine-year journey through three companies. It was a matter of tenacity, persistence, and not much momentum," admits Guber, searching for a replacement mot juste: "It was . . . synchro-destiny."

❑ ❑ ❑

The person whose career *Jaws* most profoundly altered was, of course, the man who made it. Spielberg hadn't wanted to make the movie, originally, at all. He worried about following his monster truck movie, *Duel,* with a monster shark movie, and told producers Brown and Zanuck that he didn't want to become known as the "shark-and-truck director." He didn't want to make "movies," he wanted to make "films," and had his eye on a musical about rum-runners called *Lucky Lady.* Brown had dissuaded him, saying, "If you make this movie [*Jaws*], you can make all the films you want." After *Jaws* opened, Spielberg set his sights on a script called *The Bingo Longo Traveling Club*—about a traveling black baseball team in the thirties—which had been written by his friends Hal Barwood and Matthew Robbins, and was being developed by Rob Cohen at Universal. Here was a film, if ever there was one.

He phoned Cohen up to ask him, "Don't you like the way I direct?"

"What are you talking about, you're brilliant."

"How come you haven't offered me *Bingo Longo*?"

"'Cause I didn't think you'd be interested, it's a small picture."

Jaws had, he realized, changed everything. The future in which he directed films about black baseball stars, like the future in which he directed Paul Newman musicals about rum-runners, now seemed like some parallel universe out of *The Twilight Zone.* For one thing, he was famous, and not just movie-director-famous, but film-star-famous. "As disorganized and strung out as it was back in '75," Spielberg says, "they still managed to find my face on television enough times that I began to lose my anonymity. I felt like I'd lost my virginity for the second time." The teenage connoisseur of junk culture was now part of the pop culture firmament, sucked into the TV he had grown up watching, but now looking out. After *Jaws* opened, Spielberg embarked on a worldwide publicity tour of seven countries, and was trailed everywhere he went by translators, TV cameras, and thickets of microphones. "I've never been tapped on the shoulder so many times walking around in public," he says. "That was the big change in my life." All movies, said François Truffaut, grow out of the movies that precede them, and *Close Encounters of the Third Kind* grew directly out of *Jaws*'s success, its plot as globe-trotting as Spielberg now was, and also featuring translators, mapmakers, microphones, TV cameras . . . If Spielberg was now virtually living the life of a Beatle, and *Jaws* had been his *Sgt. Pepper,* then *Close Encounters* was his *Magical Mystery Tour*—a boy-in-the-bubble riff on his own international megatude, or at least that of his movies. "I was riding such a wild whirlwind that looking through a microscope at a personal story wasn't as compelling as looking through a telescope at the cosmos," he says, "so I went on to choose projects that had a feeling of conduction, energy, size."

He had first pitched his idea for a picture about alien visitation to producers Michael and Julia Phillips at their Malibu beach house in 1973. They had put Spielberg in touch with screenwriter Paul Schrader, who turned in a script entitled *Kingdom Come,* which centered on a modern-day St. Paul who worked for the government, debunking UFOs. "But then one day, like St. Paul, he has his road to Damascus—he has an encounter," said Schrader. "He goes to the government; he's going to blow the lid off the whole thing, but instead the government offers him unlimited funds to pursue contact clandestinely, so he spends the next fifteen years trying to do that. But eventually he discovers that the key to making contact isn't out there in the universe, but implanted inside him." Spielberg didn't really care about the idea of a metaphorical encounter, or for the script's air of Watergate-era conspiracy—he wanted embrace, annunciation, not conspiracy, cover-up—and wanted as his hero not some privately funded saint but someone like himself, who lived in the suburbs, went to the movies, and ate crappy food.

"I refuse to send off to another world, as the first example of earth's intelligence, a man who wants to go and set up a McDonald's franchise," countered Schrader.

"That's exactly the guy I want to send!" said Spielberg.

As the script faltered, so did the chance of a green light from Columbia. Of all the studios trying to weather the financial tempest of the seventies, Columbia was the closest to outright collapse. Flush with the success of *Easy Rider* in 1969, it had promptly signed up the film's producer Bert Schneider to reproduce the trick and cash in on the newly emergent youth market, but successes such as *Five Easy Pieces* and *The Last Picture Show* soon segued into a series of flops—*A Safe Place; Drive, He Said; The King of Marvin Gardens.* Columbia found itself awash in red ink, and by the end of 1973 close to bankruptcy, having amassed more than $220 million in bank debt. After a corporate reshuffle, the studio found itself with a new CEO, Alan Hirschfield, and a new president, David Begelman, a legendary gambler. Initially suspicious of plowing all his money into that much-feared beast, a blockbuster, Begelman relented after *Jaws* opened.

"After *Jaws*, the money spigots opened," recalled Michael Phillips. "When Spielberg came back it was a whole new ball game. Suddenly he was a much better risk to the studio's point of view and he was given free rein to come up with the best his imagination could conjure. . . . [Begelman] was in a position to really invest, to really bet the farm. They needed to, Columbia was teetering on the brink of insolvency, and here they had the hottest director in town and a subject matter that seemed a natural fit for him. So they bet the farm." Seeking to shield the company from the risk of *Close Encounters*, Begelman sought overseas investors, from EMI in Britain and a group of German tax shelter investors, who between them provided $7 million. Even so, he had everything riding on the movie: *Variety* calculated that *Close Encounters* would have to be among the top twenty all-time box office hits just to break even.

"Without much tact to speak of, some executives from Columbia took me to lunch a week before my first day of shooting," says Spielberg, "and basically said, 'We're in financial straits right now, and you have our entire company resting on your shoulders. If you go too far over-budget like you did on *Jaws*, you could bring this company down.' They literally said to me, 'You're responsible for whether Columbia ceases to exist or continues.' They put that pressure on me, said, 'Now go make a good movie.' That was the bottle of champagne they broke over my head. I was reeling from that on my first four weeks of shooting." The movie's main set was built in a World War II dirigible hangar in Mobile, Alabama—450 feet long, 250 feet wide, 90 feet high—into which cinematographer Vilmos Zsigmond packed as many lights as he could: 4,000-watt spotlights, Navy Signal lights, Arc lamps, Brute Lights, HMI-focused spots, 2,000-watt quartz lights—all requiring as much as 4,200,000 kilowatts of electricity to power up, 500 times as much as your average home. "*Close Encounters* was a heavy, heavy situation," said Zsigmond. "We used an incredible amount of power. We took generators from Hollywood down to the hangars in Mobile; we used all the generators there were." Not even the 150 tons of air-conditioning could cope with the resulting temperature inside the hangar, which, helped by the Alabama summer, soared to 130 degrees. It was so hot that the hangar had its own internal climate: actual clouds formed, and rain. "The summit has real evergreen trees growing on it, and a maintenance man is climbing up the road watering them," wrote actor Bob Balaban in his diary of the shoot. "The greenery is doing beautifully."

The nerves of all concerned were not doing so well. "It was a nightmare," said Zsigmond. "There was a lot of pressure from the studio. Nobody could conceive how much light we needed." A bitter feud started up between Zsigmond and producer Julia Phillips, who wanted him fired, convinced that his lights were the source of the picture's budgetary ills. "Every time I walk down to the big set I feel like I'm making a descent into hell," she later wrote. "The longer we shoot here, the more like hell it seems. Sometimes on a really bad night I can still see a scene being shot, with Vilmos walking into it, and telling his crew that we just need 'vun leetle inky-dinky over here.'" Such paranoia is rife on movie sets, but it was exacerbated in Phillips's case by the vast quantities of cocaine she was then consuming, sometimes openly, off the table at meetings. Spielberg refused to fire Zsigmond, in the process becoming his producer's hate-object-du-jour, and relations between director and producer began a long, slow descent into acrimony.

The movie's budget, meanwhile, continued to climb, the initial shooting budget of $2.8 million rising to $4 million, then $5.5 million, then $7 million, then $9 million, then $12 million and beyond, as Spielberg's conception for the movie kept growing. Each night, after he knocked off shooting, he would head back to his rented house, which he shared with editor Michael Kahn, and screen movies for his crew— The Canterville Ghost, Pinocchio, The Searchers, Battleground—and each morning he would come to the set with a raft of new ideas for the day's shooting. The four shots they had to complete each day became five, and five became six. "Gotta shoot fast!" Spielberg urged his crew one day, to which the movie's gaffer, Earl Gilbert, replied, "Steven, if you would stop watching those fucking movies every night, we would be on schedule."

Originally scheduled for release Easter of 1977, the movie was put back to June, and then the fall. By the end, the budget had reached $19 million, the producers had popped the cork to celebrate the end of shooting six times, and Spielberg had gotten through five cinematographers. While special effects supervisor Douglas Trumbull completed the movie's effects, Spielberg's attention turned to the marketing of the movie. When *The Sugarland Express,* his first theatrical film, had failed to ignite at the box office, Spielberg had blamed it on poor marketing. "The right graphics campaign and plan of attack for releasing a picture are as important as finding a good script and making a good movie," he said. For *Close Encounters,* Spielberg wanted the opposite campaign to that for *Jaws,* an information blackout, not a blitz. He had insisted on total secrecy for the project from the word go—closed sets, closed dailies, locked doors wherever possible—and he designed the posters himself: a road tapering off to the vanishing point, light blooming on the horizon, and underneath, the tag line, "We are not alone." Even the title was a come-on, an example of what Spielberg called an "encyclopedia title" like *The Exorcist:* you had to look it up in the encyclopedia to find out what it meant.

Julia Phillips took the poster up to David Begelman for his approval.

"It looks like headlights," he complained.

"Well, we'll make it more mysterious—it's just the rough," replied Phillips. "I like it. Steven likes it. . . . This is a big picture with a title that has essential meaning. But it's not presold like a best-selling book or a Broadway musical. We have the opportunity to familiarize the public with the title, which also explains what the movie is about. The graphic isn't finished yet, but it's a strong hook and it will reproduce very nicely in black-and-white. The idea is to buy a lot of double truck ads in Sunday papers around Christmas, so people will be just panting to see this piece of shit next Christmas."

If they fixed the headlights, said Begelman, they had his okay, but Phillips was only just getting started; she had big plans for the movie, wanted albums, board games, toys, convinced that *Close Encounters* would turn into "a cottage industry." That summer, Meco's cover of the *Star Wars* theme music had stayed at the top of the charts for five weeks. Phillips became fixated on the idea of a ten-inch disco hit using

John Williams's five-tone theme for *Close Encounters*. She approached Paul McCartney, who wanted to write his own music, so she set up a meeting with George Clinton. "We could call it CE3funK!" she enthused, and called up her friend, producer Jon Peters, who told her that he had negotiated profits of a dollar per record for his *A Star Is Born* soundtrack. But that was Streisand, and Phillips found Columbia's merchandising wing "still operating in that stone-age where people don't know that a single movie is cottage industry, where ancillary rights are still regarded as 'boilerplate.'" Too late, Columbia would realize its mistake, and after the release of the film, Spielberg would set up his own company, Entertainment Merchandising Inc., with L.A. businessman Sam Grossman to market spin-offs from his movies.

On October 19, Spielberg showed the movie to an audience at the Medallion Theater in Dallas—his "lucky theater," where he had first tested *Jaws*. The version they saw ended with Jiminy Cricket singing "When You Wish Upon A Star," from *Pinocchio*. "I pretty much hung my story on the mood the song created," said Spielberg, but for that very reason, the movie didn't really need it and after the audience's report cards came back, he removed it. "The people who liked it didn't love it and the people who didn't like it were adamant," he said. Unbeknownst to Spielberg, though, a reporter from *New York* magazine, William Flanagan, had bribed his way into the screening, and on October 31, he published a scathing review—"In my opinion the picture will be a colossal flop"—which triggered panic selling on Wall Street as Columbia stock plummeted. Actor Bob Balaban received a call from a reporter, pumping him for information about the soundtrack. "'Is it a song from a children's movie? Don't answer if the answer is yes. If it's no, keep talking.' It [felt] like something out of Watergate," noted Balaban.

It would be the last time that Spielberg tested a movie, and the last time that a single critic would have anything like Flanagan's influence on a blockbuster. The growth of marketing would see to that, although perhaps the biggest marketing coup scored for *Close Encounters* was one of those completely unforeseen hiccups in the zeitgeist that Spielberg alone seemed able to attract: in July of 1977, the entire eastern seaboard of America experienced a huge power blackout. Two thirds of the nation kept its lights on only by moving electricity from regions where it was surplus to places where it was scarce. New York shipped power to Ohio and Michigan. Pennsylvania sent power to neighboring New Jersey. Voltages were dropped in Florida, dimming lights and producing snow on television screens. Cities in Georgia, Alabama, and Mississippi suffered rotating thirty-minute blackouts. Demand for electricity was so great that the United States had to buy extra electricity from Canada. After a decade of energy crises, this was the final straw: someone had turned the lights out on America.

And on November 16, Steven Spielberg turned them back on again. Upon its release, *Close Encounters* took in $81 million, en route to taking $270 million worldwide, single-handedly saving Columbia from liquidation. As the final credits rolled, said one observer at the studio, the company's head of advertising "leaped in the air like a giddy child, whooping and giggling and pounding Spielberg and Trumbull like players who had just won the seventh game of the World Series."

"I saved their ass," says Spielberg.

Biographers of Spielberg and Lucas generally have a pretty tough time of it. Both men's matte normalcy refuses to buff up into the lustrous gleam we usually expect of our geniuses. The biographer arrives at his subject's door, sleuthing for clues—portents of future greatness, auguries of what is to come—only to find their subjects slumped in front of the Mickey Mouse Club, wallowing in the same pop culture plasma pool as the rest of us. "George's favorite story was Goldilocks and the Three Bears," writes Dale Pollock of Lucas. "The future director of *Jurassic Park* had an early fascination with dinosaurs," notes Joseph McBride, unlike the other 70 million children in America, who were of course, boring their way through the latest textbooks on subatomic physics. You can see the problem. The portraits are either of slink-off-the-page banality, or—the opposite tack—eerie banality, of TV zombies from Midwich Cuckooland. "The beak was matched by a bird's gaze, motionless, eerily unblinking," tries John Baxter, "and he moved in an avian way, darting and topping, his actions apparently unmediated by intellect." You're not sure whether such a creature would grow up to direct *Jurassic Park* or evolve into one of its stars.

Twenty-four pages into the Baxter, however, and you come across this great fact: Spielberg's grandparents would occasionally come from New Jersey to visit the family in Ohio, and he loved it when his mother said it was "something to look forward to." It was one of the first phrases he learned to say. If you had to know just one fact about Spielberg, and throw away the rest, that would be it, I think, for from it everything flows: both the keening narrative instincts that drive his films along—replace those grandparents with T. rexes or UFOs and you pretty much have the entire oeuvre—and also the delicate art of audience beguilement that drives audiences along to his films, commonly known as hype. Spielberg movies don't begin with the credits; they begin the moment you first hear about them. Half the fun with a movie like *Close Encounters* was the humming sense of anticipation that kicked in when you first saw those deadpan, gnomic posters, or first asked what its title meant, and wondered what a close encounter of the first or second kind were, and whether they'd be worth having. The other half was the humming sense of anticipation you felt while *watching* the thing, for the film is, at its baldest, one long teaser trailer for forthcoming attractions, with the aliens glimpsed, in fractionally greater increments, in everything from beached supertankers and planes to rampaging toys and Hoovers. "America is the first country in the world to take its fads seriously and to beat its chest about them and to say, 'Look what we can produce, look at the kind of gross national product which our culture alone can produce," says Spielberg. In which case, *Close Encounters* is chest beating at its most lyrical. In its vision of America, roused from its slumber by the whirring concert of its consumer clutter, the film amounts to a sort of junk *Sorcerer's Apprentice,* with Spielberg playing Prospero to America's gross national product. The film's sprightly mischief comes from exactly the same place in the national psyche that produced Watergate board games, Nixon impeachment T-shirts, and CB radios—which, during the energy crisis, allowed truckers to radio to one another the locations of gas stations with gas—for it is a movie all about the fun to be had in times of national crisis: when the lights go out in the Neary house, the children cheer.

If you ever wondered where all those great national fads of the seventies—lava lamps, pet rocks, Slip 'n Slides—went to die, then Roy Neary's house would be your first port of call, for it is an eruptive mess of toys and train sets, hobbyhorses and doll's heads, a junkyard of yesterday's enthusiasms. *Close Encounters* is a great movie for household mess, which functions in much the same way that garage junk does in *Star Wars,* somewhere between an insistent fetish and a guiding aesthetic, and its net effect is to make you wonder at just how much *stuff* there was in American lives in 1977. There is the mess of Neary's living room, not least after he shovels his front garden into it, the mess of his kids' bedrooms, then the mess the aliens make of Jillian's (Melinda Dillon) kitchen. And it is out of this mess that the possibility of alien visitation seems to grow, like just another fad or craze. "It's better than Goofy Golf!" Neary tells his kids. The first time he sees UFOs, he is alone. The second time he goes out there, he brings his wife and children—"Remember those articles about the aurora borealis in *National Geographic*?" he asks his wife (Teri Garr). "Well, it's better than that!" The third time he goes out, everyone is there, all the crazies and hillbillies, whole families with their picnic hampers, playing cards, and painted signs. "It's like Halloween for grown-ups," says Jillian.

Or July 4th for moviegoers. The one thing the whole thing *really* resembles, but which nobody points out, is the pre-release buildup for a blockbuster movie: an audience of Americans are drawn from all over the country, by an "implanted vision" they get from watching TV, to congregate together, to watch a show of music and lights . . . "They were invited!" insists the French UFOlogist, played by none other than film director François Truffaut, which clinches it: the aliens are opening a blockbuster, and tonight is their premiere. You could be forgiven for not noticing this in 1977, though, for blockbusters were only just achieving their status as preeminent national spectacle and so could reasonably remain absent from their own cultural radar. By the time of *E.T.,* in 1982, Spielberg would have Elliott playing with *Star Wars* dolls, for it would be inconceivable to make a film about an eleven-year-old and have him not be a *Star Wars* fan; and by the time of *The Phantom Menace* in 1999, George Lucas would return the nod by giving *E.T.* a walk-on at the galactic senate, but the toys that run around Neary's floor hail back to an altogether more innocent era—Robbie the Robot from *Forbidden Planet,* Frankenstein's monster. *Close Encounters* was the last time when Spielberg could reach for the nearest toy in a movie and not be in any danger of it being one of his own. It thus marks the high point of his innocence as a filmmaker, far more so than *E.T.,* if only because back in 1977, he still had no idea of what Spielbergian meant: this was the last movie of his that wouldn't betray that knowledge, for it was all being mapped out for the first time, the suburban sprawl, the flying toys, the spilled fridges and sprinkled lawns. We would, for instance, see many monster-in-the-rearview-mirror gags in his movies—from the Nazis that Indy sees in his mirror in *Raiders,* to the T. rex in *Jurassic Park* glimpsed in a side mirror, whose decal reads "objects in mirror are closer than they appear"—a nice joke, although you only get it on video, and not quite as good as the moment in *Close Encounters* when Richard Dreyfuss pulls in at a turnstile to read his map, sees some headlights in his rearview mirror, and waves them on, only for the audience to see them go up over the truck. Dreyfuss said that when he read that in the script, he could *hear* the audience react.

The important thing is that he could hear at all. *Jaws* had played to theaters so rowdy they almost drowned out the movie, razzing up the audience to match its own internal hoopla levels. *Close Encounters,* too, is full of the sounds by which seventies blockbusters usually heralded their global importance—the excited babble of simultaneous translation, the crackle of air traffic control—but the movie's key scenes play out in a midnight hush so pure that you can hear the crickets chirp, or the whirring of a child's toy, or a dog bark in the distance. It is almost as if Spielberg had listened to the expectant silence that descended on the world after *Jaws,* like snow, and then turned that silence into a movie. Said sound effects editor Frank Warner of the UFOs: "We decided that [their] presence would be expressed simply as silence—or more accurately, a cessation of normal ambient night exterior sounds—crickets, birds, etc. . . . When an accustomed sound stopped, it became a signal that something big was about to happen." The rebuke to the sound and fury of today's blockbusters—with their crank-up toward immediate Dionysian blowout—could not be more acute. The special effects of *Close Encounters* were, you have to say, pretty special, with something of the magic of headlights seen from the safety of your parents' car on a long journey home—a fly-past of flared coronas, blurred halos, and snowy overexposures. *Close Encounters* was thus the first film to suggest that when mankind finally gets to make contact with intelligent life from another galaxy, we might, in all our wisdom, have forgotten to put the right type of film in our cameras.

Roy Neary, meanwhile, takes his place amid the aliens, arms outstretched in what would become Spielberg's signature sign-off—the image that ends films as disparate as *Indiana Jones and the Temple of Doom, E.T.,* and *Schindler's List,* of a man surrounded by children, or a filmmaker before his adoring audience, the bow of the maestro. It is this movie, though, on which the reputation of the young Spielberg ought to rest—rather than, say, *E.T.,* a far more cunning piece of work—and certainly the place his natural benevolence received its fairest, most open-hearted outing. It tends to be the thing that most divides critics about the director—his unshakable proclivity for the upbeat—and certainly it's true that we prefer our artists a little more down in the mouth. It's like the old Montherlant dictum about happiness writing white: they're easier to spot that way. You're on to a much safer bet liking someone like Martin Scorsese, whose genius shows up in all the fully approved forms—plowing a lonely course outside the studio system, obsessively burrowing down into an identifiable subset of obsessions, tearing films from his breast like chunks of his own flesh—than you are liking someone like Spielberg: devoid of visible self-destructive impulses, alighting on film after film as if giving his imagination an aerobic workout, athletically slam-dunking one box office record after another . . . if *that guy* also turns out to have been the most talented filmmaker of his generation, then what, frankly, was the point? What was the point of all those hours passed in the dark confines of the art house, boning up on Ukrainian cinema, watching the unwatchable? But there you go. What can you do. If you have to point to any one director of the last twenty-five years in whose work the medium of film was most fully itself—where we found out what it does best when left to its own devices, it has to be that guy. These early films of his now play like a bracing crash course in the history of the medium, with a young man's excitement for his newfound toy: first, a step on the gas with *Duel,* then a quick exercise in collective fright, *Jaws,* and finally, with *Close Encounters,* a deep push on the bass pedals of straightforward awe and wonderment: let's see what this sucker can *really* do.

So what can it do? Well, it turns out it's pretty good at bright lights, music, and faces. Spielberg's eye for ordinary American features— squidgy-faced cops, beaker-featured technicians, hairy hillbillies—is here as scrupulously unbeautiful as anything in Walker Evans. Melinda Dillon said she felt like Lillian Gish being directed by Griffith as Spielberg coaxed her through her reactions; and indeed, the film may be the closest modern audiences will ever come to knowing what it was like to dig out your nickel, and take your seat for the first cinematographs, flickering silently overhead: "A tense, well-knit, immobile mass of human faces, their eyes alertly fixed on the screen," is how one spectator at New York's Bijou Theater described his fellow audience members in 1909. He could as easily have been describing the climax of *Close Encounters,* with its row upon row of transfixed spectators, bathed in a baptism of light, watching the First Picture Show. Everything about the shoot marks it out as the film that should have been Spielberg's downfall—his overreaching epic, his *Intolerance*—but even at its furthest reach, the film draws us close to home: even when the aliens start leaving huge supertankers strewn about the desert, it resembles nothing so much as the carelessness of a child, strewing toys around its playpen. It's almost enough to give optimism a good name.

CHAPTER 4

THE EDUCATION OF ELLEN RIPLEY

"The founding term in the film is human (S). . . . The anti-human (-S), is, of course, the Alien, and the not-human (S) is Ash, the robot. The cat, then, functions in the slot of the not-anti-human (-S), an indispensable role in this drama."
— James Kavenagh, "Son of a Bitch: Feminism, Humanism and Science in *Alien*," *Science Fiction Studies*, 1980

"Okay Ridley, I'll figure it out myself."
— Sigourney Weaver on the set of *Alien*, 1978

Taking time out from the lengthy post-production on *Close Encounters* in the summer of 1977, Spielberg flew out to Hawaii to join George Lucas the weekend *Star Wars* opened. Earlier in the year the two of them had swapped points on each other's movies, along with guesses as to whose grosses would be bigger, writing them down on napkins over dinner one night. Lucas was convinced Spielberg would beat him, that he'd made just a kid's movie—"I promise you, *Close Encounters* will make four to five times more than *Star Wars*," he had told him—while Spielberg was convinced that Lucas would clean up. "I told him *Star Wars* was going to be the big commercial blockbuster," says Spielberg. "I said I was making the art house version of *Star Wars,* and thank God we didn't open the same weekend because they would have demolished us."

In Hawaii, it was clear whose hour it was. Spielberg found an "ebullient" Lucas, "as ebullient as George gets," spilling over with news of *Star Wars*'s second weekend grosses. The two men took a walk on the beach outside their hotel, and Lucas started building a sandcastle—something he did for every movie of his, to wish it luck—while Spielberg sat back and watched the tide come in. "You know what I really want to do, I really want to do a James Bond film," Spielberg said, "but without the hardware, much more like *Dr. No.*" He had spoken to the executives at Universal, he said, and would do it if he could get Sean Connery to make a comeback. Lucas looked up.

"I've got a great idea for a James Bond film. You can start from scratch. It's even better, it's got all the action; it's an action-serial thing, just like James Bond. There's not a single piece of metal in the entire movie."

And so he told him about the idea he had for a movie about an archaeologist hero taking on the Nazis.

"That's fantastic," said Spielberg. "I'd love to do that."

"Well, I've retired," said Lucas. "I'm not directing anymore, so it's yours." He was just beginning to describe the film's climax, when he was called back to the phone; it was Twentieth Century Fox with the latest *Star Wars* figures. The sandcastle was worth $193 million. Later, the two men would build another, for *Raiders of the Lost Ark*, and that sandcastle would be worth $209 million.

According to Spielberg, "George was always more competitive with me than I was with him," although, says John Milius, "They were both as bad as each other, always looking over their shoulder to see what everyone else was up to, who had the biggest hit." The rivalry between two directors, whatever its proportions of faux-brinkmanship to the real thing, would dominate the box office of the next half a decade, as they batted box office records back and forth between them like bored emperors, thoughtfully taking turns to provide the summers of 1980, 1981, 1982, and 1983 with their number one hits—the first of the blockbuster auteurs. It's not what critics usually mean when they use the word "auteur"—what they usually mean is a director, preferably French or Italian, but failing that, working well outside the

Hollywood mainstream—but it is, funnily enough, what the French meant by the word when they first introduced it. In 1954, when François Truffaut coined the term in his 1954 essay for *Cahiers du Cinéma,* he used it to refer to Hollywood, and not its artists but its artisans: critically unsung journeymen like Hitchcock and Hawks, toiling away within the studio system, but somehow, by some inverse alchemy, turning out work that no other director could have put his hand to. How else explain the difference between *Star Wars* and *Close Encounters?* Both sci-fi blockbusters from 1977, from the two men who are most often blamed for the anonymous corporate sheen of the blockbuster, yet as different as moondust and Gorgonzola: one staring at the heavens and seeing in them a warmly inverted reflection of the winking city lights below, the other whipping the star field into a passing blur, glimpsed from within a speeding cockpit.

Their reactions to their success could not have been more different, either, with Spielberg riding out the express train that his career had become in Hollywood, while Lucas opted out altogether, moving Lucasfilm up to San Francisco, where he would produce, not direct, the *Star Wars* sequels, micromanaging them from above—Oz behind his curtain. "That's when things changed really," says Joe Viskocil, the miniature pyro expert who had blown up the Death Star. "When we were shooting *Star Wars,* it was like we were in high school film class, in essence. We were like kids, if we had an idea it didn't matter if it was in someone else's department, whether it be matte paint or models. It was a roundtable discussion. Then everything changed: on *Empire* it was 'you have to do one thing and one thing only. You cannot interfere with everyone else.' It wasn't a cool class of classmates helping each other out, it became conservative, less creative. It was a whole political thing. It was a little bit colder. You're walking through the halls and they're crystal-clear and clean and sterile. It didn't have that flying-by-the-seat-of-your-pants kind of thing."

It's hard not to detect a certain amount of psychic fragility to Lucas, and in the self-protective recoil he had from his own success: the sheer shock of blockbuster success is greatest to those standing in its immediate blast area, and Lucas is not a man who likes his shocks. Like Jules Verne—who traveled the length and breadth of the universe in his fiction but who went into a funk if he so much as set foot outside Paris—

Lucas is decidedly an armchair astronaut: one of the things he found most off-putting about shooting *Star Wars* on location in London, reported producer Gary Kurtz, is that the light switches went up rather than down. "You have to remember that George is a guy who came out of school and wound up being a superstar and amassing a fortune very, very quickly," says Scott Ross, the general manager of Industrial Light & Magic in the late eighties. "He is incredibly shy. He's not a very people person. He had this real distrust of lawyers, a real distrust of accountants and management executives, and one of the reasons he wound up staying in the Bay Area was to get away from all of that. And also to an extent that's the reason he started Pixar, so he could make movies with a limited amount of people—literally put himself in a dark room, and direct and edit the whole thing by himself." If directors' careers are conversations with an audience, then Spielberg's would be ongoing, attentive, endlessly responsive and curious, and Lucas's rather more like the man at the dinner party who says one bold, brilliant thing, and then shuts up—in his case for twenty-two years.

But much more than any of Spielberg's films, it would be *Star Wars*—that one bold, brilliant thing—that exerted an influence on American movies like no other since *Birth of a Nation*. Its immediate impact was easy enough to spot: a fleet of imitators zooming into theaters in the form of *The Black Hole, Battlestar Galactica, Buck Rogers in the 25th Century, Battle Beyond the Stars, Starcrash.* It was an attack of the clones, all united by a design scheme closely modeled on a galactic disco, an obscure but unshakable belief that the key to *Star Wars*'s success had been R2-D2—*The Black Hole* boasted a tubby robot named Vincent, *Buck Rogers* a robot dog called Twiki—and a mysterious tendency to turn into a TV series: within months both *Buck Rogers* and *Battlestar Galactica* had slipped from theaters and onto prime time, if reconverting back into the cathode-ray static from which Lucas had first drawn nourishment as a kid. But beneath the immediate schlockwave, the deeper reverberations sent out by Lucas's success were being picked up by a generation of filmmakers, like sonar. Working as a designer on *Battle Beyond the Stars,* for instance, was the young James Cameron, who had seen *Star Wars* and thought: that's the movie that's been playing in my head all these years. "That was the movie that I wanted to make. After seeing that movie . . . I got busy."

Ridley Scott also remembers the summer of 1977 well. He had just released his first film, *The Duellists,* a handsomely staged adaptation of a Joseph Conrad novel, starring Keith Carradine and Harvey Keitel, which had scooped the Special Jury Prize at the Cannes Film Festival. Accompanying the film to America, however, Scott was furious to find that Paramount had given him seven prints and opened the film in only one theater in Los Angeles, the Fine Arts on Wilshire Boulevard. Meanwhile, up at the Egyptian Theater on Hollywood Boulevard, *Star Wars* was sucking up everything in sight like a giant vacuum cleaner. The deck had tilted decisively, and handsomely staged adaptations of Joseph Conrad novels no longer seemed quite so alluring. "From the second I arrived outside the Egyptian, I'd never seen or felt such anticipation," recalls Scott. "The actual air was agog. The air was excited. I'd never seen so many crowds outside a theater. To me this was what cinema at its best should be. A mass medium, a mainstream audience, and everybody standing outside, having queued for days. We got some pretty good seats, about thirty feet from the front, so I got the best sound and this picture was in my face, and frankly I couldn't believe it. I'd done my little film, which I was happy about, but this film was massive. It actually changed my mind about what I would do next. I'd been developing one thing, and then decided, really, how can I go down that route? I must go in another direction and so instead I made *Alien.*"

"*Alien* is to *Star Wars* what the Rolling Stones were to the Beatles," said producer David Giler. "It's a nasty *Star Wars.*" Produced by the same studio, Fox, still under the management of Alan Ladd, the *Alien* script had been sitting on a desk at Fox for almost a year without so much as a flutter of interest, according to screenwriter Dan O'Bannon: "They wanted to follow through on *Star Wars,* and they wanted to follow through fast and the only spaceship script they had sitting on their desk was *Alien,* so they green-lighted it, *wham.*" It certainly couldn't have been the quality of O'Bannon's script. A hard-core sci-fi nut and neophyte screenwriter, fresh from USC, O'Bannon had written something called *Starbeast,* and it came crammed with clichés from sci-fi movies of the fifties like *Forbidden Planet* and *It!*

The Terror from Beyond Space. There were pyramids, and holograms, and an all-male cast, who spoke at length about "what should be done" in stiff, officer-class locutions, but never got around to doing very much:

> STANDARD steps forward and slaps ROBY across the face.
> The others are shocked.
> HUNTER: Hey now, what is this?
> STANDARD: Ask him.
> ROBY: I understood why you did that.
> STANDARD: Good . . .
> After a hard stare at ROBY, STANDARD gives him a curt
> nod and turns his attention to the machinery.

It read like *The Last Days of the Raj*—all curt nods, hard stares, and stiff upper lips in space. "It had not even B picture merit," said producer Walter Hill. "Nobody could take it seriously. It had a 'Jesus gadzooks' quality about it." Hill had just set up a production company, Brandywine Films, with his partner, David Giler, and landed a production deal at Fox, when a friend passed them O'Bannon's script, and while they both hated it, they admired what Hill called the "low cunning" of its setup—"you had a monster that could not be killed without destroying your own life-support system." Giler sensed that the key to the film would be to treat it like an A movie, with full production values, and so he and Hill sat down and rewrote the script, in just under three days.

Hill was the writer-director behind such films as *The Warriors* and *The Driver,* and he wrote scenes that played out like a one-liner competition at a tough-guy convention. "Character is action," he once said. "In my films, when somebody puts a gun in your face, character is how many times you blink." He dropped the pyramids, created a computer called Mother, made two of the characters women, introduced a note of discord between the officers and the working-class crew, and streamlined the whole thing with his headlong, hard-boiled style— somewhere between "staccato and blank verse," said Giler, and it went something like this:

> A red stain.
> Then a smear of blood blossoms on his chest.

The fabric of his tunic is ripped open.
A small head the size of a man's fist pushes out.
The tiny head lunges forward, comes spurting out of Dallas's
     chest trailing a thick body.
Spatters fluids and blood in its wake.
Lands in the middle of the dishes and food.
Wriggles away while the crew scatters.

Halloween haiku. It is to Hill, then, that we owe much of *Alien*—its headlong momentum, its oil-besmirched air of class war, the character and sex of Ripley—and it was his script that hooked Scott, taking him forty minutes to read: "It usually takes about four days. It was just Bang! Whoompf! straight through. It was unpretentious, very violent, yet a lot of character painting came through, and I just thought it was an amazing piece of entertainment. Also to me it was more than just a horror film, it's a film about terror." He sensed that it would play even faster than it read.

Scott was a funny mixture of rough and smooth—gruff and distant, visually fluent but slightly inarticulate—and the result was a fierce bottleneck of temper that erupted whenever he felt other people at his shoulder, peering too closely at his immaculate storyboards. He had been born and raised in South Shields, in the hub of England's Industrial North, then gone on to art school in London before a successful career directing commercials, and something of that mixture of fluting sophistication and hard-edged industrialism seemed to have percolated through into a visual style that was fetishistically attuned to the textures of rain, rust, rot—the very textures of Britain's national decline, from which punk was also then exploding. To walk down a London street in 1978 was to be confronted with the flotsam and jetsam of Britain's imperial past and nose-pierced, ripped-jean present—a country in the blender.

"I'm a neatnik, a pathological neatnik, and so I notice these things," says Scott. "When I'm in and out of London I notice whether it's looking tidy or untidy and it drives me crazy. So I just applied that rule [to *Alien*]. I'd been flying to and from the United States a lot at that time, and I'd noticed how 747s were gradually getting beaten up. I was in a lavatory on a 747, and I noticed that even there someone had done some graffiti. And then alongside that there were instructions on the use of the lavatory in four different languages. So I applied all this thinking, except having jumped ahead, say, a hundred years. And I still believe I probably didn't go far enough." Scott called together a large crew of production designers, including Ron Cobb, who had helped supply *Star Wars* with its chunkier hardware, and Hans Rudi Giger, a Swiss artist whose paintings lay somewhere between Art Nouveau and the slaughterhouse: writhing bacchanalian landscapes of morphing flesh, bone, and pewter-gray metal. Spotting a copy of Giger's book *Necronomicon* on the table at Fox, Scott says he "had never been so sure of anything in my whole life." Fox wasn't so enamored, thought it too dark and dingy, but Scott stuck to his guns and flew to Switzerland— Giger was terrified of flying—to persuade him to work on the film.

One of the things that *Star Wars* had done was spearhead a return to the old soundstages, left vacant by the fashion for location shooting during the seventies. Now, they were in business again, and Giger arrived at Shepperton Studios in London in the middle of a steaming hot summer, dressed head-to-toe in black leather. The crew teased him, trying to persuade him to take off his jacket, but he wouldn't do it. "I don't think he dares take off those clothes, because if he did you'd see that underneath he's not human. He's a character from an H. P. Lovecraft story," noted one crew member. "When Giger first started working, he went to the production secretary and said: 'I want bones.' And I remember seeing all these trucks pull up one day loaded with boxes. They had been to medical supply houses, slaughterhouses, and God knows where else, and the next day the studio was full of bones and skeletons of every possible description. There was a row of human skulls in flawless condition. Three snake skeletons in a perfect state of preservation. A rhinoceros skull. He had everything." The sets that Giger fashioned were astonishing: vast ribbed caverns, like monstrous chest cavities, that swallowed up anyone who visited it. Sigourney Weaver took her parents on a tour of the set, just before shooting started: "It was like wandering through some Playboy orgy room," she said. "There was a huge spaceship with vaginal doors, and their beautiful female bones. They were gulping 'very interesting, very interesting.'"

Weaver was then an unknown—fresh from a stint on Broadway,

but with little movie experience. Arriving to her audition almost an hour late, she nevertheless gave off an air of hastily gathered composure, which together with her height greatly impressed Scott, Giler, and Hill. "So waddaya think?" Scott asked Fox's Alan Ladd.

"I think she looks like Jane Fonda," said Ladd, who needed a little more persuading and insisted she test. There were only three weeks to go before shooting started, so Weaver found herself acting opposite Giger's almost fully completed sets, in a costume she'd cobbled together from old army surplus gear. She didn't want it to look like "Jackie Onassis in Space," she said. "We wanted it to look more like pirates." Ladd asked the women in the Fox office what they thought. They liked Weaver. The day after she got back to New York, she was told she got the part, for $33,000.

The shoot was tense. Although he had *The Duellists* under his belt, Scott was treated, and reacted, like a first-time director, with his every decision minutely scrutinized by the Fox executives, and testily defended by the director. According to art director Roger Christian, within four days of shooting, there were nine Fox suits on the set, "just counting the minutes on Ridley and complaining—why wasn't he shooting?—and he was shooting so fast. They gave him no pre-light time so he was trying to find the look in the first two days and one of the producers came to me on the fourth day and said, 'Why is it taking so long?' . . . It did get to Ridley. I remember one incident, I was standing right next to him, and he went off like a rocket. It was like . . . power coming out. He punched his fist right through the ceiling of the bridge because he did not understand why everyone was on his back."

Operating the camera himself, Scott spent most of his time hidden beneath a plastic cowl—emerging only to fiddle with his sets, spread incense over them, refusing to shoot until it was evenly distributed, and lit just so. Actor Tom Skerritt complained that one time he left the actors waiting for three days. Scott would later say that he ignored his actors deliberately—playing them off against each other to induce the air of surly distrust that envelops the bridge of the *Nostromo,* but he ran a fine line between ignoring his actors in retrospectively justifiable cause and simply ignoring his actors because he didn't really get the creatures. During the scene in which Veronica Cartwright, John Hurt, and Skerritt clambered over the alien planet, clad in heavy spacesuits—lined with nylon and short on air—Skerritt and Hurt almost passed out. It was 112 degrees that summer and Hurt suffered from claustrophobia. "They were passing out like flies," said Cartwright. "It was unbelievable, poor John, by the time he got to the other end, he had to have a nurse there because he would sweat so profusely he couldn't even see. He was just this big ball of sweat."

"He is one of those directors who will come up to you after you've done a scene and say, 'Well, I don't fucking believe that,'" said Weaver. "At first I'd be a little taken aback and wonder, 'Where's the stroking, where's the diplomacy,' and there just wasn't any. I remember one time when I asked for his help on a problem I was having with Ripley. And he thought about it for a long time and then he came over to me and said, 'What if you are the lens on'—and he named a sophisticated camera— 'and you're opening and shutting?' And there was a long pause. Finally I said, 'Ridley, I'll have to think about it.' And he looked kind of crest-fallen because he hadn't helped me and said hopefully, 'Well, let me think, too.' He really wanted me to be part of the process. But having me as the iris of a lens? I said, 'Okay Ridley, I'll figure it out myself.'"

"Sometimes what [actors] do forget about my job," says Scott, "is that I'm carrying millions of chapters of minutiae in my head. They tend to come not with the overview but their part. Usually when I'm being attacked, I'm thinking about the fabric of their suit, or their shoes, or some other part of the story, and suddenly having to address in great detail about a specific part of the narrative, I'm not necessarily going to be on my toes. And rage flushes it out." One morning, Weaver and he crossed paths in the parking lot, when she saw him getting out of his Rolls-Royce. "Where did you get that? From your dad?" she called out. "What could I tell her? I'd already been running my own successful business for ten years at that point. I had also never had anybody question everything I did before *Alien*. I was repeatedly called on to justify my every move, whereas my natural inclination is to say, 'I know what I'm doing. Just let me get on with it, all right?' So the tension on the *Alien* set, I think, was partly due to my own insecurity and partly because I was being asked what, in my opinion, were so many stupid questions . . . so yeah. On *Alien*, you could say there was tension."

The rough cut of the film was ready eight days after shooting wrapped, and ran to three hours and twelve minutes. Ladd remembers it as "the most tense movie I've ever seen in my entire life. My wife and I went for lunch afterward and some of the people who were there weren't able to eat." Scott admits he took it too far; he'd been watching Tobe Hooper's *The Texas Chainsaw Massacre,* and was aiming for the same bone-at-breaking-point tone. "Our rough cut was just too intense. Originally, there was a stronger degree of terror. Just subtle things, half-seen, half-heard things earlier in the picture. Consequently you have the audience holding on from the beginning. That's no good." He and editor Terry Rawlings went back and let a little more air into the movie, a bit more in the way of breathing space. "The whole thing was an exercise in seeing how far back you could cock the pistol before you had to release the trigger," says Rawlings. "It was finding that moment. How long can you wait? How long can you go along those air shafts before it all gets too much for the audience? Now, of course, things are frantic from the word go but with *Alien* it was a waiting game."

How long was the wait? How long has the *Nostromo* been drifting through space before its crew are woken up? We never find out. All we know is how long it takes for what wakes up to polish them off: just over forty minutes. As for how long they have been traveling, we hear only that they are still ten years away from Earth—a quietly devastating figure—and we hear them bickering with one another. "Quit griping," snaps Kane (John Hurt). "I like griping," snaps back Lambert (Veronica Cartwright). *That* long.

    To anyone fresh from the bright-eyed camaraderie of *Star Wars,* the fug of fatigue and cigarette smoke that hung over the cramped cabins of the *Nostromo* was a revelation: not just griping in space, but *smoking.* And after they'd gone to all the trouble of taking all that oxygen up there, too! We'd never seen anything like it. Nobody ever lit up during *2001: A Space Odyssey,* despite its tedium, and you never got any bickering over pay in *Star Wars,* but then, for all the reach of Lucas's Empire, you never got to see any real work. As Kevin Smith pointed out in his 1994 comedy, *Clerks,* the Death Star appears to have built itself. "A construction job of that magnitude would require a helluva lot more manpower than the Imperial army had to offer. I'll bet there were independent contractors working on that thing: plumbers, aluminum siders, roofers . . ."

In *Alien* you got to see the work. You got to see the empire's plumbers, siders and roofers, its engineers and worker ants, all mortgaging off years of their life to trawl the inky backwaters of space, in a ship that was just that: a dank and rattling freighter, named the *Nostromo,* after another Conrad novel, and not just any Conrad novel but his "masterpiece," i.e., his least read. This was serious. Generally speaking, blockbuster films until then weren't in the habit of namedropping great unread books—*Jaws* got by perfectly well without invoking *Moby-Dick,* or *Star Wars* without quoting Joseph Campbell, although if you really want to know how grown-up the whole thing felt, here was the killer: we couldn't even see the bloody thing. Released with an 18-certificate in the U.S. and an X in the U.K., *Alien* was one last wave from Hollywood's pre-teen-market era, although at the time it felt horribly unjust: adults had stolen our blockbuster. What was rightfully ours was being held against its will, until it came out on video. In the meantime, our plans to liberate *Alien* were restricted to a number of spin-off books released that summer, including a complete shot-by-shot set of storyboards, thanks to which I was immaculately prepped for everything the film had to throw at me by the time I got to see it—all the stomach bursts and face grabs, body snatches, head smashes, and skull crushes. Everything except the sex. That, the storyboards hadn't prepared me for.

So *that* was why they'd kept this film under wraps. *Star Wars* had pretty much been a prepubescent's paradise, with Lucas taping down Carrie Fisher's bosom with gaffer tape, in case his audience got ideas. "No breasts bounce in space, there's no jiggling in the Empire," remarked Fisher, with characteristic waspishness. But sex was everywhere in *Alien,* from its gynecological corridors and vulvic doorways to its crabby, postcoital atmosphere—everywhere, that is, except where you might normally expect to have found it, which is to say, between the characters. Originally, there was to have been a scene showing Ripley sharing a cuddle with her captain, but as Scott realized, it came just after the Alien had gotten onboard, slowing down the action, and besides, by that time the film had already notched up its big sex scene, involving something wet, and slimy, with its eye on John Hurt. The

exact implications of what happens to Hurt have engendered more
fevered analysis than any single scene in any blockbuster, even more
than the Tony Curtis–Laurence Olivier bath scene in *Spartacus.* What
happens next is that Hurt gives birth to the Alien, or "chest-burster" as
it was affectionately called by Scott and his crew, although in truth, the
alien doesn't burst through Hurt's chest so much as gently *push*
through, like a puppy nuzzling through wet tissue, and then bolts,
sending the cutlery flying, and launching more graduate theses than a
month of Jean Baudrillard lectures. A "particularly horrifying confusion of the sexual-gynecological with the gastro-intestinal" decided
James Kavenagh, in his seminal essay "Son of a Bitch: Feminism,
Humanism, and Science in *Alien*" (no. 13, October 1980) for *Science
Fiction Studies,* which devoted an entire symposium to Scott's film.

The shock waves of blockbuster movies were now traveling further
afield than just Wall Street; they were reaching the leafy groves of aca-
deme, which would soon be spilling over with essays with vaguely ter-
rifying titles like "Being Keanu" and "Totally Recalling Arnold: Sex and
Violence in the New Bad Future." *Alien* was, though, the first—the
newest, baddest future on the block, and siring a small cottage industry of academic analysis devoted to its subtextual nooks and semiolog-
ical crannies. Feminists warmed to the fact that all the white males
become dead white males at a faster rate than the nonwhite males.
Marxists nodded approval of the film's grimy, Conradian take on late
capitalism. And Freudians, needless to say, had a field day, for a film
more in need of a trip to the analyst would be harder to find. Even
Jones the cat received his own diagram:

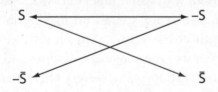

As Kavenagh explained: "The founding term in the film is human
(S), represented by the image of Ripley as the strong woman. The anti-
human (-S), is, of course, the Alien, and the not human (S) is Ash, the
robot. The cat, then, functions in the slot of the not anti-human (-S),
an indispensable role in this drama." The world of alien studies was

not all neatly drawn diagrams and smoothly processed deconstruc-
tions, however, and was soon to be ripped asunder by a bitter and acri-
monious debate, one pitting sister against sister, brother against
brother, comrade against comrade. It is with due caution and some
trepidation that we therefore approach the singular, divisive issue of
Lieutenant Ellen Ripley's knickers.

For some, the sight of Ripley stripped to her undies at the end of the
film, as she prepares to do final battle with the Alien, undid all the film's
good work. Judith Newton found the third-act survival of the two
women and one black character "especially promising"; but bikinis, she
noted sternly, are "not standard gear for space duty. . . . Ripley, though
in many ways a fine and thrilling hero, is robbed of radical thrust." To
the rescue came Kavenagh, who in "Feminism and Anxiety in *Alien*"
(*Science Fiction Studies*, vol. 7, no. 3, 1980) wrote: "I would disagree with
an ideological denunciation of the film as simply another exercise in
conventional sexism on the basis of the scene in which Ripley removes
her uniform to appear in T-shirt and panties. Such criticism would be
hard-pressed to avoid repressive and self-defeating assumptions about
what constitutes sexism, and irrelevant assumptions about what constitutes the film and its ideological discourse." A cunning move—the
panties weren't sexist; the *accusation* that the panties were sexist was
sexist—but maybe a trifle over-defensive? It was left to Barbara Creed
(*Science Fiction Studies*) to arbitrate, with an air of weary summary:
"Much has been written about the final scene, in which Ripley un-
dresses before the camera, on the grounds that its voyeurism under-
mines her role as successful heroine." She proposed a diplomatic
solution, designed to unite both pro-panties and anti-panties camps:
what if the panties "signify an acceptable and in this context reassuring
fetish object of the normal woman"? Then, "the final sequence works,
not only to dispose of the Alien, but also to repress the nightmare image of the monstrous-feminine with the text of patriarchal discourses."
Voilà. Easy when you know how.

Fun as it always is to see academics getting their knickers in a twist,
it is perhaps too easy to laugh at this stuff: Popular film has always
attracted a certain amount of academic attention, the dominant model
being those tweedy articles in the fifties examining the *Godzilla* and
UFO invasion movies for signs of nuclear-age anxiety, or cold war

nerves. It is a model buttressed by a clear sense of intellectual superiority—the academic plumbs the innocent pop-culture artifact for mean-
ings it didn't even know it had—but it doesn't get you very far with the
modern blockbuster, since it ignores the possibility that the meaning
might just be there because someone—the filmmakers—put it there.
This rather alarming possibility would continue to flummox blockbuster exegeticists—in 2003, one *Matrix* fan asked the Wachowskis
whether the religious subtext of their trilogy was "intentional," as if a
skein of Buddhist-Judeo-Christian references was something that just
happened to a movie by accident, on its way to the forum. The same
goes for much of the analysis that enveloped *Alien*. On the one hand
there is nothing very academic about a film in which an alien repeatedly plunges its jaw into the cerebrum of its victims—"it has
absolutely no message," insisted Scott, it works on a very visceral level
and its only point is terror, and more terror"—but it is a studious film,
as forensically fascinated with the life form at its center as science officer Ash (Ian Holm), hunched over his microscope like an art restorer
sizing up varnish strengths. When it comes to the burgeoning field of
post-doctorate *Alien* study, Ash graduates with full honors, summa
cum laude. Study is all he wants to do, eyeing up the Alien for its pos-
sibilities in the company's weapons division. "It's a perfect organism,
its structural perfection matched only by its hostility," he says. "You
admire it," says an incredulous Ripley. "I admire its purity," replies Ash,
"a survivor, unclouded by notions of remorse, morality. You have
my . . . sympathies."

The real question, of course, is not whether they had Ash's sympathies, but whether they had their director's. "I found it very pure," said
Scott of the script's clean lines, echoing Ash's rather creepy wording.
Did Weaver detect something of Ash's slightly inhuman connoisseur-
ship in Scott's continual fussing over his ship's design and decor? At
times, certainly, *Alien* seems to have been directed by an intelligence
you would hesitate to call human. Look at the clinical, Kubrickian
tracking shots of the empty spaceship at the start—Scott seems to
prefer it that way, all neat and unmessed—or the shot of Jones the cat
that punctuates Harry Dean Stanton's death: irises narrowing coolly,
while the poor human fights for its life. Scott clearly has a thing for
irises, for we would see that look again in the basilisk gaze of his

Replicants in *Blade Runner,* a movie too becalmed by its own beauty to be bothered with moving its plot along. *Alien,* too, is a beautiful film, most obviously when it alights on the alien planet, with its Piranesian vistas, but once the film downshifts into the *Nostromo*'s air shafts, it moves too fast to admire itself, with Scott keeping shots of his creature down to a bare minimum—a glimpse of plunging jaw, or shining skull, and that is it. Then there is Weaver, in whom the movie's lack of vanity comes, quite literally, to a head: bony and beautiful, hair pinned back to reveal that fascinatingly multiplaned face. Did Scott realize the subtle visual rhyme he had established between his heroine and her antagonist? The third film would nail it—having Ripley shave her hair, and then bring her quite literally head-to-head with the Alien, one skull against another—but back in 1979, there was very little else to hint at Ripley's eventual survival, for like *Star Wars* and *Jaws* before it, *Alien* benefited enormously from the nonstarriness of its casting, setting its crew out before us with a poker face, to let us guess who would come up trumps.

That there would be sequels was never in any doubt. Wasn't replication what the movie was about? When Ash praised the *Alien* for being a "perfect organism, its structural perfection matched only by its hostility," it sparked off an echo of Richard Dreyfuss's speech in *Jaws* about the shark being "a perfect engine" and all it wanting to do being "swim, eat, and make little sharks," which in turn triggered a complex set of synapses in the audience's brain that said, essentially, "He's Coming Back for Seconds," and caused them to cancel all social engagements the following summer. And whereas the shark of the *Jaws* sequels was, as the years went by, forced to snack on a diet of ever more indistinguishable teens, the *Alien* films had two reasons to continue—its beauty and its beast. The curious thing was that it took seven summers, with the release of *Aliens* in 1986, for anyone to get around to realizing this. These days, a movie like XXX is barely past its opening weekend before Sony takes out full-page ads in *Variety* congratulating itself on the birth of a new superhero franchise. So what happened with *Alien*?

Despite breaking *Star Wars*'s opening week records, taking in $8.5 million, it slowed down quickly, eventually taking in $40.3 million—enough to make it the number five hit film of that year, but not enough to lift the movie out of the red. Partly this was down to old-fashioned Hollywood accounting, but also because Fox had spent so much on advertising. The ads for *Alien* were devised by Stephen Frankfurt, the advertising maven who had marketed *Rosemary's Baby* with a groundbreaking trailer, featuring a slowly advancing shot of a baby carriage, and the words, "Pray for Rosemary's baby"—the progenitor, in other words, of the sort of soft-drop payoff line that would come to play so well off the blockbuster in the years to come. For *Alien,* Frankfurt came up with the line "in space no one can hear you scream" and a stunning series of trailers—elliptical, and quick as a lizard—but Fox spent $16 million, all told, on marketing the movie, and by the end of the year was still showing a net loss of $2.4 million, prompting a legal wrangle over the disbursement of profits that would, together with a series of management changes at Fox, keep any thoughts of a sequel safely buried for the next seven years. Ripley could sleep a little longer.

It was an object lesson in the unwieldy new realities of blockbuster economics. The year before, *Superman* had had much the same problem. Its producer, Ilya Salkind, had pulled together a package that had "blockbuster" written all over it: a John Williams score, a Mario Puzo script, and a Marlon Brando cameo, but Puzo's draft was too elaborate, Brando forced 80 percent of the film to be reshot after a legal battle over his footage, and the effects team's pursuit of perfect flight proved to be more costly than it looked—pushing the film's budget up from $15 million to $55 million. The film's eventual box office revenue of $82.8 million made it 1978's second biggest hit, but in terms of profit, it made Clint Eastwood's decision to team up with an orangutan that summer look like sound business sense. The same thing happened just after *Alien,* too, with *Star Trek,* much of whose costly special effects had to be junked, and whose commitment to a specific release date forced the young executive in charge of it, Jeffrey Katzenberg, to spend whatever he could to get it done on time. "Inexperienced and under huge time pressure, Jeffrey simply spent whatever it took," said his boss, Michael Eisner. "When the movie became a hit, we eked out a small profit." It had cost $35 million and took in $56 million—again, enough to make it successful, but with a profit margin that made Dolly Parton's *9 to 5* look like investment genius.

So why did Hollywood not decide, then and there, that films about orangutans and frustrated office workers were the future of the film business and that films about superheroes, or Vulcans, were nice when you could get them, but hardly worth banking on? Because although those films limped past the finishing posts, they did certifiably and reliably finish, and when they did, the flood of ancillary revenues they loosed was something to behold. *Superman*, in particular, marked the first wholly successful instance of blockbuster synergy, with every arm of the Warner Brothers conglomerate successfully feeding the next: Warner Brothers television showed short films about the making of the film; Warner Brothers records released John Williams's soundtrack album; Warner Brothers books released eight titles; and DC Comics, acquired by Warners ten years previously, brought out twenty-eight comic books; while another Warners subsidiary, Atari, brought out a Superman pinball machine. Dolly Parton fans could not compete. They doubtless thought *9 to 5* was a good movie, but they just saw it once and went home thinking: what a good movie. Teenage boys also thought *Superman* was a good movie, but only after seeing it several times and buying a pair of *Superman* pajamas, just to make sure. We didn't watch these movies so much as to lay siege to them.

Hollywood thus found itself caught in a paradox of quite fiendish circularity: it actually made more sense to spend *more* money, not less. *Variety* called it "peace of mind through profligacy." The seventies had begun with attendance levels at an all-time low, and most of the studios trying to keep their costs down, but that course had proved ruinous: reeling from operating losses of several million in 1969–70, MGM had thus turned down the opportunity to make *Jaws* and watched dismally on as the movie pumped up Universal's stock by 22.5 points. Likewise Fox, which had begun the decade reeling from the expense of *Hello, Dolly!* and *Doctor Dolittle*, had had its fortunes completely turned around by first *The Poseidon Adventure*, then *The Towering Inferno*, and finally *Star Wars*, while Columbia had been brought back from the brink by a single film, *Close Encounters*. By the end of the decade, Hollywood's total box office had nearly tripled, thanks in the main to just twenty-two films, each earning in excess of $50 million. Over at Paramount, which had fastened on to the blockbuster bandwagon faster than anyone, with *Love Story* and *The Godfather*, and whose winning streak had continued with *Saturday Night Fever* in 1977 and *Grease* a year later, the future was clear: "We want one big film a year," said Paramount marketing executive Frank Mancuso. "The rest are budgeted to avoid risk."

Risk: there was the rub. "The intoxication of a blockbuster hit can lead to an easy sense that the luck will keep striking," warned Mancuso's boss, Michael Eisner, in a memo to his staff in 1980—what he called "the Big Mistake." The next decade would see Hollywood torn between these twin urges, its progress having something of the lopsided gait of a victory march mixed with a survival dash, as the studios lashed themselves to the sides of the blockbuster, only to find the bloodstream of these behemoths slowed by ever-shrinking profit margins and ever-rising budgets. If someone could only figure out how to keep their costs down, promised the president of the Motion Picture Association of America, Jack Valenti, then a "pot of gold" awaited them at the decade's end. Hollywood's endless summer had begun.

TIME LINE

1978

1. *Grease* (Paramount) $96,300,000
2. *Superman* (WB) $82,800,000
3. *National Lampoon's Animal House* (Universal) $70,900,000
4. *Every Which Way but Loose* (WB) $51,900,000
5. *Jaws 2* (Universal) $50,400,000
6. *Heaven Can Wait* (Paramount) $49,400,000
7. *Hooper* (WB) $34,900,000
8. *California Suite* (Columbia) $29,200,000
9. *The Deer Hunter* (EMI-Universal) $28,000,000
10. *Foul Play* (Paramount) $27,500,000

1979

1. *Kramer vs. Kramer* (Columbia) $59,900,000
2. *Star Trek* (Paramount) $56,000,000
3. *The Jerk* (Universal) $43,000,000
4. *Rocky II* (UA) $42,100,000

5. *Alien* (Fox) $40,300,000
6. *Apocalypse Now* (UA) $37,900,000
7. *10* (Orion/WB) $37,400,000
8. *The Amityville Horror* (AIP) $35,400,000
9. *Moonraker* (Universal) $34,000,000
10. *The Muppet Movie* (ITC/AFD) $32,800,000

*Figures show U.S. domestic gross

CHAPTER 5

FIRST ACTION HERO

"I was into my fifth week of dysentery, and I was riding in at 5:30 A.M. with nothing to do except submit to wild imaginings. So I stormed Steven with the idea of just dismissing this maniac. I'd never unholstered my gun in the entire movie, so I said, 'Let's just shoot the fucker,' and we did. That's getting character in action."
— Harrison Ford on shooting *Raiders of the Lost Ark*

Indiana Jones is not a very good archaeologist. His sprinting has pace, his whip handling real snap, and his classes in archaeology are unusually well attended, but as a practitioner, Dr. Jones is, one regrets to say, singularly unproductive. In the opening sequence of *Raiders of the Lost Ark* we see him recover a Peruvian statuette from a booby-trapped cave, only to deliver it to the feet of his rival Belloq (Paul Freeman). Never one to miss a beat, Indy fixes his sights instead on the Ark of the Covenant, only to lose that, too, to Belloq, who crows, "Once again, what once was yours is now mine." He recovers it one more time, only to lose it, finally, to the American government, who stash it at the film's end in a cavernous, Kane-style vault. A quick glance forward to the other films in the series confirms that his luck does not improve much. Of the three Ankara stones he spends so much of in *Indiana Jones and the Temple of Doom* trying to retrieve, two he loses into a ravine and the third he gives away to a crowd of deserving villagers. The same with the Holy Grail in the third movie, which according to Jones "belongs in a museum" although what he obviously meant to say is that it belongs at the bottom of a deep lava-spitting crevasse. The trilogy records a massive strike-out. Indiana Jones's contributions to the sum total of archaeological findings are precisely, zero. One hopes that Marcus Brody's museum houses a large and profitable gift shop.

A fault in an archaeologist is, however, a major plus in the hero of a blockbuster film franchise, for it is precisely Indy's failure to acquire any baggage that allows each film to reset its bean counter and begin again: the women are different every time; all he takes with him are his hat and his whip, snatched from under the closing doors in the nick of time. Everything else returns to zero, cancels out, comes full circle. In this, he is very much a George Lucas creation, for there is no thriftier imagination in modern movies; just as *Star Wars* had shaped up as a sort of intergalactic rag-and-bone shop of floating junk, endlessly recycled and reused, so, too, with the Rube Goldbergish world of *Raiders,* a world abhorrent of waste, in which economy and equilibrium rule, in which the junk is just that little bit older, and even Old Testament caskets double up as a handy "telephone to God." The two films were conceived at roughly the same time. "I'd been putzing around with these two ideas, and came up to the point where I had to make a decision and so I decided to go with the *Star Wars* film," says Lucas. "So I put the other one on the shelf, and then every once in a while a friend would come along and I'd say I've got this great idea for a movie, I want to see it made, why don't you come and make it, and I'd tell them the story, and they'd go, 'Oh I don't know, an archaeologist looking for supernatural objects . . . I'm not sure that's going to work.'"

Initially, he had Philip Kaufman penciled in to direct it, but Kaufman peeled off to make *Invasion of the Body Snatchers*, which is when Lucas gave it to Spielberg, when the two men were in Hawaii, the weekend that *Star Wars* opened. "I committed then and there, on the beach," says Spielberg. After they had returned to Los Angeles, Lucas went over to Spielberg's house in Malibu to work out the deal they wanted. "Let's make the best deal they've ever made in Hollywood, and let's do it without the agents, just you and me," Lucas told him. They decided they wanted a percentage of the distributor's gross plus the sequel rights and eventual ownership of the movie. They wrote it all down on lined note paper, shook hands, and then sent Lucas's agent, Tom Pollock, out to the studios to see who would bite. "We took it to every single studio in town and got turned down by everybody," says Lucas, "except Michael Eisner, and Eisner got a lot of heat for it, because of the $20 million budget. Nobody thought we could do it for that. They said it's going to be a $50 million movie, and there was a lot of controversy around Steven at the time, because he'd gone over-budget on the last two movies he'd done, and they were afraid of him and said, 'Well maybe if it was a different director . . .'"

At Universal, Ned Tanen took the deal in to Lew Wasserman, who was outraged—threw it across the room, screaming, "Nobody runs the business but me!" Said Tanen: "He was so angry—because of what they were trying to do and, also, because of his frustration. He knew it was changing and he couldn't control it anymore." What the deal asked for, effectively, was for the filmmakers to be treated as equal partners with the studio, who were really no more than distributors for Lucas and Spielberg's film. "George was very much into the idea that the studio and he should be dealing as equals," said Pollock. "He was saying, 'I'm making the movie, we're putting up the money and doing the marketing. We're fifty-fifty partners.' It was a radical concept, to be as simple and fair as that. But Lew hadn't been confronted with it before, and he felt, if we start doing this, then what's left for the way we do business? His attitude was, we don't want to be fair, we're taking all these risks."

Why was Wasserman so horrified? To understand that you have to delve into the huge changes that the studio system was then undergoing and whose resounding after-shock, to this day, leaves most polite conversation unsure as to whether to smile or scowl when the word "studio" comes up. Generally speaking, the word "suit" is required to settle the matter. Do we summon up an image of a thirties hit factory, with barbershops and contract players falling through fake saloon windows; or do we think of corporate glass buildings, lined with sworn enemies of creative freedom, muttering to one another about the lowest common denominator and how best to reach it? Nobody seems to know. The reason is that what people used to mean by the word "studio"—fake saloons and contract players—is all but completely dead. When MGM released *Gone With the Wind* in 1939, it was shown in MGM's theaters, staffed by MGM employees showing the public to their MGM-owned seats, an incredible setup when you think about it: the glory days of American cinema were the result of frankly communist levels of state-endorsed monopoly. But the antitrust laws of 1948 divested the studios of that monopoly on theatrical distribution, weakening their profits still further, and leaving them wide open to takeover by the big international conglomerates. "Around the seventies which is when I got into the business," says Lucas, "the moguls, the old Jack Warners and the [Darryl] Zanucks and all those guys, were leaving the business and the only one that was still around was Wasserman. They were the old-fashioned entrepreneurs who loved movies, but were having to sell their companies to corporations. In that period of about ten years all the studios got sold." In the process, the studios emptied of the talent—all the contract players and directors who used to shoot movies on the studio lot—and became, in essence, merely glorified distributors, the place where the talent went to get the money to make their movies, which were now much more likely to be independently produced films like *Jaws:* a Richard Zanuck–David Brown production, financed by Universal. "In a sense *Jaws* was the Trojan horse by which the studios began to reassert their power," writes Biskind, as always leaving room enough for the opposite to be the case: *Jaws* signaled the final nail in the coffin of the old studio system. By the time Spielberg chose to begin *Raiders of the Lost Ark* with a nostalgic pastiche of Paramount's old studio logo—a mountain blending into the real thing in Peru—the thing he was pastiching had ceased to exist. Paramount was now owned by Gulf + Western, and would eventually be subsumed within Viacom, the international conglomerate that also owns the Blockbuster video chain, and Simon & Schuster, the publisher of the book, *Blockbuster,* that you are currently holding open at page 105.

Naturally the forces of synergistic global take-down compel me to point out how much unalloyed joy Paramount has brought us all over the years, and how farsighted its CEO in 1980, Michael Eisner, was in giving the green light to *Raiders.* Eisner was initially skeptical about the budget—"a lot of people looked at that first scene with the huge rock and thought it would cost $40 million just by itself," he said—but on the other hand, here was a movie to be made by the two men who between them had been responsible for the two top-grossing movies of all time. Eisner knew Spielberg, but not Lucas, and so traveled up to Skywalker Ranch to meet with him, half expecting to find a Hearst-like recluse, housed in a latter-day San Simeon. Instead he found a soft-spoken, low-key Lucas, who, before Eisner could even say anything about *Raiders,* launched into a speech about exactly how he intended to make the movie.

"Let's take the scene where Indy gets on the plane to go to Nepal," he said. "Now we build the entire plane, or we can build a piece of the wing, use one engine, and add roaring sound effects. We'll get just as effective a result. That's how I want to do the whole film. It isn't necessary to make a perfect movie, that's just a formula for going broke. You have to make a movie good enough to achieve the desired magic. There's a difference between magic and perfection. Magic is sleight-of-hand, and so is moviemaking. We're not trying to paint a picture, we're making a film."

In ten minutes he had won Eisner over, although Eisner still wanted it in writing that Lucas and Spielberg would stick around for the sequels. "Trust me," said Lucas. That night, Eisner rang up Lucas's friends, Gloria Katz and Willard Huyck, to ask their advice. "You blew it," they told him. "George wants to be trusted."

The next day Eisner rang up and agreed to the deal, but insisted on huge penalties if they went over-budget. "They agreed without hesitation," said Eisner. "I figured either they don't care or they've got this thing figured out." Eisner's boss at Paramount, Barry Diller, still thought he was crazy. "Michael, are you sure you want to make this ridiculous deal?" he asked him, and when Eisner replied that yes, he did, Diller replied: "This one is yours, not mine." Universal was horrified. "Eisner made it! It's going to break the business!" shouted Sid Sheinberg. "Michael Eisner just made a deal that is going to destroy this business!"

As Lucas and Eisner hammered out the finer points of the *Raiders* deal, Spielberg wound up shooting on *1941,* the reason the studios had eyed Spielberg's name with such horror: an elephantine World War II farce written by two young USC protégés of his, Robert Zemeckis and Bob Gale, which had spun wildly out of control. After *Jaws* and *Close Encounters,* the director had again tried to get smaller projects off the ground—*After School, Continental Divide*—but found the studios weren't interested. They wanted blockbusters. "I said, 'I can make this movie for $2.5 million. There's three people in the entire cast. It's a wonderful story.' And they said, 'We don't want you for this kind of movie. . . . We want you to do a movie about the size of the World Trade Center. Utilize all the tricks, utilize all the effects, utilize all the soundstages, and here's the money.' And on cue, a door opens and the wheelbarrows come in with ten-thousand-dollar bills." It wasn't just studio pressure. He also found it impossible to come down off the "emotional high from these two large-scale, large-budget mega-successes. When *1941* came along, I didn't even think—I grabbed it. I said, 'This is my chaotic lifestyle, it's my lot and welcome to it,' and I took *1941* and threw myself into it." On the 145th day of shooting, the awful truth sank in: he wasn't directing the movie, the movie was directing him. When Lucas and his producer Howard Kazanjian visited Spielberg to talk to him about *Raiders,* they found he'd started to get cold feet about it. "We started looking at, or thinking about, other directors, because Steven had not committed," said Kazanjian. "We never got a firm commitment out of him until almost the very end, when we said, 'Okay folks in about three weeks we're going to start pre-production and we're ready to go: yes or no?'"

Finally, as *1941* collapsed around him, its budget having overrun to $40 million, Spielberg finally leapt on board *Raiders.* If anyone resembled a man trying to outrun a giant runaway boulder, he did.

At which point, with that death-defying leap, the seventies ended, and the eighties began. Decades are always hard things to mark, but in this case, the dividing line comes handed to us on a plate, for *1941* was exactly the kind of multimillion-dollar demolition derby that littered the back end of the seventies like blackened car wrecks: *The Blues Brothers,* or *Honky Tonk Freeway,* which lost far more money than *Heaven's Gate* ever did, recouping only 2.1 percent of its $24 million budget. If you want the film that pulled the plug on the mega-budget seventies, then you're much better off with John Schlesinger's grid-locked epic of shunted chassis and bended fender than you are with Cimino and his immigrant farmers in Johnson County. Has anyone figured out why the cinema of the late seventies took such unalloyed joy in the sight of one motor vehicle careering into another? The final endgame of the chase movie mechanics set in motion by *Bullitt* and *The French Connection* at the decade's start, brought to fruition by *Convoy* and *Smokey and the Bandit* and now reaching a state of grid-locked decadence? Something to do with the energy crisis—a thrilling defiance of Carter's nervous edicts about gas-guzzling America? If so then *Raiders of the Lost Ark* was Reaganomics incarnate: a lean, athletic entertainment that opened the new decade with a resounding crack of the whip. To say that its key note was economy—economy of budget, economy of gesture, economy of joke—is to understate matters. The process by which the film was made resembled a whittling contest between Alberto Giacometti and Woody Woodpecker.

Round one consisted of a series of brainstorming sessions, con-ducted over a period of five days in January of 1978, by Lucas, Spiel-berg, and screenwriter Lawrence Kasdan, who thought he'd been called up to "movie heaven." "That's where the fantasy of all our pent-up, wet movie dreams coalesced," said Spielberg. "Most of the time we were on our feet trying to out-shout each other with ideas." Spielberg knew he wanted the hero being chased by a giant boulder; Lucas wanted a submarine, a monkey giving the Nazi salute, and a girl slug-ging the hero in a bar in Nepal. He originally had Jones pegged as a playboy, living a James Bond lifestyle "with all these girls and these fancy cars and furs and stuff" that he financed with his archaeological digs. Spielberg felt differently: "a tuxedo is a uniform, and it's hard to reach through a uniform to a personality." He wanted a rumpled bum in the tradition of Bogart's Fred C. Dobbs in *The Treasure of the Sierra Madre,* "with five o'clock shadow and the kind of grumpy grizzled view of everything."

They wound up with a hundred-page transcript. Kasdan took it away, and six months later he delivered his script. It was "too long and too expensive," said Lucas, and so Kasdan took it away again and shaved it down some more: off went the scenes in pilot-less plane and a Shang-hai nightclub (to pop up later, in the sequel). When Kazanjian com-plained about the million-dollar price tag of a model of a four-engine plane, Lucas broke off two of the four engines: "How much money do we save if it's only this big?" Spielberg, meanwhile, was going mad with his storyboards—he had shadows thirty feet long crawling into rooms, climbing up walls, hitting the ceiling, and stretching over to meet a villain's face. These, too, he threw out: "I walked into the room and began tearing them down. I boiled it down to where I wouldn't have to shoot more than ten setups a day . . . with each shot I substituted content for coverage. Packed as much action and style and humor into each setup as I could.

"I just got it right down to the bones, right down to what I absolutely needed to tell the story I wanted to tell. On *Raiders* I learned to like instead of love. If I liked a scene after I shot it, I printed it. I didn't shoot it again seventeen times until I got one I loved." On *1941* his average number of takes per shot had been twenty; on *Raiders* it was four. "I've never seen a camera crew so flat out," said one crew member. "You'd see them asleep with their faces in their lunch." Seventy-three days later, Spielberg had his picture, having edited as he went along. Then it went over to Lucas, who cut it down some more. "It was kind of unusual," says editor Michael Kahn. "Steven and I would be through with the cut and then Steve would say, 'Okay, Mike, now you're going to go up to Lucas-Land in Marin County.' So we went up there and George made his suggestions, and then we'd show it to Steven, and they would mediate—which shots they wanted to keep. It was harmonious but different. Lucas wanted things to go faster. That was his thing: 'faster, faster.' Steven was more interested in character development and story." Said Spielberg, "Once the film began to exceed the speed limit in terms of forward velocity, that's when I stopped and said, 'Okay, I'm finished.'"

If you were twelve years old—or thereabouts—when *Raiders* came out, you probably left the theater, floating lightly about a foot above the sidewalk, thinking: right, that's it. Everyone can go home now. Someone has finally cracked it. They've broken the sound barrier, worked out what the formula is, e equals mc squared or whatever. The secret is out. Soon, a Brave New World of movie excitement will be upon us, and your next thought was to feel a little sorry for Spielberg and Lucas, who would surely, you felt, be left behind, as one unbeatably exciting action-adventure gave way to the next—a little like

Chuck Yeager in *The Right Stuff,* breaking the sound barrier all on his own, scoring his own quiet victory, while the astronauts jet off into space. Funnily enough, *The Right Stuff*'s status as a guide to the next twenty or so years of cinema history didn't turn out to be as reliable as we had all expected. The era of nonstop action-adventures did arrive, but not in the form we imagined. It was certainly nonstop, but the pace of *Raiders* would easily turn punishing, in film after film, while the "action comedy" would turn into Hollywood's great graveyard genre, swallowing such radioactive horrors as *Ishtar, Hudson Hawk,* and *Last Action Hero,* in which the action and the comedy, far from engaging in sylphlike dance, sat in opposite corners of the theater, sulking. The fusion turned out to be harder to achieve than we thought. E did equal mc squared, but nobody else understood how it was done.

So how was it done? It helped that the competition in 1981 was pretty creaky. The other action-adventurers that year were for the most part a procession of overarching eyebrows: Burt Reynolds's, frowning over the conundrum of his own sexiness in *The Cannonball Run;* Sean Connery's, furrowed with the task of figuring out the differences between *Outland* and *Alien;* and Roger Moore's, arched with amusement at the thought of his fifth outing as Bond in *For Your Eyes Only.* Here was one offer made by *Jaws* and *Star Wars* that Hollywood was happy enough to refuse: their disavowal of stars, and the same goes for *Raiders,* for while it made Ford a star, it wouldn't have worked had he been one already: Indy needed to come from behind. Despite two outings as Han Solo, Ford had followed through with roles in such über-dreck as *Hanover Street* and *Force 10 from Navarone,* and in 1980 was working as a carpenter to make ends meet, which fed perfectly into Indy's weary fatigue, his air of a man who while perfectly happy to leap across ravines, would be altogether happier at home putting up book-shelves. *Raiders* had its debt to Bond, of course, not least in its pre-credit sequence, bowling Indy along in front of that giant boulder before you'd even had a chance to take your seat, like someone greeting you with a tap of their watch, but Ford's ability to turn a stumble into a run, and to grope for rope with a blind man's fingers—all his gifts for conveying physical extremity—work to keep Indy subtly off-balance throughout. Bond was this shaken but never this stirred.

Nor did you get from the Bond movies anything like the careful daisy-chaining with which Spielberg links up his action: the truly exhilarating thing about Indy escaping that boulder is that he escapes it only to land right at the feet of Belloq—the solution to one conundrum proving the setup for the next, the film batting Indy from one danger to the next with the lightness of a badminton ball. It was these powers of concision—all the stuff that had been chopped out from beneath Indy's feet—as much as the speed, that left you breathless, giving the film its distinctive weightlessness, and pushing its tone out toward giddy comedy. "I'm making this up as I go along," says Ford, not itself an unscripted line, but it feels like it is and rings true to the picture's feel of goosey, loose-limbed opportunism: when Nazis plug a casket of liquor in Marion's bar, she stops briefly to grab a mouthful before getting on with the fight. Lucas would never have shot that, or if he did he would have cut it, but for Spielberg, such touches are, you feel, almost the reason for shooting the film. In other words, while speed excites Lucas—precisely because it seals him off from what blurs past—it seems almost to relax Spielberg, loosening him up for his most debonair dabs of characterization and his best gags: it is *Raiders,* rather than *1941,* that is Spielberg's true homage to the art of slapstick, to the finely calibrated chaos of Mack Sennett and Buster Keaton, and most of it plays perfectly well with its sound down. The moment when Indy shoots the swordsman is funny precisely because Indy says nothing, turns on his heel and gets on with the chase. Bond wouldn't have been able to resist a wisecrack—a bit of comic relief, to lighten up the action—but Spielberg works on the far healthier assumption that action is already inherently comic, in no need of relief, with a lightness all its own: when Indy spins like a top when punched, or uses a Nazi's gun, still in the dead man's hand, to shoot down another as he advances, the choreography of thrills and laughs is so tight, it is difficult to tell when the action stops and the gag starts, exactly—a twinned-tone caught perfectly in Ford's lopsided grin, which could go either way, up or down, depending on the proximity of the nearest ravine.

Here's one thing that *Raiders* didn't do: it didn't open big, as they say, taking in just $8,305,823 on its opening weekend, June 12. Spielberg remembers the look of disappointment on the face of Paramount's head of distribution, although today it would have resulted in someone losing their job, not just their composure. Nobody at Paramount knew how to sell the film. "Steven had an idea for the teaser trailer," says Sid Ganis, then Paramount's head of marketing. "'Somewhere in the deepest desert there was an artifact, nobody knew its power, nobody understood its value . . .' Then you saw sand blowing in the desert and the ark opening up to reveal the title of the movie. George said, 'No, no, no, no, no, no no.'" So they shot another trailer, this emphasizing that it was a throwback to another kind of movie, a cliffhanger; this time it was Barry Diller who put his foot down.

So the marketing was a mess, and while the film would eventually take in $209 million, more than any film in Paramount's history until that point, it did so under its own steam and in its own time, chugging around at the $1.5 million-a-week mark for the best part of the next year, so that by March of 1982 it was still taking in $1,362,289. In other words, *Raiders* arrived with little fanfare, punched above its weight, fought for its fingerhold, and then held on for dear life. Sounds like Indy. Spielberg was soon raving about his star to anyone who would listen, ringing up his friend Barbara Hershey and enthusing, "Ford is going to be the biggest star in Hollywood." Hershey then told her friend, the writer Hampton Fancher, who was working on the script of the new Ridley Scott picture. The next thing Fancher knew Scott had flown over to L.A. from England to view Spielberg's rushes. "He talked with Ford and that was that," said Fancher. *Blade Runner* had found its lead.

How much do blockbuster movies need movie stars? How much do they even need acting? "I have a sneaking suspicion that if there were a way to make movies without actors George would do it," said Mark Hamill of *Star Wars,* and it's certainly true that one of the defining marks of the early blockbusters of Spielberg and Lucas was their careful avoidance of stars—"The movie is the star," said Spielberg of *Jaws*—and both films' success caused no end of confusion for the likes of disaster-movie impresario Irwin Allen, for whom a movie was not really a movie unless it came freighted with A-list superstars. "What are they applauding?" he asked of *Star Wars,* flummoxed. "There's no stars, no love story." Needless to say, the success of both films marked a decisive setback for proponents of the Method, and to the heady New Hollywood days when a movie circled in centrifugal orbit around one or two Great Performances: *Serpico* around Pacino, *Five Easy Pieces* around Nicholson. The days when Marlon Brando could show up for work on *Apocalypse Now,* having failed to learn any of his lines and instead quoting T. S. Eliot at length—not so much appearing in the movie as taking it hostage—would soon be a distant memory. The stars were no longer the star. The movies had struck back.

The blockbuster era would require a different set of skills from Hollywood's actors: a gift for the one-liner, not the speech; for more graphic powers of delineation at the service of pacier narrative; and for the powers of imagination required to act opposite special effects. Richard Dreyfuss complained bitterly that had he known what the effects of *Close Encounters* were going to look like he would have played his scenes differently—he called it "the CE3K stare," from left to right, mouth agape. His complaint would have its echoes, not least in the repeated claims by critics that blockbusters are the enemy of great acting: look at the ensemble ingenuousness of *Star Wars,* they say, or the B-movie intensity that James Cameron asks of his players. And yet the blockbusters of the seventies and eighties would continue to throw up one great role after another: Sigourney Weaver's Ripley in the *Alien* movies, Ford's Indiana Jones in *Raiders,* Schwarzenegger's *Terminator,* Bruce Willis's John McClane in *Die Hard.* Nobody could argue that Willis's lopsided smirk is up there with Olivier's powers of declamation, but there is little question as to which betrays a better understanding of the demands of screen acting: the terse minimalism with which the actor stands his ground against the power of the film editor; the direct one-on-one intimacy with an audience with which he circumnavigates the power of the director; and a grasp of the telling gesture with which to upstage any nearby exploding buildings. Ford, in particular, had all of these, plus—courtesy of his carpenter's training—a sturdy understanding of his role amidst the joists and struts of narrative. If *Raiders* had been an object lesson in how all these come together, in harsh confluence, *Blade Runner* was an extant lesson in what happens when the center cannot hold.

The success of *Alien* had found Ridley Scott in something of a bind: he didn't want to get waylaid doing science fiction films, and yet science fiction scripts were the only ones to land on his doorstep. After the film's release, he was approached by Dino De Laurentiis to direct a film of Frank Herbert's *Dune*, but after seven months he dropped out. It was going to take too much work and his elder brother, Frank, had just died, suddenly, of cancer. "It completely freaked me out," he says. "I felt that life was too short to be spending two and a half more years on a movie, which is how long I thought it would take to make *Dune*. I needed to get my mind off my brother's death and get moving with something else."

Something else came in the shape of a script entitled *Dangerous Days*, which had been sent him by writer Hampton Fancher and producer Michael Deeley, adapted from Philip K. Dick's novel, *Do Androids Dream of Electric Sheep?* It was more sci-fi, but of a particularly melancholy sort, concerning a world-weary detective named Rick Deckard who is hired to hunt down rogue Replicants—androids with a prematurely shortened life-span of four years. If Scott was really looking for a project to take his mind off his brother's death, he succeeded magnificently in doing the exact opposite, and finding a script that positively ached with mortality. Nor would it be the burst of brisk, breezy activity he anticipated, the shoot for *Blade Runner* proving brisk only in the sense that a force-ten gale is brisk, or a freight train.

The script took a year of rewrites to get ready. Fancher had done a good job in fleshing out Dick's paranoiac novel, but it still read like a stage play: there were few exteriors, and the world his characters inhabited remained unexplored. One day during their script discussions, Scott asked him, "Hampton, this world you've created—what's outside the window?" Hampton admitted that he hadn't a clue. "Well, think about it," replied Scott, and suggested he read a sci-fi comic called *Heavy Metal*—the same comic Scott had used as inspiration on *Alien*. The next day, Fancher "came back in all excited, going 'Yeah, let's go outside the fucking window!'" Quite how far outside the window Scott wanted to go, the writer soon found out. "His imagination is like a fucking virus," said Fancher. "It keeps growing and spreading and mutating. Ridley's mind is almost too fast for his own good; very often, it pulled ahead of himself, at great speed. Then he'd tumble over it, ideas were pouring out of him so fast."

"The idea of making it on a set on a Warners backlot was almost unthinkably expensive," says Scott, "and yet that was the most practical way to go. I researched and did a little bit of traveling. I'd been to Hong Kong before, I'd shot a commercial there for Benson & Hedges, and I always remembered the sheer density of the city, and thought this would be the benchmark for my film. That would be the future. Particularly if you're on the West Coast of America, the majority I felt could be either Hispanic or Asiatic, or a strong mélange of all three. That's how I gradually built the process of *Blade Runner:* all those years of commercials, all that awareness of urban deterioration and disintegration. You have these cities that become retro, with their guts on the outside. The guts can be beautiful."

Scott kept urging Fancher to give him more clues, more mystery—more *detecting*—but the writer felt out of his depth and so Scott instead turned to David Peoples, who took Dick's world and populated it, but still came up short on plot. "Clues are not my strong point," said Peoples. "If anybody was authoring it at this stage it was Ridley. He was dominating, supervising and caring about what went on here. . . . I would sometimes be writing a scene that Ridley would be shooting the following week, and twice I guess I was writing stuff that was going to be shot that day and just frantically trying to make certain changes to solve this particular thing or that particular thing."

Principal photography began on March 9, 1981, and immediately the film started pedaling backward into the red. "After the first day of shooting the production manager called me to say we were now five days behind," remembers Alan Ladd. "Ridley had shot smoke all day." The first scenes to be shot were on the elaborate Tyrell Corporation set, with nearly six thousand square feet of polished black marble and six enormous columns, but Scott had walked in, taken a look at the columns, and said, "Let's turn them upside down." "Ridley literally changed everything. I can't think of one set we went into and shot the way we found it," said art director David Snyder. "It was brutal." Actor M. Emmet Walsh complained to Snyder that "by the time you guys get finished lighting, we're lucky if we have time for three takes." For one scene during which Walsh had to repeatedly smoke a cigar that left him choking on smoke, he muttered, under his breath, "You son of a bitch. You should be hung up by your balls and left to twist in the wind." To his horror, Scott heard him.

"I feel that way now," Scott replied.

By day three, they were two weeks behind schedule, and the film's financiers started hovering at Scott's shoulder. The film's $18 million budget was a three-way split among the Ladd Company, who would release the film through Warner Brothers, Hong Kong film mogul Run Run Shaw, and Tandem, who had been brought into the deal on the promise that they would get the next *Star Wars.* Instead, they saw nothing but rain, gloom, a woman being shot in the back, and a relentlessly perfectionist director who shot the same sequence over and over again, all day long. They questioned Scott on everything—"Why are you taking so much time to set things up? Why so many takes? We don't have the money for this"—and every time they did, he flew into a rage. "It was the first time I'd worked extensively in Hollywood, and suddenly the new kid on the block was faced with the facts of life here," says Scott. "There was an inordinate amount of explanation that had to be done.... I was not as independent as I thought I was. It got hard, I had to give a lot of explanations which I'd honestly felt I'd earned the right not to have to do after all those years. After shooting over two thousand commercials and *The Duellists,* and *Alien,* suddenly there I was still explaining myself. So I got very short-fused. I was getting pissed off. Pissed off regularly. Every day."

"It was just wretched awfulness, really," said producer Kate Haber. *Blade Runner* was a monument to stress. "Tandem was furious with Michael and Ridley, Ridley and Michael were battling Tandem, and our leading man and director got to the point where they were barely speaking to one another." Ford was driven to distraction by Scott's attention to his sets; he would look up and see Scott perched way up on a crane thirty feet in the air, peering into his lens, composing his perfect shots, and wonder: what am I supposed to be doing here? "I played a detective who did no detecting," he complained. "There was nothing for me to do but stand around and give some vain attempt to give some focus to Ridley's sets."

"Harrison wanted to be directed," says Ladd, "and Ridley wanted to fool around with light. Harrison just wanted to be reassured, and Ridley didn't want to be bothered. At that time Ridley was very shy, and didn't want to deal with actors. It was the same on *Alien.* He knew what he wanted but didn't know how to explain to the actors how to get there." Eventually the two men stopped speaking to each other, says Ladd: "Harrison wouldn't speak to Ridley and Ridley wouldn't speak to Harrison and I was stuck in the middle. 'Could you tell him to do this, or tell him to do that?' It was difficult." By the end of the shoot, Ford was "ready to kill Ridley," said one colleague. "He really would have taken him on if he hadn't been talked out of it."

"Harrison and I are very similar," says Scott. "It can be perceived that we're bad-tempered and crotchety and actually we're not. We're actually relatively good fun, [but] if you have a discerning actor, who is smarter than most, he's gonna ask questions, and you'd better have your answers. If you haven't got your answers there's likely to be a row. You have a row and your adrenaline flushes out all the other stuff you've got going through your mind and you suddenly come up with a very distilled answer . . . rage flushes it out. I get very articulate." By the time the picture wrapped, on June 30, it had gone $5 million over-budget, and on July 11, Deeley and Scott received a letter from Tandem's attorneys telling them they were "off the picture."

The first test screening of the film was a disaster. "Almost dead silence greeted the end of the film," said Deeley. "As the lights came up, the audience filed out as quietly as if they were leaving a funeral service." They found the film too hard to understand, too graphic, too slow and draggy, and the ending too abrupt. "A lot of things went straight over the head of the audience," says Scott, "partly because they were trying to follow the main line, which was actually pretty straightforward, but somehow got veiled in complexities that it didn't have. Part of this was that the proscenium was so exotic, the world you were looking at was so interesting that that was a distraction, but then that is part of the interest in watching the film. It was a new kind of film: because the world was almost as important as the story." Tandem insisted he shoot a new ending, showing Deckard and Rachael driving off happily, removing any hint that Deckard was himself a Replicant, and provide the movie with a voice-over, although according to Alan Ladd, "It was Ridley who came up with the narration. He said, 'I loved all those Philip Marlowe stories, Sam Spade and all that. We should put the narration into it.'" It was the first time Scott had experienced the preview process, and he thought, "'My God, maybe I've gone too far. Maybe I ought to clarify it.' I got sucked into the process of thinking, 'Let's explain it all.'"

Blade Runner took in only $14.8 million upon its release, and promptly disappeared from screens. As a blockbuster, then, it was a bust, but a bust of a very particular breed, for soon the film's designs began to show up everywhere from *Brazil* to the stage sets for the Rolling Stones' *Steel Wheels* tour, and when laser discs appeared on the market in 1989, *Blade Runner* became Voyager's top-selling disc, and didn't budge. In Japan, where the film was a huge success, its art directors were treated like kings, the fans too in awe to even look them in the eye. "*Blade Runner* has kind of resurrected itself," says Scott. "But it didn't resurrect itself on its own. I think MTV did it. That whole MTV generation saw the romanticism and retro neoclassicism—where it's always raining and always dark—and saw this world as a romantic world. It certainly influenced so many filmmakers particularly in that video world: suddenly every other band had a neo–*Blade Runner* background. I think gradually kids got it, then they started to see it in the video store—usually on a badly degraded tape—and finally got with it. It's a funny cycle, but it's great that it resurfaced that way."

The film thus turned out to be one of those rare, radioactive masterpieces that cinema seems impelled to throw up every now and again: toxic to all who touch it at the time, and leaving many careers in fallout, but exerting a mesmeric, winking glow that only increases with the years. Every great film epoch has to have a film like this—the seventies had *Apocalypse Now,* the forties had *The Magnificent Ambersons*—and the procedure by which they are anointed is as tight and stringent as the route to sainthood. First, the film must follow closely on the tail of a genuine masterpiece: a *Kane,* a *Godfather,* an *Alien.* Secondly, it must thus find its director in a suitably engorged state of swelled-headedness as to think nothing of mixing the whole world into his pot. Thirdly, and most importantly of all, it must get hacked up by its studio, thus ensuring that its creator's original intentions are tantalizingly shrouded in the mists of time, and causing hordes of innocent filmgoers to jack in their jobs, nail up the door, and devote their every energy to pondering what could have been.

Blade Runner gets through on all three counts, with extra commendations on the last, with Scott's director's cut, in 1992, serving only to cloud the waters even further, lengthening, rather than shortening, the debate on such crucial matters as "Is Deckard a Replicant?," "What's with the unicorn?," and "Why is it raining all the time?" In the world of blockbuster studies, *Blade Runner* nuts rank second only to *Alien* scholars in their devotion to the cause, although they are easily distinguished by the 50 percent likelihood that they will use the word "hyper-reality." Top honors surely go to William M. Kolb for his second-by-second analysis of the movie, starting at 0:00 hours ("The Ladd Company logo begins to appear"), finishing at 1:52 hours with the end credits, and in between taking us on a blow-by-blow tour of everything from Daryl Hannah's fingertips ("Pris' fingernails are discolored like Batty's") to the irises of the artificial owl (which "glow a deep amber"). You hope Kolb was wearing his glasses. Such Lilliputian-level commentary may reek of pedantry but then *Blade Runner* is a pedant's dream—a million tiny details in search of an auteur—and the hawklike gaze with which the movie's fans fix upon it is born of the movie itself, for it is a film filled with slow blinks and long gazes, and seems to find its somnolent, narcotic center in the scene in which Ford pours himself a scotch, and sits back to issue dulcet instructions to the film's coolest toy: a voice-operated photo-enhancer that allows its user to get inside any photograph and nose around it, in 3-D. Sam Spade never had it so easy: the world's first fully automated private eye. You can see why the film had such an afterlife on video and DVD, formats that allow the viewer to pore over the movie with a leisure matching Deckard's own. Scott is right, in a way: *Blade Runner* was a new kind of film, certainly one that you watched in a new way. You didn't watch it so much as get sucked into it, and lost in it, just like its director: you followed the Minotaur into his labyrinth.

And what a labyrinth. From its opening shot of L.A.'s ziggurats belching fire—as great a flame-grilled opening as that adorning the front end of *Apocalypse Now*—to its spiraling descent into the streets below, to the sound of Vangelis's arpeggiated electro-harps, *Blade Runner* is one of those movies that key into cinemagoers' eternal desire to be swaddled in wall-to-wall gorgeousness. "If you could see what I've seen with your eyes," says Roy Batty, the head Replicant, played by Rutger Hauer as Nietzsche in cycling shorts. What those eyes of his can see, on the other hand, is another matter, for if you want to know what picture it was that turned the lights out on American movies, plunging such pictures as *Se7en* and *The Matrix* into a suitably respectful pitch of Stygian gloom, then *Blade Runner* is your picture: there was one scrap of sunshine in the original film, but Scott soon removed it with his director's cut. The source of the endless rain that falls on his pictures has been of endless fascination to Scott fans, although to anyone who had visited South Shields, in the North of England, where he was born, it's clear that what drives the bad weather in his movies is less ecological concern than straightforward autobiography. From the cigarette smoke that fills its interiors, to the rain that drenches its exteriors, *Blade Runner* wages one serious war on fresh air, further fueling the suspicion that *Blade Runner* is a film far more in love with mysterious*ness* than mere mysteries, or their solution. Scott never did get enough detective work into his picture, which lacks the bloodhound pant of the great detective flicks. Or, as Jack Boozer, Jr., puts it so eloquently in his essay "Crashing the Gates of Insight," "Where the classic detective film uncovers identity and reveals hidden motives to solve a crime—generally based on a 'realistic' representational system—*Blade Runner* interrogates identity and exposes antiquated assumptions to illuminate a crisis of identity formation—based on postmodernist concerns of hypermediation and simulation," a sentence that leaves the gates of insight not only crashed, but hanging off their hinges.

If I understand Boozer correctly, what he essentially likes about *Blade Runner* is that it doesn't actually work. He's awfully polite about it of course, and takes all the blame upon himself and his dastardly assumptions—the film "interrogates" this assumption, and "exposes" that assumption—but basically what he means is that it doesn't actually work. It is a congenital defect of critics at the higher end of the brow when faced with appraising popular movies, whose very smoothly-oiled efficiency can seem suspect; hence the perennial appearance of *Vertigo* on *Sight and Sound*'s list of best ever films: Hitchcock is a director who delights in getting his plot mechanisms buffed up to a nice humming shine, and so the *Sight and Sound* team praise the one film of his in which this is not the case—it's all loose ends and lopsided angles, its plumbing out on display for the critic to pick over at his leisure. The same with *Blade Runner,* a beautiful mutant of a film, and the only sci-fi film of the last thirty years to make the *Sight and Sound* list, but its failure to connect with a popular audience should stretch our sympathies in both directions. Arriving hard on the heels of *Raiders,* it suffered from a distinct case of keeping up with the Joneses, and left many audience members puzzling over Ford's inability to properly absail from the side of one building to the next, instead slamming unceremoniously into the side of it. What, did he forget his whip? For Scott, the film's failure at the box office marked a decisive fall from grace; he would spend much of the next decade tooling around with more earthbound genres, and giving off the slightly disgruntled air of a John Ford who had been forced to make office comedies. It was the eighties' first real case of blockbuster burnout. Sci-fi's Icarus had been grounded.

TIME LINE

1980

1. *The Empire Strikes Back* (Fox) $209,398,025
2. *9 to 5* (Fox) $103,290,500
3. *Stir Crazy* (Sony) $101,300,000
4. *Airplane* (Paramount) $83,453,539
5. *Any Which Way You Can* (WB) $70,687,344
6. *Private Benjamin* (WB) $69,847,348
7. *Coal Miner's Daughter* (Universal) $67,182,787
8. *Smokey and the Bandit II* (Universal) $66,132,626
9. *The Blue Lagoon* (Columbia) $58,853,106
10. *The Blues Brothers* (Universal) $57,229,890

1981

1. *Raiders of the Lost Ark* (Paramount) $209,562,121
2. *On Golden Pond* (Universal) $119,285,432
3. *Superman II* (WB) $108,185,706
4. *Arthur* (WB) $95,461,682
5. *Stripes* (Columbia) $85,297,000
6. *The Cannonball Run* (Fox) $72,179,579
7. *Chariots of Fire* (Columbia) $58,972,904
8. *For Your Eyes Only* (MGM) $54,812,802
9. *The Four Seasons* (Universal) $50,427,646
10. *The Fox and the Hound* (Disney) $43,899,231

*Figures show U.S. domestic gross

CHAPTER 6

MORNING IN AMERICA

"Imagination, not mendacity, was the key to Dutch's mind. He believed both true and untrue things if they suited his moral purpose—and because he believed in belief."
—Edmund Morris, *Dutch: A Memoir of Ronald Reagan*

"I *do!* I *do!* I *do!* I *do!*"
—Gertie, believing in fairies in *E.T. the Extra-Terrestrial,* 1982

If you were to go back to the tapes Spielberg made of the first screenings of *Jaws,* you would hear an odd thing at just around the 115-minute mark. After seven minutes you would notice the screams when the first girl is killed, and at twenty minutes, the screams for the little boy. At fifty minutes you would hear the reaction to Ben Gardner's lolling head, and then again to the shark when it comes at Brody when he's chumming. And at the 115-minute mark, amidst the audience screams as the shark kills Quint, you would hear the odd thing: the sound of one man clapping.

That man is Robert Zemeckis, the director who would go on to make such films as *Back to the Future, Who Framed Roger Rabbit,* and *Forrest Gump,* here making a suitably Gump-like appearance in cinema history, which is to say, just an inch to the left of it, doing the wrong thing. Having inveigled his way into one of the early screenings of *Jaws,* Zemeckis called the next day at Spielberg's office to congratulate him, "And I was going on and on about how the movie's great, and he said, 'Yeah, but I'm a little upset. When Robert Shaw got eaten by the shark, somebody was applauding!' I said, 'No, that was me!' He said, 'It was you? But weren't you sad that Robert Shaw got eaten?' I said, 'Yes, I was, but it was done so great!' It's not like I had any problem with the Robert Shaw character."

Zemeckis was a protégé of Spielberg's who had followed his course through the ranks at Universal. "According to legend," says Bob Gale, Zemeckis's writing partner, "Spielberg was hanging around at Universal, somehow had gotten himself an office and managed to convince people that he was a director and got himself a TV directing gig. So Bob decided that he would start hanging around at Universal, too." Observing the set of the TV series *McCloud*, Zemeckis swiped a couple of scripts from the production office, and together with Gale knocked out a 120-page spec script for the show. For a few months Zemeckis and Gale pursued a lucrative career writing scripts for TV shows that never got made by Universal, and when he wasn't writing Zemeckis was knocking on doors, showing his student film, *A Field of Honor*, to anyone who would sit still for twenty minutes. "He barged right past my secretary," says Spielberg, "and sat me down and showed me this student film he'd made at USC, and I thought it was spectacular, with police cars and a riot, all dubbed to Elmer Bernstein's score for *The Great Escape*."

The "Two Bobs," as they were known, were the Abbott and Costello of junk cinema—forever riffing back and forth on this or that piece of pop culture minutiae. "Bob [Zemeckis] was the first person I met in my life who had the LP soundtrack album to *The Great Escape*, which was the first movie that I saw twice," says Gale, who met Zemeckis at USC, where they were in the class just behind George Lucas's year. Between Gale's Jewishness and Zemeckis's Catholic upbringing, the two of them had a full herd of sacred cows to slaughter, and at USC they found a perfect foil for their punkishly lowbrow attitudinising. "The graduate students at USC had this veneer of intellectualism, and the undergraduates didn't have that yet, or ever. So Bob and I gravitated toward one another because we wanted to make Hollywood movies. We weren't interested in the French New Wave. We were interested in Clint Eastwood and James Bond and Walt Disney, because that's how we grew up." While everyone else was sitting around praising the lack of bourgeois narrative conventions in Jean-Luc Godard, Gale and Zemeckis would sit there celebrating the lack of bourgeois narrative conventions in the Three Stooges movies—not the Marx Brothers, who by the mid-1970s had acquired a distinct patina of intellectual respectability, but Larry, Curly, and Moe. Gale remembers later going to see John Carpenter's *The Fog,* and being appalled by the laxity of the storytelling: "The Fog didn't have any rules!" he says, the outrage still fresh. "Sometimes the Fog comes under a crack under the door. Sometimes it knocks on the door! You'd watch that movie and just go: huh. The Fog is going to do whatever the director says it's going to do. We looked on that kind of storytelling as really insulting to the audience."

Storytelling was the altar at which they worshipped, their God— that and skeet shooting. Together with Milius and Spielberg, Zemeckis and Gale made up a rowdy foursome that were often to be found firing off rounds at the Oak Tree Gun Club. For Spielberg, it was the one chance to hang out with the big brothers he never had, although he would later complain that the shooting gave him tinnitus. "Milius and Bob both have particularly bombastic personalities, more so than Steven and I do," says Gale. "They would just get really demonstrative and jump around. After that we'd go to Tommy's hamburger stand at Panorama City, and sit around and eat greasy chili burgers and get crazy in the parking lot," with Spielberg shooting the whole thing on super-eight. Says Milius: "It was said you didn't ever want to get Steven and me and Zemeckis and Gale in the same room because it would exceed critical mass. People would start screaming and howling and laughing, and just trying to yell ideas, and everything would just break down into chaos. It would get louder and louder and louder until the place detonated."

Much the same could be said of the film they all made together: *1941,* Zemeckis and Gale's comedy about Los Angeles as it is swept by fears of Japanese invasion. The group's collective cynicism wasn't a good fit for Spielberg, whose fascination with the dynamics of mass panic fastened, for the first time, on a completely false alarm. You weren't sure who the joke was on: the Californians for heeding the false alarm, the audience for paying to watch an epic comedy about one, or Spielberg, Gale, and Zemeckis for spending $40 million making it. The movie had nothing in its satirical sights except its own momentous bulk, and so was forced to self-detonate. "Everything they tell you not to do on your first screenplay—we violated all those rules," says Gale. "We were writing dogfights down Hollywood Boulevard, stuff set in Pacific Ocean Park, a park which didn't even exist anymore. This was a really expensive movie and Steven just loved the exuberance of that, that we were just blowing the shit out of everything."

Even after *1941* blew up in the director's face, Spielberg remained convinced that Zemeckis and Gale had talent, and swung Zemeckis a deal at Universal to make his directorial debut, *I Wanna Hold Your Hand,* about a bunch of Beatle fans who try to sneak their way onto *The Ed Sullivan Show;* Spielberg assured Ned Tanen that if Zemeckis looked like he was flunking it, he would step in and direct, but the film also bombed. Zemeckis and Gale seemed to have fallen into a peculiar rut: they could write scripts that everyone thought were great that somehow didn't translate into movies people wanted to see. Their stories—gleaming Rube Goldberg chains of ironic happenstance—were almost too perfect, too airless, and they almost didn't need filming; the only thing you could do with them when you filmed them was let them ramify further until they amassed like prize marrows. "It was actually a much better script than it was a movie," says Zemeckis of their third flop, *Used Cars.* "The script was a lot simpler and less noisy than the film. I began to loot the *Saturday Night Live* class. I also began to loot *Second City.* Before you knew it, I had cast more characters than the screenplay had room for, so the film began to spill over."

It was while promoting *Used Cars* in 1980, however, that Gale took time off to visit his parents in St. Louis and had a brain-wave. Leafing through his father's school yearbook, he found himself wondering: could I have been friends with the type of guy who ran for class office? His next thought was: wouldn't it be neat to make a movie in which a kid travels back in time to sort out his parents? He came back, told Zemeckis, and they started kicking the idea around, with the indolent zigzagging rhythm that characterized their partnership. They would turn up in the morning and shoot the breeze for a bit, and then, says Gale, "at a certain point we'd run out of things to bullshit one another about. It always took about an hour, maybe two hours, where we'd hash out what had been going on with our families, what we'd read in the paper, because that way we didn't have to sit down and work but eventually we'd run out of things to say to one another and we'd have to get down to it. . . . The most important thing is that we leave our egos outside the door. I can say I think 'that's the most stupid thing I ever heard,' and he will know it's not an insult, I'm not saying he's stupid, so he can then go, 'Well why do you think that's stupid, I think that's a great idea.' And we can let each other have it and the synergy would develop."

They sat down and thought of all the things that a time traveler from the eighties might take for granted, then asked themselves: were they visual and could they be delineated simply? They wrote down all their ideas on a series of 3-by-5 index cards—"Marty invents rock 'n roll" or "Dad writes best-selling book"—and pinned them up on the wall, where they could see the whole movie, laid out a scene at a time, and then they started connecting the dots. They'd pull the card off the wall and act it out for each other using whatever props they had at hand, and then Gale—the better typist—would type it all up. Their writing sessions shaped up like a mixture of jam session and military op. The time machine was originally built out of an old refrigerator, but then they realized the fun they could have if it were something as square as a DeLorean, not to mention the added turbo-boost they would give the script if Marty were mobile. "We just wrote and wrote and wrote that script," says Zemeckis. "We really kicked it. It was a real bouncing-off-the-walls movie. We just locked ourselves in a room until we got it right."

Their first draft was met with rejection from every studio in town. Time travel movies don't make any money, they were told; there wasn't enough sex; take it to Disney. They took it to Disney, who told them it was too raunchy. Only Spielberg wanted to do it. "Steven was the only guy who said, I want to do this," says Zemeckis. "And I said, 'Steven, if I do another movie with you that fails, the reality of the situation is that I will never work again.' And he said, 'You're probably right.'" The word was indeed getting around town: Bob Zemeckis can't get work unless Steven Spielberg is the executive producer, and so he took time off, got married to actress Mary Ellen Trainor, did some traveling—and rewrote *Back to the Future* with Gale. Appropriately enough, for a film that so delights in difficulty, the film rose directly out of these years in the Hollywood wilderness, as Zemeckis and Gale collected their rejection slips, tried and failed to get work, and returned again and again to Marty and his DeLorean. The script became their DeLorean: if they could only get it up to the necessary 88 miles per hour needed to power the 1.21 gigawatts needed, it would be their ticket out of there. "It was the pits," said Zemeckis. "I couldn't get a job for like three years. I guess you're stigmatized. They kept saying anything you guys do doesn't make money. It was unbelievably depressing."

Zemeckis and Gale weren't the only ones to benefit from Spielberg's patronage in the early eighties. The studios were desperate to have his name on a film, and the result was a small rivulet—later a roaring channel—of young directors and writers who swam in and out of the various development deals Spielberg had with studios like Universal and Columbia: Gale and Zemeckis, but also Joe Dante, whose movie, *Piranha,* Spielberg judged "the best of the *Jaws* rip-offs," and whom he got to direct *Gremlins;* Chris Columbus, the writer of *Gremlins,* whom he commissioned to write *The Goonies* and *Young Sherlock Holmes,* all of which would be released under the "Steven Spielberg Presents" imprimatur. Spielberg was fast turning into his own brand name, one stamped on films as a guarantee to audiences of the fact that, if he hadn't directed a script himself, he had at least, at some point, been in the same room with it. "I can't think of any director who has started paying homage to himself so quickly," wrote Pauline Kael, and certainly these were dark days for Spielberg fans, who learned to be a little more circumspect with their affections—you had to be on your toes, and read between the lines a little if you were to make sure you got the genuine article—rather like being a Coca-Cola drinker in the twenties, when Co Kola, Coke-Ola, Coke, Koke, Kul-Ku Kola all hit the stands. Which would you get, a Goonie or a Gremlin, and which was better? It was all very bewildering.

One such bit of cross-pollination was *Night Skies,* a script Spielberg commissioned from John Sayles, about a gang of marauding aliens who descend on a farm and terrorize it, *Straw Dogs*–fashion, in a sort of twisted sequel to *Close Encounters.* Spielberg wanted Sayles to direct it, and Rick Baker, who did the effects for *An American Werewolf in London,* to design the film's ringleader alien, Scar, who kills animals with one touch from his long bony finger. But halfway through development at Columbia, Spielberg radically reappraised the idea: the thirteen aliens made way for just the one, like Jesus shedding his disciples. Columbia started to get cold feet and when their marketing department concluded that what they had on their hands was just a Disney movie, and that "no one over four years old will go to see this," Frank Price put the script in turnaround, so angering Spielberg that he had it written into his contract that he need never have any dealings with Price again. Columbia, which had plowed $1 million into developing the idea, kept 5 percent of its eventual net profits—a 5 percent that would generate more money for Columbia in the year *E.T.* was eventually released than any of their own films.

Spielberg's story about *E.T.*'s genesis—as recounted to various interviewers over the years—is almost as moving as the finished film. It came to him, he said, while he was shooting *Raiders of the Lost Ark* in Tunisia. "I was pretty lonely. I really had no one to talk to—no one to be intimate with really, except Harrison and his girlfriend Melissa Mathison. So I opened up to them a lot." A soft-spoken, sensitive woman who had spent a lot of time baby-sitting her neighbors' kids, Mathison had written the script for *The Black Stallion,* another film about a fatherless boy who decides to recruit outside his own species, and also a movie that was largely silent—with boy and horse communicating just by gesture, as Elliott would with E.T. One day, during a moonlit car ride from Nefta to Sousse, Spielberg told her the story "and she wept. I thought, 'Gee, she has a tear in her eye. Was it the way I told the story? Was it my performance or was it the story?' And I realized that it was not my performance at all: so I asked Melissa if she would write it. She said absolutely and dropped everything. We began working on the outline right in the middle of the Sahara Desert."

Spielberg is good at Eureka moments—his films are filled with faces lit up by dawning realization—and everything about this story, its mixture of epic setting and intimate detail, its shining moon and lone tear, mark it out as such a classic piece of Spielbergiana that it feels churlish to point out that he'd first put the idea to Mathison several months before, while *Raiders* was still shooting on a soundstage in London, and that Mathison had turned him down. She was having difficulty with a script she was writing for Coppola, and had just read her initial draft and "hated it," she said. "I've just decided never to write again." It was only later that she reconsidered, and during that car ride from Nefta to Sousse, Ford and Spielberg managed to talk her into it.

Starting in October of 1980, Mathison would work for a week on *E.T. and Me*—as it was then called—at her office in Hollywood and then drive out to Marina Del Ray, where Spielberg was editing *Raiders* in an apartment by the beach. They'd sit down with a handful of 3-by-5 cards and a tape recorder and thrash the story out, with Mathison pulling the story toward ecological earth tones—she was very keen on the gardening angle, on E.T.'s "squishy, earthy muddy kind of feeling"—and Spielberg balancing that with more contemporary cornicing. Mathison wanted E.T. rolling an orange to Elliott's feet when they first met; Spielberg wanted a baseball. Originally Spielberg had E.T. landing in a disused car lot, but Mathison wanted a forest. "Forests are magical," she said. "There are elves in forests." Spielberg wanted E.T. to be young, like the puckish aliens in *Close Encounters;* Mathison thought he should be very, very old. They compromised—he was six hundred years old out of a possible twenty thousand—and pasted together the eyes of Albert Einstein on a baby's face to get the right mixture of innocence and experience: E.T. would sit low to the ground, like a pear, and would have a long telescoping neck, so that he could maintain eye contact with everyone, but also so Spielberg could show there was no guy inside a suit—a revealing mixture of sweetness and guile.

"He said, I want to see him, but not see him too much," said cinematographer Allen Daviau, and as always with Spielberg, the lighting gave you the biggest clue as to the film's creative animus: not since Greta Garbo had a movie character walked around in such an immaculate microclimate of perfect lighting. Said one of Garbo's cinematographers, "She was always taken in close-ups or long shots, hardly ever intermediate, or in full figure. The latter do not come out well." Add a potbelly that doesn't do good things in profile, and you have E.T.— Camille for the Atari generation. It was a weepie, a love story—as Spielberg said, "Boy meets creature, boy loses creature, creature saves boy, boy saves creature," and the release of the movie was sized accordingly, with the film opening in just 1,100 theaters. He wanted word of mouth—for news of E.T. to spread in the same way news of E.T. spreads in the movie: from Elliott to Gertie, from Gertie to Mom, like a rumor or best-kept secret. "That was the entire logic behind the campaign," he says, "but there is something beyond the five senses that gets into the air that becomes a collective national curiosity. With very little advertising, and very little indication of what *E.T.* was ever going to be about, we sneak-previewed that film in about five theaters and we sold them all out. They were 90 percent filled. You've got to give the public credit for being able to sniff it out. They can smell it faster than we can sell it. I never made a movie, except the sequels to the Indiana Jones films, which I had any expectations of going through the roof. I didn't think *E.T.* would go through the roof. I didn't think *Jaws* would go through the roof. I've never had the chutzpah to predict that kind of stuff."

It went through the roof. Finally, here was Spielberg's much longed for attempt at a small-scale, personal movie and, naturally, he had another nine-hundred-pound gorilla on his hands. The film opened on June 11 and took in $11.9 million its first week of release. It then increased its grosses, taking in $12.4 million the next week, $12.8 in the third, $14 million the week after that, and it didn't slow down until week five. Three months in and it was still earning $13 million a week, with Spielberg earning $500,000 a day. And here was an odd thing: where previous hits like *Raiders* and *Empire* had whetted the public's appetite for other movies, none of *E.T.*'s competitors—*Tron, Blade Runner, The Thing*—benefited from *E.T.*'s release. There was no spillover. The only movie *E.T.* made you want to see, it seemed, was *E.T.*—an undying loyalty born of Elliott's own. *E.T.* inspired monogamy, and was received in America with the sort of national fanfare that is normally accorded visiting dignitaries or heads of state. A book of children's letters to the creature was published ("I like you better than Annie. I got a book about you. Good bye."). The U.N. decided to award its peace medal to Spielberg, even though *E.T.* has very little to say on the subject of world peace, unless you count the "No Nukes" T-shirt worn by Elliott's brother. Universal was happy to concur, printing a new poster for the movie, one echoing Michelangelo's Sistine Chapel image of God reaching down to touch Adam, which read, simply, "Peace." Spielberg watched as news of the box office spread from the trades to *The Wall Street Journal*; the film made the cover of *Rolling Stone,* and *People* and *Us,* and was to appear on the cover of *Time* magazine—were it not that twelve hours before the issue went to press, the Falklands War broke out, pushing *E.T.* into the top-right-hand corner. "I say this with all humility," said Melissa Mathison later, "which do you really remember: the Falklands War, or *E.T.*?"

It is a good question. When *Jaws* was released, political cartoonists had seized on the shark as a symbol representing variously: inflation, taxes, unemployment, male chauvinism, Ronald Reagan, and the Hawaii Media Responsibility Commission. When *E.T.* came out, it wasn't just cartoonists who seized on *E.T*'s potential as a political shorthand. When polls showed that Attorney General Jeff Bingaman, the Democratic nominee, had moved to within seven points of Republican senator Jack Schmitt in the race for New Mexico, his aides had *E.T.* buttons made up, while on CBS, Dan Rather joked, "E.T., phone home: Jack Schmitt needs help." A decade later, and it wasn't just political aides, but politicians themselves who were busy making political hay from blockbuster movies. When the first president George Bush found Pat Buchanan catching up to him in the polls during the 1992 campaign, who did he put the call to? "I want you to vote, and at the same time send a message to Congress," Arnold Schwarzenegger told a cheering crowd in New England. "Hasta la vista, baby." The next day, Buchanan hit back: "I have a message for The Terminator: I'm still here. So hasta la vista, baby." Buchanan's advisors should perhaps have told him that when someone "hasta la vista's" you, you can't just turn around and "hasta la vista" him right back. For one thing, it gives voters no means of distinguishing between your policies and those of your opponent. For another, as everyone knows, backsies don't count.

At what point it was decided that those seeking to lead the free world should best do so by tagging their flagging popularity levels to the backside of make-believe killer robots and space aliens is a matter for future historians of American political rhetoric to puzzle over. But Reagan's presidency would be the place for them to start, the point at which blockbuster movies bequeathed that startling offspring: politics-by-blockbuster. "It is the motion picture that shows us not only how we look and sound, but—more important—how we feel," said Reagan, not the first movie fan in the White House, but the first to fully utilize the demagogic potential of the movies, sprinkling his presidency with off-the-cuff reviews and references in a way that both established his own down-home ordinariness and neatly glanced off his own acting career—an impeccable mix of self-deprecation and self-aggrandizement of the sort that only Reagan could pull off. At Camp David, congressmen were astounded to find arms talks devolving into a discussion of the movie *WarGames,* whose teenage hero drew admiration from the president. "I don't understand these computers very well, but this young man obviously did. He had tied into NORAD!" During the Lebanese hostage crisis, he emerged one morning to tell the press, "I have seen *Rambo* and now I know how I should act the next time." Most famously, he named his Strategic Defense Initiative after Lucas's *Star Wars*—after an advisor assured him "the good guys won"—causing Lucas to sue for breach of copyright and to prevent any "association with a noxious subject, particularly nuclear holocaust," as his lawyers pointed out. "*Star Wars,* your Honor, is a fantasy. It's something that doesn't exist"—but then nor would SDI, in the end, and the judge, clearly one with the zeitgeist, ruled against Lucas. The nation's most expensive but ultimately fictitious weapons program could indeed be named after its highest-grossing, and equally fictitious, movie.

The presidential endorsement of blockbusters is nothing new, of course. President Carter was a big fan of *Close Encounters,* Richard Nixon of *Patton,* while the art of the presidential puff goes right back, in fact, to D. W. Griffith's *Birth of a Nation,* which arrived in theaters emblazoned with a quote from President Woodrow Wilson—"like watching history written with lightning." But in Reagan's White House, the tradition of the White House movie screening—previously private affairs—became regular, well-publicized gala events. These movie evenings, usually scheduled for Sundays, generally began with dinner for thirty-two guests at four tables in the family dining room, after which everyone adjourned to the theater—an aqua-and-white room furnished with folding chairs and tray tables, complete with bowls of popcorn, and upholstered armchairs for the Reagans and their most important guests. The Reagans watched *Reds* this way, in the company of Diane Keaton and Warren Beatty, and *Man of Iron, From Mao to Mozart, Ragtime,* and *E.T.* Remembers Spielberg: "The film was over and Reagan thanked myself and the cast, and made some lovely comments about how the film had affected him, and then he looked around and he said, 'There's a handful of people in this room who know that everything in this movie is completely true,' and of course, and because I was so much into UFOlogy my jaw dropped but I somehow didn't have the courage to ask what he meant."

Poor E.T. There are few fates more detrimental to your health as a fictional movie character than being Much Loved, but being a Much Loved National Symbol—plucked from your movie and forced to press the flesh on the world stage—just about beats it. True, he had faced similar indignities in the movie, and weathered them well. There was the time Gertie dressed him up in her best doll's clothes—"*noo,*" moans Elliott softly—but that was as nothing compared to the drag-act of being draped in the flag of international peace by the U.N.; and yes, there was the time he almost passed away on the scientists' operating table, as lifeless as a chloroformed frog—"what have they done to you, E.T.?" wails Elliott—but that was not nearly as injurious to his standing as being wheeled around town as a Reaganite flunkie. Such are the vagaries of interpretation that beset any movie character unfortunate enough to wander onto the world stage.

By comparison, his transformation into a child's toy was, you might think, the least jolting of his various transformations. Even before shooting had commenced, producer Kathy Kennedy had been dispatched to negotiate merchandising rights and promotional tie-ins with various manufacturers, but she found it tough going, for despite *Star Wars*'s success, it was still early days for the film merchandising business. "I showed them *E.T.*'s picture and they went 'uuggh,'" she said. Schwinn bikes also turned down the opportunity to appear in the film—which is why Elliott instead rides Kuwahara trail bikes, a Japanese import—as did Mars chocolates, so they went instead with Reese's Pieces, whose sales climbed 65 percent after the movie was released; Hershey's was running three shifts, six days a week to meet demand. According to Spielberg, "There were billions of dolls that were manufactured and illegally distributed from Asia and other areas around the world and shipped in on huge 747 cargo jets. We received the negative publicity, because everyone assumed this must be Universal—marketing such a beloved character and corrupting *E.T.*'s purity and innocence with commercialism—but the only doll we ever merchandised was with Kamar. We didn't have the attitude 'hey people are going to make it anyway, why don't we do it better?' We didn't even have time. The illegal merchandise came flooding into the country like a huge dump tank of toys. We were guilty of merchandising it more than anything in Universal's collective history, but compared to the way things are merchandised today, it was a little pebble in a large lake."

Nonetheless, it churned up a sea of foaming outrage. "Spielberg [has] turned his film into a toy factory, trivializing the movie almost beyond recognition," wrote Michael Ventura in *L.A. Weekly*. Another critic called *E.T.* "a film designed to tug your heartstrings and pick your pockets at the same time," although this paradox proved easier to process for some of the nine-year-olds in the audience. Wrote one of the correspondents in that book of letters to E.T., "I thought it was extraordinary, neat and successful."

As a critical estimation of *E.T.*—not to mention a description of Spielberg's driving animi as a filmmaker, or all that one requires of a good blockbuster, for that matter—this is unimprovable: sound in its particulars, unfazed by the gimcrack ingenuity of the medium of film, and leading us toward a gentle reminder of one very important fact: *E.T.* is a kids' movie. It's a very good kids' movie, possibly the best kids' movie ever made, but the time may have come to reclaim *E.T.* for the audience for which it was intended. What the rest of America was doing slobbering all over it is anyone's guess, although, this being Spielberg, there is a lot of America in the movie and, frankly, it looks a peach: a glorious recession-free idyll of lawns and sprinklers caught in the roseate glow of dusk and dawn. When Reagan promised "morning in America" this is probably what the country looked like in his head. It is customary to pay classics the compliment of their timelessness, but one look at Elliott's bedroom—a mad jumble of Elvis Costello posters, Space Shuttle models, and Anglepoise lamps—is all you need to know that this is one movie hell-bent on being set in 1982. "This isn't a room," says his mom, "it's a disaster."

But it is also an education. The last time the aliens came calling, in *Close Encounters,* they also found a mess, but a mess of a very different kind: the junkyard of Richard Dreyfuss's living room, teeming with discarded hobbyhorses and old enthusiasms, and all the more reason to get out on the highway, looking for the lights on the horizon, arms stretched wide for deliverance. But all Elliott wants to do is hug E.T.

tight, and squirrel him away back at home—*E.T.* is a nester's movie, a window onto homebody videotape-watching, "Reach out and touch someone" America—and it is here that E.T.'s education begins. It is with Elliott's *Star Wars* figures that Elliott first explains about life on earth, and it is with Elliott's plastic wrap that E.T. then explains where he comes from—at least two reasons why the accusations of merchandising cash-in just slightly miss the mark with this film, for toys are clearly everything to E.T. They are how he hides himself from the prying eyes of Mom (passing himself off as a doll in the toy cupboard), how he learns to speak English (using Gertie's Speak & Spell), and finally how he phones home. "You go for that level of verisimilitude today, and you're accused of product placement," says Spielberg. Indeed, *E.T.* marked a decisive end of the director's extended period of innocence. It is the film before the Fall. There are few more perilous moments in the career of faux-naïf artists than the point at which they find their voice, and *E.T.* brought to full ripeness the style that would forever be associated in the public mind with the "Spielbergian"—for now everyone knew what that term meant, what its vital signs were and where it had been done best.

One of the most curious things about *E.T.* is not so much that it is a Good Spielberg film, but how closely it resembles, and avoids, being a Bad Spielberg film. The distinction is absolute, with Good Spielberg and Bad Spielberg being as separate in the public mind as Jekyll and Hyde. Good Spielberg is the guy who made *Jaws,* and *Close Encounters,* and *Raiders of the Lost Ark:* the brisk young tyro, full of cackling humor and spritely anarchy, who can't turn his nose up at the prospect of pandemonium and whose ruthless abilities as a dramatist cut like a knife through water. Bad Spielberg is the guy who made *The Color Purple,* and *Always,* and *Hook* and the final ten minutes of *Schindler's List:* the gluey sentimentalist with a sweet tooth for fairytale endings, who can't resist the opportunity for public address, clambering aboard his films as if they were pulpits, or as if apologizing for his own dramatic technique. What, then, are we to do with *E.T.?* It looks like Bad Spielberg: the lighting has the same over-honeyed, pre–Janusz Kaminski burnish that would engulf *Hook;* and it sometimes sounds like Bad Spielberg: "I don't know . . . how to feel," says Elliott, doing a very good impression of an adult's idea of a child in grief. And the last time I looked, *E.T.* harbored not only a fairytale ending but an impressively ambitious Marshall Plan for the immediate annexation of the nation's tear ducts. But somehow, it isn't Bad Spielberg. For one thing it has Drew Barrymore, delivering the last uncute performance by an under-ten in his movies, all brisk no-nonsense and random truth-blurts. "I don't like his feet," she says, and refers to E.T. throughout as the "man in the moon," for which Mathison deserves a medal: the line so thoroughly germinates from within a six-year-old brain, filtering what she sees through whatever stuff she's picked up on TV or at school, and it so gently pricks the film's bubblelike immersion in its own fantasy—you can imagine Elliott getting all huffy at her for saying it—that allows audiences to lose themselves in that world all the more. Fantasists with a sense of humor are a rare breed indeed—far rarer than realists with the usual dose of cynicism—and E.T. is probably the best example of Spielberg's weird, double-jointed ability to both sell a fantasy to an audience and also to see what that fantasy looks like from the outside. He digs his own ribs.

"For me E.T. was both the quintessential story of my childhood and at the same time the end of my childhood," says Spielberg, "and it gave me the courage, based on its success, to start to tackle more adult subjects like *The Color Purple* and *Empire of the Sun,* and *Schindler's List* and *Amistad. E.T.* gave me a kind of free pass to fail." He had found his voice; the trick would now be to lose it, and it would be a long haul. "After *E.T.* people expected a certain kind of movie from me, a certain amount of screams and cheers and laughs and thrills. And I was caving into that. I knew I could give it to them, but I realize it made me a little arrogant about my style. It was all too easy." Or, as the critics like to say, he was about to "grow up," a career path eventually followed by all the blockbuster auteurs, as they hankered for the sort of critical responsibility denied them all the while they made movies to satisfy their inner teenager.

All except Lucas. The rest of the eighties would be a tough time for him, too, but for a different reason, as he struggled to find life after *Star Wars,* and came up empty. In 1984, he gave up the presidency of Lucasfilm, to try his hand at producing—*Howard the Duck, Willow, Radioland Murders*—and when those movies failed, he resumed it again, not to make movies, but to concentrate on the technical side of his business, starting up Pixar in 1984, to develop the digital tools that would, within a decade, revolutionize the industry.

"George was really thinking ahead," says John Lasseter, director of *Toy Story*. "He basically created his own division to come up with digital sound editing, digital film editing, digital optical printing, digital compositing, then computer animation. At the time, crazy nutty ideas. Now, tell me a movie that doesn't use an Avid or a Lightworks. Every bit of sound editing is now digital. There hasn't been a traditional optical printer used in fifteen years, and look at the effect computer animation has had. It was a pretty significant time, and a small group of people, so he was really forward-thinking. He put his money where his ideas were." Others found Lucasfilm more constrictive: a sterile, spooky place where everyone went around in jeans and sneakers and said "neat" a lot, just like their employer. When Scott Ross went up there to become general manager of ILM (a division of Lucasfilm) in the late eighties, he did so expecting something resembling the creative nucleus of Spielberg's Amblin, but found "an incredibly cloistered environment, like entering a nunnery. There weren't any managers to speak of, and executives to speak of. George was in a very strange space. He had just come off *Howard the Duck* and *Willow,* and was not really in the moviemaking business. We were being told by our CEO that we shouldn't be in the film business, that we should look at other businesses like real estate and theme parks. And we were also being told: 'No one can make movies within my organization except me.' We were losing the likes of Joe Johnstone and David Fincher, who came to work at ILM because they both wanted to make movies. We thought this is crazy, why don't we form our own company?" Johnstone would go on to make *Honey, I Shrunk the Kids* and *Jumanji,* Fincher to make *Alien 3* and *Se7en.* When Lucas sold off Pixar, along with John Lasseter, to Steve Jobs, he was setting loose the talent that would go on to make *Toy Story,* while Scott Ross would go on to found Digital Domain with James Cameron. Lucasfilm was hemorrhaging talent at an alarming rate.

"I left because I wanted to make movies," says Ross, "just like everyone else. Everyone there had a screenplay in their back pocket, and a lot of the newer filmmakers—the Camerons of the world—were looking to create digital effects for less money and not fall into the mind-set of the Lucases and Spielbergs. It was the next generation." The blockbusters of the early eighties had been almost exclusively generated by just two men, but Lucas's and Spielberg's monopoly on the upper registers of the box office was about to be broken; a generation for whom *Star Wars* and *Jaws* had worked like dog whistles, and who had been slowly amassing in the wings, finally broke cover in the summer of 1984. If you wanted to know who would be dominating the box office for the next decade, in fact, all you had to do was keep an eye out for the guys with the time travel script sticking out of their back pockets.

TIME LINE

1982

1. *E.T. the Extra-Terrestrial* (Universal) $359,197,037
2. *Tootsie* (Columbia) $177,200,000
3. *An Officer and a Gentleman* (Paramount) $129,795,554
4. *Rocky III* (MGM) $125,049,125
5. *Porky's* (Fox) $105,492,483
6. *Star Trek: The Wrath of Khan* (Paramount) $78,912,963
7. *48 Hrs.* (Paramount) $78,868,508
8. *Poltergeist* (MGM) $76,606,280
9. *The Best Little Whorehouse in Texas* (Universal) $69,701,637
10. *Annie* (Columbia) $57,059,003

1983

1. *Return of the Jedi* (Fox) $252,583,617
2. *Terms of Endearment* (Paramount) $108,423,489
3. *Flashdance* (Paramount) $92,921,203
4. *Trading Places* (Paramount) $90,404,800
5. *WarGames* (MGM) $79,567,667
6. *Octopussy* (MGM) $67,893,619
7. *Sudden Impact* (WB) $67,642,693
8. *Staying Alive* (Paramount) $64,892,670
9. *Mr. Mom* (Fox) $64,783,827
10. *Risky Business* (WB) $63,541,777

*Figures show U.S. domestic gross

ACT II
1984–1993

COMETH
THE TITANS

CHAPTER 7

TIME TRAVELERS INC.

"I am afraid I cannot convey the peculiar sensations of time-travelling. They are excessively unpleasant. There is a feeling exactly like that one has upon a switchback—of a helpless headlong motion! I felt the same horrible anticipation, too, of an imminent smash."

—H. G. Wells, *The Time Machine,* 1895

"YOU CAN'T SCARE ME, I WORK FOR JAMES CAMERON"

—T-shirt worn by *Terminator* crew members, 1984

James Cameron went to lunch thinking: I've got to pick a fight with Conan the Barbarian.

When Mike Medavoy first suggested Arnold Schwarzenegger for the role of Reese, the hero in *The Terminator,* Cameron thought it a lousy idea. Reese had the bulk of the film's exposition to reel off—all the stuff about future war and techno apocalypse—and Cameron didn't want it reeled off in an Austrian accent. He had to show willing, though, and so decided to go to lunch with the Austrian, pick a fight with him, and then come back and say: the guy's an asshole, the deal is off.

Over lunch at the actor's favorite restaurant, the Schatzi in Santa Monica, however, Cameron found himself charmed. Schwarzenegger seemed to love the project—was full of advice, in fact, for whoever

141

would end up playing the part of the Terminator: he had to be able to reload his weapon blindfolded, he said, shoot without blinking his eyes, and walk with his head tilted forward. Cameron found himself gazing up at Schwarzenegger's face, marveling over its planes and angles, thinking, "This guy has got the most amazing face." Eventually he piped up.

"Y'know Arnold, we've been talking for an hour and a half, two hours, and virtually everything you've mentioned about the script has been the other guy. Do you want to play him?"

Even as he said it, he thought: he's going to be insulted, he wanted to play the hero. But to his amazement Schwarzenegger agreed, settled the bill—Cameron was too skint—and they went back to their offices. The only remaining problem was to persuade Schwarzenegger's agent, Lou Pitt, who didn't want his client playing a heavy. Executive producer John Daly got him on the phone and pleaded with him: "I know, Lou, but he is the title character, after all, and yes, I know he's the villain, it's true, he is the bad guy, but it's the title character after all, Lou . . ." That afternoon the deal was drafted and signed. *The Terminator* was a go project.

It was a crucial change. In the original script, *The Terminator* had been a lithe assassin with blue eyes, military crop, and an upturned trench coat. Cameron had been thinking: Jürgen Prochnow. What he had instead was 220 pounds of Austrian bodybuilder who could no more blend into a crowd than he could crochet. "He fills the space, and you have to go with that," said Cameron. "With Arnold, the film took on a larger-than-life sheen. I just found myself on the set doing things I didn't think I would do—scenes that were supposed to be purely horrific that just couldn't be, because now they were too flamboyant." The movie's center of gravity shifted down, and its tone pushed out, toward—if not black comedy, then an air of flabbergasted extremity, thunderstruck glee. When Cameron had written the line, "I'll be back," he hadn't meant it as a payoff—one of those tough-guy apothegms with which Bond or Dirty Harry brought their violence to a full stop. For one thing, it preceded the act of violence it supposedly punctuated: the Terminator driving his car through the police headquarters window. But next to Schwarzenegger's sheer mass, it played that way in theaters: audiences simply knew that "I'll be back" didn't mean "Give me five minutes while I park the car." It promised carnage. It was just like the "You're going to need a bigger boat" in *Jaws:* a punch line made in retrospect, by the audience, not the film. Something seemed to have sprung up between the screen and the auditorium—some change in air valence, a static charge, switching the moral current of the movie. The villain was playing like a hero.

Cameron has his own reasons for so transfigurative a fantasy. In 1981, he had been fired from his first directing job, on *Piranha Part Two: The Spawning,* while it was being edited in Rome. Furious, he had snuck into the editing suite one night, using his credit card to slip the lock. "So there I am. I'm looking at all these boxes and I see the word "fin," which is Italian for end, so I figure these must be the trims. I teach myself how to run the Cinemonta . . . it was horrible." There was a good flying piranha picture in there somewhere, but *Piranha Part Two: The Spawning* was not it. Cameron contracted a fever of 102, and crawled into his bed, scurrying forth only to steal the other rooms' left-over dinner trays, where he dreamt about a robot rising phoenix-like out of a wall of fire—literally death warmed up. He woke up, grabbed a piece of paper, and started writing. "It all unfolded backward from that scene," he said. "I was alone in Rome, I didn't speak the language, I had no money, the producer had just cut off my per diem and I wasn't feeling very much a part of the flow of humanity. It was very easy for me to project this character."

Returning from Rome, Cameron sold the rights to *The Terminator* to his producer and business partner, Gale Anne Hurd, for one dollar—it was a "blood oath" he said, designed to bind them together in partnership "against all the scumbags we knew we would have to go into business with in order to get the movie made." When Hurd first started taking the script around the studios, she found they either wanted to buy the script off them, or split them up, and pair her up with a more experienced director. But the more they heard "This is a great project but we want a real producer and a real director to do it," the more convinced they were that they were sitting on something good. Hurd was the daughter of a private investor from Palm Springs who had spent much of her teens reviewing Heinlein novels for her local paper; she had studied economics at Stanford, graduating Phi Beta Kappa, before getting a job as Roger Corman's assistant at New

World, the schlock shop that had given so many filmmakers their break in the seventies—Jonathan Demme, Martin Scorsese. Back then, it had been *Easy Rider* rip-offs and Summer-of-Love exploitation flicks. Now it was *Jaws* rip-offs and *Star Wars* clones like *Piranha Part Two, Battle Beyond the Stars,* and *Humanoids from the Deep.* It was after storming out of a screening of the latter, appalled by its sexism, that she first came across Cameron, working away on his models outside. She assumed he was the head of the model shop: "He was acting as if he were the head of the model shop."

Cameron had joined New World, figuring, "I would just insert myself there and spread like a virus." Starting out as a model-maker, he had soon moved on to heading up his own effects department, picking up all the low-budget, down-and-dirty tricks—back projection, miniature work, white frames flashed up to simulate gunfire—that would get *The Terminator* made. "Science fiction films were notoriously under-budgeted until George Lucas came along," he noted. "What's happened, though, is that filmmakers have become hardware happy. The audience has become visually educated and sophisticated, and even a bit jaded, by the big guys. My strategy was not to do big special effects from the beginning to the end; the story is set in Los Angeles, 1984, and the main character is the girl next door. Everything plays out from beginning to end against an everyday backdrop."

"Jim and I worked really really closely, writing and rewriting different scenes," says Hurd. "The key thing, and it's the heart of the movie, regardless of what people remember, is the love story: Michael Biehn's character travels through time because he has fallen in love with this woman's picture. Then it was okay, how do we get to that point?" Eventually they secured a budget of $4.6 million from Orion Pictures, although production was almost instantly derailed by Schwarzenegger's commitment to film a sequel to *Conan the Barbarian.* With the production of *The Terminator* in hiatus, Cameron went shopping for writing work, landed himself the script for *Rambo: First Blood Part II* and also met up with producers Walter Hill and David Giler, who wanted him to write a sort of *Spartacus* in space. They never quite saw eye-to-eye on the project but just as the meeting was petering out into embarrassed pleasantries, and Cameron was getting up to leave, Giler made one last attempt to snare him.

"Well, there's always *Alien II*. It's been kicking around for years and no one's done anything with it. You want to take a crack at that?"

Cameron felt like he was digging out an old bone in the backyard, "dragging out something that no one had been thinking much about." Giler and Hill had only a basic concept—"Ripley and soldiers," they told him, but Cameron loved it: "I thought the concept of grunts in space was wonderful." And so, while waiting for Schwarzenegger to finish *Conan*, Cameron holed up in his apartment in Tarzana, drew the blinds, arranged three desks, each with a stack of yellow legal pads, and sat down to work on three scripts—*Alien II, Rambo: First Blood Part II,* and polishes to *The Terminator*. "I sat down and I figured, 'Okay, I've got two and a half months,' and I broke it down into days, and I broke it down into hours, and I figured out how many pages I could write in an hour. It worked out to about 0.8 pages an hour. I plugged in 0.8, x-number of hours, x-number of hours to rewrite, plus five days for research, and came up with a total figure that was two days longer than I had." To clear his head for each, he played a different piece of music on the stereo "to throw the other stuff away, get into a '*Terminator* mood,' or whatever." For *Rambo* it was Wagner's *Ride of the Valkyries,* for *Alien II* it was *Mars, Bringer of War* from Holst's *The Planets.*

It would soon become his preferred working method. "When Jim makes a movie he writes two," says friend Scott Ross. "What he does is he sleeps during the day and he wakes up in the night and from 8:00 P.M. until 1:00 A.M. he'll write one movie, and from two o'clock until seven he'll write the other movie. He cocoons himself and nobody ever sees him, and then he comes out and now he's got these screenplays, and now he wants a close group of his personal friends to read the screenplays and give him feedback. He want lots of feedback and if you don't give it to him, he gets very upset because he needs to know if he's good. Once he's made a decision and decides this is the way to go, then he will just go and all hell breaks loose."

Action movies are bad for you. You must know that. Everyone knows it to be true. They impair your capacity for rational thought and ability to complete even the most basic pieces of moral arithmetic. "It's as bright, shiny and noisy as a video game, and so fast-paced that even bogus thrills count," *New York Times* critic Vincent Canby wrote of *Die Hard* when it was released in 1988. "It leaves no trace whatsoever. It's an utterly silly movie that . . . renders even basic reasoning skills super-fluous. . . . [It] has the form of a movie, one made with a great many sophisticated skills, but it works on the audience less as a coherent movie than as an amusement park ride." The only problem with this view—leaving aside for a second the fact that *Die Hard* turned out to be one of the best films of the eighties, let alone action movies, a national treasure of coherence, sophistication, reasoning, etc.—is that *Die Hard* happens to agree with you. *Die Hard* knows it's bad for you. It says so. "Just another American who saw too many movies as a child. Another orphan of a bankrupt culture who thinks he's John Wayne . . . Rambo . . ." taunts Hans Gruber (Alan Rickman). "Actually I was always partial to Roy Rogers myself," responds John McClane (Bruce Willis), like the good film historian we all are these days.

When did this happen? When did the action movie reach this star-tling degree of debonair belligerence, such no-flies-on-me swank? When did everyone get so *wise?* In the seventies, the job of action director was essentially a specialty act, a renegade career path, the province of lone wolfs like Walter Hill and Don Siegel—tough, leath-ery types who peeled off from the Hollywood pack to pay their silent debt to Sam Peckinpah and Howard Hawks with movies that were set in the city—*The Taking of Pelham One Two Three, The Driver, Dirty Harry*—but which felt like Westerns, lean and loping, with hides like an old boot. In the eighties, everyone joined in. Action moviemaking became a loud, raucous party, much closer to the suburbs of Holly-wood, if not bang-smack in the middle of it, with a lunchtime booking at Spago, thronged with young pups fresh from the world of advertis-ing or rock videos, where they had honed their editing skills to within passing semblance of the skills necessary to shoot action. In the process, the action movie would undergo a complete makeover, losing its air of civic sweat and moral unease, to make way for a brasher, bright air of hard-edged modernity. Heroes who probed the thin fault line between cop and vigilante (*The French Connection, Dirty Harry*) became cops who enthusiastically trounced you for a parking ticket (*48 Hrs., Lethal Weapon*); action heroes with a lurking resemblance to inhuman automatons *became* inhuman automatons (*RoboCop*). Villains who were terrorists (*The Enforcer*) gave way to villains who only pretended to be terrorists, in order to pull off a high-end bank heist (*Die Hard*), and from being people the audience called "the bad guys" to people the film's heroes referred to as "the bad guys." Perhaps above all, the dress code for American movies was about to undergo its biggest overhaul since tuxes and tails went out in the forties. It was to be out with Spielberg's bathers in their skimpy beachwear, or Sylvester Stallone, baring his flesh like a saint approaching annunciation, and in with RoboCop in his full metal jacket. Superman's daringly low halter top was about to give way to the full body armor of Batman; Indy's rumpled civvies to Tom Cruise's crisp white navy uniforms; the sight of Ripley in her panties—from which we all, quite frankly, needed to move on—to that of Ripley strapped into her power-loader. In short, the age of flesh tones—and all the pink vulnerability they signified— was over. Hollywood's Heavy Metal Age was about to begin.

The exact point at which everything changed is hard to determine, but if you had to pick the point where the era of *Dirty Harry* made way for the era of *Die Hard,* you would, I think, want to pick Jim Cameron's Tarzana apartment in the spring of 1983; and in particular the point exactly midway between the *Rambo* desk and the *Terminator* desk. Cameron would later disown *Rambo,* saying, "the action was mine, the politics is Stallone's," and indeed, his draft has a breezier, Bondish snap to it, with John Rambo bundling out of a Blackbird spy plane and free-falling seventy thousand feet. He also rectified a glaring oversight of the first movie, *First Blood,* in which Vietnam vet John Rambo is hunted by his own military commanders to within an inch of his life, but signally fails to take anyone else's. Must have been a typing error. In *Rambo: First Blood Part II,* he makes up for lost time, enthusiastically plowing through villages, mowing down armies, and swatting helicopters from the skies like flies. A one-man biochemical army, a porcupine of bristling muzzles and barrels, this John Rambo is "a pure fighting machine with only one desire . . . No fear. No regrets . . ." Would that this were true. In Sylvester Stallone's hands, John Rambo turns into one big bag of regrets, sauced with self-pity and mixed up into one big trembling martyr, peeking out from behind his wall of weaponry with a stare closely modeled on a recently orphaned basset hound. It was basically Rocky-in-a-bandanna—a noble punching bag, masochistically soaking up punishment on behalf of a demoralized nation, a noble brute with his mind on higher matters. "The mind is the greatest weapon," says Rambo, before strapping some rocket launchers to his torso, in case his mind wanders.

The mistake, as hindsight now makes clear, was to give him a mind at all, and to root that ruthlessness in anything resembling human psychology. Who needed it? How much more effectively that power chord ("no fear, no regrets") plays when it glances off the sleek chrome surfaces of the Terminator, this time stripped of the bandanna and the sweaty geopolitics: "It doesn't feel pity or remorse or fear, and it absolutely will not stop, ever." Where Rambo started out a fighting machine and ended up fleshy punching bag, the Terminator takes the opposite course, starting out as a semblance of a human being, whose flesh peels away to reveal a chassis of gleaming exoskeleton—or as the script puts it, "Death rendered in steel." The evolution of the antihero in American film is a little like the search for the basic building blocks of matter conducted by physicists at the start of the last century—first molecules, then atoms, then neutrons, then neutrinos, quarks, and so on, as each seemingly irreducible element is split into something even more compact and durable, each baseline assumption collapsing into yet another fresh start. Audiences thought Robert Mitchum a little thuggish and taciturn, but he was a model of garrulity when set next to Lee Marvin; and those who thought Marvin a little hard to read would find him an open book when Clint Eastwood came along . . . and so on down the chain, endlessly ramifying, endlessly subdividing.

Until you hit the Terminator: speaking only seventy-four words and killing twenty-four people, Cameron's creation remains the closest anyone has come to locating cinema's answer to the unsplittable atom, cinematic base-matter. I could be wrong. In fact precedent suggests that one day a director will in fact introduce a character who simply walks onscreen, says nothing, and blows up; but until that day, the Terminator remains an unsurpassed model of ruthless implacability. Other directors would attempt to spark up a little chemistry between the Austrian and his co-stars—striking matches off the monolith—but the key to Schwarzenegger, as Cameron realized, is not chemistry, but physics. The director would stand over him issuing instructions—"I want you to lay there, Arnold, then when I tell you I want you to start lifting up with your head, then your shoulders, then I want you to sit up, then I want you to look straight ahead"—and if anything went wrong, he would explode. "He was like an encyclopedia of technology, and if a shot was a half inch off the way he visualized it, he would go crazy," said Schwarzenegger. "I would do a scene and would ask him how it was. He'd say something like, 'It was disastrous, but probably a human being could do no worse.' He was talking to me like I was the Terminator. It got pretty freaky at times."

Perhaps the best advice on dealing with the director came from actor Michael Biehn. "You don't fuck with his movies," he said. "When he throws a tantrum, it's almost like the movie is throwing a tantrum." A sobering thought, for *The Terminator* is not a movie you would wish to pick a fight with. If *Rambo* was a movie in a sulk, then *The Terminator* is a movie in a rage—one long, hard, beautifully-controlled rage. It is a heavy-metal hymn to the textures of chrome and concrete, all specified with glinting exactitude in Cameron's script, from the Hunter-Killer mobile ground units ("a blast-scarred chrome leviathan with hydraulic arms folded mantis-like against its torso"), to the "phased plasma pulse-rifles in the 40-watt range." It's the "40-watt range" that brings you up short now: as if anyone, reading that in 1983, had any idea what a plasma pulse-rifle was, or what wattage they come in. But Cameron knew. Cameron's script for *The Terminator* is driven by an almost messianic sense of self-announcement—*Mein Kampf* as rewritten by J. G. Ballard—a Cassandraish revenge fantasy in which disbelievers are punished with a swift death, poor fools!, while the future takes shape around them. It's all there on the page, like manifest destiny awaiting its hookup: "Sarah dodges to one side and LOCKS THE BRAKES. The bike slides, fishtailing. The truck roars past, hitting the air brakes." If you didn't know that before he made films, Cameron drove trucks for a living, and that before he drove trucks, he studied physics, you would be able to guess, I think, from that. What the speeding fighter was to George Lucas, and the airborne bicycle was to Spielberg, the skidding eighteen-wheel Kenworth tanker is to Jim Cameron. In *Terminator 2,* Arnie would even surf one down the highway—a vision of juggernaut cool, and as close to a heraldic image as the Cameron oeuvre possesses.

John Daly tried to shorten the final film's reel only to be angrily rebuffed: "When the truck blows up, the film has to end," he said. "Fuck you! It's not done yet!" screamed Cameron and threw him bodily out of the editing suite. They tested the film in a shopping mall in the San Fernando Valley, where it caused a near riot amongst its teenage audience. Even so, Orion's head of marketing refused to put the studio's full marketing muscle behind the film, telling Hurd and Cameron that a thriller like *The Terminator* would drop 50 percent of its box office in its second week, and would disappear altogether by the third. "*The Terminator* was simply considered a down-and-dirty cheap exploitation picture whose shelf life would be very short," says Hurd. "This is what was told to Jim and me while we were making the movie. It was an uphill battle, we felt like Sisyphus at every turn."

Orion released the film in October—a dumping ground, well away from the main summer competition—where it took in $5 million its first week, and the same again for six weeks, running rings around its immediate competition, *Dune* and *2010*. Cameron and Hurd made one last-ditch attempt to squeeze more advertising out of Orion and flew at their own expense to New York to have dinner with Orion's executives, only to fall out all over again. Cameron tried to order a bottle of champagne only to be told it was too expensive, and when Hurd suggested that Orion take out some trade ads congratulating them on their success—she was trying to get *Aliens* off the ground at Fox—they again refused. "Even after its initial success," complained Cameron, "which was even more than I expected, they still had no interest in beefing up the ad campaign or giving it any added support at all. They treated me like dog shit."

Orion may have been right to keep *The Terminator* away from the summer of 1984. The first summer to bear any resemblance to today's demolition derby, it boasted four films taking in over $100 million—*Beverly Hills Cop, Indiana Jones and the Temple of Doom,* Joe Dante's *Gremlins,* and *Ghostbusters*—which between them accounted for over a third of the summer's box office, pushing it toward "a spectacular record" of $4 billion, according to the MPAA's Jack Valenti. This, too, would become something of a summer tradition, the trick being to reach for the nearest superlative and politely forget the effect of both inflation and rising

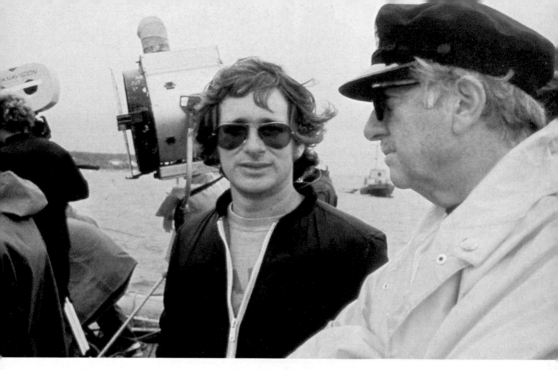

HOLLYWOOD'S ENDLESS SUMMER BEGINS: "Back in the days when we were making *Jaws*, I looked upon all this as something we had no control over," says Spielberg. "The blockbuster was created not by the film director or the studio's marketing machine. The blockbuster originally was made by the general public." *Below left*, the cover of *Time* magazine for June 23, 1975. On the same day the director's secretary gave him a note of the first weekend's grosses, *below right*: "I kept waiting for the next weekend to drop off and it didn't, it went up and it went up and it went up."

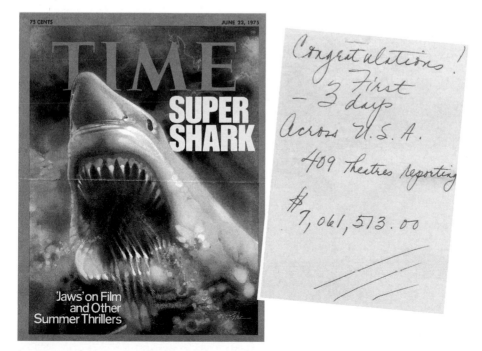

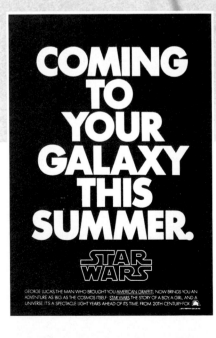

THAT ONE BOLD BRILLIANT THING: "*Star Wars* wouldn't get made today," says George Lucas. "It barely got made *then*." *Above*, one of Ralph McQuarrie's original sketches of Darth Vader.

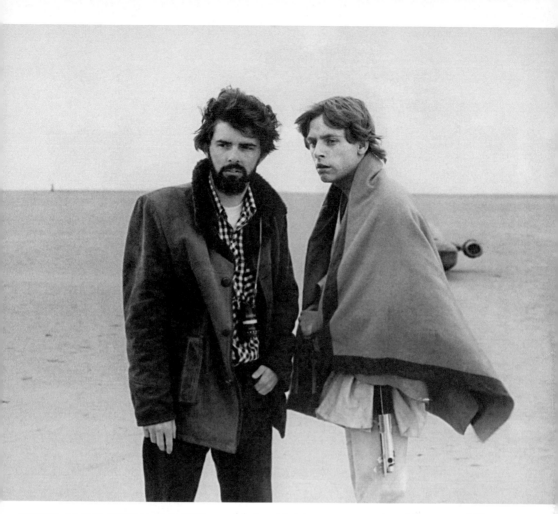

CRASH LANDING ON TATOOINE: "We would sit with him, try to convince him not to kill himself. He was so disappointed he couldn't get anything he wanted, the crew was making fun of him," said Lucas's friend Willard Hyuck. "He was really in a very fragile state. The final insult was the English crew voted [on] the last day of the movie whether they were going to do overtime. They voted no."

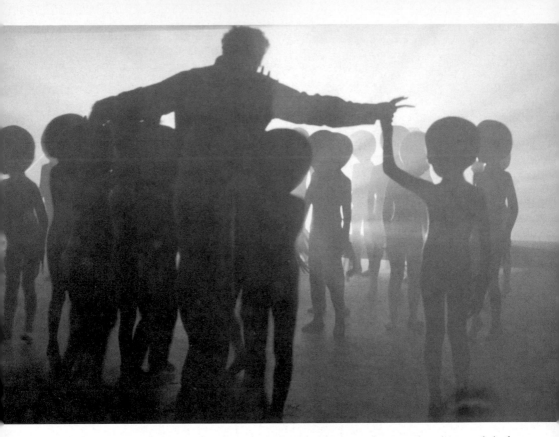

THE NIGHT THE ALIENS SAVED COLUMBIA: "Some executives took me to lunch a week before my first day of shooting," says Spielberg of *Close Encounters of the Third Kind*, "and said, 'You have our entire company resting on your shoulders. You could bring this company down.' They literally said to me, 'You're responsible for whether Columbia ceases to exist or continues . . .' I saved their *ass*." *Below*, with editor Michael Kahn.

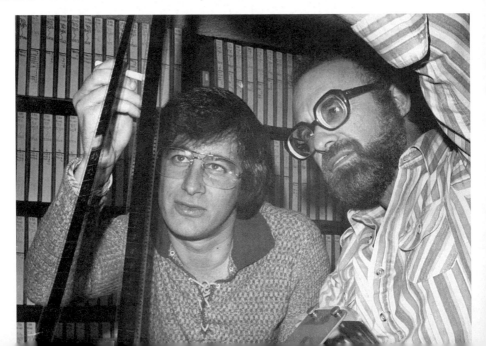

NOT SO CLOSE ENCOUNTER: "*Alien* is to *Star Wars* what the Rolling Stones are to the Beatles," said producer David Giler. "It's a nasty *Star Wars*"—as the shoot proved. "He is one of those directors who will come up to you after you've done a scene and say, 'Well, I don't fucking believe that'," said Sigourney Weaver of director Ridley Scott. "Yeah, you could say there was tension," says Scott. *Right*, one of Scott's original storyboards showing the *Nostromo*.

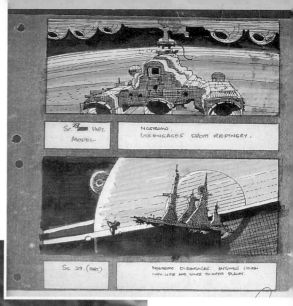

Sc 29 PARS.
MODEL.

NOSTROMO.
DISENGAGES FROM REFINERY.

Sc 29. (PART)

NOSTROMO DISENGAGES. ENGINES COUGH
INTO LIFE AND WAKE THUNDER PLANET.

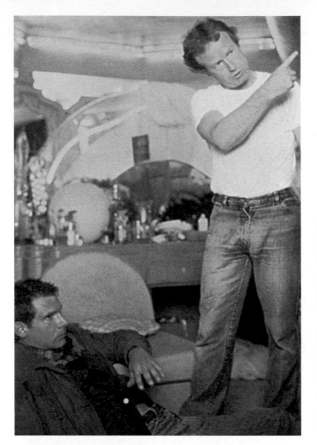

KEEPING UP WITH THE JONESES: Harrison Ford, *left*, with Ridley Scott on the set of *Blade Runner*: "It was just wretched awfulness, really, a monument to stress," said producer Kate Haber. "Our leading man and director got to the point where they were barely speaking to one another." Ford, *below*, shooting *Raiders* with Spielberg. Eating canned food from the UK, Spielberg was the only member of the crew not to come down with dysentery.

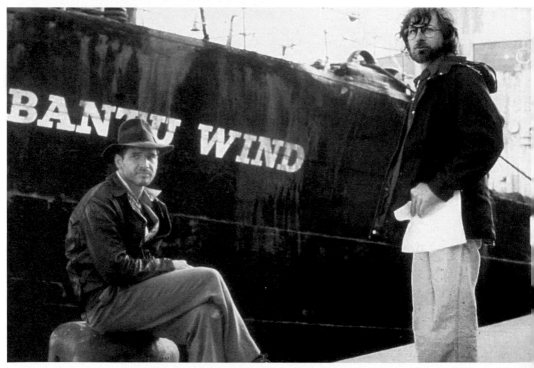

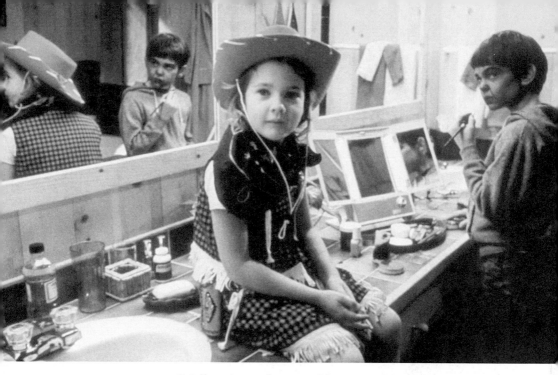

THE AGE OF INNOCENCE ENDS: Spielberg in conference with a young Drew Barrymore, one of the stars of *E.T.*—"A whisper from my childhood," said the director. "A movie designed to tug at your heartstrings and pick your pocket at the same time," said one critic. "Extraordinary, neat, and successful," adjudicated one nine-year-old.

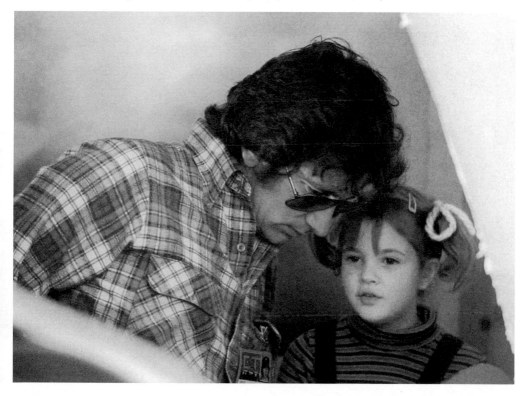

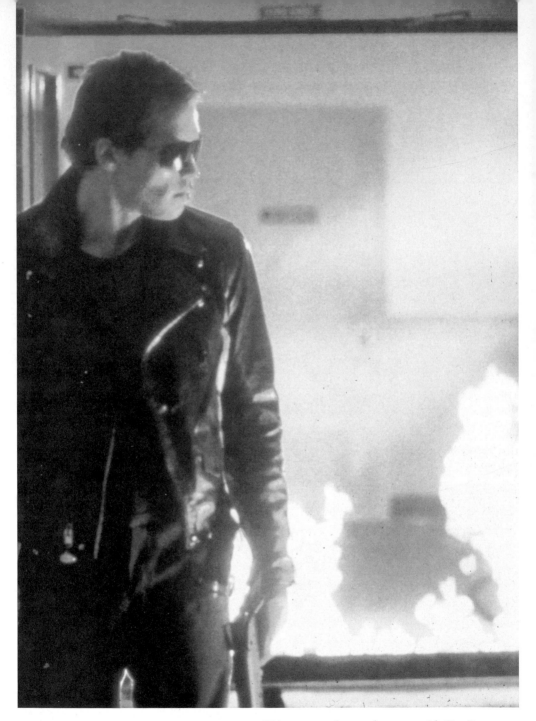

THE ARRIVAL OF THE AUTEUR-AS-TERMINATOR: "It's not peaches and cream with Jim," says *Terminator* designer Stan Winston of James Cameron. "He knows what he wants, and that's very, very, very tough to work with. He can direct, he can draw, he can write, he can paint. Unfortunately he knows your job." Said Arnold Schwarzenegger: "I would do a scene and would ask him how it was. He'd say something like, 'It was disastrous, but probably a human being could do no worse.' He was talking to me like I was the Terminator. It got pretty freaky at times."

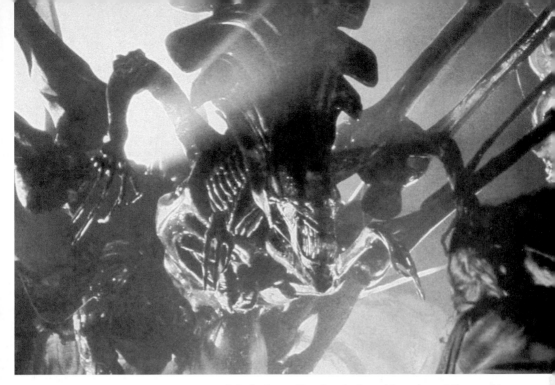

THIS TIME IT'S WAR: James Cameron and Gale Anne Hurd quit the table twice while working out the *Aliens* deal with Fox. "It was the amount Sigourney was asking," says Hurd. "They were considering writing a sequel that didn't include her, and Jim and I couldn't imagine what that movie would be. We couldn't simply rewrite the script for someone else. It's not that easy when the entire theme of the movie is all about facing your deepest fears. How do you do that when no one else survives?"

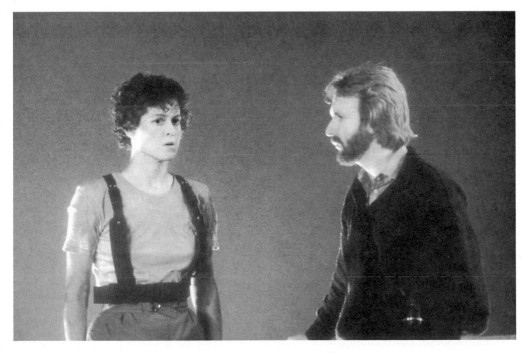

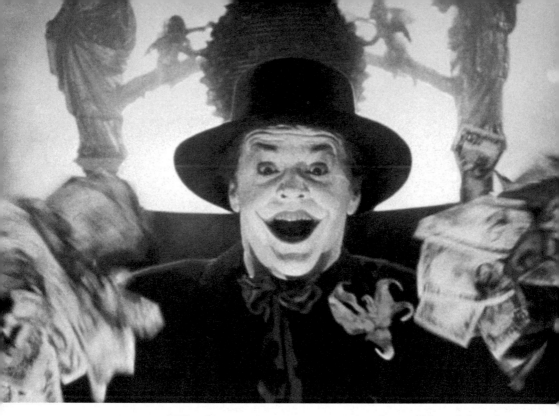

THE FLOODGATES OPEN: "What happens is, you get engaged in this world, and then there's no way out. There's too much money," said Tim Burton, director of *Batman*, for which Jack Nicholson, *above*, received $5 million for his role as the Joker. *Below*, East Germany eyes the assorted *Batman* merchandise. "Everything—we made everything," said producer Jon Peters.

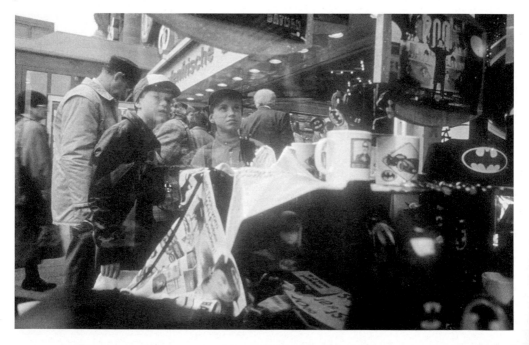

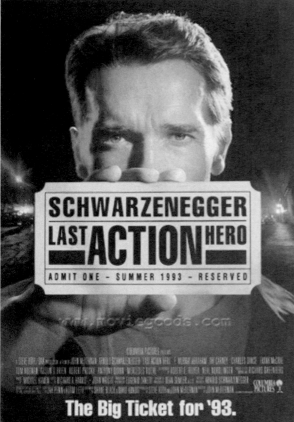

The Big Ticket for '93.

BATTLE OF THE BLOCKBUSTERS: In the blue corner, *Last Action Hero*, weighing in at $82 million, with 20 million dollars' worth of tie-ins with Mattel and Burger King. "The goal was to create a blockbuster. Instead it was a debacle," says Sony's Sid Ganis. "Instead of withholding, we strutted. So that all the press could say to us was, 'oh yeah, oh yeah' and they said it time and time again."

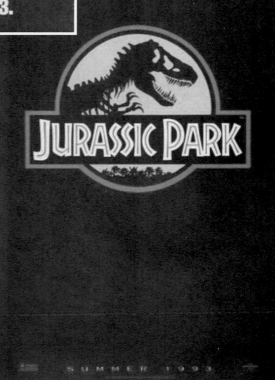

AND IN THE RED CORNER: Spielberg's *Jurassic Park*, weighing in at $55 million, with 28 million dollars' worth of tie-ins with McDonald's, Kenner and Sega. It took $900 million worldwide, just slightly more than the gross national product of Mozambique. In France, it was perceived as "the second invasion of France, this time not to liberate but to occupy," says Spielberg. "They have arrived," warned *Le Parisien-Libéré*.

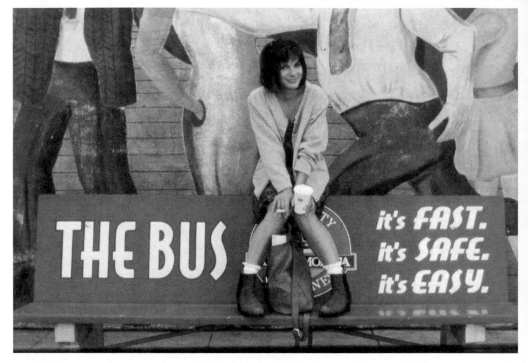

THE EUROPEAN INVASION, PART I: "You want the audience to go *ohmigod* he's not going to do that, he cannot do this, this is impossible, he cannot go there," says "Flying Dutchman" Jan De Bont, director of *Speed* and *Twister*. "And then you go there." The sequel was not so much fun for the director: "Movie companies are part of these gigantic corporations, and they need product and they need product at a given time. It's like you're launching a new Coca-Cola product and it's got to be done by June 17, because Pepsi is going to bring out something a day earlier."

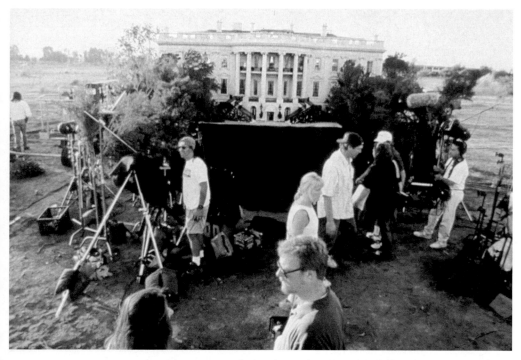

AND PART II: Detonating the White House for *Independence Day*. "Only a German would do that," says director Roland Emmerich. "The 9/11 thing, when it happened, I'm watching TV like the entire world," says the film's explosives expert, Joe Viskocil, "and I'm saying to myself *I have done these shots*. I felt like shit. I really did. I mean aliens are one thing, and terrorists are another. I started thinking maybe I did my job too well, and this might have been the nucleus of an idea for somebody to say, 'Hey, let's crash a plane into the White House'."

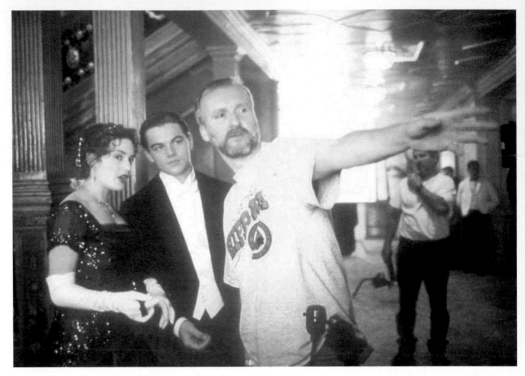

THE WORLD'S FIRST BILLION-DOLLAR BLOCKBUSTER: "How did we get here?" asked stars Leonardo DiCaprio and Kate Winslet, onboard *Titanic*. "There were lots of pointed fingers and arguing, a lot of scared people, at as high a level and as bright a light as one could imagine: some $200 million in the production and $100 million of cost overrun," says effects supervisor Scott Ross. "It was the worst experience of my life."

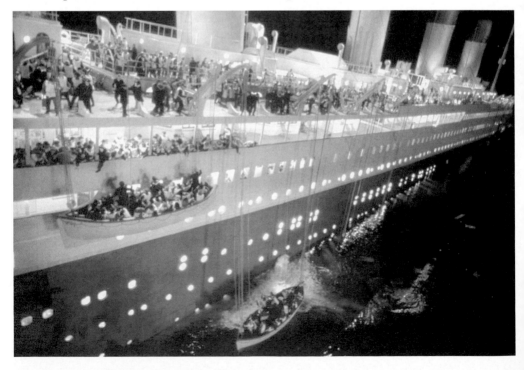

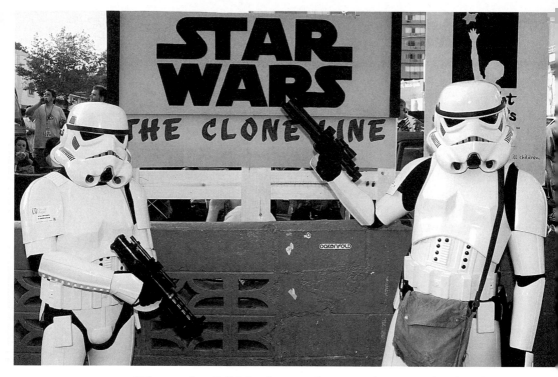

RETURN TO TATOOINE: "I knew when I did the first one that I was doing exactly what the fans didn't want me to do," says Lucas of the *Star Wars* prequels. "I knew that I was taking huge chances, and doing things that were very uncommercial with a very commercial property." *Above*, the fans queued up anyway, and if they couldn't make the queue, they watched the queue via live webcam broadcasts.

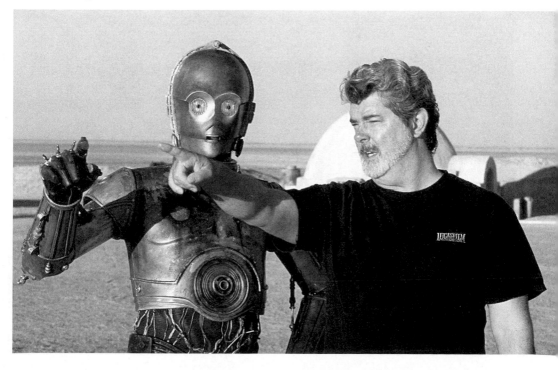

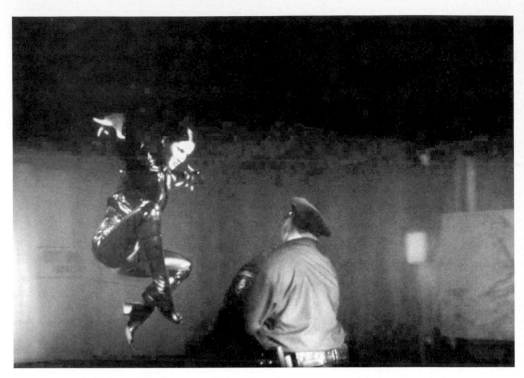

INDIE–BLOCKBUSTER CROSSOVER KINGS: The distance between the arthouse and the popcorn seats has never been smaller. After early indie success with *Bound*, Larry and Andy Wachowski let loose with their *Matrix* trilogy, while Peter Jackson, *below* moved from the small low-budget success of *Heavenly Creatures* to *The Lord of the Rings*, the first fantasy blockbuster to strike Oscar gold.

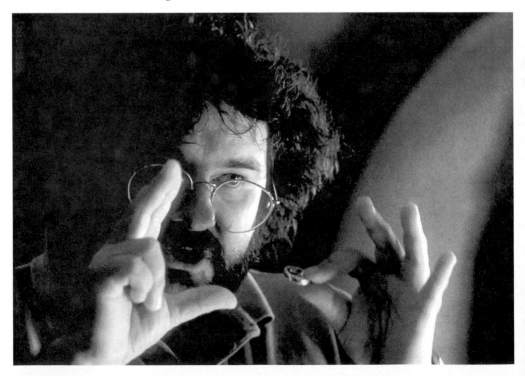

ticket prices. Thus 1981 had broken 1980's records, with takings of $3 billion—"the biggest summer in the history of movies" said the *New York Times*. So, too, 1982 had broken 1981's records, with takings of $3.5 billion—"the hottest season in U.S. history" said *Time*, while 1984 topped the lot with $4 billion—"the biggest spring in the history of the business" said one Fox executive, in the *Spinal Tap*–ish idiom in which everyone was henceforth doomed to speak.

The second part of the tradition, equally important, was to scan the tea leaves for auguries of woe—in the shape of rising budgets, shrinking profit margins, video games, or recorders—and pronounce the whole business dead on arrival. In 1980, critic David Thomson noted a "climactic crisis in American film," and in 1981, Paul Schrader volunteered, "We are supporting a dying business," while according to the *New York Times*, the summer of 1982 showed "every sign of a town in crisis," and so on and so forth until 1984's Cassandra, producer Robert Radnitz, warned, "He who lives by the blockbuster shall die by the blockbuster." How was Hollywood doing in 1984? Somewhere in the vague ballpark between sparkling good health and imminent demise, boom and bust all in one, with the summer shaping itself accordingly somewhere in the middle. For one thing, it was getting bigger, like Stephen Hawking's universe. The number of films in production that year had risen by 41 percent, and the summer was forced to expand, if studios were to avoid stepping on each other's toes. "It's like a party balloon," said a marketing executive at Columbia. "Once you stretch it, it's easy to fill." Originally stretching from June to September, it had been first pushed back when Fox opened *Star Wars* in May, and in 1984, the same studio pushed it back still further when they released *Romancing the Stone* in April, where it happily ate up $76 million. It was a landmark movie in one other important regard, for finally, the impossible had happened: Robert Zemeckis finally had a hit on his hands.

It wasn't much—a director-for-hire gig at the behest of the film's star, Michael Douglas, who had seen and loved *Used Cars*—but it meant that after a three-year spell in the Hollywood wilderness, Zemeckis was suddenly hot, and every studio was falling over itself to make *Back to the Future.* "Nothing had changed, right?" he mused. "All that was different was that now I had a hit film. I thought the only honorable thing to do is to go back to the original guy who had faith in the project," although as he also admitted, "I had selfish motivations, too, because by this time Steven's name had become synonymous with a certain type of film. I mean, he had become a brand name, and to have him associated with *Back to the Future* was like a perfect fit." Spielberg's transformation into a brand name wasn't the only thing that had changed since Zemeckis and Gale first started writing the movie, back in 1980. Reagan had entered his second term in office, which meant they could keep their Reagan joke ("Who's vice-president? Jerry Lewis?" scoffs Doc Brown). Also, one of Reagan's first acts had been to order an attack on two Libyan jets in 1981, so it is Lebanese terrorists who provide the plutonium that powers the DeLorean into 1955. But by far the most alarming historical upheaval to which the writers of *Back to the Future* had played mute witness was the release of the *Porky's* movies.

When Zemeckis and Gale had started writing the movie, it was the first *Porky's* movie that was doing the rounds. By 1983, it was *Porky's II: The Next Day,* and by 1985, when their film finally got made, it was *Porky's Revenge.* The nation's youth seemed to be lining up for leering, hormonal comedies about locker room jocks, and here were Zemeckis and Gale endlessly repolishing an egghead movie about time paradox, in which the only sex on offer was the sight of Marty McFly retreating chastely from the advances of his mom. It was a telling difference— like Spielberg, their sympathies tilted toward nerds, not jocks—but it was enough to send the Two Bobs into a panic: every time they looked out their office, another *Porky's* movie leered lasciviously at them from theater marquees. "We didn't have any scenes in any locker rooms," worried Zemeckis. "We didn't do anything in the girls' shower. Gosh, we're in a high school in this movie, and we never went into the girls' shower! At one point Bob and I got into this emotional funk and paranoia and we wondered, 'Is there too much storytelling in this movie?'"

They had been writing *Back to the Future* for so long, in fact, that they had started to screw up their own time line. The more they wrote, the bigger the distance they opened up between themselves and the fifties, and the bigger the distance they opened up between themselves and the fifties, the older Marty McFly's parents got—Zemeckis and Gale had to keep inventing siblings for him, to explain why Marty was staying so young. A year would tick by and they would add a brother. Another would tick by and he sprouted a sister. They were getting ensnared in their own clockwork. "Even Steven was on our case wishing we could shorten the first reel," says Gale. "We said 'no, all that stuff pays off.' We believed in the twenty-five-minute rule, which is that the audience will sit still for anything for twenty-five minutes and if by the twenty-five-minute mark they think something's going to happen, they're confident the moviemakers have a handle on this and they're hooked."

They began shooting, for Universal, with Eric Stoltz in the lead role, but five weeks into the shoot, it was clear things weren't working out. "Bob [Zemeckis] became very unsettled about whether this was a comedy anymore," said Spielberg. "And he came to me with forty-five minutes of cut footage. At the end of the screening, I said, 'We've got to do something drastic, because this isn't funny.'" They decided to fire Stoltz. It was, said Zemeckis, "the hardest meeting I've ever had in my life and it was all my fault. I broke his heart." The role went instead to Michael J. Fox, who had been their original choice, until his commitment to the sitcom *Family Ties* had ruled him out. The commitment still stood, so now they shot around Fox's schedule. "For the next three and a half months, the combination of *Back to the Future* and *Family Ties* swallowed me whole," noted the actor: "A teamster driver would pick me up at 9:30 A.M. and take me to Paramount, where I would spend the day rehearsing that week's show, culminating in a run-through at approximately 5:00 P.M. each afternoon. Then, at six, another teamster driver would pick me up and shuttle me to Universal studios or whatever far-flung location we were based that evening, where I would work on the film until just before sunrise. At that point, I'd climb into the back of a production van with a pillow and a blanket, and yet another Teamster driver would take me home again—sometimes literally carrying me into my apartment and dropping me into my bed. I'd catch two or three hours sleep before Teamster driver number one would reappear at my apartment, let himself in with a key I'd provided, brew a pot of coffee, turn on the shower, and then roust me to start the whole process all over again."

Nobody could accuse Fox's performance in *Back to the Future* of being the purest of Stanislavskian exercises, but all this was perfect prep for a movie in which Fox would spend all his time chasing the clock in an attempt to catch up with himself, quite literally given that half the movie had been shot once before, with Stoltz in his role. "I wince a little when they suggest where to put the camera and someone will say, 'Last time we did this scene . . .'" said Fox. After the movie's first test screening, in San Jose in May, production on *Back to the Future* was accelerated still further. "I think it's the most commercial movie since *E.T.* We have the potential to catch lightning in a bottle," declared Universal's Sid Sheinberg, who buttonholed the filmmakers to see how fast they could finish post-production on the film. "The movie originally wasn't going to come out until August," says Gale, "but after the sneak preview, Sheinberg said, 'We have to have it out by July 4th. Can you guys do it?' 'Well, if you want to spend the money . . .' And he said, 'Whatever it costs, get it out by July 4th.' We were the movie that ruined production schedules for Hollywood. We were in the theaters nine and a half weeks after we wrapped photography. It was insane." A bushwhacked Zemeckis was to be found in the editing room, complaining to journalists: "I had it all worked out perfectly. The movie was going to open on the 21st and we were going to move into our new house last weekend. Now I have to leave for Atlanta in a press junket, and my wife, who is pregnant, won't stay in the house by herself. . . . This is not how I plan to make movies from now on."

New Yorker critic Pauline Kael had a problem with *Back to the Future.* She found many things to admire, tagging it a "likeable screwball comedy," and praising Zemeckis and Gale's "wit in devising intricate structures that keep blowing fuses." But the fact remained: "I'm not crazy about movies with kids as the heroes." She must have had a tough time of it in that summer, for 1985 was the year *E.T.* finally showed up in Hollywood's bloodstream. Having been broken down into its constituent enzymes, just as *Jaws* had, it was now showing up everywhere in the form of films featuring magical forests, kids riding BMX bikes, and cherubic alien visitors. And not just Spielberg productions like

The Goonies, or *Explorers. Mad Max Beyond Thunderdome* also boasted a small squadron of "lost children," while in *Pale Rider,* Clint Eastwood encounters a little girl who finds a friend in the heavens. The day Dirty Harry starts pram-sitting, you know something is up. "When the causes of the decline of Western civilization are finally writ," wrote *Variety,* "Hollywood will surely have to answer why it turned one of man's most significant art forms over to the gratification of high-schoolers."

There's no getting around this one. *Back to the Future* really *is* a movie about a teenager, and not just that, but a movie about a teenager who travels back to the fifties—the very birthplace of the breed—in order to visit the condition on his parents, too. If you are looking for a movie that perfectly symbolizes the state of arrested development that is American cinema, *Back to the Future* is your movie: an episode of *Leave It to Beaver* as scripted by Feydeau, a teen sex farce with no sex, a family comedy that contemplates incest, and as sturdy a disquisition on man's place in the webbings of fate as any movie with Huey Lewis on the soundtrack has ever quite managed to be. The real question, of course, is not whether fifty-something *New Yorker* film critics want to watch movies with teenage heroes, but whether teenagers want to watch movies with teenage heroes. These days, the studios have woken up to the fact that the last thing a sixteen-year-old wants is a film that makes overt acknowledgment of his tender age. He doesn't go to movies to see an image of himself, not unless it is an image of himself in blue-and-red spandex, slicing across the Manhattan skyline. He wants to watch what he imagines the adults are all watching: bitching movies about killer robots and superheroes and two-hundred-foot lizards. The adults aren't, of course, watching those movies. We are otherwise engaged, having long since matured and moved on to better things. We're far too busy reading *Harry Potter* and watching *Finding Nemo,* and wondering why it is that only movies for the under-tens have any good plots, and pining for the days when movies for teenagers did, too.

The moment you realized just how fully *Back to the Future* was going to distinguish itself from all the other Spielbuggies zooming around that year is relatively easy to pinpoint: it is the point at which Marty

McFly, having seen Doc Brown gunned down by Libyans, and flown back to 1985 in the DeLorean, suddenly finds it completely useless, there being no plutonium in 1955 with which to power it. It is hard to overstate the importance of this piece of news. In film after film, in 1985, teenagers were using their science class to invent magical devices that granted them their every wish—to travel through time, whizz through space, secure a face-to-face meeting with Kelly LeBrock—but here was Zemeckis's biggest effects gizmo, his time machine, suddenly rendered as useful as an orange-press. "*Back to the Future* has this reputation for being this big special effects movie, but in fact there are only about thirty special effects in it," says Zemeckis, "and they're mostly lightning. But because of the nature of the story, everyone thought it was loaded with effects." Today, nobody bats an eyelid when the Wachowski brothers allow Trinity to download the helicoptering skills she needs to extricate herself from whatever corner she happens to be hemmed into—a quite astonishing cheat—but once Marty has been whisked back to 1955, all he has to get him back are his own powers of ingenuity and the quarter in his pocket, which he naturally uses to phone a friend.

It is the first of many such drop-ins on Doc Brown in the series, which—appropriately enough for a movie written by two men who locked themselves together in a room for three years—has an affable, loose-fitting feel for male friendship. The series's take on romantic attachment is a snatch of pure comic book—the affections of Marty's mother zing from person to person like a Ping-Pong ball, while Marty's girlfriend, Jennifer, spends much of the second movie asleep—but no matter what historical era Marty finds himself in, or what manner of fix, he can always put in a call to the guy with the perma-stare and the Afghan-in-a-wind-tunnel hair. Christopher Lloyd's performance gets even better when you find out what a pussycat the guy was: he would turn up for rehearsals, not say a word to anyone, and then, the moment the cameras rolled, explode into a mad fizz of limbs and pseudo-scientific exposition—all the braininess of the script coming to a boil, and running over into affectionate self-satire. The Doc is a direct descendant of that "gentle lunatic" Charles Goodyear, pawning all his possessions in pursuit of odorless rubber, and all the other amateur inventors, toiling away in the backyards of America to bring better ballpoint pens to the nation. "Build a better mousetrap and the world will beat a path to your door," said Ralph Waldo Emerson, and there are few better mousetraps than *Back to the Future,* as great a tribute as could be imagined to old-fashioned American ingenuity—a very different thing from mere cleverness. All of Zemeckis and Gale's previous films were as fiendishly clever as *Back to the Future,* giving their characters the runaround like rats in a maze, but this was the first of theirs to invite their protagonists in on the joke, for Marty is both pinball and player, and even has his own Wizard. "There's nothing you can't do if you don't set your mind to it," he tells his father—interestingly enough, much the same conclusion that Sarah Connor came to at the end of *The Terminator*—"There's no fate but what we make," in her rather tone-deaf rhyme. "God, a person could go crazy thinking about all this," says Sarah finally, and for the most part she eschews thinking too hard about it, instead choosing the more sensible course of driving away from it, at speed, in a hot-wired car. Together, though, the two films form a small but distinct subgenre. All around them, in movies like *Working Girl, Flashdance,* and *Top Gun,* characters were chasing their dreams, making it count, chasing their tomorrows, starting up small ghost-busting agencies and other such eighties activities; but *The Terminator* and *Back to the Future* were the only movies whose protagonists chased their tomorrows to quite so literal a degree—time travel movie as self-improvement manual.

This is probably not what H. G. Wells had in mind when he wrote *The Time Machine.* What he had in mind was something a little sterner, with a distinct rap of the lectern to it. Wells's novel was basically a whither-Western-civilization lecture, whipping through historical periods like a slide show to demonstrate just how quickly and remorselessly Western civilization was going the way of the dodo. The notion that our lives are stuck fast in preordained grooves is, however, a curiously European invention, at its heaviest over Russia but still discernible in the fog that clung to Wells's London, and it has never exported that well to America, generally getting stuck in customs for a quick interrogation as to whether it has been, or ever intends to be, a member of the communist party. Needless to say, it is entirely absent from the brash, acrylic surfaces of *Back to the Future*, which strips time travel of its world-historical duties, and instead drops it into the gleaming chassis of a teen sex farce. Wells delivered a dire warning, which flattened his narrative into placard; Zemeckis gives us a pep talk, with Marty playing his fate like a craps game. Zemeckis was at one point to have made a biopic of Houdini, which makes sense, for few modern directors' names so cry out for the prefix "the Fabulous and Amazing" to be attached to it, but like most directorial hobbyhorses, probably best left unridden, for there is no higher tribute to the art of escapology than *Back to the Future*, which piles up difficulty around its hero like coils of rope, and then sits back to watch him wriggle free.

The film opened on 1,100 screens and took in $10 million in its first weekend, $11 million in its second, soon topping the $200 million mark, one of very few to do so since *E.T.* It was indeed "bottled light-ning" as Sheinberg put it, although the art of bottling had come on apace in the few years since he released Spielberg's film. This time around, Zemeckis and Gale had the studio's newly founded product placement department to contend with. "They were trying to cram all kinds of stuff at us," says Gale. "Shell gasoline for example would have paid more for a placement than Texaco but Shell didn't change their logo. The same with Pepsi versus Coke. Coke bottles in the fifties and Coke bottles in the eighties were the same." Meanwhile, the California Raisins Board had been told that *Back to the Future* could do for their product what *E.T.* had done for Reese's Pieces. "They came at me with this proposal to put raisins in the movie, and I'm saying what brand? Sun-Maid Raisins? No just raisins. Can't we have a bowl of raisins at the dance? A bowl of raisins looks like a bowl of dirt. How is that going to photograph if we can't put a brand name anywhere? They had taken $50,000 from the California Raisins Board for this placement that wasn't going to happen in the movie. Finally what we gave them was the bum on the bench; in 1985 when the DeLorean comes back at the end, it says 'California Raisins' on that bus bench. When the California Raisins Board saw that they were livid."

"I didn't build the time machine to make money!" screeches Doc Brown in the sequel—a queasy echo of the filmmakers' own plight, for the second time around, the product placement department, like the special effects, would prove to be a little harder to resist. "When you make a movie that's successful, it becomes a piece of real estate," said Zemeckis. "It becomes a franchise and the reality comes at you very quickly, which is 'We're making a sequel and you guys can either help us or not but a sequel is going to be made.'" Says Gale, "We knew we were stuck with where the first one left off: something has to be done about their kids because that's what Doc Brown says. That was just a joke! We never thought about what that movie might be, and here we were, writing one around it." The result would be a broken-backed movie, its first hour devoted to the task of cleaning up the mess generated by that one line, before—in one truly ingenious touch—delivering Marty McFly back to the events of the first movie, through another time-space wormhole. "When Bob came up with that, I went, 'Holy shit, nobody is going to go with that,'" says Gale. "And he said, 'No, we have to do this because we have a time machine, we have to do this, nobody has ever done this.' The trick to writing a sequel is that people want to see the first movie but they don't want to see the first movie. They want the same except different. That's what we gave 'em."

Or as Marty puts it, "Talk about déjà vu." Variations of this cry would echo throughout the eighties, as screenwriters grappled with the same task—providing the same movie but different—and decided that up-front shamelessness was by far the most honest tactic. "What is it with this town?" asks Roy Scheider in *Jaws 2*. "Another basement, another elevator," muses Bruce Willis in *Die Hard 2: Die Harder*. By the mid-eighties, most of the major film franchises of the first half of the decade had come of age, ripe for harvesting—it was time for more helpings of Rambo and Indiana Jones, for *Ghostbusters II, Beverly Hills Cop II, "Crocodile" Dundee II, Rocky IV,* and *Star Trek V: The Final Frontier*—and, nestling like a viper amid this waving grassland of roman numerals, a movie that would completely change the way people looked at sequels, and bring the form some measure of redemption. Even its title was different, boasting not roman numerals, but simply an additional letter "s," so easily missed, as if to warn of the dangers of unchecked growth.

TIME LINE

1984

1. *Beverly Hills Cop* (Paramount) $234,760,478
2. *Ghostbusters* (Columbia) $229,242,989
3. *Indiana Jones and the Temple of Doom* (Paramount)
     $179,870,271
4. *Gremlins* (WB) $148,168,459
5. *The Karate Kid* (Columbia) $90,815,558
6. *Police Academy* (WB) $81,198,894
7. *Footloose* (Paramount) $80,035,402
8. *Romancing the Stone* (Fox) $76,572,238
9. *Star Trek III: The Search for Spock* (Paramount) $76,471,046
10. *Splash* (Disney) $69,821,334

1985

1. *Back to the Future* (Universal) $210,609,762
2. *Rambo: First Blood Part II* (TriStar) $150,415,432
3. *Rocky IV* (MGM) $127,873,716
4. *The Color Purple* (WB) $94,175,854
5. *Out of Africa* (Universal) $87,071,205
6. *Cocoon* (Fox) $76,113,124
7. *The Jewel of the Nile* (Fox) $75,973,200
8. *Witness* (Paramount) $68,706,993
9. *The Goonies* (WB) $61,389,680
10. *Spies like Us* (WB) $60,088,980

*Figures show U.S. domestic gross

CHAPTER 8

RIPLEY REDUX

"It spins, moving straight for Ripley. Firing from
the hip she drills it with two controlled bursts which
catapult it back. She steps toward it, FIRING AGAIN.
Her expression is murderous. AND AGAIN."
— *Aliens,* first draft, May 28, 1985

"This time it's war . . ."
— *Aliens* poster, 1986

During post-production on *The Terminator,* James Cameron and
Gale Anne Hurd started dating. It was a gradual transition,
according to Cameron: "We'd gone from spending twenty-four
hours a day together making a movie to spending twenty-four hours a
day together because we wanted to." On weekdays they would leave
home and race to the office down the freeway—he in his Corvette, she
in her Porsche, both bought with the proceeds from *The Terminator*—
the perfect eighties power-couple, caught in the slipstream of their
own success. The weekends were more romantic. "We went off-road
on a four-wheel drive, took the hot-air balloon out, and a huge wind
came up, and we ended up crash-landing," said Hurd. "We went horse-
back-riding, ice-skating, we shot AK-47s out in the desert, and that
was just one weekend."

"The women that he's been associated with in his personal life
have been very strong characters," says Scott Ross, friend of the direc-

tor and co-founder of their effects house, Digital Domain. "He's like a moth to a light. He's attracted to these strong burning women but when he gets there he can't deal with it. And he will always win. It's almost like he needs this ongoing angst in his life between himself and a woman. I think it's an issue between him and his mother. His mother is very intimidating and incredibly intelligent and his father is quiet and stands in the background but his mother clearly seems to wear the pants in the family, and I think that's made a big impact on his work." In fact, not since the heyday of Hawks would a body of films so ostensibly bent on singing of arms and the man, prove so hospitable to the sight of women packing heat. Cameron's machismo, like Hawks's, is unisex.

Most of his friends tried to talk him out of doing *Aliens*. They thought it a losing proposition; if it was good it would be because Ridley Scott had made such a good film; if it was bad it would be his fault. "Yeah, but I really like it," he would reply. "I think it'll be cool. Can't I just do it?" His script unfurled from a single, simple question that had nagged at Cameron throughout Scott's original film: where had the alien eggs come from? "They've seen the eggs, they've seen the parasite that emerges from the eggs, they've seen the embryo laid by the parasite emerge from a host person, and they've seen the embryo grow up into a supposedly adult form. But the adult form—one of them anyway—couldn't possibly have laid the thousand or so eggs that filled the inside of the derelict ship." In the first film there had been a scene that showed the alien cocooning the captain, Dallas, and Harry Dean Stanton, in order to turn them into eggs, but it had ended up on the cutting room floor. "In my story," said Cameron, "the eggs come from somewhere else. At least that was my theory. So working from that theory— acres and acres of these quite large eggs, two and a half to three feet tall—I began to focus on the idea of a hierarchical hive structure where the central figure is a giant queen whose role it is to further the species."

Cameron wrote through the Christmas of 1984, before finally delivering his first script outline in January of 1985. "If you think of the first *Alien* movie as a fun house, *Aliens* is a roller-coaster ride," he told producers Walter Hill and David Giler. Twentieth Century Fox, however, refused to believe that the film could be done for $15.5 million, as Gale Anne Hurd said it could; a budget estimator at Fox put it at nearer $35 million, and the studio refused to finance the film. Cameron and Hurd both quit.

"We walked out and said 'thanks we'll do something else,'" said Cameron. Fox's bluff was called and by March, the project was back on track again, only to hit another problem in the form of the film's star, Sigourney Weaver. Cameron had written the whole thing around Weaver's character without anyone contacting the actress, so he finally took matters into his own hands and phoned her up to talk her into it. She was in France at the time, shooting *Une femme ou deux,* and at first she was a little nonplussed, thinking: "I can't believe why no one even mentioned it to me...." "I didn't really want to do a sequel, I was pretty skeptical of what I thought was an attempt to cash in on the success of the original.... I thought why do something that has already been done?" She and producer David Giler had joked about it, on and off, for years. "Well if we ever do the sequel and you cooperate, you can be in the picture," Giler told her on one occasion. "If you don't, then your hyper-sleep capsule lid and you will dissolve into dust."

She was suspicious that Cameron was doing it just to cash in, but the director pointed to the seven-year gap since the first film: didn't that indicate the film was being done for love not money? He told her that the story was focused dead-center on Ripley, and that he couldn't do the film without her participation. Weaver thought it showed "a loyalty that is quite unusual in this business" and agreed, but having gotten only $33,000 for the first movie, upped her demand to $1 million—then unheard of for an actress. Fox put its foot down and told Cameron and Hurd: do it without her. "It was the amount Sigourney was asking," says Hurd. "They were considering writing a sequel that didn't include her, and Jim and I couldn't imagine what that movie would be. It all happened over a rather short period of time. We couldn't simply rewrite the script for someone else. It's not that easy, when the entire theme of the movie is all about facing your deepest fears, how do you do that when no one else survives?"

When things reached a deadlock, Hurd and Cameron quit for a second time—"We thought it was a dead issue at that point," said Hurd. "We thought the movie was off"—and flew to Hawaii in April for their honeymoon. "We spent half of our honeymoon making calls to England and L.A. to set up the *Aliens* deal," said Cameron. "Jim had to do this logical, cost-benefit analysis of why getting married would be a good idea," reported back Hurd. "We came out in the black."

When they returned in May, *Aliens* was on again, with Weaver on board for $1 million, a budget of $18 million, and a start date of September at Shepperton Studios in London, and a decommissioned electrical engineering station in Acton. *Alien* had been a hot, groggy shoot, taking its cue from the tension that hovered around Ridley Scott, but *Aliens* was shot during a dark, freezing British winter, warmed only by the blaze of Cameron's temper. It was the by-now-characteristic fireworks display, with the director firing first actor James Remar, who played Hicks, and then cinematographer Dick Bush. An old Shepperton stalwart, Bush was old-school: the director would shoot things the way he, Bush, decided to light them, and he lit up the dark cavernous aliens' lair just a few amps short of a car salesroom. Cameron was not happy.

"This is Jim's movie, Jim's vision," protested Hurd, thinking: oh no, this is not going to work.

"Well if that's the case," replied Bush, "and I can't do my job, which is to light it the way I want it, you'd better find someone else."

Giler told Hurd, "You've got to fire him," and so they brought in a replacement, Adrian Biddle. It was the beginning of a long and grueling war of attrition between the American producers and the largely British crew, who were all Ridley Scott loyalists, highly suspicious of this young American hotshot couple flying in to make a sequel to their beloved movie. They nicknamed Cameron "Grizzly Adams" and were openly contemptuous of Hurd, this dainty woman stepping across the power cables in her immaculate shoes. "It was very up-front, their discomfort with women," says Hurd. "People would come in and sit down and would say, 'Who is really producing this film?' and I would say, 'I am really producing this film,' and they would laugh and say, 'No, no, no, you're the director's wife, lovely to meet you, but who will I really be reporting to?' and I would say, 'Actually me.'

"'Well if that's the truth, I want to be completely up-front with you, I won't take orders from a woman,'" said one, according to Hurd. "'Well, you clearly won't be working on this film.' I thought it might be an isolated occurrence, but it happened quite a few times."

Things finally came to a head over the endless breaks that the crew insisted on taking—for tea, to go to the pub for lunch, for lottery raffles. "It was union-regulated, whether you wanted it or not," said Giler. "If you murdered the tea lady, there'd be someone there the next day at the same time." When one crew member took the opportunity to go around giving out tickets for a raffle, Cameron finally exploded. "No man, we're working here. Fuck the draw! There's a last shot we've got to get." He destroyed the tea-trolley—mashed it into a cube—and called in the entire crew and told them, "If you guys don't shape up, we're going to go someplace else, we'll fire the whole crew."

"They were having a party," said Lance Henriksen, "and Jim was at war to finish this movie."

It was a grueling shoot for Weaver—freezing cold in a T-shirt for most of it, weighed down with her co-star, Carrie Henn, whom she had to carry in many scenes, and further loaded down with guns and ammo when she was a staunch opponent of firearms. She would stand there in daily handgun practice, loaded up to her eyeballs with ammunition, thinking, "Here I am a member of the gun control lobby in a picture where I do nothing but shoot guns." When she first read the script, she'd done the usual thing and sniffed out her dialogue, skipping the stage directions—never a wise move with a Cameron script, which bristles with all the usual chunky toys, like a one-movie answer to the arms race: "She checks her weapon. Attaches a BANDOLIER OF GRENADES to her harness. Primes the flamethrower. Checks the rifle's magazine. Racks the bolt, chambering the first round. She checks the marking flares in the high pocket of her jump pants. She drops an unprimed grenade . . ."

"Part of the attraction of doing the film was that it was a design fest, an opportunity to do all sorts of wonderful hardware," said Cameron. "I like hardware a lot." He and production designer Peter Lamont lined his sets with the dismantled parts of old 747s, Canberra and Vulcan bombers, just being phased out of the Royal Air Force. "I invented a pulse gun by combining a Thompson submachine gun with a Franchi SPAS-12 pump-action shotgun, and there's a smart gun, based on the Spandau MG42 with thermal imagery sights. And our artillery and aircraft are so advanced that we had to have help from the aerospace industries, they were just terrific." He liked hardware a lot.

"I knew we were playing into something trendy with *Aliens,*" said Weaver, "the Rambo commando complex where the hero single-handedly mows down his opponents. If I see my role as a Chinese warrior, or as Henry V, then I'm interested in it. It's a chance to do a classic part. If I see it as gunplay, I'm not interested. The use of weapons is always the least important aspect to me, even if it's the most effective with the audience. I tried to see *Rambo* but I couldn't sit through it. I think I underestimated the degree to which Cameron would pay so much attention to guns." Still, he was suitably deferential to his star, who had as great a claim on being the auteur of the *Alien* movies as anyone. "I was the throttle, she was the brakes," said Cameron, who duly made note of every one of her detailed queries about the character of Ripley.

"Her script must have had five thousand notations in it," says Hurd. "It was all about 'Ripley would not do this, she is working on a loading dock, she would be making every decision from a functional point of view, working on a loading dock you are not going to have long hair that gets caught . . .' every intonation, every line, every motion came from a deep character place." In particular, Weaver found the idea of a character waking from a fifty-seven-year sleep fascinating. She believed that Ripley's mind didn't stop working in that period—that she hadn't skipped those years, but had racked them up internally, in hyper-sleep. "Ripley isn't the eager young ensign anymore," she said. "Her own daughter has grown old and died before the film even begins. In *Aliens* she got to go back and fight the monsters because she has no choice. Nothing is left for her here."

When officer John McClane flies to L.A. to see his wife at her office Christmas party, he does not expect to find instead a gang of Teutonic bank robbers in Savile Row suits and haircuts suggesting the Vidal Sassoon convention has just wafted into town. But being the cop he is, he knuckles down to the job at hand, namely preventing Nakatomi Plaza from being turned to tinderwood. The central joke of *Die Hard* was contained in that square-off between man and building, which glanced with breezy insouciance off a film like *The Towering Inferno:* what in the seventies would have taken an entire tower block of A-list actors to overcome, now only needs just one example of New York's Finest. By the time of *Die Hard 2,* however, McClane is a different fish altogether, for, of course, he has not returned to night duty in New York, the producers having correctly judged that the sight of him chomping on donuts on the corner of 86th and Second couldn't really hold a candle to the sight of him beating another bunch of Teutonic hardmen to a pulp. John McClane was now, it seemed, the first port of call for any visiting terrorists, hot off the plane—less the hero of the *Die Hard* movies, as simply the guy who the *Die Hard* movies keep happening to. "Another basement, another elevator," he muses. "How could this shit happen to the same guy twice?"

To which the only real answer is: ask Sylvester Stallone, for it was *Rocky* that changed the way Hollywood thought about sequels. During the sixties and seventies, they generally followed a law of diminishing returns, with each film expected to make only about 60 percent of its predecessor's money. Thus the first *Airport* movie made $90 million, the second $50, the last $30. Some of the *Rocky* movies, on the other hand, made more money than the first—*Rocky* grossed $117 million and *Rocky III* $123 million—a pattern swiftly followed by the *Star Wars* sequels, *The Empire Strikes Back* and *Return of the Jedi,* which grossed $330 million and $280 million respectively, and which further suggested that sequels need not drop off drastically in quality either. *The Empire Strikes Back* set the standard for the industry at large: darker than the original film, it began by plunging audiences deep in the middle of a snowy shoot-out that leaves the rebels scattered to the space winds, the Empire in the ascendant; and Luke now tempted to join the dark side of Darth Vader, now revealed as his father—a plot development that confirmed three broad sequel rules. One, the hero must briefly swap sides—Superman, RoboCop, and Indiana Jones all spend some of their second films enjoying a spell as a villain; two, the villain must reciprocate and acquire some humanizing psychological motive; and third, and most important: all successful sequels are family affairs.

From a scriptwriter's perspective, the advantages are obvious: to threaten the same person again would be a bore, but mess with their family and you have another movie on your hands. Introduce a relative and you've doubled the surface area of your hero's vulnerability.

Go back to the very first horror movie sequels—*Son of Kong, Bride of Frankenstein*—and you find that they furthered the franchise by first furthering their blood line. So, too, with Indiana Jones, who finds a father; Mad Max, who adopts a son, as would even the Terminator, proving that not even robots are exempt from this biological law. In film after film, the edges of the screen acquire the gilt edge of a family album, enclosing and conferring familial status on everyone within. Stick around long enough, and you're family. Because sequels reveal Hollywood's money-grubbing instincts at its purest, their ascent to the top of Imminent Threats to Western Civilization has been fairly swift, challenged to the top spot only by video games and theme parks, but they are a form like any other, with their own rules and requirements. There is nothing particularly ignoble about refusing to give up the ghost, and in the case of Jason, Michael Myers, and Freddy Krueger, it would have severely dented their credibility: what would it have said of their staying power if they had scared the living hell out of one movie, and then called it a day? What would it have said of their dedication to the job?

Sequels also have privileged access to a subject that is off-limits to most movies and virtually taboo in Hollywood: the passage of time. In a town that is unusually wrapped up in the blur of the present moment, sequels are one of the few forms to register the creaking weight of years; and while for most movies this is a source of either deep regret or fuddled comedy—"You're getting too old for this shit," says Danny Glover to Mel Gibson in *Lethal Weapon 4,* by which time he really was—for some, like *The Godfather* films, it amounts to much more: to have checked in with Al Pacino's face at three different times in his career, to see what cares it had weathered, amounted to one of the great coups de théâtre that Coppola's trilogy pulled off. The same for the *Alien* films. The first film had a beautifully elastic sense of time, registering both millennia and milliseconds, and nothing in between, like all nightmares. In the first of Cameron's master strokes, the action of *Aliens* picks up fifty-seven years later, a long enough period of time for Ripley to have lost her daughter—a heartbreaking blip, gone as soon as we hear of her—and also to accommodate the audience's seven-year distance from 1979. *Aliens* was thus the first blockbuster sequel to put the time *between* movies to good use, suggesting that while our backs were turned and our attention was elsewhere—watching *Ghostbusters,* or whatever it was that we were doing—the forces of darkness had been steadily amassing, readying to strike. Ripley, meanwhile, is a changed woman, wracked with bad dreams that leave her pooled in sweat, and about as keen to return to the fray as a cat to a bathtub. With Sigourney Weaver's performance in *Aliens,* a mauling at the hands of nine-hundred-pound summer blockbuster ceased to look like something you recovered from easily, something you sprang back from bright-eyed and bushy-tailed. "Just tell me one thing, Burke," she asks. "You're going out there to destroy them, right? Not to study."—a good question, and one which neatly divides *Aliens* from its predecessor, for Ridley Scott's film had been intent on a form of study, taking its slow, patient rhythms from the life-form at its center; watching it was like watching cancer cells forming. *Aliens,* on the other hand, has no time for Scott's air of forensic disquiet, and its creatures obey hokier, jack-in-the-box rhythms. It's a coarser film, no question, but there is no resisting its headlong charge. Scott gave us a Freudian fever dream, Cameron a bruising martial epic. You take your pick.

The idea of franchise crop rotation—of sprinkling each film with the virtues of a different director—is now a commonplace feature of the summer landscape. If the first *Mission: Impossible* was a Brian De Palma film, we expect the second to be a John Woo extravaganza and look forward to the day when the producers put the call in to Pedro Almodóvar. But *Aliens* was the first to do this: while never failing to take *Alien* into all the places we wanted it to go, most of them enjoyably lethal, it never failed to be anything other than a James Cameron film, right down to its last rivet. Coming so closely on the heels of *The Terminator,* *Aliens* suggested that Cameron was modeling his career on the progress of a large, angry rhino, although for all the panting pandemonium of his style, Cameron's films are a master class in the fine art of audience orientation—the whys and wherefores of mayhem. Action movies may have been on their way to being the default setting for any number of directorial careers—the summer would soon resound to the gentle sound of breaking glass and shrieking metal—but the success rate would be much the same as if you'd asked every director in Hollywood to drop what they were doing and start shooting musicals. Too many directors treat the chaos of an action sequence as a cover for their own confusion—slicing-and-dicing their action sequences to ribbons—but Cameron keeps his head. There are many explosions in his work but none that blow up out of nowhere, many collisions, but none that haven't followed a carefully plotted course; and while Weaver was right to be on his case about the guns—she has always seemed one move ahead of her directors in the *Alien* films, warming up the chilly Scott, and tempering Cameron's steel—she needn't have worried, for no director's work is as energized and perplexed by the problem of How the Mighty Fall.

What gives Cameron's plots their strength is that military might fails as much as it prevails. In *T2*, Schwarzenegger's Terminator would meet its match in the T-1000, a model not bigger and brawnier than he is, but made of a liquid metal alloy that changes shape at will, mercury to his might, and as timely a take on asymmetrical warfare as you could have wished for in 1991, what with George Bush having just attempted to kick out Saddam Hussein with "overwhelming force." If only he were as keen a student of James Cameron as he was a breathless fan of Arnold Schwarzenegger, he might have saved himself, not to mention his son, a lot of bother. Or look at what happens in *Aliens*, for the marines descend to the planet's surface, only to find that their guns cannot be fired without triggering the planet's nuclear reactor, while the armor that once protected them now imprisons them. Hung heavy with hardware, their military superiority leads to a Vietnam-like rousting. Despite Cameron's evident ear for the foul tongues of his grunts, he also has a fine tactician's eye, closer to that of a general or a chess player: the twist by which the aliens outwit the marines' motion sensors by approaching not head-on, but above, perpendicular to the expected attack line, is one of the great Knight-takes-Rook moves of modern cinema, one that gets even better when you remember that the aliens still have their queen to play.

And so, after all the escalation: reduction, attenuation, as Ripley regroups the scattered marines around her in a formation more closely resembling a family—with Hicks as father, Newt as daughter, and the android Bishop as her one gay friend—and takes on the queen alien with the skills she picked up in the docking bay, in what amounts to the mother of all movie climaxes, not least because it consists of two very angry mothers, bearing down over one frightened little girl. Who would have thought it? One of the best action movies of the eighties, and it's a maternity battle. "Get away from her, you bitch," screams Ripley, a line not only purpose-built to send Camille Paglia rocketing out of her seat, but which confirmed the *Alien* films as doing for maternity roughly what *The Godfather* films did for paternity in the seventies, providing a scalpel-sharp disquisition on the matter of what it is to have a family and what it is to defend one—the ties of blood and the letting of it. This may be a rather grandiose way of looking at a bunch of movies about space aliens, but then you could say the same thing about a bunch of movies about mafioso thugs. Coppola's mixture of aesthetic scruple and gangland violence has proven a far more winning ticket with critics—the same ticket on which Scorsese and Tarantino have ridden to acclaim—although the time may have come to question the rather dubious connection that seems to exist between film critics and the mafia. I don't mean an actual real-life connection—the dons haven't got the film critics in their pockets, although they may as well have. The narrowest strip-mining of a small patch of gangland America has rendered Coppola's and Scorsese's reputations as critical darlings all but unassailable, whereas the likes of Scott and Spielberg and Lucas and Cameron are seen as toiling away in the Twilight Zone, only to be praised when they recant, give up the spaceships and aliens, and come down to earth. It's a more sophisticated version of the prejudice that grips the Academy for historical films over fantasy films—for films about events that demonstrably did happen, as opposed to films about events that demonstrably did not. Weaver got nominated for an Oscar for *Aliens,* which was a considerable advance, but there was no way she could win. Spaceships and aliens—as opposed to blood oaths and horse's heads—are definite proof that the events concerned demonstrably did not happen: absolute, undeniable evidence that someone, somewhere, has been making this stuff up.

You might think this is a pretty good way of judging how much creativity has been poured into a film—how much stuff in it was made up. The time may have come to admit that *The Godfather*'s status as mahogany-hued classic has always overlooked its roots in the roiling Guignol of Mario Puzo's imagination: like Corleone, Coppola reached for greatness but his feet were mired in pulp. That horse's head looked real enough, but Puzo made that stuff up, I'm afraid, just as surely as

Ridley Scott made up all that stuff about aliens with retractable jaws falling out of airlocks. Coppola is often held up as the first casualty of the blockbuster age, and *The Godfather* a prime example of the Type of Film That Couldn't Get Made Anymore—the last Custer-like stand of all the darkness that was rudely expunged from American cinemas by the bright lights of Lucas and Spielberg in 1977—but the *Alien* films suggest otherwise. Maybe all the darkness didn't get sucked out of the airlock, but crept on board the *Nostromo,* to encircle the tenebrous family saga that unfolded from her decks. The heart of darkness is beating still. For, like *The Godfather* films, the *Alien* movies do amount to a family saga, of a particularly warped sort. *Alien*³ would begin by wiping out the surrogate family that Ripley had collected around her at the end of *Aliens*—Hicks, Newt, and Bishop—in order to clear the decks for another clan that has a claim on her, the one she has been trying to extinguish all along. And so, after the flight of the first movie, the fight of the second, we arrive at the weary embrace of the third, like exhausted boxers, or old lovers. "Now do something for me. It's easy. Just do what you do," whispers Ripley. "Don't be afraid. I'm part of the family. You've been in my life so long, I can't remember anything else." Or as Michael Corleone said, in another context, "Just when I thought I was out, they drag me back in." Not only that but the third *Alien* movie was a mess. How much more like *The Godfather* films can you get?

This scene, occurring about halfway through David Fincher's movie, had the whisper of the blackest of jokes: the suicide and the Grim Reaper, foxing each other, one only too keen to die, the other preferring to condemn her to grim life. And boy was it grim in Fincher's movie. It's not too hard to see why *Alien*³ didn't exactly coin it in at the box office. Having exhausted the efforts of six writers and two other directors before it got to Fincher, he inherited a wounded lion of a movie, but one still capable of the odd roar. With its air of celestial melancholy, its Bosch-like furnaces, and positively medieval gloom, it seemed to have drifted light-years away from the bright lights of the multiplex, and closer to the dolorous realm more normally patrolled by the art film: the world's first $80 million art movie. As of the summer of 2003, we are a little more acclimatized to the idea. What with Ang Lee's *The Hulk* prompting articles asking, "Has art house saved the superhero?" and *The Matrix Reloaded* prompting enough philosophical exegesis to stun a small bison, the time may indeed have come, in fact, to mobilize world opinion in the reverse direction, and begin the campaign to Keep Summer Movies Dumb. Certainly, the more fascinated *Alien* films grew with the richness of their own thematic texture, the more they neglected their humble duty to terrify, and by the time of *Alien: Resurrection*, the series had unspooled into mere marginalia, of archival interest to those who wished to know what happens when you give an *Alien* movie to a Frenchman to direct. In the long battle between the blockbuster and the art house, nobody stopped to think what purposes that conflict served, on both sides; or that the only thing that might stop the summer blockbuster dead in its tracks, like an elephant before a mouse, was the possibility that someone, someday, might consider it art.

CHAPTER 9

WAR ZONES, HIGH CONCEPTS

"I feel the need. The need. For speed."
—Maverick, *Top Gun*, 1986

"Speed is everything."
—Sun Tzu, *The Art of War,* fourth century B.C.

In May of 1983, Jerry Bruckheimer sat outside his partner, Don Simpson's, office, waiting for him to finish talking on the phone. This normally took some time, so he settled in with a copy of *California* magazine, and flipped it open to a photograph that immediately caught his attention. "It was a picture of this helmet with a visor down, and a plane reflected in the visor," he says. "And then two airplanes beside the helmet, and the guy's in a cockpit." The photograph accompanied an article about the navy's dogfight school in Miramar, California, entitled "Top Guns." Bruckheimer thought to himself: it looks like *Star Wars* on earth, and rushed into Simpson's office to show him the picture.

"We gotta buy this! We gotta buy this!" Simpson yelled. They called in writer Chip Proser and pitched the idea, such as it was. "It was two guys in leather jackets and sunglasses standing in front of the biggest, fastest fucking airplane you ever saw in your life," said Proser.

"Don said, 'This is it. This is the concept.' But it wasn't even a concept. It was just an image." Proser passed.

What *was* it? As an idea it wasn't much: *Star Wars* on earth. But hadn't the whole point of *Star Wars* been that it was dogfights—i.e., *Top Gun*—in space? The industry buzz word for what Bruckheimer and Simpson had on their hands at this point would be "high concept" and like a lot of industry buzz words, almost everyone has taken credit for it, and it doesn't actually mean very much. Basically, it was a term for a creative idea for those who are not in the business of having them—producers, executives—and who therefore felt a little embarrassed walking into a meeting clutching just a plain old concept. A high concept, on the other hand, was an idea in shoulder pads—an idea pithy and punchy enough to survive the "aggressive advocacy and yelling system" that had sprung up at Paramount at the beginning of the decade, where Simpson cut his teeth as a young executive. Stewarded by TV executive Barry Diller, the studio had turned into a grooming zoo for Hollywood's alpha males—Simpson, Michael Eisner, Jeffrey Katzenberg—or the "killer Dillers," as they were known. "At the time I didn't know how unique this way of doing things was," said Dawn Steel, one of the few women in a sea of testosterone. "I thought all studio executives stood on tables and screamed."

All the clues to Simpson's later success with Bruckheimer lay with the movies he saw made at Paramount under Diller's stewardship. When Eisner first arrived at Paramount, Diller had bought him a 1976 buff Mercedes convertible 450 just like his own; on his first day behind the wheel, Eisner sped down Santa Monica Boulevard, only to be pulled over by a cop; on the drive home, he got to thinking about the life of this cop, protecting the rich and famous of Beverly Hills, and the next day gave the idea to Simpson to develop. Simpson called in writer Danilo Bach, and pitched it to him. "There was no story," said Bach. "There was just this vague idea about a cop who turns Beverly Hills upside down." Thus was born *Beverly Hills Cop:* the first motion picture by a major studio to be adapted from a speeding ticket. In 1981, Eisner promoted Simpson to head of production, trying to steer him toward a film called *White Dog,* about a dog trained to hate blacks. "*White Dog* is *Jaws,*" he told him, but Simpson was more interested in *An Officer and a Gentleman,* "a little romantic movie," according to

Eisner, but Simpson saw something in Douglas Day Stewart's script about young navy cadets, and was soon all over the project. "Don loved the mano a mano stuff," said Stewart. "He never got the love story." Simpson would sit up at night, loaded on cocaine, dictating long, rambling memos about the script, which his assistants typed up the next morning. "The script got longer and longer as Simpson made more changes and more changes," said director Taylor Hackford. "'This character could really happen,' 'This scene could be wonderful.' He was too fucking creative."

What would *An Officer and a Gentleman* have been like had Simpson had fully his way with it? For one thing it wouldn't have starred Debra Winger (whom he told "You're not fuckable enough for the part"), and it wouldn't have had the Joe Cocker theme song. ("This song is no good," he told Hackford.) The marching chant about "napalm sticks to kids," that would have gone, along with those skies the color of porridge, and the suicide attempt, obviously. It would have still had those crisp white navy uniforms, though, and a hero on a motorbike. What you would have been left with, in fact, would have been *Top Gun*, a high concept *An Officer and a Gentleman*, just as *Beverly Hills Cop* was a high concept *48 Hrs.*, and *Flashdance* was a high concept *Saturday Night Fever*. That is to say, versions of those films that had been shorn of peripherals, strip-mined for their pockets of triumph, their character arcs reduced to telegraphic shorthand, and strung out along a gleaming bead of hit songs—that's what high concept was, or felt like to watch: like being told about another even better movie by a highly excitable intermediary.

When Simpson had gone to the navy for cooperation to film *An Officer and a Gentleman*, he had been turned down because they thought the script portrayed them in a bad light. When he pitched them the idea for *Top Gun*, they had no objections, nor could they really, since the script hadn't been written yet. It was still just an idea. "What happened was Don just started to spin a tale," said Bruckheimer. "He told the story of the movie. At this point there was no movie, so he made it up. What's interesting is that the movie ended up very close to the story he told, but he just told it off the top of his head." They called in screenwriters Jim Cash and Jack Epps to flesh the idea out, and six months later they handed in their first draft. Simpson hated it; the "narrative arc" was off, and the girl was all wrong: an aer-obics instructor. Couldn't they make her an astrophysicist? They asked for a second draft, which was, to Simpson's mind, even worse. He went back to their original choice of Proser, and after him to writer Warren Skaaren. Eleven drafts later and they had the script they wanted, although by this time, Paramount had begun to get cold feet. Jeffrey Katzenberg, once Simpson's assistant and now head of production, called a meeting with the two producers, a meeting whose purpose, Simpson knew, was to put the project in turnaround, and so he placed a call to his old boss, Michael Eisner, and begged him to come to the meeting. Sure enough, Katzenberg sat them down and began to explain that Paramount already had an aviation film, *Call to Glory,* on the books. "I was biding my time till Eisner walked in," said Simpson, "because if I knew one thing, I knew I could sell a movie to Michael Eisner. I had been doing it for a decade. When he walked in, I jumped from my seat."

He spoke for several minutes, keeping one eye on Katzenberg and another on Eisner to see how they were reacting. The whole film came out of him in an inspired tumble, its narrative arc sketched in an instant, its characters laid out, their wrongs set forth, then righted, their inner potentials filled out, then fulfilled, conflicts opening up and resolving in seconds, climax following climax in what amounted to the best pitch of his life, hammered out in the white-hot heat of inspira-tion and panic. Eisner turned to Katzenberg and said, "Jeff, these guys are so passionate about this, we have to do it."

At which point we will leave them, in glorious freeze frame, as they would want it: Simpson on his feet, delivering the pitch of his career, Bruckheimer at his side, the two of them basking in the radiant light of Eisner's acceptance. It was maybe their finest hour: not the movie *Top Gun,* not the making of *Top Gun,* but the pitch for *Top Gun.* As Bruck-heimer noted, the finished movie wasn't much different from the movie Simpson made up on the spot. Sure, it had actors, and jets, and hit songs, but no matter how it tried it could never hope to match the powers of passionate brevity, the exultant concision, of that pitch. If only they had left it at that—the ultimate in high concept. But then the career of Bruckheimer and Simpson has proven itself subject to a high concept paradox all its own: they were the very embodiment of brash, boisterous eighties yahooism, so naturally they inspire nothing but fond thoughts; but compared to the vivid Day-Glo vulgarity of the *idea* of Bruckheimer and Simpson, the movies of Bruckheimer and Simpson now run a close second.

Top Gun comes closer than most to distilling their fragrant essence. Many a hero of theirs would have father issues, a beautiful girlfriend, an ill-fated buddy, and a motorbike, in various combinations, but *Top Gun*'s hero, Maverick (Tom Cruise), is the only one to get the full deck. And while many of them would be fondly thought of as mavericks, or rumored to be mavericks, or flatteringly referred to behind their backs as mavericks, Maverick was the only one to actually be *called* Maverick, just to be on the safe side. But then one of the most striking things about *Top Gun* today is how safe it feels. Its plot unfolding beneath cloudless, Cold War skies, in which no combat takes place, the villain of the piece turns out to be Maverick's rival, Iceman (Val Kilmer), although one of the reasons it's always a surprise to remember that Kilmer is even in the movie is that he's given so little to do: he doesn't get to sabotage Tom Cruise's fuel tank, or challenge him to a dogfight, still less a punch-up. All he does is make catty remarks in the locker room. That's the only enemy in the movie, really—any comment that might scratch or dent the immaculate confidence of its pilots creating holes in the fragile ego-sphere. You might have thought that if you left a movie to its producers to pull together, rather than its director, you'd get nothing but beefy hard-boiled action, but weirdly, you get the opposite—movies hollowed out by talk, boast, braggadocio, reputation-bolster and beef-up. "You're here 'cause you're the top one percent," Viper (Tom Skerritt) tells Maverick's class. "You're the elite, the best of the best. We're gonna make you better, because your job is damned important." Compare that to the foul-mouthed dressing-down that Lou Gossett gave Richard Gere at the beginning of *An Officer and a Gentleman,* and Viper's speech can only come across as the most fluting flattery, but then Hackford's film put Richard Gere through a mill of muddy humiliations before allowing him his final moment of freeze-framed glory. In true Bruckheimer-Simpson fashion, *Top Gun* starts in triumph, runs a few victory laps, finds a few other causes for celebration, reroutes through a decorous setback or two, and then moves on to full ego floss. "You're a great flier. You fly cowboy style," Viper tells Maverick, "reckless, wild, out of formation half the time. . . . You buck the system and do everything the hard way." Ah, the iron voice of military discipline. The film's release sparked a massive surge in applications to join the navy, although one can only wonder at the quality of couch potato they found waiting in line, or how they broke the news that the job didn't involve giving Kelly McGillis a ride home on their motorcycle, or working hard to build up the Kenny Loggins section of their album collection.

The films of Bruckheimer and Simpson have never been the place to go for career advice, of course. Viper's kind words are no more likely to be the sort of thing whispered into the ears of those seeking to fly F-14s than *Flashdance* was a manual for welders, still less those attempting the delicate career transition from welder to lap dancer. What the navy should have done was reroute all their applicants to leafy enclaves of Beverly Hills, for there is one career, and one career alone, for which their credo of passionate recklessness is a fantastic fit: that of movie producer. It is the great tragedy of Bruckheimer's and Simpson's careers that they never quite realized this, and never made the one great movie they had in them, about a couple of fast-talking sharpies, with matching black Ferraris and matching black Levi's, who roll up and take Hollywood for a ride. Such autobiographical urges were, unfortunately, beneath them: "Some directors who shall remain nameless do regard movies as an extension of their internal emotional landscape, but Jerry and I decide on the movie we want to make," said Simpson. "I don't believe in the auteur theory. The movie is the auteur." Nonetheless, no body of work better testifies to the muscular status battles of the Hollywood bear pit than their films, or to its landscape of verdant palms, flashy cars, well-manicured valets, and sotto voce personal assistants. *Beverly Hills Cop* isn't a very good movie about cops but it *is* a good movie about Beverly Hills; and it got a green light from Eisner when the producers told him about the movie's art collector villain: "You're describing the guy I'm having lunch with!" Similarly, *Top Gun* is not a good movie about the navy, still less a good movie about whatever idea about the navy that Simpson gleaned from *An Officer and a Gentleman*, but it is a great movie about the feeling that Simpson experienced when, as Paramount's head of production, he saw *An Officer and a Gentleman* become a huge hit.

There's no better film on the subject. If you want to know what manner of exultation floods your being when a movie you have produced takes in $129,795,554 at the box office, then watch *Top Gun*, a movie all about the importance of being top dog, flying high, a number one hit movie all about being number one. What did that mean, exactly, by 1986? *Top Gun* was released on May 16–18 in 1,028 theaters and took in $8,193,052, the highest gross of any movie that week. Sylvester Stallone's *Cobra*, meanwhile, released the week before, was busy advertising itself as "the No. 1 grossing film in America," but was playing in 2,131 theaters, almost twice as many as *Top Gun*. So, using a per-screen average, *Top Gun* came out the winner. Or did it? For using a per-screen average, *Top Gun* was easily bested by *A Room with a View*, which averaged $6,717 in just ninety-three theaters—Tom Cruise's smirk wiped from his face by a bunch of Edwardians in white linen, which clearly couldn't be right. So which movie was "number one"? It was impossible to say. The title had become a shifting standard, almost meaningless, and not even beginning to hint at which film was the most profitable.

But then watching *Top Gun* in actual movie theaters was one of the more retrograde things you could do with it. You could also buy yourself some *Top Gun*–style aviator shades and bomber jackets, you could buy the soundtrack album, featuring Kenny Loggins's "Danger Zone" and Berlin's "Take My Breath Away," as two million people did that summer. The more dogged of literalists could always express their enthusiasm for the movie by going and joining the navy, although by far the best option was to wait a year and see the movie on video, where it seemed a lot happier than it had in cinemas. Up on the big screen, it strutted and puffed to fill the space and seemed a little defenseless against critics' taunts that it was merely an overdressed pop video or navy recruitment commercial. Watched a few years later, with friends at home, in an air of companionable irony, and it seemed much more relaxed, its machismo unfurling into more amiable camp, the thrill ride now playing as straightforward nostalgia trip. Within one week of *Top Gun*'s release on video in 1987, Paramount sold 2.5

million cassettes, generating $40 million, which is to say half again as much as it had made in theaters.

Amidst the mass of statistics thrown up by Hollywood, this one is worth hanging on to for it really tells you something, and takes you places. In the words of Deep Throat, in *All the President's Men*, "Follow the Money," and if you follow it, you find yourself taken on a whistlestop tour of Hollywood's "ancillary" revenues—video, pay-per-view, cable—all of which had grown up around the movies by the mid-eighties, like parasitic vines that now held the whole infrastructure in place. In 1987, Hollywood's video revenues were $7.5 billion, almost twice that generated by films in theaters. That is an industry-changing statistic, the sort of statistic that actually affects what you see on the screen, for it renders any comparisons between *An Officer and a Gentleman* and *Top Gun* moot: they are movies from a different medium. Not wholly different, but different enough to throw critical judgment subtly off-track. So while critics might complain that *Top Gun* was a louder, cruder version of *An Officer and a Gentleman,* and attribute it to the fact that Don Simpson was an insecure bully, the reason Simpson came to the fore when he did, was that by 1986, cinema had become an insecure bully, too: having to shout to make itself heard in this new multimedia environment, and in the process making itself hoarse. As cinema, *Top Gun* was pure vapor trail, evaporating instantly, making only the briefest of pit stops in theaters, before jetting off into the ancillary stratosphere, which was where the real money was to be made.

"We do not make motion pictures for which we don't have the full stream of rights," Michael Eisner told *Variety*. "It's all tied to one purpose, creating a stream of rights that may start off in motion picture theaters, then move to cable, network, off-network, and foreign; or might start in the legitimate theater, or may go directly to cable. It doesn't matter where it ends up. The point is that we will own the software to every one of those media needs." What this numbing brand of corporatespeak meant in practice was that the public's bum on a theater seat counted for less than it ever had, and it marked a vital sea change in the way movies were put together—the way blockbusters were built. "The attitude changed in the eighties," says producer Peter Guber, who had been part of the team at Columbia that green-lit *Close*

Encounters back in 1975. "A movie like *Close Encounters* was essentially idiosyncratic. They weren't thought of as tent pole franchises, or as aiming for blockbuster status. There was a conscious effort that the film had to perform at a higher level because of its cost, and there was greater expectation. But the attitude changed in the eighties: they became targets of opportunity. People looked to these pictures as a means of moving the company's stock up, of generating this locomotive for all the other businesses that you wanted to drive with the movies, and to create people's careers in the company, because it created such attention, and created such white heat. You managed an asset. What you were doing was managing an asset toward that soft landing. That's a real difference."

Few were as good at generating that white heat, and managing those assets toward their soft landings, as Guber. Back in 1969, he had accurately predicted, in an essay entitled "The New Ball Game/The Cartridge Revolution," that "the home entertainment center will become the backbone of the national economy" and after his success with *The Deep* in 1977, he had teamed up with fellow producer Jon Peters, whose rise to the top of the Hollywood food chain was the sort of thing Jackie Collins gets paid good money to invent, having gone in the space of a year from being Barbra Streisand's hairdresser, to her lover, to her producer on *A Star Is Born*, the film that single-handedly launched the soundtrack tie-in industry. Together, the producers rode out the disco wave with such hits as *Thank God It's Friday*, but it was only in the late eighties that they came into their own. As the number of blockbusters required to fill the summer increased, and the number of directors who could provide them remained finite, it was to the producers that the studios turned in their hour of need—to producer teams like Bruckheimer and Simpson, or Peters and Guber, who could be relied upon to pull movies into shape, building them from the top down, to their specifications, rather than from the bottom up, to a writer's or director's.

Peters and Guber's way with creatives was notorious: Peters got through fourteen screenwriters, three directors, and four musical collaborators in the course of producing *A Star Is Born*. Spielberg had the producers banned from the set of *The Color Purple*, while George

Miller, the young Australian director entrusted with bringing *The Witches of Eastwick* to the screen in 1987, later said of the experience: "I knew when I made *Witches* why America lost the Vietnam War: patrols of ten people went off in ten different directions. Everyone interfered, the producers, Peter Guber and Jon Peters, went crazy on that one, particularly Peters." Miller called the producer "genuinely thought-disordered. The mind can't focus on one issue. You know, it's coming from fifteen different directions. . . . It depended upon the last movie he'd seen. If *Aliens* was out, he'd say 'oh, we've got to make it like *Aliens.*' And the next week it was a Whoopi Goldberg movie. The tone of it was completely dictated by whatever was scoring high at the box office at that time."

Originally, the ending of *The Witches of Eastwick* was to have consisted of Susan Sarandon, Michelle Pfeiffer, and Cher realizing that Jack Nicholson may, in fact, be the devil. Peters didn't want any maybe about it; he wanted Nicholson to transform into a huge, hundred-foot demon who smashed their house to smithereens. Miller was distraught: "I kept trying to say, 'People, this isn't going to work. This is just nonsense.'" And so it was that *The Witches of Eastwick* tried its hand, at the very last minute, and without any warning whatsoever, at being *Friday the 13th.* The scene was over so quickly, and followed so smartly by the end credits, that audiences weren't entirely sure that what they'd seen had in fact happened, but a quick glance along the aisle at the row of puzzled frowns and upturned palms confirmed it. The movie had gone, very briefly, mad—a brief shriek of what was to come.

Within Hollywood, the horrors of the *Eastwick* shoot only confirmed what they already knew about working with Peters and Guber. "I always heard [*Witches*] was such a nightmare," said director Tim Burton. "I tried not to listen too much." Burton had his own reason for ignoring the obvious, for he had just been elected by the producers to bring their next film, *Batman,* to the screen. "Torture," Burton would later call the experience. "The worst period of my life."

TIME LINE

1986

1. *Top Gun* (Paramount) $176,786,701
2. *"Crocodile" Dundee* (Paramount) $174,803,506
3. *Platoon* (Orion) $138,530,565
4. *The Karate Kid Part II* (Sony) $115,103,979
5. *Star Trek IV: The Voyage Home* (Paramount) $109,713,132
6. *Back to School* (Orion) $91,258,000
7. *Aliens* (Fox) $85,160,248
8. *The Golden Child* (Paramount) $79,817,937
9. *Ruthless People* (Disney) $71,624,879
10. *Ferris Bueller's Day Off* (Paramount) $70,136,369

1987

1. *Three Men and a Baby* (Disney) $167,780,960
2. *Fatal Attraction* (Paramount) $156,645,693
3. *Beverly Hills Cop II* (Paramount) $153,665,036
4. *Good Morning, Vietnam* (Disney) $123,922,370
5. *Moonstruck* (MGM) $80,640,528
6. *The Untouchables* (Paramount) $76,270,454
7. *The Secret of My Success* (Universal) $66,995,879
8. *Stakeout* (Disney) $65,673,233
9. *Lethal Weapon* (WB) $65,207,127
10. *The Witches of Eastwick* (WB) $63,766,510

1988

1. *Rain Man* (MGM) $172,825,435
2. *Who Framed Roger Rabbit* (Disney) $156,452,370
3. *Coming to America* (Paramount) $128,152,301
4. *Big* (Fox) $114,968,774
5. *Twins* (Universal) $111,938,388
6. *"Crocodile" Dundee II* (Paramount) $109,306,210
7. *Die Hard* (Fox) $83,008,852
8. *The Naked Gun* (Paramount) $78,756,177
9. *Cocktail* (Disney) $78,222,753
10. *Beetlejuice* (WB) $73,326,666

*Figures show U.S. domestic gross

CHAPTER 10

THE LONG DARK NIGHT

"Tell your friends. Tell all your friends."
—Michael Keaton, *Batman,* 1989

Where do movies come from? It used to be relatively easy to say. A movie started life as an idea by a director, or a script by a writer. The script then secured funding via a producer, who submitted his budget to a studio for approval, hopefully getting a green light, and thus began the film's long journey to the screen. That journey was fraught with peril, and could get snarled up at any stage, and frequently did, but that essentially was the order: idea, money, execution. *Batman*'s journey to the screen was different, a three-legged race in which idea, money, and execution all exerted their lopsided pull on one another, all at the same time, giving it an altogether more drunken gait, as it wound its way through three different companies, as many directors, and innumerable scripts, in a game of Chinese whispers whose only guiding principle, at any one point, was the idea that a *Batman* movie might be a neat thing to have in existence. It wasn't how movies used to get made, if you were lucky, but *Batman* was a taste of the future: it would increasingly be how blockbusters got made.

You could, for instance, say that the film started life as that single-spaced, nine-page memo, presented by the comic book aficionado Michael Uslan to Peters and Guber back in 1980: "No longer portrayed

185

as a pot-bellied caped clown, *Batman* has again become a vigilante who stalks criminals in the shadow of night." Peters and Guber signed a deal with Uslan, who then heard nothing back from the producers for several years, as they migrated from their film company, Casablanca, to PolyGram, and from PolyGram to Warner Brothers, where Peters and Guber signed a production deal in 1982. And it was at Warner Brothers that the project began to pick up some heat—some of Guber's "Big Mo"—for Warner Brothers also owned DC Comics, and therefore all the merchandising rights to the *Batman* comic strip. The project thus had "synergy"—that longed-for cross-pollination that occurs when the different arms of a large corporation come together to help promote a single "entertainment property." In this case, the property was Batman—not the movie, but the idea of Batman, his platonic essence, an essence that would be incarnated in the movie, just as it would be incarnated in the merchandising, but reducible, in the end, to neither. "The concept of blockbuster results—the idea that a film could generate enormous revenue—was still being tested," says Guber. "It had been tested with *Star Wars* and several other films but it wasn't yet the concept of a franchise picture: the idea that you could build a series of pictures out of it. *Batman* tested the boundaries of how enormous merchandising could be driven by toy manufacturers who would wrap the toys pre-Christmas or pre-summer and participate in the advertising. They helped promote the film, which helped promote the merchandising, which helped promote the sequel."

He went knocking on doors, up and down the Warner Brothers lot. "We went and managed to enlist the support of people like Dan Romanelli, then the head of merchandising, and discussed how this could resuscitate the whole merchandising company. We went through the whole company that way so that when the time came to make the picture, there was momentum, there were a group of supporters inside the company who made it easier for the senior management to make the decision."

Romanelli, for one, was delighted with the attention. "Years ago we used to be ignored. It was 'who cares what those guys want?'" he says. "It was a case of 'oh give us some T-shirts for the kids.' Now, a lot of not only filmmakers but executives here at the studio embrace us because they know that it can be a significant part of the overall marketing success of a film. You go into Wal-Mart: there's 10 million people a week. That's very impactful. You can't ignore that." Romanelli had learned from the release of *Superman* in 1978 that some films were more "toyetic"—easily turned into toys—than others. "Here was the problem," says Romanelli. "*Superman* was a phenomenon but *Superman* doesn't need anything. *Batman* needs all his toys to get around. *Batman* has amazing toys. Superman just flies and he's off. It was all very frustrating for us." *Batman* was different: in Sam Hamm's script he was happily sprouting toys by the truckload, and although he was a hero, he looked like a villain. He was toyetic. "A boy doesn't necessarily want to be some dog or some character, but he wants to be *Batman*," says Romanelli. "The role playing is critical. If you can't relate, you may love that character but you don't want to *be* that character." The film's merchandisers were given unprecedented access to the production, with faxes of the film's designs flying back and forth across the Atlantic, before the producers invited the film's licensees over to look at the real thing—hundreds of them swarming over Anton Furst's darkly fascistic Gotham City sets. "They were very excited," noted Furst dryly, although Burton was aghast. "Cereal manufacturers and fast food companies, who wanted to make bat-shaped toys and hamburgers were looking over my shoulder the whole time," he complained. "It was quite horrifying."

The producers had come by the director through a circuitous route. When they signed their original development deal with Warners, in 1982, it had been with the late Frank Wells, but the management at the studio then changed several times, and *Batman* had gone through a six-year hiatus, during which time the project was attached to several different writers and directors—Tom Mankiewicz, Steven Engelhard, Joe Dante, Ivan Reitman—before Burton popped into the frame in 1986. A less-likely man to helm a big studio blockbuster would have been harder to find. Spindly, pipe-cleaner frame, topped off with an unruly crow's nest of hair, from which complete sentences would occasionally emerge only under extreme duress—Burton looked like some lesser-known cousin of the Addams family. From the time he was a kid, people had taken one look at his heavy-lidded eyes and asked if he was on drugs. Brought up in the Los Angeles suburb of Burbank, beneath the flight paths of LAX airport, he used to lie on his lawn and watch the vapor trails left by the passing jets. "Anywhere USA" he called it. Fitful and unfocused, he only seemed settled when drawing or when watching horror movies on TV—*King Kong, Frankenstein, Godzilla, The Creature from the Black Lagoon.* He'd be glued to the screen, without a flicker of fear: just eating them up. In many ways, it was an upbringing with broad hints of Spielberg's, but marked by a more amused, ironic distance from the images he watched. These creature features reached him through a richly developed sense of the absurd, playing to him like *Rebel Without a Cause,* but with the monsters in the James Dean role. "I felt most monsters were basically misperceived," he said, "they usually had much more heartfelt souls than the human characters around them."

He got a job as a draftsman at Disney, but found himself unable to fake the house style ("mine looked like roadkills") before scoring a hit, in 1986, with *Pee-wee's Big Adventure*—a cross between Jacques Tati and *I Dream of Jeannie.* It was this charming bit of pop surrealism that—somehow—convinced Peters and Guber that they'd found their man, although the studio executives at Warners took a bit more convincing. "Warners was a complete, total freak-out," said Peters, "scared to death [of] shooting a $30 million film with a third-time director whose first two films cost about a dollar and a half." They decided to wait and see how his follow-up, *Beetlejuice,* did at the box office, before committing, and so a pattern was established: during the week Burton would shoot *Beetlejuice,* and on weekends he would hole up with screenwriter Sam Hamm to sketch out *Batman.* "It was kind of charming in a way because Sam and I would meet on weekends to discuss early writing stages, and we had a great script, but they kept saying there were other things involved," noted Burton. "They were just waiting to see how *Beetlejuice* did. They didn't want to give me the movie unless *Beetlejuice* was going to be okay. They wouldn't say that, but that was really the way it was."

Hamm and Burton had inherited a script by Tom Mankiewicz, which basically followed the contours of his screenplay for *Superman,* and told the story of how Bruce Wayne grew up, from lonely orphan into adult crime-fighter. "You had to wade through twenty years just to get to the first shot of the guy in the costume that we've all come to see," complained Hamm. Their solution: at the start of the picture Batman would already be Batman, but the Joker would not yet be the Joker, who now took center stage, like all the misunderstood monsters Burton had soaked up as a kid. Critics would say that Jack Nicholson stole the movie, but you can only steal what doesn't belong to you, and the movie was his from the beginning. Batman, meanwhile, graciously backed into the shadows—a dark, tormented loner—as Burton tried to find some angle on the character, some kink, through which his sympathies could find some sort of purchase. Burton was "never a big comic book fan," he said. He also had "real trouble with vigilantism." Nor did he like action movies ("I don't like guns") or big studio productions ("I'm for anything that subverts what the studio thinks you have to do"). You have to ask, therefore, whether a big studio action movie about a comic book vigilante was ever going to be an' exact match for Burton's talents.

"The thing I liked about *Batman* as a comic book property was that they're all fucked-up characters," he said, seeking solace in the potential kinkiness implied by the act of dressing up in black leather every night. What he didn't want, above all, was "*Death Wish* in a batsuit," and so cast Michael Keaton, his nervy, crackerjack star from *Beetlejuice.* "What's nice about *Batman* is that he's not strictly a physical force," agreed Keaton. "He's essentially a cerebral force. He doesn't just go out and kick ass." There was only one problem with this: Jon Peters. "When we got into this I thought, what a great opportunity to have this guy kick some ass," said the producer, who wanted *Batman* "to be New York, to be street." "*Death Wish* in a batsuit" was almost *exactly* what he had in mind, although any differences between the director and producer were momentarily shelved when the grosses of *Beetlejuice* finally came in—over $70 million. Warners was finally persuaded to go with Burton and gave them the green light.

"Suddenly we were developing the picture with a hot director," says Guber. "Once we got Jack Nicholson on to play the Joker, the film suddenly had novelty. And it had certainty: it was a presold highly recognized property. That combination—novelty and certainty—generated the enthusiasm that got it made." Even so, they were taking no chances with their twenty-seven-year-old director and cocooned him in a sturdy and experienced production team that included first assistant director Derek Cracknell and editor Roy Lovejoy, both of whom had worked on *Aliens,* line producer Chris Kenny, a veteran of the Bond films, and second unit director Peter MacDonald, the action specialist who had worked on *Rambo II.* Turning up for his first day at Pinewood Studios, where Anton Furst's vast sets dominated most of the eighteen soundstages, on a chilly English October day, Burton muttered to himself, "This movie's so monumental." He had forgotten to wear a winter coat.

Jon Peters was on a roll, having embarked on an affair with the film's female star, Kim Basinger—"My sweetheart hoodlum" she called him. Throughout the shoot he was the very image of big-balled largesse; showing off the sets to visitors; hiring and firing so many chauffeurs that the crew kept a tally; and playing merry hell with Burton's script. "He's supposed to be Batman, not Wussman," complained Peters, and brought in *Top Gun* screenwriter Warren Skaaren, and then *Brazil* co-writer Charles McKeown for rewrites, expanding the Joker's role, amping up the antagonism between him and *Batman,* and introducing more action in the form of some kick-boxers. "If Jon pushed for something in the film, it would be two angles," said Chris Kenny. "Romance and action."

"That was the real nightmare on this picture," said Burton. "I don't quite understand why it became such an enormous frantic problem. We started out with a script by Sam that everyone liked, although we all recognized there were a few little things that needed changing. Our meetings literally went like this: 'The script's great, the script's great, the script is really great, okay the script's great, but we think it needs a total rewrite.' What made the situation worse in this instance was there was this big hubbub about making the script better and—zoom—we were suddenly shooting. In certain scenes the actors and myself were blocking out new lines on the day we had to shoot them. A couple of days near the end of production I was close to death over this insane situation. The responsibility of having this crew of over a hundred men waiting to shoot something unwritten was quite upsetting. Once you start shooting, you just can't be at that stage."

Things finally came to a head at the climax of the movie—in which Vicki Vale (Kim Basinger) was to have been killed by the Joker, sending Batman into a vengeful fury. Peters decided that audiences wouldn't accept Batman beating up a fifty-year-old man, and so without telling Burton, he reworked it: the Joker would take Vale captive, and drag her up to the top of Gotham cathedral's bell tower. It would require an additional thirty-eight-foot model of the cathedral—costing $100,000, when they were already well over-budget. Burton hated the idea, having no clue how the scene would end: "Here were Jack Nicholson and Kim Basinger walking up this cathedral, and halfway up Jack turns around and says, 'Why am I walking up all these stairs? Where am I going?'

"We'll talk about it when you get to the top!" Burton called back.

"I had to tell him that I didn't know. The most frightening experience of my life. I knew they had to go up to the bell tower and they better do something up there. That was always a given. But what? Help me! Help me!" he said. "It was one of those nightmares where you're feeling big and small at the same time. Here you've got this big production with all these people waiting around and you're supposed to be shooting this sequence that suddenly goes wrong. I thought, 'My God, why didn't I see it to begin with? How did I let this happen?'" Nicholson was very supportive of his young director—"Get what you need, get what you want, and just keep going," he told him—but finally, on a rainy night that seemed to have been going on forever, Nicholson finally snapped and started ranting at Guber and Peters: *life was too short for this many hours in makeup, he'd been snookered, everyone else had known how long it would take . . .* "He was very angry and screaming, but with his face frozen in this smile," says Guber. "Jack had his full makeup on—it was kind of a surreal experience—and he was screaming at me and John: 'I can't believe this film is ever going to see the light of day!'" Another argument erupted over who was going to foot the bill for the crew's black leather *Batman* jackets: originally Peters's responsibility, he had shucked it, causing Nicholson to snap at Basinger, "Tell that guy whose cock you've been sucking for the past six months that he's an asshole for not paying for the jackets!"

As shooting wound down, though, Peters's sense of showmanship came into its own as he orchestrated a publicity campaign that would prove a template for blockbuster blitzes of the next decade. First up was the question of how to deal with the batfans who had been outraged at the casting of Keaton. "By casting a clown, Warner Brothers and Burton have defecated on the history of *Batman*," wrote one in the

Los Angeles Times, and soon *The Wall Street Journal* had slapped the news on page one: Wall Street's ears picked up, Warner Brothers' share price slumped, and every financial analyst friend of Peters's was on the phone to him, asking him what was going on. "It deflated everybody," he said, and persuaded Warners to spend $400,000 on a trailer he cut himself that caused four hundred fans to line up at the Bruin Theater in Westwood to pay their $7 to see it. The trailer was magnificently oblique—showing just scenes from the movie, no music, no narration—and Peters used much the same trick with the posters, showing just the bat logo, and the film's release date, June 23. "I never thought he'd get away with no name and no writing," marveled Anton Furst. "Jon told me, you'll never know the battles I had, right up to pinning people against the wall."

"I wanted to do, like, foreplay, to create the magic and myth of it all," said Peters. In March, the foreplay began in earnest, when Warners plastered the bat logo across city billboards and movie theaters in ten major cities across America; on May 23, they bought time for a $1 million ninety-second nation-wide TV commercial. "And then we disappeared again," said Peters. "Vanished. Like Batman." When retailers began reporting a small bump in interest in bat memorabilia, the producers started testing the waters with some merchandise—just a sprinkling of T-shirts and hats—only to find that the water was already seething with pirated goods. In Britain, over Christmas, the news show *TV-AM* had been taken off the air due to labor disputes, and the broadcasters were forced to show reruns of the old *Batman* TV series, and it had sparked a small wave of batfashion that was now spreading west across the Atlantic. Warners' merchandising wing was delighted.

"When the pirates are selling out there, too, they only go after the stuff they know will sell. They can't take any risks," says Dan Romanelli. "We recognized we had a real phenomenon on our hands. It was spectacular. . . . My son, who was six years old at the time, going to school in Encino, I gave him a bunch of *Batman* pins and said 'Give them out to your friends, Danny.' He said, 'No, no.' I said, 'Go on do it, do it for Dad.' And he came back to me a couple of weeks later saying, 'I need more pins.' Then one day I was in his room and he's on the phone selling the pins. I caught him and he got upset and I said, 'No, no, don't get upset: you're actually selling these things? How much are you getting?' 'Four dollars each.' I gave him a big kiss. We've got a success." In the end, some three hundred items would be spawned by one hundred licensees, generating more than three times as much revenue as tickets for the movie. "It's really a case of the tail wagging the dog," said a spokesperson for Hecht's Metro Center store, where fifteen thousand items sold in three months. By May, J. C. Penney in L.A. had sold forty thousand T-shirts, and continued to sell them at such a rate that licensees ran out of black material. "It's the biggest thing I've ever had in nineteen years," said one astonished retailer. "It's . . . *bigger than the California raisins.*"

"Everything," boasted Peters. "We made everything." Burton, meanwhile, was to be found doing a very good impression of a vole caught in a threshing machine, as he vainly attempted to fight the demands of the movie's assorted merchandisers and tie-in merchants. "They're saying to me, these record guys, it needs this and that, and they give you this whole thing about it's an expensive movie so you need it. And what happens is, you get engaged in this world, and then there's no way out. There's too much money," he said. "My major concern is that there is so much awareness and hype. I keep thinking, 'I hope there's a movie attached to all of this.'" Although as he noted later, "The interesting thing about hype is that everyone thought the studio was creating it, when in fact you can't create hype; it's a phenomenon that's beyond a studio, it has a life of its own."

What *is* hype, exactly? Where does it come from? Nobody seems to know. Newspapers use the word to refer to the publicity blitzes concocted by the studios—"studio hype." The studios, on the other hand, use it to describe the self-induced feeding frenzy of the press—"media hype." The film director, meanwhile, sits in the middle, observing that it has a "life of its own." Hype, it seems, is something of a catch-all, a nonce-word, covering a multitude of sins, none of them ever your own. I anticipate, you expect, others hype. It's a bit like trying to work out the genesis of clouds. Even its commonly presumed etymology is fake: "We live in a world of hyperbole," said a Doubleday editor in 1980. "Hyperbole has become so common that we now refer to it by a cozy contraction. We call it 'hype.' We decide to apply it, as if it were a wax compound for shining up a car." But hype is not a shortening of "hyperbole" but of "hypodermic needle," and refers to the hopped-up state of drug users; when newspaper columnist Billy Rose praised a 1950 movie for having "no fireworks, no fake suspense, no hyped-up glamour," his assumption was not that hype was something applied to a movie's surface, buffing it up to a nice shine, but that it was something internal, intravenous—which is much the way it works in Hollywood. As Will Rogers once remarked, "The movies are the only business where you can go out front and applaud yourself," in which case the blockbuster is the only species of movie in which the hype is at its loudest within that movie itself. One of the more curious aspects about the hype for *Batman*, for instance, is that it never quite cleared. After all the hype, that's what *Batman* turned out to be about: it was about hype. "Tell your friends, tell all your friends," whispers Batman to his first criminal catch, before letting them go, having realized that the benefits of good word of mouth far outweigh the benefit of having two more petty criminals behind bars. He then gets involved with newspaper photographer Vicki Vale (Basinger), who ensures that Batman's name is spread city-wide, and it is the quality of Batman's media coverage, in fact, far more than his actual deeds, that most enrages the Joker, flushing him out of hiding.

"Can someone please tell me what kind of a world we live in where a man dressed as a bat gets my airtime!" he complains, before shooting up his TV set. "Wait'll they get a load of me!" he says and hits back with a PR campaign of his own, hijacking the airwaves to run a series of advertisements for himself—parodies of the hard-sell adverts of the fifties, with *Batman* in the opposite corner, representing the matte-black, soft-sell eighties. Can somebody please tell me what kind of a movie it is where all the villain wants to do is be more *popular* than its hero? This is how the central battles in *Batman* are played out, not on the streets, but at press conferences, across the airwaves, and in the newspapers. It is a PR war for the soul of Gotham City, and it resembles less the battle between two superhero colossi, than it does a presidential race, with two candidates endlessly finessing their public personae. It goes some way to explaining why Jon Peters had so much trouble trying to inject some genuine antagonism into the meetings between Batman and the Joker: they're like two presidential candidates who have somehow slipped their entourages, and accidentally meet, away from the spit and fury of the hustings, only to find themselves getting along fine. There's nothing between them personally. It's all for the folks back home.

The one thing you don't see much of in *Batman,* though, is folk. For all the energy that Batman and the Joker expend to win the hearts and minds of Gotham, it's a strangely underpopulated place: at a press conference in front of the town hall, a gaggle of extras do their best to suggest a pullulating crowd, but Burton's heart is not really in it—he doesn't have the bullying instinct for crowd scenes. He can't summon the demagogic charge that you catch off all the great popular film directors—Capra, a great rouser of rabbles, or Hitchcock, never happier than when losing his heroes in a sea of faces. Nothing signaled Steven Spielberg's entry into their hallowed company better than the crowd scenes in *Jaws,* with their ebb and flow of push and panic; there's even a nun in there, just to remind us that this is the seventies. The thrill of the crowd pushes straight past Burton, who much prefers the sequestered darkness of the batcave or the lonely eyrie of *Batman*'s perch atop a skyscraper—he is one of cinema's natural loners, like Nicholas Ray. But he is no action director, and everything in *Batman*—its stop-start pace, its damp squibs of dark wit, its hero's entrapment within a costume that gives him all the mobility of a neck brace—suggests sulky self-sabotage on its director's part: revenge on a hero he just didn't get. There's not much to get, but you do need an honest instinct for hero worship to shoot a comic book, and Burton's temperament is naturally mock-heroic; he can't fake the tones—the athletic heft, the blockbuster high style—needed to sweep a movie like this along. Despite what he thought, "*Death Wish* in a batsuit" is almost exactly what it should have been. Reading the rewrites ordered up by Peters, it's not to hard to figure out what was going on: the producers were using the Joker to smuggle back into the movie all the showmanship they felt their recalcitrant director was refusing to provide, and the movie belongs, in the end, to them. "Have fun, 'cause the party's on me!" shouts Nicholson at the end, a version of Peters's own high-rolling largesse, distributing cash to the greedy Gothamites, in what amounts to the movie's last word on the delicate art of winning public favor: we can be bought.

□ □ □

Peters and Guber were right—up to a point. The summer *Batman* opened was one of the blockbuster's landmark summers, just as 1984 had been before it, and whose records it casually smashed. "There's a point beyond which no one can project," said one box office analyst. "Anticipation is so high, the question this summer seems to be, how high is high?" The anticipation was guaranteed, however, if for no other reason than that 1989 saw the tidal wave of sequels set loose on the mid-eighties finally engulf moviehouses—*Lethal Weapon 2, Ghostbusters II, The Karate Kid, Part III, A Nightmare on Elm Street 5: The Dream Child, Star Trek V: The Final Frontier, Friday the 13th Part VIII: Jason Takes Manhattan, The Return of the Musketeers, Eddie and the Cruisers II: Eddie Lives!, Indiana Jones and the Temple of Doom, Police Academy 6: City Under Siege, The Fly II,* and *Back to the Future Part II.* "We're thinking of calling it *The Abyss II*," said Fox's Tom Sherak, entrusted with the task of promoting one of the season's few non-sequels, James Cameron's *The Abyss.* If for nothing else, 1989 deserves a place in the history books as the year in which the fewest people had an original idea for a movie than at any other time in Hollywood's history.

What this meant for moviegoers was an equally dense barrage of promotional campaigns, all vying for their attention. That year, the discerning moviegoer could choose between entering the James Bond *License to Thrill* sweepstakes to win a weekend getaway to Key West, the Indiana Jones Pepsi-Cola sweepstakes, and a *Honey, I Shrunk the Kids* McDonald's promotion. You could win a trip to Tasmania courtesy of *Young Einstein*, you could follow the *Great Balls of Fire!* publicity junket to Memphis. You could trot along to the Hollywood Palladium to listen to Run DMC sing the *Ghostbusters* theme, and try and win yourself the Ectomobile, all the while chewing on your Slimer Bubble Gum. Or you could go for a replica of the Batmobile, courtesy of a promotion on MTV, and jig around to "Batdance" by Prince—"an ode of the movie," as he called it, which is rock-star-speak for "they only used thirty seconds of one of my songs in their lousy movie but you might as well have them anyway."

Alternatively, you could always go see a movie. Or *the* movie, for

WEEK	1	2	3	4	5	6	7	8	9	10
E.T.	$22m	22	26	24	23	23	19	19	16	15
Batman	$70m	52	30	24	18	13	11	8	5	4

Batman soon became the blockbuster to see, unless you wished to announce your recent decision to join an order of Trappist monks. It opened in 2,194 theaters and took in $42.7 million its first weekend, "the biggest opening weekend in history," proclaimed Warner Brothers, and proceeded to take in $100 million in under ten days—another record, breaking Hollywood's four-minute mile. But it also slid from pole position faster than any movie that has ever made that much money, too, taking just $30 million in its second weekend, a drop of about 25 percent, and the weekend after that, $19 million, a drop of 36 percent. Blockbusters never used to fade like this—*E.T.* had stayed at the top for ten weeks (see graph), and increased its grosses as it went along, while *Back to the Future* had stayed up there for thirteen. But *Batman* came and went in the blink of an eye—that year, even *Look Who's Talking* had greater staying power at the number one spot. The most popular movie of all time was also just the flavor of the month. Far more so than *Jaws*, it marked the beginning of the long, slow erosion of audience word of mouth—asked how much influence he thought the negative reviews in *Variety* and *Time* would have, Peters responded, "None"—and with it, a crucial shortening of the audience's reaction time, which is to say our ability to respond to a movie, and then signal our collective approval or dislike by either staying away, or flocking to it in greater numbers. Who could tell, looking at *Batman*'s grosses, and their tail-off, to what degree people had enjoyed the film or not? "The audience can smell it faster than we can sell it," Spielberg had said of *E.T.*'s release. As of 1989, we had just a little less time in which to do so. The art of selling bats had caught up with the art of smelling rats.

Batman was the movie Hollywood had been waiting for. Up until this point, the studio executives had not been under the illusion that they could manufacture these things themselves. They could, in Sid Sheinberg's phrase, seek to put lightning in a bottle, but as that phrase revealed, they saw themselves as being in the bottling business, not the lightning business. For the lightning, they still had to wait on the talent—those erratic creatures, the writers and directors. *Batman* was different. Peters and Guber had pulled together a great-looking package, sprinkled it with stars and synergistic tinsel dust, picked the wrong director, ridden roughshod over him, made an okay movie, and then bulldozed their way into public consciousness for long enough to make it, briefly, the fastest grossing movie ever. *That* got the studio's interest, for that, they knew a little bit more about. That, they knew how to do. The signal it sent out was as clear as the batsignal above Gotham City: if you build it, they will come.

TIME LINE

1989

1. *Batman* (WB) $251,188,924
2. *Indiana Jones and the Last Crusade* (Paramount) $197,171,806
3. *Lethal Weapon 2* (WB) $147,253,986
4. *Look Who's Talking* (TriStar) $140,088,813
5. *Honey, I Shrunk the Kids* (Disney) $130,724,172
6. *Back to the Future Part II* (Universal) $118,450,002
7. *Ghostbusters II* (Sony) $112,494,738
8. *Driving Miss Daisy* (WB) $106,593,296
9. *Parenthood* (Universal) $100,047,830
10. *Dead Poets Society* (Disney) $95,860,116

*Figures show U.S. domestic gross

CHAPTER 11

EXTINCTION

"Most actors take themselves too seriously. I don't take any of this too seriously. The trick is to have a sense of humor—not to take it too seriously. That's what it's all about, a sense of humor."

—Arnold Schwarzenegger on the set of *Last Action Hero,* 1993

On holiday in Hawaii in the Christmas of 1990, Jeffrey Katzenberg sat down and wrote himself a letter. Running to twenty-eight pages, and some 11,000 words, it was entitled "The World Is Changing; Some Thoughts on Our Business," and in it, the Disney executive pondered the ills facing Hollywood as it entered the nineties. "It seems that, like lemmings, we are all racing faster and faster into the sea, each of us trying to outrun and outspend and out-earn the other in a mad sprint toward the mirage of the next block-buster," he wrote. "Not surprisingly this box office mania is fostering a frenzy among actors, writers, directors, and their agents." Star salaries had risen to astronomical heights, he noted, during a year that "should have demolished once and for all" the notion that such stars can guar-antee big box office. "How can one explain what happened to the 1990s vehicle for 1989's 'most bankable star,' Jack Nicholson, to say nothing of the heralded return to the screen of Robert Redford?" he said, referring to Nicholson's *The Two Jakes* and Redford's *Havana.* He also took pot shots at Warren Beatty's *Bugsy,* a production Disney had had the sense to turn down, as should everyone, he said, when offered "a big period action film, costing $40 million. . . . We must hear what they have to say, allow ourselves to get very excited . . . then slap ourselves a few times, throw cold water on our faces and soberly conclude that it's not a project we should choose to get involved in." Perhaps sensing that any reasonable reader, particularly a Disney employee, might point out that Katzenberg had just come off just such a big, period, Warren Beatty action film—*Dick Tracy*—Katzenberg conceded, with timely candor, that *Dick Tracy* "made demands on our time, talent and treasury that, upon reflection, may not have been worth it." He concluded, "The time has come to get back to our roots. If we remain on our current course, there will be the certainty of calamitous failure. . . . We should now take a long and hard look at the blockbuster business, and get out of it."

Hollywood is an apocalyptic town. Situated on the westernmost coast of America, fringed by desert and wracked by earthquakes, its denizens have often imagined themselves as part of some fiercesome drama, preferably directed by Cecil B. DeMille, in which the honest God-fearing folk of Los Angeles are swept into the sea on a tidal wave of runaway budgets, ballooning scripts, and other such unnatural disasters. Katzenberg's memo joined a long and illustrious tradition of panicky memos that stretch as far back as Darryl Zanuck's to Fox top brass in 1946 about the rising budgets ("the most alarming report I have read at any time in the twenty years I have been producing pictures") and David Selznick's about the cost of *Gone With the Wind* in 1938 ("we have simply got to do something about the Cukor situation"). More recently, people had been predicting Hollywood's death-by-blockbuster for years; Katzenberg's boss at Disney, Michael Eisner, had pulled off a similar bit of hedge betting back in 1980, with an internal memo at Paramount, in which he warned, "The intoxication of a blockbuster hit can lead to an easy sense that the luck will keep striking . . . success tends to make you forget what made you successful, and just when you least expect it, the big errors shift the game."

Katzenberg's memo was an instant classic of the genre: couched in its own brand of woolly seminar room blather ("we must not be afraid to say we love what we do"), it was strictly confidential, so naturally it appeared in *Variety* one week later, under the headline "Thoughts of Chairman Jeff," where it had soon inspired a parody from a disgrun-

tled Disney employee ("This is why we should be aggressive on all
fronts—at the dining table with major stars . . . at the back door of the
Betty Ford Clinic, with a pen and contract in hand"). Crucially,
Katzenberg had pulled off the one trick to these things, which is to give
voice to opinions so vague that few people could disagree with them,
and assent to which therefore costs you nothing. It was Jerry Maguire's
memo in reverse—The Thing We All Say But Don't Really Think—too
platitudinous to be even hypocritical, and it was greeted with a receptive round of noncommittal murmuring and head nodding amongst
Hollywood's top brass. Nineteen ninety had been a terrible year, with
every one of the majors emerging from the summer with at least one
big cash-hemorrhaging blockbuster to its name—Warner Brothers
with *The Bonfire of the Vanities,* Universal with *Havana,* Disney with
Dick Tracy, Paramount with *The Two Jakes* and *Days of Thunder. Thunder* was the first film Bruckheimer and Simpson had to show for their
new $300 million deal with Paramount, but it had been sucked into
existence too soon, by a gap in the studio's summer schedule; according to one executive, "We knew the script wasn't ready, but we needed
a movie for Memorial Day. We needed to work off this tremendous
overhead we were paying Don and Jerry. We had a window on Tom
Cruise. Suddenly we all felt more fondly about the script." *Top Gun* had
cost $19 million: *Thunder* cost $70 million, and as it neared completion, Don Simpson sent off a fax to Katzenberg, which read, "You can't
escape the Thunder!" Katzenberg, then $47 million into *Dick Tracy,*
with an added $54.7 million going on marketing, faxed him back: "You
won't believe how big my dick is!" Perhaps Katzenberg was right.
Maybe it was time for Disney to get back to its roots after all.

As all of these behemoths floundered, the summer of 1990 instead
belonged to *Pretty Woman* and *Ghost.* For just a moment, another
audience other than teenage boys opened up, another future unfurled
before everyone, and together with Katzenberg's memo, a kind of con-
sensus was forged. Action blockbusters were out; romantic comedies
about hookers with hearts were in. "More and more projects don't add
up for us," said Frank Price at Columbia, before announcing a 1991
production slate heavy on romantic comedies: "There's no more
important bond than the one between men and women," he suggested.
Over at Paramount, Frank Mancuso agreed: "Everyone's been looking

for a bigger piece of the pie, but the pie has stopped growing," he said, before cutting the number of films in development by half and dropping their production deal with Bruckheimer and Simpson: the kings of high concept were out in the cold. The nineties thus began much as the eighties had: with a hangover, and a firm list of New Year's resolutions, as executives all over town promised to kick the blockbuster habit and join Katzenberg in his vow of abstinence.

It lasted as long as most New Year's resolutions. It was several months—at *least*—before Disney had picked Bruckheimer and Simpson off the floor and given them a new deal ("I know that 'conventional wisdom' holds that they can only make giant big-budget movies," insisted Katzenberg. "As usual, the conventional wisdom is wrong"). Over at Universal and Columbia, meanwhile, the party was just about to get started all over again, thanks to a wave of foreign cash, from the Japanese electronics giant, Sony, which had just bought Columbia for the staggering sum of $3.4 billion, and installed dynamic duo Jon Peters and Peter Guber at the top, buying them out of their contract at Warner Brothers for a further $500 million. *Vanity Fair* called it "Pearl Harbor Revenged." Newly ensconced in the Thalberg Building, Peters and Guber embarked on a spending odyssey so great that it "distorted the economic balance of the entire business," according to one Merrill Lynch analyst. They bought themselves a fleet of corporate jets; commissioned *Batman* designer Anton Furst to redesign the Columbia lot in Art Modern style, and refurbished the Thalberg Building to the tune of $100 million, installing state-of-the-art electronics and sound systems, and even buying their own florist shop so executives could have fresh flowers delivered to their offices every day. Guber's wife, Lynda, was given an office and lucrative production deal; as was Peters's ex-wife, Kristine; even his son's girlfriend found her way onto the payroll. Their offices became known in the company as the Hall of Shame. "There are the pharaohs and there are the citizens," noted one employee. Above all, they started hiring executives, luring them away from other studios with six-to-seven-figure salaries: from Warner Brothers Mark Canton—who had helped the producers squire *Batman* to the screen, from Paramount Sid Ganis, who had worked on the *Star Wars* trilogy and *Raiders* films, to head Columbia's marketing department; and from Orion Mike Medavoy, who had bankrolled the original *Terminator.*

They hired so many executives that outsiders started calling the studio "the elephant's graveyard." An inverted pyramid, top-heavy with suits, Sony began to take on the nature of a controlled experiment designed to see how far a film studio's staff could get from the actual process of making movies, and still make movies. It was like the glory days of Paramount in the early eighties—only in negative, without the hits. Still reeling from the $50 million *Hook* and the $40 million *Bugsy,* Sony started buying up scripts left, right, and center, spending $750,000 on a script called *Fire Down Below,* $1.2 million on a script called *Radio Flyer,* and another $30 million developing it. Neither ever saw the light of day. "We were all working behind period antique desks, walking on teak wood floors, and smelling freshly cut flowers every day," noted Medavoy. "The process started to go haywire when Guber started soliciting each department's opinion on every film and then throwing that into the mixture. Guber couldn't make decisions on his own and wanted some plausible deniability if a film didn't work. He would ask the domestic distribution, foreign distribution, marketing, and even home video departments what they thought of the various scripts. I considered the strategy to be lethal . . . it's impossible to argue with a committee."

If Guber was hyperkinetic, then Mark Canton—his new head of production—was "Guber on steroids," said Medavoy. "He was constantly backslapping someone or dropping names of stars he had wined and dined the previous night. 'You see that hat?' he once asked me when I walked into his office. Jack Nicholson gave it to me.'" Katzenberg's austerity memo got short shrift from the executive. "We used to say, 'We want it, no matter how much it costs,'" Canton told reporters. "Now we've adopted the mantra of all well-run businesses: 'We want it, but only if the price is right, or if Arnold is in it.'"

Schwarzenegger had been the only star to emerge from the 1990 bloodbath with his reputation intact—*Total Recall* had grossed $261.4 million worldwide—and Canton was desperate to work with the star, seeing him as the key to any future film franchise. In the summer of 1991 thought he had found just the vehicle in the shape of a script

called *Extremely Violent.* Written by two neophyte writers, Adam Leff
and Zak Penn, the script was a parody of the kind of big loud action
movies that had shaken everyone's fillings loose during the eighties.
Two friends from Wesleyan University, Penn and Leff had rented every
video they could find—all the *Lethal Weapons*, all the *Die Hards*—and
then sat down and asked themselves all the crucial questions. "When
does the second most bad guy get killed?" "Does the hero have a Vietnam buddy?" "What holiday is the film taking place on?" They knew
exactly who they wanted for their hero, and tailored the script to the
talents of Schwarzenegger. "We wanted the movie to have a really
overblown superhero," they said, "as big and ridiculous as possible."

Canton optioned the script for $350,000 and sent it to the star's
agent, Lou Pitt, for him to read over Christmas. To his delight, Pitt
called back, "Come to lunch. Arnold is interested."

Columbia went to DEFCON 1. "When you're dealing with Arnold
Schwarzenegger, you go into a high stage of alert," said one executive.
"You can't let anything fall between the cracks." The squad of executives, headed by Guber and Canton, made their way to Schwarzenegger's favorite restaurant, the Schatzi in Santa Monica, where James
Cameron had first met the star and signed him up for *The Terminator.*
Schwarzenegger had ten different scripts he was trying to choose between—including something called *Sweet Tooth,* about the tooth
fairy—and told Guber he would only choose his film on certain conditions. He wanted $15 million plus complete power of veto over every
aspect of the production, from choice of director down to the marketing of the film.

They agreed to everything and screenwriter Shane Black was called
to do a $1 million rewrite on the script, which centered on a young boy
who was sucked into the movie screen, where he meets his favorite
action hero, Jack Slater, before plucking him back into the real world—
a sort of *Purple Rose of Cairo* for the *Die Hard* set, it was sweet-natured,
magical, and a little . . . toothless. Columbia wanted a PG-13 movie,
but Black was determined to push the envelope a bit. Beefing up the
violence, he introduced a satanic villain, and walls that dripped blood.
It was this version of the script—now titled *Last Action Hero*—that
secured director John McTiernan. "Shane had done enough service in

the salt mines of action movies to ridicule them in an acid way," said McTiernan. "The script had so much venom that I loved it."

McTiernan rang up Schwarzenegger, who was on the point of committing to *Sweet Tooth*, and told him to hold up: "This thing is great, you have to read it."

Schwarzenegger wasn't happy. He loved the pace and the action, but felt the script lacked any elements of "bonding between this kid and his hero." Having just come off *Terminator 2*, in which he had starred opposite a teenage boy, he was convinced that this was the way forward for his career—one of the more bizarre hippo-in-a-tutu reinventions since Garbo decided to laugh. "While it was okay for the Arnold of the eighties to kill 275 people onscreen, it is not for the Arnold of the nineties," he said, and set his mind on veteran screenwriter William Goldman, who had just scored a feel-good hit with *The Princess Bride*. It was Goldman, he told Canton, or the deal was off.

At first Goldman refused, saying the script was too bloody, but after a three-way conference call between him, Schwarzenegger, and Canton, the writer agreed. For $750,000, he would fashion a suitable vehicle for the Arnold of the nineties. He eliminated the bloody walls, rewrote the satanic projectionist as a kindly old man, promoted the secondary villain, and made the boy eleven instead of fifteen. McTiernan was delighted: "Goldman gave Arnold a character to play, and he excised 150 toilet jokes."

Arnold, however, *still* wasn't happy. Now the script was too soft, and so more writers were brought in; the final tally of writers who worked on the script eventually numbered eight, by which time Schwarzenegger finally committed, but to what exactly? It was less a script than it was a script-shaped hole, into which everyone projected their ideas for what that script should eventually be, all at magnificently crossed purposes. They "were making a deal and not a movie," said McTiernan. "They had sold it to themselves and to each other by making it as vague as possible about what they were really doing. It was all things to every different person. Then when it began to become specific you'd have people charging in different directions saying, 'No, we're doing this, now, we're doing that.'" Canton saw an Arnie movie; Schwarzenegger saw a "kinder, gentler" Arnie movie; McTiernan saw an Arnie movie parody. Sony's new marketing chief, Sid Ganis, didn't know what to call it. "There's no genre for this movie," he told reporters. "It only looks like an action movie. It's about an action movie star. I think it's more—what it is, it's it's, uh, it's fantasy."

Sony simply saw its first major blockbuster—a film that would announce their entry into the big league of studio heavyweights—and in August of 1992, a team of seventy executives met in a "war room" under the Thalberg Building, on Sony's Culver City lot, to discuss the film's $20 million media package. Canton got up and talked about tie-ins with Sony Music, Sony Electronic publishing, Mattel, MTV, Reebok, and Burger King. Sid Ganis talked about the $25 million promotion of the film, which would declare it the "ticket of '93," in preparation for its release on June 18. Finally Schwarzenegger mounted the podium, cigar in hand, and announced, "I want to be involved with every single facet of this film from start to finish. I'm behind you. I'm accessible to each and every person in this room."

"He got everybody so pumped up," said one observer. "It's what Arnold does best." As Schwarzenegger spoke, however, production commenced in Hawaii on a movie that would prove to be *Last Action Hero*'s downfall: *Jurassic Park*, Steven Spielberg's adaptation of the best-selling Michael Crichton dinosaur novel for Universal, also owned by a Japanese electronics firm, Matsushita, and scheduled for release on June 11 of 1993. Canton, however, refused to budge. It would be a battle of the blockbusters—a multimillion-dollar version of chicken, from which the Sony team would not be the first to flinch. "The summer of '93 will make or break me," declared Canton. "This is the big one, this is the best thing I've ever done." A fellow executive dryly noted that he'd said that once before, about *Bonfire of the Vanities*.

"Once you have a release date for a big picture, the momentum is like a tsunami. It takes a real act of derring-do to step in front of it and say stop," says Guber, whose Big Mo was about to reveal its dark underside. "It's got so much momentum—the toys are being sold, the videos are being sold, the marketing machine, everything starts to work. It's so hard to hold your hand up and say, 'Whoa whoa whoa, the script ain't right yet. Or the actor passed. This one isn't as good,' or, 'Wait a minute there's a problem with this director.' It's very, very, very hard to stop it. Once it gets going, you're throwing yourself in front of a moving train and it'll run you over. They'll consume you. They become a self-fulfilling prophecy. What's up on the screen is not the toys. It's not the soundtrack. It's not the video sales. It's the script and its interpretation by the filmmaker. And if that's six degrees off at launch then a year and a half down the line when the film's all put together, it's five thousand miles off track. You have to make sure it's on the page before it's on the stage." In the case of *Last Action Hero,* the rocket was literal: the centerpiece of the film's publicity campaign would be a giant $50,000 billboard for the film plastered onto the side of an unmanned NASA rocket, due for launch in June. Schwarzenegger was delighted with the idea. "I like the idea of every month the movie comes out, to put a new spin on it. To have the rocket out there, then the ride simulator. It makes it look like we are dealing here with a monster movie, a giant monster. And then we will announce the Burger King tie-in."

If anyone involved in *Last Action Hero* harbored any doubts about the production, they lost them in contemplation of their star, a promotional dynamo, reeling off interview after interview in which he warmed to his new theme, proudly displaying his new inability to take himself at all seriously. "Most actors take themselves too seriously. I don't take any of this too seriously. The trick is to have a sense of humor—not to take it too seriously. That's what it's all about, a sense of humor," he told a reporter from *The New York Times,* while two journalists from *Premiere* bore firsthand witness to Schwarzenegger's booming largesse. "Acting as a producer for the first time in his career, Schwarzenegger operated like a field marshal out of his forty-foot trailer on the Sony lot," they later wrote. "Equipped with a special telephone that allowed him to punch directly into offices in the Thalberg Building, he would summon executives—who would immediately be seen streaking out of their offices and tearing across the lot to Camp Arnold." A prototype for an Arnie action figure, complete with flamethrowers and missile launchers, was dismissed and disarmed after Schwarzenegger passed judgment: "That was okay for the Arnold of the eighties, but not the Arnold of the nineties." On another occasion, he summoned Sony's head of marketing to discuss the film's posters. "My hair isn't flying," he complained. "No matter how much hairspray you have, with wind in the hair, it should fly all over the place." The posters were redrawn to Schwarzenegger's specifications—"from a totally static look to something that represents what the film is saying, which is . . . bang!"

Schwarzenegger's bombastic levity seemed to permeate every corner of the production. "He creates an extraordinary atmosphere on set, because everybody in the film industry is rampant with insecurity and paranoia," noted his co-star Charles Dance. "Everybody's nauseatingly nice to each other for fear of the next job. But the more I worked, the more I realized the good atmosphere actually came from Arnold." One evening, the star stopped by Dance's trailer, to expound on his connection with audiences. "You see, Charles, you make your art films, but I make films for the Polyester People." At a test screening of the movie at Long Beach in May, however, the first cracks began to show. The numbers were terrible and the report cards even worse, with audiences finding specific fault with the gentler, kinder Arnold. "I don't want to see Arnold being dragged down to where he's helpless like that," said one girl. "He's standing there talking about the boy's father's death, and the rain—it's very upsetting." The Polyester People had bitten back.

Everyone—Canton, Guber, Schwarzenegger, Ganis, McTiernan—repaired for an emergency meeting at the Schatzi afterward. The possibility of changing the release date was raised and dismissed: they would lose $10 million a week for every week of summer lost, argued Canton. "I wasn't about to argue with those sorts of figures," said McTiernan; and so the report cards were shredded, the screening was hushed up, some reshoots were ordered, and the production hunkered down for a feverish post-production schedule of just ten weeks—almost half what it would normally have been—which saw the editors working eighteen-hour-days, six days a week, with a nervous Schwarzenegger hovering over their shoulders, ordering in food from the Schatzi and hiring a masseuse to relieve tired necks. The accelerated schedule forced the movie budget past its original $45 million, up to the $60 million mark and beyond, and the press began to circle: *Last Action Hero* giving off all the thrashing signals that usually indicate a production in distress.

The bombshell came on June 6, with a story in the *L.A. Times*, entitled, "PHANTOM SCREENING: YOU HAVEN'T HEARD THE LAST ABOUT *LAST ACTION HERO*," in which journalist Jeff Wells claimed to have uncovered the movie's disastrous test screening, except he placed it in Pasadena, not Long Beach, and the date was off by about a month. It was all Columbia needed; Wells had invented a screening that "demonstrably did not take place." A furious Sid Ganis rang up the *Times* to complain, and issued an extraordinary ultimatum: "Columbia Pictures will be out of business with the entire *Los Angeles Times* editorial staff as of noon on Monday, June 21, unless you guarantee that your paper will never again run a story written by Jeff Wells about (or even mentioning) this studio, its executives, or its movies." If the paper did not comply, then Columbia would ban all of its writers and editors from future screenings—an unprecedented fiat. No studio had ever declared war on a newspaper before, and especially not the *Los Angeles Times*.

"The goal was to create a blockbuster. Instead it was a debacle," says Ganis now. "And the reason was—it wasn't a bad movie. My son has watched it and he's told me: it's not a bad movie. What happened was we just handled it all wrong and I—the man who had done the *Star Wars* trilogy—I was the one who handled it. It was me who fucked it up. Instead of withholding, we strutted. So that the press all they could say to us was, 'oh yeah oh yeah' and they said it time and time again." When asked about the runaway budget, Guber shrugged it off with a bullish joke. "A modestly priced *Last Action Hero* would wind up being *The Last* starring Arnold Schwarz." When asked about the reshoots, Ganis's press office insisted, "Columbia does reshoots on practically all its pictures" and that the writing of additional dialogue was "customary during the post-production period." Even when the news broke that their NASA rocket would not be launched until several months after the film was released, they insisted it "still works nicely for our worldwide marketing plans." A NASA spokesman later revealed that it had "never even had the rocket on its launch docket on June 18."

"It's like Nixon in the last days of Watergate," said one Columbia employee of the atmosphere in the Thalberg Building; one producer refused to show up for work, because it was "just too poisonous."

Schwarzenegger was the last man standing, a promotional powerhouse to the end. At a dinner at the Hôtel du Cap in Cannes that summer—beneath a giant inflatable Arnie balloon—he announced that he had given more than eighty-two interviews in a day, and that he had honed his answers so efficiently that the average interview took under three minutes. "The movie is a ten," he told the KTLA morning news. "I think it will be spectacular."

"You seem to establish a connection with your fans," suggested his interviewer, gingerly.

"It's really the fans who lift you to this pedestal. . . . This is the best movie I've ever done."

The movie came out, and took in just $15 million in its first weekend. "We're very, very, very happy with it," declared Ganis. "We're heading for big numbers, I won't predict how big but we feel good." It then nosedived, dropping 47 percent to $8 million in its second week, as *Jurassic Park* devoured everything before it. "Arnold believes that one point represents $1 million over the opening weekend," said Mc-Tiernan. "He knew on Wednesday that it was all over." The critics moved in for the kill: here, finally, was the bomb to end all bombs, a blockbuster turkey worthy of the name, standing proud and ready for plucking. "It was supposed to be a movie within a movie," said the *Chicago Tribune*. "Turns out it's a movie without a movie." "A noisy monstrosity," wrote the *Hollywood Reporter*. "A joyless, soulless machine of a movie," said *Variety*, "enough to make you nostalgic for *Hudson Hawk*."

Needless to say, Sid Ganis's son was right. It wasn't that bad. It was just another boisterous, berserk action movie, no better than *Lethal Weapon 3* and no worse than *Die Hard 2*. Compared to the hubristic passion play that we had all been led to expect, what finally peeked out from behind the posters was an extremely meek and mild-mannered parody, directed more at the glossy world of TV than the movies—a sunlit land in which everyone smiles and no one gets wounded—and rising to only one moment of genuine po-mo brio, in which Arnie gives his version of Hamlet's "To be or not to be!" before detonating Elsinore—"Not to be . . ."—boom! So what happened? How had the film picked up a reputation just a few toxicity levels below brain cancer?

In his book about the making of *Heaven's Gate, Final Cut*, Steven Bach recounts the final unveiling of Michael Cimino's beleaguered epic to the public gaze in 1980: "No one saw it. They saw, instead of the movie on screen, the movie they had been told about by forests of newsprint, by cascades of critical condemnation . . . that 'unqualified disaster' they tried to discern through the lights and shadows of the truncated one before them. . . . They seemed to feel cheated somehow for it was, was . . . a movie. . . . The phenomenon reduced was, well, no phenomenon at all. It was just a western, and not so thrilling at that." Writing in 1982, Bach was on to one of the stranger paradoxes of the blockbuster era: even the failures are events. The press have always pounced on turkeys, of course, but the aura of anticipation surrounding *Heaven's Gate* was something else again, a force field of inverse glamour so great that it obscured the actual movie just as surely as any amount of studio hype. It was a species of anti-hype, in fact—a direct, antibody response to the amount of hoopla pumped into the public bloodstream by the studios—and containing a dire prophecy of what was to come. In an age of marketing overload, the plucking, basting, and roasting of turkeys would become something of a cathartic public ritual, somewhere between an exorcism and a witch hunt, with the press in the role of witchmaster general.

By 1986, America's two main news services—United Press International and Associated Press—had started transmitting weekly box office statistics; as did Cable News Network, on Monday nights; and *USA Today*, on Tuesday. The tracking of movie grosses had become one of America's favorite spectator sports. At first the studios had resisted the idea—who wanted their laundry washed in public?—but soon realized that it could be turned to their advantage, by advertising their films as the "Number One Hit Movie in America." "The media got into a contest over these big blockbusters, saying 'who's number one for the weekend?'" says Guber. "That had never happened before. So the pressure was on to get more screens, so you could be number one, and herald your picture your second week as the number one picture in America. Which didn't mean that it was the most profitable film—enjoying the best per-screen average, or the best return on investment. It was just a popularity contest: the most number of admissions. . . . It became an anathema to every executive that Friday night opening a blockbuster, you got sphincter arrest, waiting for the midnight results across the nation. It was like entering a war zone." War has always been a favored metaphor in Hollywood, although usually it is only used by directors, whose model is firmly Napoleonic: the general (the director) marshaled his infantry (his crew) and led them into battle (shot his movie), and emerged at the end, bloody and glorious. The fighting was just like the fighting in movies—valiant and prolonged. It was the Charge of the Light Brigade. But the battlefield that was Hollywood by the early nineties was as different from traditional warfare as the First World War had been from the Napoleonic Wars, and for much the same reason: Hollywood had, with the blockbuster, discovered its big guns, which had exactly the same effect as the invention of the machine gun and tank. The fighting became entrenched, prolonged, and bloodier, obeying more fitful stop-start rhythms, with months, sometimes years of preparation being settled in the space of a single weekend. The effect on the nerves was disastrous. During the Battle of the Somme in 1916, one Australian lieutenant wrote, "All day long the ground rocked and swayed backwards and forwards from the concussion . . . men were driven stark raving mad . . . any number of them could be seen crying and sobbing like children, their nerves completely gone . . . we were nearly all in a state of silliness and half dazed." It was one of the first documented instances of shell shock—a condition signaled by sudden attacks of amnesia, torpor, the shakes, and strange, off-center walks. "You never dreamed of such gaits," wrote one doctor, "the craziest, untext-book things . . . with the feet far apart, the arms out, the man balancing himself and making several attempts with his hind foot before taking a step."

It is the most humane and sympathetic hearing that *Last Action Hero* never got: the movie was exhibiting all the classic symptoms of clinical shell shock. The pressures of going over the top had cracked its nerves. In a way, it offered a far more telling insight into the behind-the-scenes fiasco that had been its making than any Hollywood satire ever could, its fluctuations of tone registering every rewrite and reshoot with gossamer delicacy, its lumbering gait an exact index of the inverted pyramid that was Sony's chain of command. It was moviemaking by committee in which the committee still hadn't called it a day: watch it today and they're still up there on the screen, haggling over plot points. Should Jack Slater be a figure of fun or not? It's still being decided. Is this movie aimed at adults or kids? We'll come back to you on that. Should that laugh be a scream, or vice versa? Call my agent in the morning. The movie didn't need releasing, still less reviewing, it needed love and attention, it needed rehab. It needed *finishing*.

In time, the reviewing of these beasts may acquire the taint of cruelty that attends the baiting of bears in the sixteenth century, or public mockery of the mad. But then the critics weren't really reviewing the movie. They were doing something far more modern; they were reviewing the hype for the movie—a much more satisfying and useful task. If *Batman* had shown that the critics' opinion of a film was about as noticeable as a gnat-bite to a hippo, then the role of the critic would have to change; it was only in the surrounding hoopla that they could find anything like the drama they craved but failed to get on the screen, and in the case of *Last Action Hero*, the drama came with a highly satisfying third-act comeuppance in the shape of Spielberg's dinosaurs—arriving at the final hour to redress the public's woes, like avenging angels. "Lizard Eats Arnie's Lunch," ran *Variety*'s headline, although in truth, it was no contest and never had been. On the one hand you had Schwarzenegger, ruled by the old Newtonian laws of mass and muscle; and on the other you had Spielberg's dinosaurs, devised by computers whose rules were as different again as Einstein's had been from Newton's—a world in which T. rexes could be whisked up to bone-shattering speeds with the flick of a mouse. The future would belong not to leviathans like Schwarzenegger but to the likes of Keanu Reeves and Will Smith: lean, springy types who could hold their own in this new world of cartoonish bend and bounce. In its way, *Jurassic Park* heralded a revolution in movies as profound as the coming of sound in 1927. Does anybody remember what movies were playing the week *The Jazz Singer* came out?

On the other hand, does anybody remember the *plot* of *The Jazz Singer?*

TIME LINE

1990

1. *Home Alone* (Fox) $533.8 (53.5%)
2. *Ghost* (Paramount) $517.6 (42.0%)
3. *Pretty Woman* (Disney) $438.2 (40.7%)
4. *Dances with Wolves* (Orion) $424.2 (43.4%)
5. *Total Recall* (Sony) $261.4 (45.7%)
6. *Back to the Future Part III* (Universal) $242.5 (35.7%)
7. *Die Hard 2* (Fox) $237.5 (49.4%)
8. *Presumed Innocent* (Paramount) $221.3 (39.0%)
9. *Kindergarten Cop* (Universal) $202.0 (45.3%)
10. *Teenage Mutant Ninja Turtles* (New Line) $201.7 (66.9%)

1991

1. *Terminator 2: Judgment Day* (Sony) $516.8 (39.6%)
2. *Robin Hood: Prince of Thieves* (WB) $390.5 (42.4%)
3. *Beauty and the Beast* (Disney) $352.9 (41.3%)
4. *Hook* (Sony) $300.9 (39.8%)
5. *The Silence of the Lambs* (Orion) $272.7 (47.9%)
6. *JFK* (WB) $205.4 (34.3%)
7. *The Addams Family* (Paramount) $191.5 (59.3%)
8. *Cape Fear* (Universal) $180.5 (42.8%)
9. *City Slickers* (Columbia) $179.0 (69.3%)
10. *Hot Shots!* (Fox) $175.1 (39.0%)

1992

1. *Aladdin* (Disney) $479.4 (45.3%)
2. *The Bodyguard* (WB) $410.9 (29.7%)
3. *Basic Instinct* (Sony) $352.7 (33.4%)
4. *Lethal Weapon 3* (WB) $319.7 (45.3%)
5. *Batman Returns* (WB) $282.8 (57.6%)
6. *Home Alone 2: Lost in New York* (Fox) $279.6 (62.1%)
7. *A Few Good Men* (Columbia) $236.6 (59.8%)
8. *Sister Act* (Disney) $231.6 (60.3%)
9. *Bram Stoker's Dracula* (Columbia) $192.5 (42.9%)
10. *Wayne's World* (Paramount) $183.1 (66.5%)

*Figures show worldwide gross, in millions of dollars, followed by the percentage of that generated in the U.S.

CHAPTER 12

PLANET HOLLYWOOD

"They note with delight GATT's roiling the French,
The folks who make teeth around the world clench.
The French claim our movies, TV and such,
Will put their own filmmakers in Dutch.
They clamor their culture's in peril, the French,
Terrified Spielberg will make them retrench.
Overshadowed by *Jaws* and *Terminator 2*,
How will Gérard get his Depardieu?"
    — *The New York Times,* 1993

"If you give them food it's relief.
If you leave the labels on it's imperialism."
    — *A Foreign Affair,* directed by Billy Wilder, 1948

have no embarrassment in saying that with *Jurassic* I was really just trying to make a good sequel to *Jaws*," said Spielberg. "On land." It was another best-selling thriller about another island, beset by another set of snapping jaws. It would, though, end up demonstrating all that had changed in the intervening years since *Jaws* was released. For one thing, Universal was now owned by the Japanese firm Matsushita. Like Sony, they were looking to the film as their first film franchise, to launch them into the nineties and give their global synergies a full body workout. For another, the audience had changed, comprising the children of those who had first queued up to see *Jaws*.

215

"Frankly I don't think that *Jaws* would do as well today as it did in 1975," Spielberg would say when *Jaws* was rereleased a few years later, "because people would not wait so long to see the shark. Or they'd say, there, too much time between the first attack and the second attack, which is too bad, we now have an audience that doesn't have patience with us. They've been taught, by people like me, to be impatient with people like me." *Jurassic Park* would mark the director's first major entanglement with these front-row raptors.

Most importantly of all, Spielberg himself had changed, for he was now fifty-seven, a father himself, with his eye on an altogether different prize: *Schindler's List,* which he would also direct for Universal, once he was done with his dinosaurs. Sid Sheinberg knew that this was the script that was burning its way through the director's mind. According to Spielberg, he had approached Sheinberg as early as 1991 with Steven Zaillian's latest draft in his hand and said, "'I have to act now, I have to make this film right now,' and Sid said, 'We just need *Jurassic Park* for the summer of '93, please make *Jurassic Park* first.' And so I agreed. I shot *Jurassic Park,* I cut the whole thing together, and then six weeks after the last shot of *Jurassic Park,* I was on an airplane heading for Poland. There was a huge overlap: *Schindler's List* and *Jurassic Park* were almost directed in the same breath."

The director had first come across Michael Crichton's novel in 1989, while developing with the author a movie about a Chicago emergency ward, which would eventually become the TV series *E.R.* Spielberg happened to ask him what he was working on next and Crichton told him about *Jurassic Park,* which was then being proofed by his publishers. "You know, I've had an obsession with dinosaurs all my life," Spielberg said. "I'd really love to read it." Crichton slipped him some galleys and Spielberg called back the next day, saying, "I'd like to make it."

"You mean you want to produce it or direct it?" asked Crichton.

"Both."

"I'll give it to you if you guarantee me that you'll direct the picture."

Despite their unwritten agreement, Crichton's agents had other ideas and instigated a bidding war. In May of 1990, CAA set a $2 million minimum on the book and circulated it to six studios and directors, including Warner Brothers, who wanted it for Tim Burton, Columbia, who wanted it for Richard Donner, and Fox, who wanted it for Joe Dante. After a fierce round of bidding Universal secured it for Spielberg, and Crichton set to work on his script—one of the conditions of the CAA deal.

Seven months later, he turned in a draft nobody was happy with. "Steven was really good about identifying what was wrong," said Crichton. "He said, 'The movie starts too fast.'" Spielberg's head was brimming with images: he spoke of snorting breath fogging a glass window; a giant foot squishing in mud; muscles moving under skin; a pupil constricting in bright light, about how to convey the weight, speed, menace of the dinosaurs, about their different characters, and about a Tyrannosaurus sprinting at sixty miles an hour, chasing a jeep. Screenwriter David Koepp was called in, and the first thing he did was throw out a lot of Crichton's characterization. "Whenever they started talking about their personal lives, you couldn't care less," he said. "You wanted them to shut up and go stand on a hill where you can see the dinosaurs. When we announced the sequel, I got this packet of letters from an elementary school class somewhere outside San Francisco, and one of the kids wrote that we should add a Stegosaurus and this and that, but whatever you do, please don't have a long, boring part at the beginning that has nothing to do with the island. In other words the premise of these movies is so exciting the usual cat-and-mouse game just doesn't work. The kid is only eight, but he's right, and I kept his letter on my desk. On my tombstone, it'll say my name, the years I lived, and then 'IT TOOK TOO LONG TO GET TO THE ISLAND.'" It was a telling difference of diagnosis from Spielberg—who thought the movie started too fast—and the first sign of a dilemma that would return to haunt the film.

Originally, the dinosaurs were to have been models and puppets. When the film had begun pre-production in the summer of 1991, the call was put in to the leaders in each field—Phil Tippett and Stan Winston. Working alongside them, more as an experiment than anything else, was Industrial Light & Magic's Dennis Muren, who was one of the pioneers of computer technology, if not its leading light, having delivered the world's first completely computer-generated character—a stained glass window knight, in *Young Sherlock Holmes* in 1985—and then provided James Cameron with a large water snake for *The Abyss* in 1989, and the T-1000 terminator for *Terminator 2* in 1991. Still, he "wasn't terribly thrilled about the idea" of re-creating sixty-foot dinosaurs: living, breathing creatures with rippling hides and wrinkling skin.

"I didn't have any clue if we could render skin and light correctly," says Muren. "Computers are good at replicating things over and over and over again, like word processing: copy and paste, copy and paste. It seemed like the stampede scene would be a good idea to try something. So we did a test of that and a test on a full-size Tyrannosaurus rex and those two tests we showed Steven and that changed the whole movie. That changed the whole deal." Among those present at the test screening were Muren, Spielberg, Phil Tippett, and George Lucas, who was crying when the lights came up. "It was like one of those moments in history, like the invention of the light bulb or the first telephone call," Lucas said. "A major gap had been crossed, and things were never going to be the same." Spielberg found himself consoling model-maker Tippett. "There we were watching our future unfolding on the TV screen, so authentic I couldn't believe my eyes. It blew my mind," says Spielberg. "I turned to Phil, and Phil looked at me and Phil said, 'I think I'm extinct.' I actually used Phil's line in the movie, gave it to Malcolm to say to Grant."

The normally sedate offices of Industrial Light & Magic erupted into a menagerie, as technicians pored over wildlife footage, filmed each other running around in the parking lot, and engaged in heated arguments about the average cruising speed of a T. rex. "We had a zillion arguments about it," said animator Steve Williams. "Some people argued that it was probably like a lion: it never ran unless it had to, and if it ran, it would do so for a very short period of time and move very fast. Using that logic, I had to throw physics out the window and create a T. rex that moved at sixty miles per hour, even though its hollow bones would have busted if it ran that fast." It made the T. rex look too lightweight. Williams ran it slower, which better honored the animal's mass, but this time it looked too slow and ponderous. It was the old dilemma—size versus speed—the two twinned, but opposing, forces that ruled the blockbuster from the beginning, and from which the dramas of *Jaws* and *Star Wars* had been fashioned, Death Star against

X-wing, *Orca* against Great White, but here brought into fresh conflict again on the computer screen.

Jurassic Park's lengthy pre-production—up to two years—gave Universal plenty of time to plan for its upcoming bonanza. The release strategy was planned fifteen months before the studio saw a frame of film—"in certain territories like Japan you have to book play dates sometimes a year and a half in advance," one marketing executive said. In August of 1992, just as *Jurassic Park* started live action shooting on the Hawaiian island of Kauai, Universal called together a series of key meetings between its executives and various licensing agents and promotional partners. The merchandising and marketing opportunities of Crichton's story were obvious—"Never before has the name and logo been a plot point in a movie to this extent," pointed out one executive. The *Jurassic Park* logo was also a perfect way for Spielberg to keep his dinosaurs from the public gaze, although McDonald's was at first taken aback by the thought of being denied access to the movie's stars. In October, they along with forty or so other promotional partners were invited to Universal Studios for a strategy meeting, during which they, not Universal, pitched for the right to be involved with the film. "McDonald's got up there and shared with the lunch box guy and the pajama guy their vision for what *Jurassic Park* was going to be," noted one observer. "It got to be a *Jurassic Park* lovefest." As the winning spirit caught fire, they nicknamed themselves the "Dinosaur Dream Team," comprising Kenner, who promised $6 to $8 million, Sega ($7 million), and finally McDonald's, who committed $12 million to a "Dino-size" meal promotion, thus rounding out the three must-have categories for any self-respecting film franchise: toys, fast food, and video games, a total package worth $28 million. In the end some 100 licensees would market 1,000 dinosaur products, with 10 percent of the retail price going to Spielberg's production company, Amblin, together with further flow of cash from Ford, who after a "casting call" of jeeps, won out over Crichton's original choice of Toyota Land Cruisers, because Spielberg wanted, in this instance at least, to buy American.

The irony was not lost on David Koepp. "It's a kick in the head that the fate of a Japanese company is, in part, hanging on a project written by the author of *Rising Sun*," he said, "which warned of the dangers of foreign investment in America. Even more ironic are *Jurassic*'s warnings about the greedy amusement park owners messing with nature by manufacturing *Jurassic Park* lunch boxes and the like. The same greedy merchandisers are making a truckload of money on our movie, I had to laugh as I typed out the dialogue. Who are the good guys here and who are the bad guys?" The film would prove the biggest grandstand yet for what David Denby called "corporate irony": the fact that films made by multinational corporations should so often be drawn to denunciations of corporate commerce. *Jurassic Park* would be the first movie to warn against the evils of theme parks that would itself be turned into a theme park—one that came complete with its own warnings about the hazards of hastily-completed theme parks. "You stood on the shoulders of geniuses to accomplish something as fast as you could, and before you knew what you had, you patented it, packaged it, slapped it on a plastic lunch box, and now you want to sell it," Dr. Malcolm tells Hammond, the park's creator in the movie. Spielberg, too, saw the irony, but only in muffled form, sensing elements of himself in Hammond, the Disney-like impresario. "In a way, *Jurassic Park* tells the story of any studio head, having a bad year, who needs a hit," said the director. "I mean Universal's not had a great couple of years and they're counting on this film. I've sort of jokingly said to the guys John Hammond is as anxious for *Jurassic Park* to work as you guys are."

On November 30, 1992, principal photography wrapped twelve days ahead of schedule and on budget—much like *Raiders of the Lost Ark*—and Spielberg immediately flew to Poland to start shooting *Schindler's List*, overseeing the editing and post-production of *Jurassic* via a satellite linkup to his house in Kraków. Even though he had reassured Sheinberg that *Jurassic Park* would receive his fullest attention, before *Schindler's List* called him away, Universal's executives were still not convinced, so Spielberg called up George Lucas "to kind of front for me—he promised that when I wasn't around, he would look in on my movie, thereby making Universal relax a bit." Spielberg and editor Michael Kahn would work on one movie during the day and in the evenings finish the other, beaming in the computer-generated dinosaurs from Industrial Light & Magic's facility in San Francisco. "The dinosaurs were just partial, we had to rhythm out the scenes without them," says Kahn. "Here we are starting to edit *Schindler's List* and what's coming back to us on a big monitor in the editing room are the first shots of dinosaurs and it blew us away: the first dinosaurs you see in the movie were the first ones that we saw, and if that hadn't've worked, nothing would have worked."

Jurassic Park thus did for Spielberg in the nineties roughly what *Raiders* had done for him back in 1981—it was a briskly shot, leanly budgeted pick-me-up, following a severe wobble, to get his confidence back up for greater things. Back in 1981, the wobble had been *1941,* the greater thing *E.T.* In 1993, the wobble was *Hook,* the greater thing *Schindler's List.* How much confidence do you need to make a movie like *Schindler's List?* Somewhere in the rough ballpark of $900 million, just slightly more than the gross national product of Mozambique. In one sense, *Jurassic Park* worked perfectly: it gave the world its dinosaurs. There they are, at the twenty-five-minute mark, standing in a field for all the world to see—"no quick cuts, no shaky cameras to hide things," as Dennis Muren told *ShoWest* in 1993. "It's right there for you to look at, in bright daylight, fifteen seconds of dinosaurs moving. It's just about perfect." The cast dutifully adopt their regulation-issue shock-and-awe expressions, although how it crept up on them, given that it is as large as a house, standing in a field so wide and open you expect to see people practicing their golf swings, is anyone's guess. On balance, Hawaii may not have been *the* best bit of casting to play a savage, primeval jungle.

In other words, this is Spielberg's "You-ain't-seen-nothing-yet" moment, and he fluffs it. Koepp's script had them walking in a forest, coming across a tree trunk, then three more, the trunks turning out to be legs—a much more Spielbergian alternative to the version Spielberg gives us, but then *Jurassic Park* feels weirdly off balance throughout, the rush to get to the dinosaurs throwing all of Spielberg's usual cat-and-mouse artistry off track. The first thirty minutes are among the worst of his work, and his beginnings are usually beauts: all debonair mystery and stealthy acceleration. *Jaws* begins with such fluently mounting dread that we are thirty minutes in before you realize that nobody has said the word "shark." We have seen a shark attack, and seen the words "shark attack" printed up on a police report, but nobody says the word until Dreyfuss enters the picture. The same for

Close Encounters, which goes forty minutes without anyone mentioning UFOs. In *Jurassic Park,* it is five minutes before people start in with the dino chat, and they never seem to let up: we get a lecture on their DNA, we get Richard Attenborough's guided tour of their park, we get a roundtable debate on the ethics of their cloning, before the film plonks us down in front of our first dinosaur at the twenty-five-minute mark. Spielberg recovers his manners in time to give his T. rex a proper introduction—at first, it's a no-show, like any self-respecting lion in a wildlife park, but then as night falls, so does the rain, and some of Spielberg's characteristic obliquity reasserts itself as he holds our attention with a rippling cup of water and swaying treetops. For twenty minutes or so, the picture finds its feet—there is some great business with a jeep—but it soon slackens and dies again, and after repeated viewings of the film, I have failed to locate anything resembling an ending. The kids have their runaround with the velociraptors, and you think—nice warm-up, and settle in for the payoff, only to find the cast floating off in a helicopter with smiles on their faces. *Finis.* Did the climax go looking for the beginning, wherever it was? The picture is all middle, like an anaconda caught mid-lunch.

The digestion problems are mostly Crichton's. He never did figure out what all the chaos theory was doing in his book—apart from facilitating the major plot development in which everybody sits down for a nice chat about chaos theory—and he has a remarkable tendency, in moments of high drama, to seek refuge behind the nearest computer screen. Here is a T. rex attack à la Crichton:

```
*/Jurassic Park Main modules /
*/
*/ Call Libs
Include: biostat.sys
Include: sysrom.vst
Include: net.sys
Include: pwr.mdl
*/
*/ Initialize
SetMain [42] 2002/9A {total CoreSysop %4 [vig. 7*tty]} if
ValidMeter (mH) (**mH).MeterVis return
```

```
Term Call 909 c'lev {void MeterVis $303] Random (3# *Max-
Fid) on SetSystem (!Dn) set shp_val.obj to lim(Val{d}SumVal
if SetMeter (mH) (**mH). ValdidMeter (Vdd) return
on SetSystem (!Telcom) set mxcpl.obj to lim (Val{pd})NextVal
```

I quote from memory. Did he fall asleep while writing it? *Some-one's* head hit the keyboard. Stranger still is Spielberg's unfathomable fidelity to it all—the computers, the chaos theory—all except Crichton's ending, which had the army arrive to blow the park to kingdom come, rather satisfyingly. Spielberg, by contrast, obeys a rule that would be followed by all the sequels, and refuses to let a single dinosaur suffer so much as a scratch by human hand—worthy instincts in an environmentalist, to be sure, but severely limiting if you are making a monster movie. The man who made *Jaws* couldn't have cared less about hurting the feelings of sharks, let alone those of best-selling authors. Back in 1975, Spielberg had gutted Peter Benchley's best-seller with suitable dispatch and then ran his audience through the mangler, with a young man's ruthlessness. He wasn't making a sequel to *Jaws* at all, of course. *Jurassic Park* was just as demographically spatch-cocked in its way as *Last Action Hero* between adult and child audiences: Spielberg wanted *Jaws* but he also wanted a movie capturing something of the wonder he felt for dinosaurs as a kid. He wanted his audience both running in fear, and casting admiring looks back over their shoulder as they ran.

This unseemly demographic tussle was a relatively new development: the man who made *E.T.* wouldn't have acknowledged the difference. He spoke with one voice, and it spoke to everyone, but since then Spielberg's cinematic voice had essentially broken, peeling off into the tentative bass of *The Color Purple* and *Empire of the Sun,* on the one hand, and the slightly strained falsetto of *Always* and *Hook,* on the other—and *Jurassic Park* has the same glottal catch in its throat. Its cheery endorsement of night-vision goggles ("Night-vision goggles: cool!") has a distinct touch of the disco-dancing uncle to it, and all the toys we see lining the shelves of the park—which critics fastened on as a sign of a sinister self-promotion—in fact testified to something far more melancholy: a final end to the time when the pop culture landscape into which Spielberg used to plug so enthusiastically could reasonably exclude his own stuff. He was caught in his own viewfinder; the youthful enthusiast of pop culture now its chief producer; the only guy in the toy shop, its shelves lined with his own toys, as far as the eye can see, and not a customer in sight. There is genuine, Midas-like desolation to the sight of Hammond spooning jelly into his mouth as his island kingdom crumbles around him.

Spielberg began his career with another such island, but that didn't stop the hordes of holiday-makers descending on Amity in a clamorous rush, filmed with great affection; he is a people's director, all right, and *Jurassic Park* is spookily devoid of them, boasting an entire population one minute, and nobody the next. So that's what's missing from the film: America—its people, its consumer clutter, its gabble, energy, rush. Which is one reason why, although it beat *E.T.*'s overseas box office record, taking $563 million, it never beat its domestic record of $399 million. For once, the records tell you something, for *E.T.* had felt like a secret shared by the entire nation, a "whisper" from Spielberg's childhood that everyone strained to hear. *Jurassic Park* let loose with a roar that carried the world over, for what did it matter that it strained to entertain, where *E.T.* did so effortlessly? Such strangulations of tone do not show up, once a film has been translated into Hindi. What did it matter that it felt so cut off from the American mainland? A bonus, in a way, as it circled the globe with 3,400 prints, buoyed by a $25 million marketing campaign. In Japan, where Spielberg's celebrity was so great that his face appeared on the film's posters alongside his dinosaurs, it was showing six times a day, starting at 7:00 A.M. In Argentina, it took in $2 million in two weeks, in Colombia $1.1 million, and in Brazil, $6.1 million in three weeks. In Russia, black-market bootlegs of the film—complete with accidental footage of the theater floor—were selling for 7,000 rubles within weeks of the movie's opening; while in Jerusalem, it caused controversy with its implicit endorsement of Darwinism—"Dinosaurs are symbols of heresy," pronounced Rabbi Zvi Gafner, "while our kosher certificate symbolizes faith." But by far the biggest uproar was to be heard in France, where Spielberg's dinosaurs charged into 450 theaters—a quarter of the country's 1,800 total—looming at French citizens from posters outside 279 McDonald's restaurants, and took in $9.5 million in five days, while *Germinal*—an adaptation of Emile Zola's novel about the nineteenth-century coal miners—snuck home with only $3.5 million. "They have arrived" proclaimed *Le Parisien Libéré.*

The film benefited from spectacular timing, arriving not just in time to smush *Germinal,* but also wandering straight into the middle of a row brewing over the GATT free trade agreement. Seven years in the making, covering some $4 trillion worth of international trade, and designed to allow 177 countries to trade freely, negotiations had come unstuck over the issue of American movies: should they be allowed into the agreement, thus ending French quotas designed to protect their film industry, or should they be regarded as a vital national resource, to be provided by each nation for itself? "What is at stake, therefore at risk, in the current negotiations, is the right of every country to create its own images," declared President François Mitterrand, while actor Gérard Depardieu warned, "European cinema is in danger of dying. My fight isn't anti-American, it's anti-industrial. The movie industry in the United States is like a war machine." The film director Bertrand Tavernier, meanwhile, took the battle to America's backyard with a stinging comparison: "We cannot allow the Americans to treat us the way they dealt with the redskins," he told the European Parliament in September—a metaphor continued by Jack Valenti, the tough-talking Texan who, as president of the MPAA, headed the American delegation to quash French resistance. The French were "stringing their trade bows tight, and the smell of export conquest is in their parliamentary nostrils," he argued in the *Los Angeles Times.* "There is a war going on at this very moment that could shatter your future."

It was the Battle of the Little Big Horn, with *Jurassic Park* wandering straight into the middle of it. French culture minister Jacques Toubon declared the movie "a threat to French national identity" and claimed that it was every Frenchman's "patriotic duty" to see *Germinal* instead; *Libération* called on Prime Minister Edouard Balladur "to confront, with renewed muscle, the yankosaurs who menace our country." As the GATT talks trundled on in Geneva, the row spilled over into that year's Venice Film Festival, where France's ex-culture minister, Jacques Lang, stood up to an audience including Robert Altman, Sydney Pollack, and Gus Van Sant, and launched into an impromptu denunciation of America's "commercial totalitarianism." It was, said the *New York Times,* "a cross between a Felliniesque circus and a bad day at the United Nations." A few weeks later, Spielberg issued a statement: "I am both puzzled and saddened by views publicly offered by some of my fellow artists in Europe whose work I admire [but with] whose support of quotas as restrictions I beg to differ. If artists demand freedom to create without constraints, we must also demand freedom to travel without restrictions. . . . We cannot lock our borders any more than we can close our minds." In *Variety* a week later, a reply surfaced in the form of a joint letter from directors Pedro Almodóvar, Bernardo Bertolucci, and Wim Wenders: "Dear Steven, We are only desperately defending the tiny margin of freedom [allotted] to us. We are trying to defend European cinema from complete annihilation. . . . There will be no European film industry left by the year 2000."

The French would win the GATT talks, for what it was worth: the status quo would be preserved, American movies were not to be included in the free trade agreement, but kept at bay with quotas. "It's not a victory of one country over another," declared Lang. "It is a victory of art and artists over the commercialization of culture." The ironies, though, were about as thick as the walls of the Bastille. France's unassailable sense of superiority as a cinematic nation went back to the sixties, when the New Wave had swept the likes of Godard and Truffaut to international fame. Denouncing the type of the heritage-industry filmmaking that had dominated French cinema until then, they had instead drunk deep of American movies, which rolled into French theaters when the French relaxed their quotas after the war. In other words, French cinema's moment of greatest glory came from the time when its borders were most porously receptive to American cinema, having lost the fight to guard their national treasures with imposed quotas. They had now fought that same battle again, in 1993, and won, but at a time when those treasures consisted of nothing greater than *Germinal*—precisely the sort of heritage filmmaking Godard had denounced. They were defending an empty castle.

Fears about American culture's global dominance are nothing new. In 1950, when producer Walter Wanger heard the number of prints of American films exported every year, he called them "120,000 American ambassadors," hailing a victory for "Donald Duck diplomacy" and calling Hollywood "a Marshall Plan for ideas . . . a veritable celluloid Athens," more important to America "than the H bomb."

When Clark Gable took off his shirt in *It Happened One Night* (1934), a deputation of Argentine businessmen protested to the U.S. embassy about the sudden drop in undershirt sales, and when Gable instructed an Italian boy how to eat a hamburger in *It Started in Naples* (1960), the scene sparked off an impassioned debate among Italian chefs about America's deleterious effect on Mediterranean cuisine.

At first sight, the modern blockbuster would seem easily the most effective intercontinental missile since the studios wheeled Clark Gable out to the launch pad. By 1992, the entertainment industry had become America's second largest export after aerospace—$3.7 billion—accounting for 85 percent of the total European market. In 1991, *Dances with Wolves* topped the charts in nine different countries, *Terminator 2* in six, closely followed by *Pretty Woman, Home Alone,* and *Total Recall,* but just how American was *Total Recall,* exactly? It may have looked a prototypical slab of big, dumb, American blockbuster, but it was directed by a Dutchman, starred an Austrian, financed with French money, and was distributed by a Japanese-owned studio. It barely touched American soil, in fact, before zipping off to its expectant international audience. By 1993 most of the Hollywood studios were owned, like Universal and Columbia, by international conglomerates. Many of Hollywood's hottest young directors—Paul Verhoeven, Renny Harlin, Jan de Bont, Roland Emmerich—were transplants, and by 1993, the year of *Jurassic Park,* Hollywood's total overseas profits had outstripped its domestic profits for the first time in its history—a vital tip of the seesaw, for it would be the foreign market that increasingly dictated to Hollywood what films it made. Even *Last Action Hero* would make back most of its money overseas, where it took in $71.2 million: when foreign critics complained about the gung ho belligerence of such All-American figures as Rocky, Rambo, or any of Schwarzenegger's various incarnations, they forget that they are essentially creatures of the overseas markets—Frankenstein's monsters whipped up by the international trade winds: a monosyllabic brute needs no subtitles. In fact, as the nineties progressed, the whole question of American cultural imperialism would get turned neatly on its head. Instead of asking how and when American films came to so dominate the rest of the world, American moviegoers were quite entitled to ask: how and when did the rest of the world hijack American movies? When did Hollywood get turned into the global jukebox—pumping out what Michael Eisner called "planetized entertainment"?

"*Jurassic Park* was a political hardball that was used as a symbol of the fattened American invasion, the second invasion of France, this time not to liberate but to occupy," says Spielberg now. "That was the party line on it, and I was caught up in the middle. The blockbuster began in America, so no matter who the writer and director and producers are of those films, even if it's an Italian director, and a French writer, and a British producer, if it makes a lot of money, almost too much money, it will be accused of being an American blockbuster. The world is shrinking. The Internet has shrunk it to half its original size. We are closer neighbors in cyberspace than we ever have been in our collective history." Whether this is a good thing is another matter. Artistry—even artistry of the multimillion-dollar blockbusting variety—is built on particulars not universals. Globalism is bunk: internationalism cheapens imaginations, cutting them off from the very thing that juiced them up in the first place. As Spielberg says, the blockbuster did begin in America; it was the quintessential American form, and was nursed into life by two quintessentially American artists, Lucas and Spielberg, who were preternaturally plugged into their homeland audience. This didn't stop their films from traveling; on the contrary, it helped them. A film like *Jaws* or *Star Wars* worked overseas for precisely the reason that it was not the sort of thing a foreign audience found in their own backyard. The fact that half the people who watched *Close Encounters* or *E.T.* had never been to a Goofy Golf course, or didn't celebrate Halloween with pumpkins, or didn't know their Slip 'n Slides from their Pet Rocks, didn't harm those films as they touched down in country after country. We still got it instantly. If anything, it only made them more fascinatingly foreign, more coolly exotic. Their Americanness was a plus.

When did the Americanness of American movies become a problem for the rest of the world? Ironically, it was at precisely the time when American movies had least claim on being American. "A new era in human history has begun," declared Time Warner when it merged in 1989, "the world is our audience"—an echo of the motto adorning George Lucas's THX Dolby system: "The world is listening." In truth, it was the world that was now speaking, and it was Hollywood's turn to listen, and to learn a new sort of cinematic esperanto—speaking all things to all men, but nothing to anyone in particular. The blockbuster *was* the Trojan horse the world had been fearing but it was pointed the opposite way, not out toward global domination, but inward, toward the Hollywood Hills. America had effectively trumped itself, devising a toy that was so alluring and lucrative that it could not hope to hang on to it for long. The blockbuster was now the world's plaything, and the world would play with it and play with it until it broke.

TIME LINE

1993

1. *Jurassic Park* (Universal) $920.1 (38.8%)
2. *Mrs. Doubtfire* (Fox) $423.2 (51.8%0
3. *The Fugitive* (WB) $368.9 (49.9%)
4. *Schindler's List* (Universal) $317.1 (30.3%)
5. *Indecent Proposal* (Paramount) $266.6 (40.0%)
6. *The Firm* (Paramount) $262.3 (60.4%)
7. *Cliffhanger* (Sony) $255.0 (32.9%)
8. *Sleepless in Seattle* (TriStar) $227.9 (55.6%)
9. *Philadelphia* (TriStar) $201.3 (38.4%)
10. *The Pelican Brief* (WB) $195.3 (51.6%)

1994

1. *The Lion King* (Disney) $766.9 (40.8%)
2. *Forrest Gump* (Paramount) $679.7 (48.5%)
3. *True Lies* (Fox) $365.3 (40.0%)
4. *The Flintstones* (Universal) $358.5 (36.4%)
5. *The Mask* (New Line) $320.9 (37.4%)
6. *Speed* (Fox) $283.2 (42.8%)
7. *Dumb and Dumber* (New Line) $246.2 (51.7%)
8. *Four Weddings and a Funeral* (Gramercy) $244.1 (21.6%)
9. *Interview with the Vampire* (WB) $221.3 (47.6%)
10. *Pulp Fiction* (Miramax) $212.9 (50.7%)

1995

1. *Die Hard: With a Vengeance* (Fox) $365.0 (27.4%)
2. *Toy Story* (Disney) $354.3 (54.1%)
3. *GoldenEye* (MGM) $351.3 (30.3%)
4. *Pocahontas* (Disney) $347.2 (40.8%)
5. *Batman Forever* (WB) $335.0 (54.9%)
6. *Apollo 13* (Universal) $334.1 (51.5%)
7. *Se7en* (New Line) $330.1 (30.3%)
8. *Casper* (Universal) $282.3 (35.5%)
9. *Jumanji* (Sony) $264.7 (37.9%)
10. *Waterworld* (Universal) $255.2 (34.6%)

*Figures show worldwide gross, in millions of dollars, followed by the percentage of that generated in the U.S. In 1992, five films—half of the top ten—made more money at home. In 1993, it was four. In 1994, it was two. By 1996, it would be just one: *Jerry Maguire,* thus proving that despite the growing internationalism of the market, some things—*Teenage Mutant Ninja Turtles, The Addams Family,* Tom Cruise's comic timing—just don't travel.

ACT III
1994–2004

DECLINE AND FALL

CHAPTER 13

OOPS, APOCALYPSE!

"We gotta get outta here!" "C'mon, c'mon!" "Let's go, c'mon!" "Ohmigod, ohmigod, ohmigod!"
—the cast of *Twister*

"Ohmigod, ohmigod, ohmigod!" "Let's go, c'mon, c'mon!"
—the cast of *Independence Day*

"Open fire!" "Cease fire!" "Move!" "Ohmigod!"
—the cast of *The Rock*

"**Y**ou want to blow up the White House?"

The executives at Fox were seated in a row on the sofa at the studio's Culver City headquarters, and were understandably worried. Just a few months earlier, Timothy McVeigh had parked a Ryder truck of explosives outside the Federal Building in Oklahoma City, killing 166 people; two months before that, an Egyptian cleric was found guilty of a plot to blow up the U.N. Building in New York and was also implicated in the 1993 bombing of the World Trade Center, which killed six people. And now, here was this lanky, excitable German film director with tufty hair and a big wide grin, who thought the public was ready to see the White House turned to match wood.

"Everyone is frustrated with politics right now," Roland Emmerich told the Fox executives. "They'll cheer it."

"Yes . . . but the *White House?*"

Emmerich's partner and producer, Dean Devlin, tried a different tack. "We would agree with you," he said, "if it were a terrorist doing it, but . . . it's space aliens." This would be, he said, an "up-and-at-'em feel-good war film," full of rah-rah patriotism, "like the ones that got made just after the Second World War, before Vietnam came along." With aliens, you could still have some of that fun back. Nobody cared about hurting the feelings of a bunch of Martians.

Emmerich and Devlin had their own reasons for wanting the shot: when they first wrote the movie, during a three-week brainstorming session in a rented house in Puerto Vallarta, Mexico, it had jumped out of them as a sure thing for the trailer. They knew about the paramount importance of marketing from their experience with their previous film—*Stargate*—which had been the sleeper hit of 1994, with no help from Warner Brothers, according to Devlin. "We had had a lot of prob-lems in the marketing of the film," he says. "Real disagreement. Be-cause the film had a different distributor in every country, some of them were able to do more of what we wanted and some of them weren't. It was frustrating, because every place where we liked the mar-keting, it did well, and where we didn't, it didn't."

This time around, they hadn't left it to chance: they'd made the marketing of the movie part of their deal. After finishing up in Mexico, they'd put the script out to the whole town, and waited for a bite. "It was a very exciting weekend," says Devlin. "We gave it to our agents on Wednesday, they sent it out to the studios by Thursday afternoon, by Thursday evening we had three offers, and by Friday every single stu-dio had made an offer. We spent the entire day on Friday meeting with each studio, and a bidding war began and we put into the bidding war the ad campaign that we wanted, so that not only did you have to buy the movie, you had to agree to sell the movie in the way that we wanted to sell it. We pitched them the idea of this teaser and at the end of the teaser the White House blows up. 'Earth take a good look—it could be your last.' We had the catch line 'The world ends July 4th.' We didn't want to have our best shot to have a bad campaign." The Fox team was so enthusiastic they wouldn't let them leave until they made a deal.

"Fox stepped up on every level. By Monday morning we were in pre-production."

Devlin and Emmerich were both first-generation blockbuster fans: suckled and weaned on the films of Spielberg and Lucas, with B-movie serum coursing through their veins. Emmerich had gone to film school in Munich in 1977, the year *Star Wars* came out: "I was blown away from the very first frame: you saw that small ship, and then the imperial cruiser kept getting bigger and bigger," he says. "For me German movies were boring and dull, and everything that came from the new Hollywood was cool." He didn't want to make movies in the tradition of Fassbinder and Wenders, featuring drifters or drug addicts, and set east of Stuttgart; he wanted to make movies about global exodus and intergalactic catastrophe. His 1981 graduation film, *The Noah's Ark Principle,* was the most expensive student film in German history, costing 900,000 marks—more than most feature films—and earned him the nickname Das Spielbergle aus Sindelfingen ("Little Spielberg from Sindelfingen"). "Roland was the only person in Germany making movies like that," says Volker Engel, a friend from film school who worked as a special effects technician on Emmerich's film *Moon 44.* "They were incredible."

Like many European filmmakers, Emmerich found his way to America by working up through the salt mines of the action movie, following in the backdraft of one of the muscle-bound European stars who made it big in the eighties, as Paul Verhoeven had done with Arnold Schwarzenegger. In his case it was Jean-Claude Van Damme and Dolph Lundgren, the stars of his first Hollywood movie, *Universal Soldier.* "I went to a video store and rented all their movies, which I shouldn't have done. I thought: 'We had to come up with a cool story because these guys can't act.' And so Dean and I conceived they both had to die, and then be reanimated as robots." Though a Jewish New Yorker, Devlin professed himself a "popcorn child of Hollywood": a sci-fi geek and webhead, whose brain positively fizzed with pop culture arcana, he had moved to Los Angeles to be an actor, and first met Emmerich on the set of *Moon 44;* he complained about the dialogue he'd been given, and ended up writing his own. They made an odd couple, the tall German and the New York Jew—Herman Munster meets Ferris Bueller—but the relationship worked, and it was while promoting their first film together, *Stargate*, that they came up with the idea for *Independence Day*. A member of the foreign press had asked Emmerich if he believed in aliens, and then expressed shock when he said he didn't. "Well, I don't believe in Santa Claus but he'd make a great movie," he replied. "What if we woke up tomorrow morning there were fifty-mile-wide spaceships hovering above the city; it'd be the most incredible, momentous day in the history of mankind . . ." He turned to Devlin. "Hey, I think I've got our next movie."

Devlin wasn't convinced. "Frankly I didn't want to do it," he says. "I thought there had been so many movies about aliens coming to earth, and Spielberg had done it better than anyone. I couldn't see what our movie was. He started to tell me the images he had in his mind and I started to get excited by the images but I still didn't have the movie." But as Emmerich started to tell him about the images in his head—"I'll make them so big they won't be flying saucers anymore, they'll be huge ships, as big as cities"—something clicked. This could be a disaster movie, thought Devlin, like all the old Irwin Allen flicks in the seventies. "Roland and I went, there's no way of doing this movie and pretending nobody's ever done this. We can't pretend that we're inventing this. Let's have some fun with it, otherwise we're just going to be trying to ignore film history," and so they toploaded it with references to *Close Encounters, The Towering Inferno, The Day the Earth Stood Still*. It would be a movie, said Emmerich, "for people who loved *Star Wars* and loved Spielberg movies and wanted these movies back."

They had a budget of $69 million from Fox—relatively modest in 1996—but they were determined to have a movie "that looked over a hundred million dollars." Emmerich put in a call to his old friend Volker Engel, in Germany, who put together a small group of German effects technicians who would be able to do the movie on the cheap. "I have to be careful here, against the Americans, but it's the German engineering factor: when we do something we do it right," says Engel. "I found out when we started working on *Independence Day*, I came to America and our production department seemed so grand: everyone seemed to know what they were doing. Yeah, right. What we encountered is that there is a lot of money but the money gets spent in the wrong directions. Because of the time pressures on these movies everything has to happen really fast and usually nobody really thinks what he's doing." With only fourteen months in which to complete production, Engel set up a relay system, farming out different effects to six different effects companies, each linked by a 270-foot motor home, which raced from house to house, ferrying explosions and aliens as it went. Fox was still trying to talk Emmerich and Devlin out of blowing up the White House, so they scheduled the shot early in the production schedule, and called up Joe "Boom Boom" Viskocil, the expert in miniature pyro who had blown up the Death Star.

Since then Viskocil had had a hand in almost every major conflagration in American movies, from the truck detonating at the end of *The Terminator,* to the global holocaust of *Terminator 2.* Viskocil had spent the best part of two decades pondering the fine art of mass destruction—how you got flames to plume outward at the right speed, or push the debris just ahead of it; how you elongate an explosion so it doesn't just go bang, but creates a staggered series of blasts to simulate a chain reaction. Viskocil didn't just blow stuff up: his explosions were mini-plots, leading you patiently from initial spark to final floating cinder. "One has to think: How would it really blow up? Is it a car? Is it a spaceship?" says Viskocil. "You have to think about the environment it's in, why it's happening, what the model is made out of, how big the model is, how big the charge should be."

"We gave him a room where for nothing but three and a half months he did nothing but shoot explosions," says Devlin. "He built up this library of fire and flame that was the most extensive ever created." For the film's pièce de résistance, he built a fifteen-foot-wide, five-foot-tall plaster model of the White House—complete with miniature furniture and potted plants—trained six cameras on it, and detonated it in one take. Devlin and Emmerich rushed the shot to the offices of Fox, to show off Viskocil's handiwork. "The first time they saw the shot they knew what the impact would be," says Emmerich.

"I have the feeling this is going to be a phenomenon," Tom Sherak, Fox's head of marketing, told them, "not a movie. A phenomenon."

"Tom, how can you say that, don't . . ." said Emmerich, knocking on wood.

"No, I feel it," replied Sherak.

Sherak had worked as a theatrical distributor before working for the studios, and knew the business backward. "I regard him as my guru in Hollywood," says Devlin. "He really taught me everything I know about how to deal with the studios." Ruddy and phlegmatic, Sherak was an old-school movie salesman, the type who would, you feel, have been equally happy selling soap, or aluminum siding, and he sported an air of happy flabbergast at the insane economics of the business he happened to find himself in. "The motion picture business has the shortest shelf life of any marketable product," he says. "You can spend $100 million to make a movie. You can spend another $35 million to market it, and you can be off the screen in seven to fourteen days. Think about those odds!" On the other hand, "There are more teens living in this country now than in the history of this country. It's driven by that, by how you get them in. By Memorial Day, a third of the state schools are out, and the entire South is out of school in the month of May. They go back to school on the 10th or 12th of August, so it starts in May now—it doesn't start in June. It's all about when the schools are out.

"You're looking to open your movie on a weekend when there isn't another movie going after your demographic," says Sherak. "You used to be able to find a free weekend once in a while, but you can't find it anymore because there are too many movies. The summer has started to cannibalize itself." Hence the importance of marketing, the average cost of which in 1996 was $20 million, up nearly 15 percent from the year before. "If we want to buy *Friends* it'll cost us $450,000 for a thirty-second spot," says Sherak. "We are a customer that needs something. The stations have it, and they charge a lot for it. You have to shout louder than the next guy." In 1975, the average cost of marketing a movie had been $2 million, but since *Jaws,* the dynamics of the summer had changed beyond all recognition. In 1975, summer moviegoing had accounted for roughly 32 percent of the year's business. By 1996, it was 60 percent, while the summer itself had expanded. In 1975, the big summer films rolled out in the weeks preceding July 4th, but in 1977 *Star Wars* had pushed it back to Memorial Day weekend. In 1996, it would begin even earlier, on May 10, when Warner Brothers was planning to bring out *Twister,* to give it a twelve-day window before the arrival of *Mission: Impossible* on May 22. Nineteen ninety-six was shaping up as another of *those* summers—like 1984 and 1989 before it—in which the seemingly crammed blockbuster season somehow found room for a few more movies. It was complete blockbuster gridlock, with forty-nine movies all jostling for pole position, and most of them costing somewhere upward of $100 million.

Fearing the competition, Fox originally wanted to open *Independence Day* on Memorial Day, and change the movie's title to *Doomsday*. "We fought this very hard," says Devlin. "And in fact the president's speech [in the movie] never said 'today we celebrate our Independence Day.' I literally ran onto the set that morning and added that line because we were in this fight with the studio over the release date, because I didn't want to lose that date. I wanted to put our flag in the sand and say don't come near us." The film would thus mark a curious landmark in the history of the July 4th movie: the first, *Jaws,* had been set during the July 4th weekend, but *Independence Day* was the first film to actually name itself after its own release date.

There was only one problem with this, pointed out Sherak: the Olympics, which started in September. He told Devlin and Emmerich: you've got a ten-week window in which to strut your stuff, and then you're going down. That was the competition: not another movie, still less another blockbuster movie, but the Olympics. Sherak went to town on the movie with "a campaign that P. T. Barnum would have been proud of," costing $24 million. In December he loosed his first scattering of trailers, following it up not with the normal billboards, but five black helicopters cruising up and down the California coastline with banners reading "No warning," then "No negotiation," then "No L.A."; and then in January paid $1.3 million to run the trailer during the Super Bowl. "The studio wanted to do something spectacular," says Devlin. "And they came to us and said 'what do you think about Super Bowl Sunday?' From that moment on, that became the standard. You had to have it out on the Super Bowl."

"We knew right away that we'd grabbed people," said Sherak. "Our phones were ringing off the hook, people were talking about it in restaurants. We accomplished what you always hope for—to hit everybody at once." It also helped open the money spigots for Devlin and Emmerich, who in early January had almost exhausted their budget—

having completed only 10 percent of the film's four hundred effects shots—and needed another $3 million. "If you wait until you screen it," Devlin told Fox. "It will cost about twenty times as much as it will cost now," but after Fox saw the rough cut they said, "What do you guys want?"

The movie finally came in for a shade under $75 million, and the filmmakers flew to New York for the movie's first junket screening in June, only to find out that the White House had called, wanting to see if a screening could be arranged for President Clinton. That night. Everyone—Devlin, Emmerich, star Bill Pullman—bundled into a jet, and flew to Washington, where they screened it for the president and his family. "It was completely surreal," says Emmerich. "To watch the White House blowing up inside the White House? The most unreal moment of my career." When the scene played in which a newscaster complains about the president—"we elected a warrior and we got a wimp"—both Emmerich and Devlin shrank down into their seats, but Clinton loved it, and when July 4th found him in Youngstown, Ohio, he joked, "Somebody said I was coming to Youngstown because this is the day the White House gets blown away by space aliens. I hope it's there when I get back"—a perfect comment, off-the-cuff, self-deprecatory, as good as Reagan at his best. By contrast, his opponent in the presidential race that year, Bob Dole, was caught horribly short. After Clinton's review of *Independence Day,* Dole hurriedly sought out a screening of the film, so that he, too, could be seen to review it, his entourage speeding south on the San Diego Freeway in early rush hour, before finding the Cineplex Odeon Century Plaza, where Dole handed over a $20 bill at the box office for two $4.75 tickets, giving him enough money back for a small tub of popcorn and a box of Goobers for him and Elizabeth. "I liked it," he told the press, before continuing, "We won in the end. Bring your family, to be proud of. Diversity. America. Leadership. Good over evil."

No wonder he lost. It took a lot more work by Dole's speechwriters before his endorsement had approached anything like the necessary standard, but a few days later, Dole had rallied, and he was proudly proclaiming that for too long Clinton's economic policies "have hovered like an alien ship over the American economy, blowing away growth and opportunity. In 1996," he said, referring to his new tax-cut plan, "America strikes back." Much better, although the real papal blessing came when the filmmakers were invited onto the set of *The Lost World* by Spielberg; as Devlin points out: "In America more people can tell you who directed *Jurassic Park* than know who the president is." Spielberg reeled off his ideas for how they could best turn *Independence Day* into a theme park ride. "He had had his people make up three different versions of the ride," says Devlin. "While he's directing the movie he's pitching us three different versions of the ride he'd like to do: one was in the spaceship with Jeff Goldblum, another one was in the town when it was attacked by aliens. Another was a virtual reality thing. They were incredible."

Finally, Spielberg told Devlin, "Enjoy it, because in six months they're going to turn on you."

"How come?" said Devlin.

"Because in six months they're not going to remember the movie. They're just going to remember the hype, all the toys, the commercialization of your film, and they're going to forget the film."

"I thought maybe that was sour grapes," says Devlin, "but six months later we were being called everything that's wrong with Hollywood. All that year, the headlines were 'the year of the independent film,' because all the movies nominated for Oscars were independent movies. But the reality is, when these movies do well, the studios are flush and when they're flush, they're willing to take chances on more interesting films. In Europe it was so misunderstood. The American government throughout the years has so angered 80 percent of Europe that by the time our movie came out every single place I went to promote the movie the first question was: 'Don't you think this movie is promoting the idea that America is the world policeman?'" He points out that the film—written by a German and a Jew—celebrates "coming together to face our enemies," although the alliance showed a slight hairline fracture when, on the set of *The Lost World*, Spielberg asked Volker Engel how many takes it required to blow up the White House.

"One," replied Engel.

"One? How did you manage that?"

"German engineering," replied Engel.

The maker of *Schindler's List* blanched.

"I meant it as a joke," protests Engel.

□ □ □

The method by which grosses are counted was, in 1996, and still is, pretty archaic—a system of faxes and telephone calls all relayed to a small room, manned by thirty-five people, at the E.D.I. unit of A. C. Nielsen—a very literal box office. On Sunday they call up theaters— covering some 25,000 screens—and put out "flash figures," which the studio then uses to project what they estimate the total weekend tally to be, which they then give to the press on Monday. There is more than enough room for error, wishful thinking, and sometimes outright lies. If you examine those Monday figures, they are never $95 or $87 million. It's always $90 or $100 million. This is called "pushing the gross," and everyone does it. A studio will call with a number, but then realize that another studio has called in a higher number, and then revise their original figure accordingly. Disney and Warner Brothers delivered estimates for *Pocahontas* and *Batman Forever* that were off by $1 million, and in 1997 Miramax had to admit that the gross they reported for *Scream 2*—$39 million—was in fact closer to $33 million.

On the Tuesday before its July 4th opening, *Independence Day* was sneak-previewed on more than 2,400 screens, playing around the clock on some of them, and causing ticket prices in Los Angeles and New York to jump from $7.50 to $8, which allowed the movie to pass the $100 million mark by Monday—a first, beating even *Jurassic Park,* although rival studios disputed the head start the movie had been given by its previews. Had it reached $100 million in six or seven days? "In my mind, 6:00 P.M. Tuesday to 6:00 P.M. Monday is six days," said Sherak. "Though a lot of studios complained about my calculations, each of us determines our own course. There's no accountability, no hard and fast rules. In the end, though, you have to live with yourself." Looked at another way, the very speed with which *Independence Day* made its money was at best neutral news, accelerating further the trend started by *Batman,* by disappearing from screens faster, too. By its second week it had dropped 30 percent, then 40 percent, to leave the number one spot free for an adaptation of John Grisham's *A Time to Kill,* starring Sandra Bullock. Future historians of American movies will have a tough time figuring this one out. The records will state merely that in the summer of 1996, millions of Americans queued up to see their most cherished monuments and institutions demolished—a scaldingly traumatic sight that held their attention for several weeks, at least, before they turned in search of healing balm, a common cause to bind their wounds, and found it in the latest Sandra Bullock movie. A fine, spirited actress, to be sure, but shouldn't total national annihilation leave, you know, more of a *dent*?

Not anymore. As of the summer of 1996, national devastation carried about the same charge as a burst party balloon. *Independence Day* kicked off a cycle of nineties disaster movies, returning the blockbuster to exactly the sort of large-spectacle, multicast extravaganzas from which *Jaws* had once delivered audiences. If *Jaws* had radically downsized its threat level to that of a single shark, then *Independence Day* radically upsized its threat level to include global catastrophe. If *Jaws* had lowered its heroism levels to the scruffy low-slung heroism of ordinary men, *Independence Day* upscaled to presidents, pilots and other national paragons. And—most importantly of all—if *Jaws* had sought out comic relief in the singular spectacle of Richard Dreyfuss and his Styrofoam cups, then *Independence Day*'s joshing tone expanded to swallow the entire cast. The film is all comedy double acts: Jeff Goldblum and Harvey Fierstein, Goldblum and Judd Hirsch, Will Smith and Harry Connick, Jr., Smith and Goldblum . . . "Oops" mutters Smith as he crashes an alien spaceship into the side of a U.S. government hangar. "Oops? What's with the oops?" responds Goldblum, and in that single exchange you have *Independence Day*, a film in which even the comic relief gets comic relief, and apocalypse is simply a bummer. Here is the way the world would end, in film after film: not with a bang, nor a whimper, but a wisecrack.

Only Bill Pullman's president plays it straight, like a schoolteacher trying to quiet a classroom of noisy kids—"Exciting? People are dying out there. I don't think exciting is a word I'd choose to describe it"— but his is a lone voice, the voice of another era almost, when global onslaught might have been cause for concern. *ID4* instead ushered the blockbuster into its late, decadent, self-parodic camp phase, offering up a hardier, titanium-skinned version of the limp-wristed, Susan Sontag–era camp of the seventies. Back then, camp was essentially the prerogative of the sophisticates in the audience, who, as part of their last defense against the assaults of big dumb movies, could profess to find them "so bad they're good." The movies didn't know they were big, bad, or dumb, of course, which only sharpened the audience's sense of superiority still further. With *Independence Day,* camp went mass market, its prerogative passing from the audience to the filmmakers themselves, who knew their movie was big and dumb ahead of time, and advertised their knowledge at every step, with the sort of dialogue so cheerily cognizant of its own faults as to leave film critics in a state of fuming gridlock. What could they say about it that it hadn't already acknowledged? The larding of references to other movies was so dense you weren't sure if the film would have end credits or footnotes. "Now that's what I call a Close Encounter!" yodels Will Smith. "Must go faster, must go faster!" mutters Jeff Goldblum, quoting himself in *Jurassic Park.* Whoever it was who said that everyone's a film critic, presumably didn't mean the movies themselves, or their characters, but that's what *Independence Day* was, a movie whose characters were all film critics, people who act, not as if they are facing the end of the world, but with the levity levels of people watching a movie about a bunch of people facing the end of the world. "This is so cool," murmurs one Los Angeleno. There would be someone like her in every disaster movie of the nineties—less a character, in fact, than a cheerleader for the film's sense of fun, an ambassador for the audience's sense of excitement. "We've got front row tickets at the end of the earth!" trumpets Steve Buscemi in *Armageddon.* "This is so much fun it's freaky!" And in *Twister,* Philip Seymour Hoffman, "This is the fun part, sweetheart!" The mid-nineties were so full of films telling us how much fun they were, it was perfectly conceivable that the audience might slip their seats, go out to the lobby for more Coke, and leave the movie to enjoy itself. It was curious, watching these movies: like being listened to and ignored, flabbergasted and bored all at the same time.

So if the characters were now playing the audience's role, what was the audience doing? Playing the director's role, naturally, sitting out in the theater in row after row of canvas chairs, names stenciled on the back, bullhorns by their side. "The audience is as inventive as a filmmaker. Quite often, they think like filmmakers much more than we think," says director Jan de Bont of this game of musical chairs. "You want the audience to go 'ohmigod he's not going to do that. He cannot do this, this is impossible, he cannot go there' and then you go there."

This was something of a de Bont specialty, having probed the outer limits of audience-sponsored audacity in *Speed*, and returning to deliver more of the same in the shape of 1996's *Twister*, released a month before Emmerich's *Independence Day*. His story was not so different from Emmerich's: as a film student in Eindhoeven, Holland, he had seen *Star Wars* and been blown away by it, less by its size, which had so impressed Emmerich, than its speed. "What I think was so unique was that he never lingered on anything. In Europe, if you had a big set piece you would want to show it as long as you can, because it's the only one you'd get in the whole movie, here it just went from one thing to the other. Right from the credits you knew ohmigod this movie is going to be different. . . . I was so overwhelmed, you can do all those things."

De Bont had come to America along with his countryman and mentor, the director Paul Verhoeven, and, like Emmerich, worked his way up through the salt mines of the eighties action movie—supplying *Die Hard* with its hard, clear camerawork, and also working on *Lethal Weapon 3*, and Verhoeven's *Basic Instinct*. De Bont harbored directorial ambitions of his own, and having seen one project after another drift away from him, he stepped out of the ring for a year to see if he could fish for scripts, and landed himself a winner in the shape of Graham Yost's script for *Speed*. "Nobody ever believed you could make an exciting movie about a bus, especially in L.A.—they drive like about thirty-five miles per hour, really slow," says de Bont, "but I saw instantly what you could do with it. This had to be a movie that once it starts can never let up but gets bigger and better. I never wanted the audience to relax, I always wanted the tension to be building and building, and never stop moving. Even with two people talking, the camera had to create this kind of energy."

You could argue that Yost's central conceit—a bus that will explode if it drops below fifty miles per hour—didn't need jazzing up, and in another decade it would probably have been served up straight, but de Bont set about topping and tailing it with two more action sequences, one in an elevator and one in a subway, and then whipping it along at such a pace that audiences never stopped to ask why Dennis Hopper was laying out such an infernal relay of tasks before Keanu Reeves—he was one of those Simon Says villains who would become increasingly familiar as the nineties progressed: why does Bruce Willis have to jump through all these hoops in *Die Hard: With a Vengeance*? Because Simon Says. The villain was basically the screenwriter, dropping tasks in front of the hero as and when called for. *Speed*, as its title suggested, homed in with such adroit ruthlessness on what you wanted out of a summer blockbuster as to provide an almost abstract distillation of thrills: it was fast, funny, crafty, and boasted a surprisingly low body count, dispensing with the crunchy heavyweight violence of the eighties for a more streamlined nineties version: more feline than butch, as incarnated in the svelte, lightweight form of Keanu Reeves.

"The main reason I cast Keanu was that to be taken seriously there has to be a vulnerability to them, and the thing about big action heroes was that they were always bigger than life," says de Bont. "I wanted someone who you weren't sure whether they would deal with it or not." If *Speed* was all slipstream, *Twister* was all updraft, the first multimillion-dollar Hollywood production about thin air, with de Bont juggling houses, trucks, tractors, even cows with some of the playful anarchy which the young Spielberg once loosed on the world, except this time the genie was not going back into his lamp. Even Spielberg—his producer on the film—wanted more in the way of the science of tornadoes, but de Bont didn't want any interruption to the adrenaline rush. The pupil was outstripping his master for blithe ruthlessness. "It was the opposite of a movie like *Earthquake*," he says, "because I felt the stormchasers have a great time doing it. I went to spend time with them and it was a great rush to see that stuff flying around. Of course, twisters can do a lot of damage but that's not what the movie is about. Sitting in the car chasing them, I thought, this is really cool. There's nothing else around you except this incredible storm. I had to fight to get all the effects in. They were like, 'We'll have them at the beginning and at the end and that's it,' and I was saying, 'No, no, no,' but ultimately they caved in and let me do it. They got so excited when they saw the effects coming in, that they moved it forward"—from May 28 to May 10, where the film took in $152.3 million in its first three weeks of release, on course to its eventual take of nearly $500 million, while *Independence Day* took in $813 million, thus making 1996 the summer of two invasions: one by a bunch of marauding aliens, and the second by a gang of marauding Euro auteurs. While Germans were blowing up the White House, a

Dutchman was razing most of the South to within a few inches' resemblance of his home country.

The last time Hollywood had seen such an influx of foreign directors had been in the thirties and forties, the glory days of the studio system, when Fritz Lang, Billy Wilder, and Alfred Hitchcock had sought to rechannel back into America some of the American pulp they had absorbed in their teens. But where those directors sought to serve it back with added topspin—Wilder's caustic wit, Lang's cynicism, Hitchcock's dry mordancy—their nineties equivalents brought less in the way of cinematic baggage with them, aiming for a style that carried no foreign accent and that was, if anything, more American than the Americans. Verhoeven made films that were simply more violent, Emmerich films that were even more grandiosely scaled, and de Bont films that were even faster than those of his Hollywood peers; they would do much to lend the nineties its air of baroque, top-loaded excess. The studios had found a fresh set of willing pups—fresh off the boat, keen and eager to please—although as both de Bont and Emmerich were to find, riding out blockbuster success was harder than it looked.

For one thing, the genre was beginning to double up on itself, with 1997 boasting not one but two $100 million volcano movies (*Volcano*, and *Dante's Peak*); two $100 million boat movies (*Speed 2: Cruise Control*, and *Titanic*); two $100 million alien movies (*Alien: Resurrection, Starship Troopers*); and two $100 million movies about superannuated old dinosaurs (*The Lost World: Jurassic Park* and the new Bond, *Tomorrow Never Dies*). Commentators were spoiled as to their choice of death-defying metaphor: "It's just too crowded. They're going to eat each other alive," said Fox executive Joe Roth, clearly with *The Lost World*'s raptors preying on his mind. "What we're seeing here has the inevitability of a train wreck," said research analyst Larry Gerbrandt. "There's going to be a lot of blood on the floor." *The Fugitive* maybe? *Cape Fear*? "We're setting off supertanker against supertanker," said Fox chairman Bill Mechanic. "If a couple of these fail there's going to be an echo all over town." Except, in his case, the metaphor was no metaphor, for Fox—the studio behind both *Speed 2* and *Titanic*—really *was* setting supertanker against supertanker, and so moved *Speed 2* up in its schedule from July 4th to June, to avoid collision, compressing de Bont's ten-week editing period down to four.

"The script wasn't ready by a long shot, but once something like that starts, it's very hard to change," says de Bont. "Movie companies are part of these gigantic corporations, and they need product and they need a product at a given time. It's like you're launching a new Coca-Cola product and it's got to be done by June 17, because Pepsi's going to bring out something a day earlier. It is impossible because you don't have any control. Anybody who has ever made a movie on water, it's the same story. Whatever you do, however you prepare yourself, you're never prepared for nature and nature never wants to play along with you. So if you need waves you're not going to get waves. If you need clouds, you're not going to get clouds. You need blue sky, you're going to get a hurricane." Alternatively, there is another method: set the atmospherics to your own internal thermostat, carry personal storm clouds around with you wherever you go, and loose lightning bolts on whoever gets in your way, otherwise known as "shooting a Jim Cameron movie."

TIME LINE

1996

1. *Independence Day* (Fox) $813.2 (37.7%)
2. *Twister* (WB) $494.7 (48.9%)
3. *Mission: Impossible* (Paramount) $452.6 (40.0%)
4. *The Rock* (Disney) $330.5 (40.6%)
5. *The Hunchback of Notre Dame* (Disney) $324.6 (30.8%)
6. *Ransom* (Disney) $301.8 (45.2%)
7. *101 Dalmatians* (Disney) $281.2 (48.4%)
8. *Jerry Maguire* (Sony) $273.6 (56.1%0
9. *The Nutty Professor* (Universal) $269.4 (47.8%)
10. *Space Jam* (WB) $250.2 (36.1%)

*Figures show worldwide gross, in millions of dollars, followed by the percentage of that generated in the U.S.

CHAPTER 14

STARING INTO THE ABYSS

"YOU EITHER SHOOT IT MY WAY OR YOU DO
ANOTHER FUCKING MOVIE."
— James Cameron, as quoted on T-shirts worn by *Titanic*
crew members

As a teenager, Cameron had "shared the sort of general feeling
that it was the coolest shipwreck in history. But I didn't know
that much about the detail of it." When oceanographer Robert
Ballard found the actual wreck of the *Titanic* and returned with photographic footage in 1991, the now forty-seven-year-old director was
hooked, thinking: "Wow. I love that. It looks like space. It looks like a
very high-tech environment except it's in the ocean. . . . It was pure science fiction imagery in my mind." By the end of 1996, the director had
made twelve visits to see the wreck in a small submersible, guiding
remotely operated cameras in and out of its dining rooms and cabins;
by the end of which, he had spent more time on board the *Titanic* than
any of its passengers. "It was a romantic notion, as much personal as
professional," he admitted later, "but I felt that doing it would imbue
the film with a sense of veracity that it might not otherwise have." The
dives weren't strictly necessary—in the finished film much of even the
present-day "documentary" footage would be digitally created. It was a
piece of pure Cameronian machismo, technological brinkmanship: the
Method Acting approach to your special effects.

Footing the bill was Twentieth Century Fox, then headed by Peter

Chernin, and his number two, Bill Mechanic. Cameron had pitched the project to them as "Romeo and Juliet on a boat." They weren't so sure about his ability to deliver Romeo and Juliet—"What people were afraid of with Jim was that he could do the techie stuff, could he do the romantic stuff?" says Mechanic—but they knew that he would deliver, pound for pound, when the ship went down. "I wanted to shoot *Titanic* like a *Terminator* movie," said Cameron. "I wanted it to have the subjective immediacy of my other films, like *The Abyss* and *Aliens,* where you're inside this thing." Nervous of exactly what film they would be getting for their $125 million, Fox sought a financial partner in Paramount, which was desperate for a big summer movie for 1997, and who agreed to stump up half of the film's budget but insisted their input be capped at $56 million—Fox would have to pay anything over that. It was, said one newspaper later, "one of the better deals since the Indians sold Manhattan." Paramount may have been expecting a wham-bam July 4th movie but *Titanic* was to be epic filmmaking as it used to be—a battle of will and world, mind over matter, with Cameron hacking his film from the coastline of Mexico in DeMillean high style—but with one important difference: where the epics of DeMille and Griffith used to be proud of their extravagance, rounding their figures up in order to impress the public, that tide had forcibly turned the other way. Mechanic would find the opposite: an eagle-eyed press gallery, ready to pounce on every hint of budgetary excess and turn *Titanic* into a sink-or-swim symbol of Hollywood's death-by-blockbuster. "Whatever figures we gave the press," he says, "they would add a few million. It was crazy. When we told them the truth, they still rounded it up."

The air of impending doom was palpable in Hollywood that year. "I think that we're at DEFCON three right now," Spielberg told *Premiere* magazine. "Everybody is looking to their neighbor to see what they're making. There's always some highwater mark, and every year it inches up. It's not going to be too long before an average film, without marketing, is going to cost $55 million. It is getting to the point where only two kinds of movies are getting made, the tent pole summer or Christmas hits or the sequels, and the audacious little Gramercy, Fine Line, or Miramax films. It's kind of like India, where there's an upper class and a poverty class and no middle class. Right now we're squeezing the middle class out of Hollywood and only allowing the $70-million-plus films or the $10-million-minus films. And that is going to spell doom for everyone." From the beginning, the press was ready and waiting for *Titanic,* which promised to fill the gap that *Last Action Hero* had only sheepishly filled: here, finally, would be the blockbuster era's *Heaven's Gate*—the film that would capsize the system, the turkey to out-gobble them all. "Every single day there was a blurb [in *Variety*] about the movie, and what the problems were," says effects supervisor Scott Ross. "The entire world was focused on this movie and everyone in Hollywood was rooting for it to fail." It was, he says, "maybe the worst experience of my life."

On May 28, after many months of dickering, *Titanic* finally and suddenly got the green light. "It was like a rocket going off," said Cameron. "I'm like okay, if I'm supposed to have this movie ready for next summer I'm going to need the green light—a month ago? Two months ago? By that point I'd spent two years of my life on the film, for no pay, so I wasn't about to write it off." In May, a construction force of 1,900 men descended on a forty-acre portion of oceanside property in Mexico's Rosarito Beach, and using ten thousand tons of dynamite blasted a hole big enough to accommodate a huge outdoor tank, using up some three hundred tons of steel, capable of handling 17 million gallons of salt water, for the 775-foot likeness of the boat, just yards from the Pacific, thus providing Cameron's cameras with a ready-made horizon line. Three sections of the ship were built, one for interiors, another built on an elaborate hydraulic system that could repeatedly raise and submerge the 1,300,000-pound structure, and a third that could be raised to a full vertical tilt, for the film's climax. "When we first started we were only going to shoot two hundred feet of it. Eventually, we did the whole ship," says production designer Peter Lamont, who managed to track down the original blueprints of the ship from Harland and Wolff, giving details of everything on board the boat—lifeboats, dining chairs, engine controls, carpets, right down to the last rivet in the engine room. "The sets were built, finished, packed in Mexico City, and transported two thousand kilometers, then re-erected at Rosarito," says Lamont. "Which was quite amazing. From the day the first piece of soil was turned, one hundred days later, the ship was there. At one point we had nineteen cranes on site. That was just the *cranes*."

When cinematographer Caleb Deschanel arrived on set, however, he found what looked like a large and unfinished building site—how will they ever be ready to shoot? he thought, there's nothing here. After an argument over the film's color palette—Cameron wanted a blaze of color, Deschanel something more sepia-tinted—Deschanel was fired. "Jim Cameron is like the scene in *Spinal Tap* where the amplifiers go up to eleven," he said. Throughout the shoot, the crew would respond to Cameron's outbursts in time-honored way, by having them printed up on T-shirts: "DON'T GET CREATIVE, I HATE THAT" "YOU EITHER SHOOT IT MY WAY OR YOU DO ANOTHER FUCKING MOVIE" "IT'S A TIMING THING, I DON'T CARE IF IT HAS ANY ORGANIC EMOTIONAL REALITY OR NOT." Most of these were delivered atop a 162-foot crane that Cameron had earmarked for his own personal use—the "Cam Crane"—fitting it with a camera basket and PA system, and in which he could scoot the length of the ship in seconds, like some mixture of Zeus, D. W. Griffith, and Big Brother, to bawl out some unsuspecting extra when a corpse took it upon himself to start swimming ("Somebody give me a fucking rifle").

It was quite a sight. "There was a moment when Kate [Winslet] and I were on the poop deck, which was on hydraulics," said Leonardo DiCaprio. "We looked down and there were, like, twenty men clinging on to the rail below us on bungee cords. And when the poop deck went to its peak, the guys jumped off and started bouncing off each other, bouncing off girders. Three stuntmen were injured in the shoot. Then you looked up and saw, like eighteen cranes with huge lights shining on you, and Jim Cameron coming from a little spot in the sky, zooming in past your close-up to the people diving below you. Kate and I looked at each other, our eyes just bugged, and we said, 'How did we get here?'"

While visiting the set, a journalist witnessed the following argument between Cameron and his stunt coordinator, Simon Crane, after his crew of stuntmen proved incapable of righting a capsizing dinghy for the sixth time in a row. "You said you could do this!" yelled Cameron. "What's wrong with them? Do it now!"

"You're lucky they got it over," shouted back Crane.

"What do you mean were lucky? That's their job!"

"Go fuck yourself."

Cameron couldn't believe his ears.

"What did you say?"

"You heard me."

"Yeah, well, you're fired!"

In a show of support for Crane, sixty stuntmen walked off the set, leaving Cameron stewing with producer Jon Landau. "Let him walk," Cameron insisted. "What do you think? Should he be able to say that to me? Say anything you want to me in private. Just don't break the chain of command on the set." Landau broke the deadlock by leading a suitably cowed Crane to apologize—not quite as publicly as Cameron wanted it, but it would do.

"I had a few shouting matches with him," says Peter Lamont, an old hand at dealing with the director, having worked with him on *Aliens,* "and we did almost come to blows one day, but there was never any animosity. It was here today, gone tomorrow. Jim is only trying to get the very, very best. When you're at his house, he's a different beast. You can go and chat like normal people but once he starts filming, once they started sending in the accountants to find out where we were, Jim could be very blunt or very elusive." Cameron's way with studio executives and accountants was notorious; during the shooting of *The Abyss,* he had dangled Fox executive Harold Schneider over the edge of a forty-five-foot diving platform and threatened to let him drop. This time around, the job of reining him in fell to Bill Mechanic, who took over as CEO of Fox when his boss, Peter Chernin, was promoted up the Fox ladder to become Rupert Murdoch's number two. "From the moment that it went to the physical production in Mexico it was well over-budget," says Mechanic. "What was really behind all the problems was that everything was all done at such a breakneck pace. They're building a ship, they've got hydraulic systems, they've got the size of the set, the sinking of the set underwater, what water does to your lighting bills, ruining your carpets and costumes. . . . The thing was just too big." By October of 1996, just one month into principal photography, Cameron had already spent $75 million and was averaging around $225,000 to $250,000 a day. Two scenes—the implosion of the ship's glass dome, and the Southampton dock—racked up an astonishing tab of $500,000 a day. It fell to the soft-spoken, bespectacled Mechanic to fly down to Mexico and try to persuade the director to make some cuts.

He found Cameron in his trailer at 2:00 A.M., strapped into the harness he had been using to traverse the ship's tilting deck with a handheld camera. "It looked really great out there tonight," said Mechanic, "and we want to do everything we can to keep it looking great, but you've got to appreciate our position. From a financial standpoint this film is wildly out of control. Nothing is going to change that. All we can do now is contain it. So here are some scenes we'd like you to cut from the shooting schedule."

He pushed two pages of cuts across the table, which Cameron picked up, scanned, and dismissed, one by one, before crumpling the pages up. "This is a stupid idea, this is a stupid idea. What kind of idiot would think of this? This won't work. You gotta have this. . . . You want me to hack apart the film I've already put four years of my life into!" he screamed. "If you want to cut my film you'll have to fire me, and to fire me you'll have to fucking kill me. If you're such a fucking expert, then you can finish the movie yourself!" He stormed out of his trailer, and took off in his car, "just basically quit," said Mechanic. "It was my lowest point. He told me where to go. He walked off. Would he ever come back? Would we ever finish?" A shell-shocked Mechanic called together the crew at four in the morning and told them, "You're gonna shut it down." For forty-eight hours, *Titanic* was dead in the water.

Eventually they worked out a compromise. "What do they want for that at the end of the day?" reasoned Cameron. "Do they want a film that's a compromised, screwed-up embarrassment? Of course not. They want a film that's something between the one that's costing way too much and the one that's a compromised, screwed-up embarrassment." He made a few concessions, and Mechanic let most of his cuts go ignored: "I had already seen enough of the dailies," he says. "The stuff that was shot early was the Kate and Leo stuff, which I thought was extraordinary and touching . . . could he do the romantic stuff? I felt he had already shown that he was doing that."

By December, however, an array of hidden costs suddenly sprang out of the woodwork; the electrical budget was short by $9 million; the completed ship weighed twice as much as anticipated, and estimates for how long it would take to jack it up went from six to thirty-six days. It was "like an artillery barrage day after day, boom, boom, boom!" said Cameron. "All of a sudden in the space of like a two-week time period, the budget jumped up like $20 million or the cost of the film had jumped $20 million. It was going up faster than I was shooting. It's impossible. It's just nuts. Things were basically really bad." On December 23, while the production was in the Christmas hiatus, Mechanic summoned Cameron and producers Jon Landau and Rae Sanchini to an emergency meeting at Fox. "We can't make any money off this movie," he told them. "Now it's not a question of how much we are going to make or not make, it's a question of how much we are going to lose."

"If we stopped shooting today we would remove enough production days to offset the overage," said Cameron, "but of course we haven't sunk the ship yet, and I don't think anyone's going to want to go see a movie called *Titanic* where the ship doesn't sink." But he was also pretty embarrassed, and offered to reassign his profit participation back to Fox.

Mechanic couldn't have cared less, and replied, "Sure you can give us your points, you can do whatever you want because there aren't going to be any profits anyway."

By this time, the press was having a turkey shoot with the movie. "A Sinking Sensation," ran *Newsweek*'s headline. "Glub, Glub, Glub," ran *Time*'s "Can James Cameron's Extravagant *Titanic* Avoid Disaster?" The watery metaphors deepened into a torrent with *Variety*'s April 15 article, "That Sinking Feeling"—the first of many to bear its "*Titanic*-watch" logo, as it charted the production's every hiccup. As production wound up on the film, attention swiveled the way of Scott Ross and his team of effects artists at Digital Domain. "We were under incredible pressure," says Ross, "work that had never been done before, a difficult director who was very controlling, a studio that was bleeding cash to keep this movie going and which it was afraid was going to be a flop, budgets that continued to escalate, additional work that continued to come in, schedules that continued to be missed by Cameron and the first unit. We thought we would have all our material by January and we wound up getting it as late as April and May."

Matters had not been helped by the increased workload necessitated by a series of accidents on set. After a stunt girl fractured her cheekbone and another stuntman broke his ankle, occasioning an investigation by the Screen Actors Guild, Cameron decided to insert the falling figures digitally; after numerous complaints about being left in cold water, Cameron had relented and allowed shooting in a warmed tank, which meant the character's cold breath had to be inserted digitally, too. By the time he finished shooting he had added more than a hundred effects shots to the film's already bulging five-hundred-effects schedule. Every time Ross and his team looked back it was another four shots—more stars in the sky here, a safety line removed there, move that crane—with Cameron looming over everyone's shoulders. "These aren't North Atlantic seagulls! North Atlantic seagulls have a four-foot wingspan! These are the wrong seagulls!"

"It was the vision and the strength and the determination and downright nastiness, at times, of the director that got the film onscreen," says Ross. "I asked him once, during the filming. I said, 'How do you do it? I'm cracking and I'm not the director.' And he said, 'It reminds me of mowing the lawn when I was a kid. If I ever have to look up at the whole lawn I'd get really discouraged. So all I do is I roll one lane at a time and when I'm finished with that one, I turn back around, I look at that lane and I go, 'Okay I'm going to do another one.' And that's how I do it.' It's his MO, it's how he deals with everything. It's just the way it is. It's an amazing way to live. He does that in every area of his life. He has blinders on and he's so incredibly focused and he believes he is absolutely right and you can get on the top of a building and scream 'you idiot' but he won't hear you. The downside to mowing one lane at a time is that you become obsessive-compulsive about how straight the lanes are and you don't see the forest for the trees. He gets lost in the detail."

Ross would eventually have to farm out the film's effects to seventeen rival firms, and would still come up $4 million in the red. At a review of their release date position in March, it fell to Ross to tell everyone that there was simply no way they could meet the July 4th deadline.

"There were lots of pointed fingers and arguing," he says. "It was a lot of scared people. Bill Mechanic's life was on the line. It was as high level and as bright a light as one could imagine. Some $200 million already in the production, and $100 million of cost overrun." Relations between the two studios had begun to sour when Paramount owner Sumner Redstone boasted to a Wall Street analyst about how clever he'd been to cap Paramount's spending at $56 million, and now, Paramount's vice chairman Robert Friedman was adamant that the film still be ready for July 4th, and pressed Mechanic to reel it in. Mechanic knew that Paramount needed a big summer movie more than they did—he had *Speed 2,* or so he hoped—and said he would only do so if Paramount put up more money to pay for the costs of accelerating the production in time for summer. "I wasn't having us be the only ones to get fried," he says. "If we were sacrificing to make something good, everybody along the line was going to make sacrifices. There were huge fights between Jim and them and between us and them. Financially I was awful, and creatively Jim was awful." Refused access to dailies, Paramount started leaking stories about the film's budget to the press, which was soon abuzz with stories from "unnamed sources" on both sides. In the end the studios refused to take calls from the other, while at Cannes Mechanic and Friedman almost came to blows.

By then *Speed 2* had revealed itself as the disaster it was, and so Mechanic moved it up in the schedule, to June, which left him as desperate for a July 4th movie as Friedman was. "Nobody would back off their position," said Cameron. "Everybody started to posture. It's like a blowfish that puffs up to scare its enemies away. Everybody was puffed up trying to scare the enemies away and they weren't being realistic, because in March we were really screwed up. We were a month behind schedule. The visual effects were at least two months behind schedule. It was impossible to hit the July date but nobody dealt with it until too late and then we all looked like idiots." When the production wrapped, the returning cast and crew were grilled for information by the media, resulting in a second wave of negative stories about the film. On April 19, the *Los Angeles Times* ran a story by Manuel Puig, entitled "Epic Sized Troubles on *Titanic,*" which quoted second assistant director Sebastian Silva as saying, "The horror stories are true . . . we were top dollar slaves." Kate Winslet also told the newspaper in May, "If anything was the slightest bit wrong he would lose it. He has a temper like you wouldn't believe," calling the shoot "an ordeal" and complaining that she had survived on four hours sleep a night, and had almost drowned after her dress snagged on a gate underwater. "I had to sort of shimmy to get the coat free. I had no breath left. I thought I'd burst, and Jim said, 'Okay let's do it again . . .' For the first time in my life on a film set, I was thinking I wish I wasn't here. In fact things were getting so intense that some days I'd wake up and think, 'Please let me die.'" Clearly unused to the demands of modern Hollywood etiquette, Winslet later retracted the remarks in a letter to the *L.A. Times* in which she said she had "learned a lot" from the director, and "deeply regretted" any impression she may have given to the contrary. Cameron denied that she had ever been in any danger, although she may have "perceived that she was," and hit back at the Puig article with his own, refuting the claims, point by point. "Am I driven? Yes, absolutely. Out of control? Never. Unsafe? Not on my watch." As July 4th approached and still no sign of *Titanic*, Cameron finally called up Fox's Peter Chernin and told him, "We shouldn't be doing this. Rushing for summer will compromise the film. It will only be 85 percent there."

"Okay," replied Chernin. "Give me a day to figure out how to play it."

On Tuesday, May 27, Paramount and Fox announced that *Titanic* would be in theaters on December 19, 1997. Up at George Lucas's Skywalker Ranch fifty sound editors slept on cots while they worked around the clock to finish the film, while Cameron hunkered down at his house in Malibu, which he had turned into a makeshift postproduction facility to work on his edit. Making a brief visit to Fox headquarters, Cameron had the misfortune to bump into Rupert Murdoch in the corridor. "I guess I'm not your favorite person," he mumbled. "But the movie is going to be good."

"It had better be better than good," replied Murdoch.

In the end, news of what sort of movie Fox had on its hands broke from an unusual source: a twenty-eight-year-old 350-pound college dropout and Internet geek Texan named Harry Knowles. In 1996, Knowles had created a film fan Web site called *Ain't It Cool?*, read by over 1.5 million people, which had turned him into the studio's latest bête noir. Compiled from the reports of a series of moles within the studio and correspondents who just happened to get lucky and chance upon a test screening, Knowles's Web site was able to break news of a film's quality weeks, sometimes months, before the studio's publicity department had a chance to click into gear. He had single-handedly killed the buzz on *Batman and Robin* before it was even out of the gate. In a sense, his Web site provided the last-chance saloon for that ever-dwindling commodity: word of mouth on a movie.

One day in the autumn of 1997, Knowles got a call from an anonymous informant, a woman who told him, "If you want to find the *Titanic,* you need to search the Twin Cities." He posted a message on his site that read "Attention Minneapolis-St. Paul residents: Contact me immediately! important life-saving mission to occur in your city" and received 150 e-mails back. After calling up local theaters and radio stations, he ascertained that there were two test screenings being held on the same day: one for a Martin Lawrence Disney comedy called *Nothing to Lose* and another for *Great Expectations,* which was being distributed by Fox: this had to be it. "Just to be sure, I divided my spies between the two screenings," said Knowles. "At first I was giddy that I'd actually pulled it off. And then as the hours wore on, I started to develop a sinking feeling." Then he received word from the first of thirty-five correspondents. "Utterly, unbelievably fantastic. I'll write you later." Knowles posted a digest of the reviews, adding that he thought the movie was going to be the highest-grossing movie of all time.

Which of course it was: the world's first billion-dollar blockbuster. Having slipped its summer moorings, *Titanic* premiered at the Tokyo Film Festival on December 19, performed a neat double midair pirouette and then went demographic-diving, just as *E.T.* had done before it. Down through the teenage boys, down into the substratum of teenage girls—the audience hinted at by the success of *Ghost* and *Pretty Woman* in 1990—and from there, it burrowed further down to their mothers, who had seen *Doctor Zhivago* and *Love Story,* before finally reaching the Land That the Movies Had Forgot, that red-hot core of molten unembarrassability that waits, obediently biding its time until a filmmaker goes looking for it. Did anyone in 1997 even have the faintest inkling this place still existed? Still less that a director best known for his intense interest in robot assassins would lead us there? These were dark days for hard-core sci-fi fans. The pages of *Starlog* magazine, normally a Cameron-friendly zone, passed over the film in glacial silence; while Cameron purists had to content themselves with the brief shots of the ship's vast engine room, pistons pumping like a row of Terminators doing bench-presses in the gym. The problem started with the stuff above decks, where with Jack (Leonardo DiCaprio) and Rose (Kate Winslet) meet up to declaim, "Jack, this is impossible. I can't see you." "No wait. Let me try to get this out. You're amazing." If there is one thing that *Terminator* fans do not take kindly to, it is sweet nothings on the poop deck. You could see them in the theaters, taking it all manfully on the chin, and waiting for the iceberg to put in an appearance, and wondering if it would be played by Arnold Schwarzenegger.

But as the film progressed, and Jack and Rose start fighting for their love, down they went, to a man, for if there is one thing Cameron understands it is the dynamics of a good fight. Jack the dreamy artist is a sop and a bore, but the sight of Jack the class warrior, girding himself for battle in tux and tails, is as purely thrilling, in its way, as seeing Rambo strap a couple of rocket launchers to his forearms. So, too, with Rose: caught in a clinch in the back of a car, and the film steams up with softcore cliché, but the sight of Rose charging below decks, up to her neck in water with an axe in her hand, is as stirring as that of Ripley, or Sarah Connor, or any other of the female survivalists who populate Cameron's work. If there is one thing he understands, in other words, it is the survival instinct, both how unpretty it is—look at the man who stops, performs a quick bit of mental calculus, and then abandons Winslet to her fate—and also how much stronger it is in women than in men, for it is Rose who survives, not Jack. The idea that *Titanic* worked because it unlocked the tender hearts of teenage girls is a fallacy, if only because the tender hearts of teenage girls is a fallacy, as the briefest foray into the fan literature around the film confirmed. "Leo's mine!!!" snarled one contributor to a Leo fanzine. "Leo's cute," said another, "for all you people who hate him get a life and fuck yourselves!" *Titanic* works, in other words, because Cameron understood just how tipped with steel the whole notion of romantic adoration is—how fringed with anger, and possessiveness. Only Cameron could have come up with this world of contest and strife, and then people it with such fighters and strivers; and the net effect of the film was not to make you wonder how the director of *The Terminator* could direct a period love story, but to return you to the big epic romances of the past like *Anna Karenina* and *Gone With the Wind,* with their firebrand heroines, and make you wonder just how much Terminator they had in their veins. When Scarlett O'Hara vows to return and fight another day, what is she saying, after all, but, "I'll be back"?

Critics, nonetheless, thought they smelled a rat. From the way *Titanic* was reviewed, you would think Cameron, far from lending technological steel to the romantic melodrama, had laid his hands on cinema's crown jewels, and was tearing through its classiest stately home, scrawling graffiti over the dining room walls. *The New York Times* called it "Edith Wharton lite." The *Buffalo News* found that Cameron "has as much chance of getting away with Noël Coward chitchat as he would quarterbacking the Packers." *The Washington Post* said it was "as if the film were written by a scriptwriter in 1912 fresh from reading stories in *Woman's Home Companion*—but completely unversed in the psychological complexities of Mr. James and Mr. Dreiser." An impressive array of highbrow reinforcements, to be sure— Henry James! Theodore Dreiser! Noel Coward! Edith Wharton!—but since when was it decreed that a film had to go ten rounds with the literary heavyweights of whatever era it happened to be set in? Personally I've always found *Singin' in the Rain* a little lacking in Joycean wordplay and decidedly short on Woolfian stream-of-consciousness, but who knows, maybe this method of reviewing movies will catch on. In 2025, film critics will probably be sitting around comparing notes on *The Terminator,* and complaining that the film sorely missed the psychological complexities John Updike might have brought to the tale, or dreaming of what might have been if only Saul Bellow had been let loose on it.

It was critical snobbery at its most knock-kneed, in other words, and Cameron took it in typically bristling form, responding to Kenneth Turan's *Los Angeles Times* review thus:"Turan sees himself as the high priest of some arcane art form that is far too refined for the average individual to possibly appreciate." Turning his attention westward, to those who "glommed onto *Titanic* as being symptomatic of a sick Hollywood, that it was somehow typical of a trend toward spending too much money on disaster epics and action films," riposted Cameron, "nothing could be further from the truth. *Titanic* is not a disaster epic or an action film. Call it a love story or a $190 million art film, whatever, but *Titanic* is not a road map to the future. It's meant to be a singular picture. The media is constantly whining about how big studio blockbusters are all the same—all formula pictures or sequels or comic book movies, all designed to create a franchise or sell Slurpee cups or bendable action figures. So we do a movie that has no franchise potential whatsoever, that is about people and emotions, and not one mindless action sequence after another—and we get pilloried for being what's wrong with Hollywood."

The subject of what was wrong with Hollywood was a subject left for Fox's Bill Mechanic to ponder, as Fox girded itself for the summer of 1998. With both *Speed 2* and *Titanic* behind him he had more than enough reason to call the business "schizophrenic"—lurching from boom to bust in an ever quicker fibrillating pattern. "When you had *Gone With the Wind*, the system was a much more controlled system," says Mechanic. "Movies were 90 percent of the leisure time activities. Movies are now probably 10 percent, so you're fighting a confluence of other media. Driving through not just the clutter of other movies, but the clutter of entertainment, concerts, music, cable, satellite, you name it. The attempt to break through that kind of clutter, and reach the most number of people, had undercut the process. The idea had taken over from the movie itself. They look like movies and they sound like movies and they feel like 'em until you get inside 'em and then that lack of caring shows. Everybody is about basically the same kind of thing, caught in a spiral of stupid budgets, with everybody relying 100 percent on these big movies when the name of the game is not making the same thing all the time. You can't afford to have twelve blockbusters a year. Everybody is guilty of it. Nobody cares about making a good movie out of those movies. The idea has gotten empty."

Mechanic was convinced that Hollywood was "heading for a cataclysm, similar to the one that happened at the end of the sixties, when Hollywood collapsed. You would have a cast of thousands, and instead of big musicals, you had big stupid musicals, instead of historical epics, big stupid historical epics. We went from the point where $100 million should be like touching scalding coals, to the point where it's something you roast chestnuts on. They weren't afraid of it. It was insane. So while you're booming you're giving it all away. There wasn't much growth left, so while your costs were insanely high and worse,

the middle-budget movies were what used to be high-budget movies. It was bifurcating the market. A high-budget comedy was $50 million whereas a low-budget comedy was $20. The high-budget costume epic was $100 million and the low-budget was $40 to $50 million."

As the summer of 1998 loomed, Mechanic decided on a radical course: to try and resuscitate Fox's middle class of movies, particularly comedies and, where possible, farm out the blockbusters to directors from the indie sector. When Jan de Bont came to him with an idea for a $100 million sci-fi western called *Ghost Riders in the Sky*, he wouldn't go near it. But he gave *X-Men* to Bryan Singer, then coming off his success with *The Usual Suspects,* and gave the green light to the Farrelly brothers to make *There's Something About Mary,* and watched as the movie took in $360 million. It had cost $23 million. He then did the same with their follow-up, *Me Myself and Irene,* which together with *X-Men* and *Big Momma's House* saw Fox's profits shoot into the hundreds of millions. Sadly, Mechanic was not around to enjoy the fruits of his success; after a series of differences with Rupert Murdoch about his choices, he was fired in 2000, citing "creative differences."

TIME LINE

1997

1. *Titanic* (Paramount) $1,835.1 (32.7%)
2. *The Lost World: Jurassic Park* (Universal) $614.4 (37.3%)
3. *Men in Black* (Sony) $586.2 (42.7%)
4. *Tomorrow Never Dies* (MGM) $343.3 (36.5%)
5. *As Good as It Gets* (Sony) $313.4 (47.1%)
6. *Air Force One* (Sony) $312.6 (55.2%)
7. *Liar Liar* (Universal) $306.4 (59.2%)
8. *My Best Friend's Wedding* (Sony) $286.9 (44.2%)
9. *The Fifth Element* (Sony) $263.6 (24.1%)
10. *The Full Monty* (Fox) $256.9 (17.9%)

*Figures show worldwide gross, in millions of dollars, followed by the percentage of that generated in the U.S.

CHAPTER 15

DOES SIZE MATTER?

"Whatever exceeds the common size is always great, and always amazing."

—Longinus, *On the Sublime,* first century A.D.

"Look at these damn things. They arrive after the movie opened. They're hard to assemble. And they look like leftovers from an old Spielberg film."

—Irate toy shop owner, on her stockpile of unsold *Godzilla* merchandise, 1998

When the grosses for his 1997 movie *Men in Black* came in, Barry Sonnenfeld was in his swimming pool with his daughter. He knew his film was doing well, because he started receiving calls of congratulation from heads of studios he'd never even met before. Finally, someone Sonnenfeld did know called—the producer, Scott Rudin—with the news that *Men in Black* had broken all previous July 4th, opening-weekend records. The call only unnerved him more.

"Scott, I gotta tell you that if the movie made $12 million or $220 million it's still the same movie," he said, not altogether accurately.

Rudin replied: "Barry, if on this weekend, of all weekends, you can't be happy, then your mother has won."

A small, roundish man, whose mind seems permanently tuned to

some private channel where repeats of world-famous disasters are being replayed around the clock, Sonnenfeld is something of a worrier. Even in a town that runs on anxiety, and in which careers are measured out in hospital bills, he stands out as a world-class worrywart, an Olympian-standard fretter. When he was shooting his comedy, *Big Trouble,* he came down with stress-induced sciatica, and he once fainted on the set of *The Addams Family* after downing too many cups of coffee: one, two, three, and down he went.

"Oh God this is just so unmanly," he wailed when he came to.

"You're not a very manly guy," replied Rudin.

Naturally, when Spielberg came to him with the script for *Men in Black,* he worried that he wasn't the right man for the job. The action was all over the place—Washington, D.C., Nevada, Kansas—in the globe-trotting manner of *Independence Day* and *Armageddon,* "big manly movies," as Sonnenfeld calls them. "I look at those movies with things blowing up and I don't know how to do them," he says. "I said to Spielberg, if you want to hire me I would totally rewrite the script and shoot it in New York. We should make *The French Connection* with aliens and the comedy is we don't acknowledge that dealing with aliens is funny. Ultimately it's going to be a small cop movie. We're making a little buddy movie with smoke and mirrors. There's no action in the movie, practically. Will runs through some police cars, and taxi cabs. It's a painfully small movie. It's not that I don't want to know how to do them, it's just the nature of how I see things, the lenses I use, everything I do somehow conspires to make the movie small."

If most blockbusters are all forward rush and thrust, then *Men in Black* was all bend, bounce, and Brownian motion, its center of gravity to be found in the scene where Will Smith accidentally releases a rubber ball that then proceeds to demolish the agent's headquarters: "That thing almost destroyed the 1958 Trade Fair," says Tommy Lee Jones— the perfect Sonnenfeld gag, dinky-sized, and quite literally off the wall. "That was our one big action sequence," he says. If you look at the list of all-time biggest box office smashes, there are very few comedies on the list, in fact there's just two, *Ghostbusters* and *Men in Black.* There is no such thing as epic comedy, as Spielberg found out on *1941,* for comedy mocks the profligacy on which epic rests, which is why most epic filmmakers—DeMille, Cameron—can only complete their tasks if unencumbered by anything resembling a sense of humor. The same with the blockbuster, whose sheer size militates against the fleet-footedness required of good comedy. Some of the best jokes in *Ghost-busters* and *Men in Black*—or *Raiders* for that matter—are jokes against scale: the Stay-Puft Man, as tall as Rockefeller Center; Indy's boulder, loosed by a few grains of sand; the tiny gun that Will Smith scorns, and whose kickback then blasts him off his feet; or Smith's response to the navy cadet who enrolls to be "the best of the best of the best . . . and he has no idea why he's here." The joke was, of course, against the "best of the best" speech given to Tom Cruise and his class of navy cadets in *Top Gun.* When Cash and Epps wrote that speech, did they have any idea what a virulent strain of hyperbole they were releas-ing into the Hollywood bloodstream? By 1998, the line had been fric-asseed, flambéed, and flipped over into self-parody, even without Smith's help. You'll remember Harry Stamper, of course, the hero of *Armageddon*—"the best deep-core driller in the world," although as Harry explains, "I'm the best because I work with the best of the best." Naturally, when an asteroid threatens earth ("one of the worst days in NASA history just got worse"), Harry braves "the worst G-forces in the history of flight" in order to do battle with "Dr. Seuss's worst night-mare," although the question still lingers as to which is worse, that asteroid or hanging out with the cast of *Con Air,* the "worst of the worst," according to John Cusack's FBI agent. Ah, the nineties: they were the best of times, they were the worst of times. The cliché was last seen some way off the coast of Hong Kong, in the SWAT team thriller, *The New Option,* about a young man's efforts to become—you'll never guess—"the best of the best" in the world of international snipers.

Men in Black came in at an unusually trim ninety-eight minutes—"much shorter than any movie that's made that much money," says Sonnenfeld proudly—and providing a welcome break from three-hour blockbusters about sinking ships, although its principled stand against the forces of Hollywood giganticism was roundly ignored by the trailer Sony tagged to the front of it, for *Godzilla,* featuring a giant foot crushing a T. rex skeleton in a museum—the tag line? "Size mat-ters." It played so well with audiences that theater owners asked Sony for the right to advertise *Men in Black* on the back of the trailer that was playing before it. "We're at the point where the marketing itself has to be entertaining," said Sony's head of marketing, Bob Levin, and indeed the summer of 1997 saw the art of the trailer lift completely free of the films they promoted, with theaters extending their limit to four, five, even six trailers showing before a movie, while a total of eleven films jostled to have their trailers attached to Spielberg's *The Lost World: Jurassic Park,* in what became known within the industry as the "trailer wars." *Godzilla* was the first to draw blood, with its anti-dino campaign, but when Spielberg's Dreamworks appended a trailer for *Small Soldiers* that featured a giant lizard being hog-tied by a bunch of action figures—tag line: "Size doesn't matter"—Sony threatened to slap a lawsuit on them.

Needless to say, none of this bore any relation to the final movies, for the simple reason that none of them had been shot yet. *Godzilla*'s trailer was a specially commissioned show reel, costing $600,000, and the first installment of what would turn out to be the most prolonged promotional pummeling an audience had ever received, lasting from July of 1997, when trailers were first tagged onto the beginning of *Men in Black,* then spreading to billboard posters in every major city, then more trailers during the New Year's Eve and New Year's Day bowl game telecasts—everything finally grinding to a climax exactly one year later, on May 20, Memorial Day 1998. If you were a seven-year-old child when you first read the slogan "size matters" you were eight by the time you saw the movie it advertised. If you were a potato crop, you would have been harvested and turned into French fries. If you were a joke, however, there was a high likelihood that you would have worn a little thin.

The slogan came about at a meeting Dean Devlin and Roland Emmerich had with Sony's marketing executives. "A very legitimate question was raised by the marketing people," says Devlin. "They said 'If I've already seen *Jurassic Park,* why do I need to see *Godzilla*? Haven't I already seen the big lizard movie?' And that's when a very clever marketing executive said, 'Well, size does matter.' And so we put it in the first teaser and sure enough it got huge laughs. The problem is, if you hear a joke too often it stops being funny. There was a real desire to try and duplicate what had happened with *Independence Day,* which seemed to be this incredibly hyped movie, but the truth is it wasn't that hyped. I think that the actual marketing costs on that movie domestically was something like $22 million, but it felt like $100 million because it became a cultural thing. You can't pay to get *Time* and *Newsweek* covers on the same weekend, but we got them. Well, they were trying to create that by buying it. The *Independence Day* trailers came out seven months in advance; with *Godzilla* it was a year in advance, and we live in a very disposable culture. Nothing lasts for a year. Nothing in the culture survives a year."

Godzilla started life back in 1993, when Peter Guber's assistant, Cary Woods, together with a producer friend of his called Rob Fried, first started agitating to film a new version of the Japanese B movie. They pitched it everywhere in the Sony organization, but were told it was yesterday's news. "We pitched the idea to Columbia and they passed outright," said Woods. "Their response was they felt it had the potential for camp." Woods was lamenting his failure to his wife, when she asked, "'Have you pitched Guber?' I explained that I can't pitch Guber—he's the boss, the head of the company. He doesn't want to get involved in production decisions. She just stared at me and said, 'Pitch Guber.'"

Woods flew down to Florida, where the Sony CEO was due to give a speech, and, within seconds, "Peter got it; he saw the movie in his head. He was like 'Godzilla? The fire-breathing monster? *Yessss!*'" Sony needed a hit badly; after the fiasco of *Last Action Hero*, they had followed up with one dud after another—*I'll Do Anything, Poetic Justice, Striking Distance,* and *Geronimo,* which lost $40 million, far more than *Last Action Hero.* Guber saw an opportunity for the company to reverse its slide, and set up the film at TriStar after securing the rights from *Godzilla*'s Japanese keepers, Toho. "I've done my bit," he told Woods. "Now it's up to you to get this thing rolling. You have to give it momentum." Woods and Fried hired writers Ted Elliott and Terry Rossio—who would later write *Shrek*—and the two came up with a script that roughly followed the outline of the original *Godzilla,* with him in the good guy role against a monster named the Gryphon. "They wrote a beautiful original screenplay," says Fried, "respectful of the organic origins of *Godzilla,* in some ways a homage to U.S.–Japanese relations, there was a new character, a new foe for *Godzilla.* They did a really good job."

They had more difficulty trying to snare a director for their project—trying Tim Burton, James Cameron, and even considering the Coens before approaching Jan de Bont, then fresh from the first *Speed*. When de Bont's budget estimates came in at $150 million, however, "Sony got frightened and pulled out," says Fried. De Bont took his cast—Helen Hunt and Bill Paxton—elsewhere, to chase tornadoes. By now, *Independence Day* was a hit, and Mark Canton, the head of Columbia TriStar, dispatched two executives to woo the filmmakers. "All we could see was farce," says Devlin. "We could see the joke but we couldn't see the movie, but it's always a strange thing when another successful director takes on a film you've said no to. You suddenly go, 'Wait a minute, what did he see that we didn't see? What did we miss?'" Once the project had swung back from its time with de Bont, the two men retired to the rented villa in Puerto Vallarta, in Mexico, where they had written *ID4*, and set to work, and by the time they finished, they emerged to find Sony in complete disarray.

The Guber-Canton regime had finally imploded, after the company reported operating losses of $42 million. Guber was asked to resign and Canton was fired, making way for John Calley, a sixty-year-old industry veteran who saw himself as something of a maverick, refusing to wear a suit and tie. Even so, before he said yes to Devlin's script, he first gave it to Bob Levin, Sony's head of marketing, to see if he could sell the movie. "In this realm, it's critical," he said. "I mean, if Bob throws up his hands and says, 'I don't know what to do with a giant lizard,' we're all going to be scratching our heads." Levin gave *Godzilla* the thumbs-up and Calley called Devlin. "I read your script of *Godzilla*. I want to assure you that I will make your movie. Is that clear?"

"Very clear," replied Devlin.

Fried and Woods were furious to see their baby snatched from them. "The Sony executive team that took over *Godzilla* was one of the worst cases of executive incompetence I have observed in my twenty-year career," says Fried. "One of the golden assets of our time, which was hand-delivered to them, was managed as poorly and ineptly as anybody can manage an asset. They took a jewel and turned it into dust. They had the wrong creative sensibility: they let Roland and Dean go. There was no understanding of the property and what it was all about. There was just this enthusiasm about having this project. They announced the release date—Memorial Day—so now they're targeting the release date a year in advance, so now the movie has to hit a date rather than allowing the movie to get made and be the best it could be. They handed the keys of the studio to a couple of guys who happened to have a hit film. They wouldn't allow any of the licensees to see the creature, they weren't even allowed to ship the toys until the day of the release of the movie, they were so obsessed with the secrecy of it. It was no big secret, but those six weeks prior to the release of the movie are when you do the bulk of your sales and they eliminated that. So when the film was disappointing they had all this excess merchandise."

Sony had lined up the usual array of marketing partners—Taco Bell contributed $60 million to promote its Gordita line of tacos—but the merchandisers, who had produced more than three hundred products, would find the *Godzilla* dolls being outsold by Teletubbies at a rate of three to one. "Look at these damn things," complained one store owner. "They arrive after the movie opened. They're hard to assemble. And they look like leftovers from an old Spielberg film." Even more crucially, Devlin and Emmerich found themselves with no time to test it, but were forced to unveil their hasty final cut to great fanfare at Madison Square Garden and L.A.'s Dome Theater. "Thank goodness we've just got the second- and third-string critics here," muttered one Sony executive.

"Everybody was mad at everybody," said another. "Devlin and Emmerich suddenly became monsters with their demands and complaints." Emmerich blames the outsized marketing campaign. "They ran the opposite campaign to *Independence Day,*" he says. "They didn't trust it. It was a good idea—'size does matter'—but because they put it on every available fucking billboard it became a joke. I remember one day I drove to my house, on La Brea, and there was this billboard, 'He's longer than whatever . . .' and I thought, 'Oh that's cool. But every day I drove home, one more billboard appeared, so by the time the movie came out, you had had twenty encounters with *Godzilla.* I said that's too much. I felt it on the street. Sony wanted to have a hit, but the audience feels it if the studio is trying too hard. They did that campaign because they had to sell merchandising products. It was like a movie and a product, which wasn't right. It didn't work. It worked but . . . it didn't work."

"One of the curious side effects of hype," Anthony Lane once wrote in *The New Yorker,* "is that the longer and more loudly a work is discussed the less idea you have of what it is actually like." In the case of *Godzilla,* however, the two experiences, waiting for it and watching it, were weirdly similar. After a year of marketers telling us how big *Godzilla* was, what did we get but a one-and-a-half-hour movie full of people telling us how big *Godzilla* was. "No creature could have made footprints this large!" exclaims Matthew Broderick. "Jesus, Mary, and Joseph, that's large!" yells cameraman Hank Azaria—a preoccupation with size that extends, in rather surreal fashion, even to such seemingly minor details such as job titles ("sounds big!"), guns ("we're going to need bigger guns"), and even piles of dead fish ("That is a lot of fish!"). If the characters in *Independence Day* were all movie critics, in *Godzilla,* they were all marketing executives, staying resolutely on-message about their creature's size.

The line about "bigger guns" was of course, a reference to Roy Scheider's famous line in *Jaws*—"we're gonna need a bigger boat"—although the crucial thing, of course, is that they didn't get it; all they had was the leaky, sinking *Orca,* from which to pitch their wits against the shark. If there was one thing that distinguished the early blockbusters of Spielberg and Lucas from their DeMillean predecessors, it was their speed, not their size; Spielberg's reputation as a purveyor of the grandiose is misplaced, his talent being not for the big but the big, glimpsed obliquely through the small: in *Close Encounters,* the first sign that UFOs were about to arrive was the elimination of the sound of crickets from the soundtrack. The first sign that UFOs were about to arrive in *Independence Day,* on the other hand, was the sight of four fifteen-mile-wide UFOs, parked above America's largest cities. The problem with such up-front thrill delivery is with the follow-through; having built up the aliens as the biggest, most invincible thing in God's creation, the film has no way to defeat them except by recourse to a handy computer program that Jeff Goldblum suddenly remembers he has in his back pocket. *Now* he tells us. You barely noticed such sleights-of-hand in *ID4*—such was its rah-rah rush—but Devlin and Emmerich's preoccupation with scale was more cruelly left exposed in *Godzilla,* for having summoned their poor creature to New York, and congratulated him on his stature, what are they to do with him, except lose him amid the very buildings he'd been towering over just seconds before—"He's in there someplace," says Broderick, gazing at the New York skyline, "He's resting"—so as to make way for some smaller lizards who could be relied upon to chase people down corridors and leap out at them from behind cabinets. So size turned out not to matter, after all.

Godzilla opened in seven thousand theaters, but having generated expectations of $300 million, took in just $55 million in its first weekend; by the end of its first week, it had taken in $74 million, before dropping 60 percent in the second week to take in just $17 million, and $10 million in its third—a catastrophic drop by most standards. "You're the first filmmakers ever to experience a $74 million opening week and still be called losers," mocked *Variety,* although an outraged Devlin was to be found responding angrily on the Internet: "Please tell me how you figure that a movie that will make a studio over a hundred million dollars in profit is a flop? Where did you learn your math?" Indeed, it took in $22 million in Japan, $21 million in the U.K., and did extraordinarily well in Latin America, taking in $12.4 million in Mexico, $7.5 million in Brazil, $6.1 million in Argentina, all in its first week, before repeating the pattern and fading fast as news of its quality spread. In a way it was the cruellest fate of all for the creature: not to be allowed the dignity of death, but to be kept alive by the life-support machine of seven thousand screens and $50 million worth of marketing, in country after country, as each lined up to peer at the poor thing—this fabled, flailing blockbuster—smashing into buildings again and again, acting out his failure for all to see. In one sense, its "failure" was a complete mirage, a leftover from another era, when it was easy to tell if a film had failed or succeeded, but now long since gone. With a final gross of $376 million, making it the third biggest movie of the year—*Godzilla* was the world's first $375 million flop, which is to say, no flop at all. It was the Flop That Wasn't.

How bad do these things have to be to properly fail, anymore? A lot worse than *Godzilla* evidently. When the causes of the decline of popular film come to be writ, the fact that *Godzilla* made $375 million will surely be some kind of inverted bizarro-world landmark. When movies that critics hate make money, you just put it down to grumpy critics, or the madness of crowds, or somesuch, and leave it at that. But when movies that nobody likes—not even its creators—make $375 million, then something is seriously wrong with the art of popular moviemaking. It wasn't *Godzilla*'s fault, or its makers: they just made a bad movie. People do it all the time. "I think that the number one thing that was wrong with *Godzilla* was the movie that we made, and I say that as the writer of the film," says Devlin. "The mistakes that we made were my mistakes. Roland did a great job directing that film and the actors did a great job with the think characters I had written for them. But all the mistakes were in the script. We had a chance to fix that but it was the only movie I've ever done that we didn't screen-test. It is my biggest regret in life because if we had done even one screen-test we would have fixed it."

Critics tend to be down on test screenings, as constituting yet another tentacle of the market, reaching Kraken-like into the theater to drag unwary filmmakers to their doom, but the fact remains that in today's Hollywood they mark one of the few remaining points of contact between a filmmaker and his audience. Devlin's plea for more feedback—more information, *any* information from the audience—is genuinely plaintive, for there are precious few other means of gauging a movie's popularity. It used to be relatively easy to ascertain: you looked at the number of bums on seats. Not the most expressive tool of communication in the history of human contact, but it did the trick. We went to a film, and if we liked it we told our friends, and then they saw it, and over time, the number of bums on seats left a collective and probably quite literal impression: you could tell exactly what sort of impact a film had had by the swell and surge of its box office, or by its tailoff and truncation, and over time, it all added up to a remarkably contoured map of our likes and dislikes—the literal shape of our affection—which the filmmakers and studio executives could read and use to make their decisions on which movies to next green-light. We made ourselves heard; we let the studios know what we liked and what we didn't—what was popular and what was not.

By 1998, that ability was sorely eroded. By 1998, what was in place was a system where it is perfectly possible for a studio to buy our curiosity for the space of a single weekend, which was all the time the studio needed to make back its money. It didn't matter whether we liked what we saw or not, only that we sat there, liking it or disliking it in sufficient numbers. To use Spielberg's formulation: they could now sell it faster than we could smell it. What could Sony infer from our presence in the theater watching *Godzilla*? Very little, in fact. They could not conclude that we liked the film or disliked it, loved it or hated it. All they could safely conclude—if they were interested in concluding anything at all, which of course they weren't, since it made $375 million—is that we were curious, of a Saturday afternoon, to see what the fuss was all about. That's all our bum on a seat now meant: the satisfaction of a vague curiosity, and vague curiosity—unlike like, or dislike, let alone love—could be bought, which is why *Godzilla* made $375 million, and why *Waterworld* made $255.2 million. While *Waterworld*'s theatrical release was the occasion for much principled disgust at the waste of $200 million, more than a few of us were curious to see what wasting $200 million looked like, and so when it came out on video we rented it. And then it was shown on cable TV, and what sort of person is it, frankly, who won't even raise their wrist and flip the channel to see $200 million going down the drain? Repeat that in country after country and bingo, the year's biggest flop is one of the year's biggest hits! By raising that remote, you've just given *Wild Wild West* the green light! This is why the press's decade-long hunt for the true blockbuster turkey—the one that would bring the whole system crashing down—was always going to come up empty. All the means by which studios had insured themselves against failure—video revenues, overseas sales, marketing budgets of $100 million—had worked only too well, forming such a thick wall of insulation as to eliminate a certain stratum of failure from its system altogether, like an alcoholic who no longer registers his hangovers, his system simply soaking up each fresh abuse. These things were now doomed to success, "failing upwards," buoyed by all the means by which the studios had insured themselves from ruin.

In the end, it was the theaters who took the punch. Someone had to, and it wasn't going to be the moviegoers and it wasn't going to be the studios. The theaters, on the other hand, had overbuilt, and by 1998, the number of screens in America had swollen, in the space of five years, from slightly fewer than 28,000 to more than 37,000. At ShoWest in 1997, a panel of concerned theater owners gathered to discuss such topics of the hour as "How much is too much?" "How loud is too loud?" and "Giant Screens: Is Bigger Better?" "The building that took place in the last half of the nineties was very rapid," says John Fithian, the president of the National Association of Theater Owners. "We did not close down older theaters fast enough to make room for the new properties that were coming online. We got to the point where there were too many movie screens. . . . The patrons wanted new amenities, but the companies got too highly leveraged in the process, and got into trouble."

It was the terms exacted by the studios for the rights to show their summer blockbusters that would finally break the camel's back. "They screwed themselves by overbuilding," says Rob Fried, "but the studios exploited and pushed them to the point of collapse." For *Godzilla*, Sony had asked cinemas to fork over an unprecedented 80 percent of their opening week profits, dropping to 75 percent in the second week, and 70 percent in the third and fourth—plus an up-front guarantee of $4 million. Given that it did most of its business in its first week, it wasn't hard to do the math; the picture wasn't around long enough for the theaters to start making a profit, and by the autumn of 1999, Carmike Theaters, the largest U.S. chain, was blaming its second-quarter earnings drop on the film, sending its shares plummeting by 5.7 percent to hit a fifty-two-week low. "Carmike clearly got killed on the terms," said one Hollywood agent. "They were told they had a diamond when they really had cubic zirconia." Within a few years, Carmike, along with eleven other of America's leading theater chains, would be filing for bankruptcy.

The terms exacted from theaters for the right to show *Godzilla* were as nothing, though, compared to the terms imposed on them a year later by Twentieth Century Fox for the rights to screen *The Phantom Menace*, the first of George Lucas's prequels to *Star Wars*. Tom Sherak, Fox's marketing chief, had done his homework: poring over the record books, he looked for all the tiny concessions theater owners had made to studios over the years, and then compiled them into one big profit-squeezing deal. It was death by a thousand cuts. *The Phantom Menace* had to run in the biggest and best theaters. If it ran on multiple screens, it had to continue to do so. No more than eight minutes of trailers were to be shown before the screening, and no onscreen ads at all for the first two weeks. Oh yes, and it had to have a minimum run of eight to twelve weeks—the whole summer, in other words, or else the theater had to pay a penalty and have their print of the film confiscated. "They couldn't say no because it was *Star Wars*," said Sherak. "They couldn't say no because they'd done it before."

In one important regard, Lucas avoided the pitfalls into which *Godzilla* had fallen, opening on only 3,800 screens—half the expected amount. "I thought it was kind of brilliant," says Dean Devlin. "So there were far less theaters, and you had to wait in line again. So you saw those lines outside and thought, 'I gotta be a part of that.' It was genius." Cinema queues had been one of the first casualties of the multiplex era, with its multiple screens and round-the-clock screenings. Whereas in 1977, the sign of a good blockbuster was a ring of people around the block, by 1999, a blockbuster meant the opposite: a film with no queues whatsoever. But not only did *The Phantom Menace* have queues, it had live webcam broadcasts of its queues: you could either line up to watch the film or you could watch the lines of those who lined up to watch it. When Fox premiered a preview of the movie's trailer in theaters on November 21, 1998—in effect, a preview of a preview—it caused box office of the film it preceded, *The Siege,* to jump 85 percent, as fans paid up, saw the trailer, and then left the theater. When Apple made the trailer available online, 10 million people downloaded it; a search on eBay found twenty-five prints of it on sale to bidders, until the sale was shut down by Lucasfilm attorneys.

The hype for one blockbuster movie tends to blur into the hype for the next, forming one long indiscriminate blur of Pepsi promotions and burger bonanzas, but the hype for *The Phantom Menace* possessed its own peculiar inverse magnitude, like that of a collapsing sun—so dense as to form a species of promotional black hole. "PR professionals are being forced to practice a kind of anti-hype," reported *Variety.* "We're almost trying to get people not to talk about it," said one publicist at Fox, which spent a minimal amount marketing the movie, just $10 million, almost half what they might normally spend, for who needed to hype it? Their marketing was carried out by the film's marketing partners—Tricon Global Restaurants and Hasbro, who had promised a stunning $600 million for the rights to manufacture toys for all three prequels. The toy-makers had also agreed to other extraordinary conditions, such as a complete moratorium on old *Star Wars* toys, which were to be held back from stores, to make room for the new ones; and the new ones were not to be unveiled in shops a day before May 3, "Menace Monday"; store owners were told that Lucasfilm would have agents go to stores, and if they found any premature merchandise, they would lose the rights to sell any *Star Wars* toys, ever again. "It's like a military campaign," said one store owner.

"It's only a movie," said Lucas, displaying a keen grasp of the words "it's" and "only," for in the end it would turn out to be both much more than a movie, and somehow much less. Either way, here was something we were all *very* curious about.

TIME LINE

1998

1. *Armageddon* (Disney) $554.6 (36.4%)
2. *Saving Private Ryan* (Dreamworks) $479.3 (45.1%)
3. *Godzilla* (Sony) $376.0 (36.3%)
4. *There's Something About Mary* (Fox) $360.1 (49.0%)
5. *A Bug's Life* (Disney) $358.0 (45.5%)
6. *Deep Impact* (Paramount) $348.8 (40.3%)
7. *Mulan* (Disney) $303.6 (39.7%)
8. *Lethal Weapon 4* (WB) $285.4 (45.7%)
9. *Shakespeare in Love* (Miramax) $279.2 (36.4%)
10. *The Truman Show* (Paramount) $248.4 (50.6%)

*Figures show worldwide gross, in millions of dollars, followed by the percentage of that generated in the U.S.

CHAPTER 16

THE EMPIRE STRIKES BACK

"The decline of Rome was the natural and inevitable effect
of immoderate greatness. Prosperity ripened the princi-
ples of decay, the causes of destruction multiplied with the
extent of conquest, and as soon as time or accident had
removed the artificial supports, the stupendous fabric
yielded to the pressure of its own weight."

— Edward Gibbon, *The History of the Decline and Fall of
the Roman Empire*, 1776

By the beginning of the nineties, *Star Wars* was as dead as film franchises get. The last film had been in 1983, there were no more comic books or novelizations, and the merchandising had all but dribbled to a halt. "In 1985, the toys were over," said Howard Roffman, head of merchandising at Lucasfilm. "You couldn't even mention *Star Wars* to retailers." So much so, that in 1991, the toy manufacturer Hasbro, which had acquired Kenner, surrendered the licensing rights back to Lucasfilm. It was, one industry analyst said later, "one of the greatest blunders in the history of merchandising."

The resurgence started in 1991, when Bantam published a novelization called *Heir to the Empire,* by Timothy Zahn, which picked up the story of Luke Skywalker five years after the events of *Return of the Jedi,* and which went straight to number one on the *New York Times* best-seller list, remaining on the list for twenty-nine weeks, and eventually spawning its own sequels and games. Hasbro began negotiations

with Lucasfilm again, and in 1995 released a new line of figures, which by 1998 was making $400 million a year. "If it weren't for the merchandizing, there would never have been the next three Star Wars," says Spielberg. "The phenomenon of the reissue started with Hasbro. I know that George was always planning to make three more films but this quickened George's plans by twelve months. This was the huge economic indicator where George said "my God the audience is out there, more than ever before," and then with the reissue, which did $135 million domestically, the handwriting was there in bold italics on the wall."

During the early nineties, the annual company meeting at Lucasfilm had followed a set pattern: someone would invariably ask Lucas, "When are you going to make the next round of Star Wars pictures?" and Lucas's reply was always the same: "At some point, in a few years, not yet." In 1996 he started a cleanup operation on the original Star Wars trilogy: one shot, in particular, had always bugged him—showing Luke's land-speeder as it entered Mos Eisley airport—but as Lucas and his technicians got to work, they became enmeshed in a problem they called "washing just part of the car." "You look and you go, 'Oh here's the dirtiest part here,' and you kind of clean that up and everything else looks dirty," says John Knoll, who led the cleanup operation. "And then you clean up the bit that looks like the next dirtiest thing and you never arrive at this point where it all feels clean because there's still something that's not quite right. And so George went through and said, 'I want to fix this and this and this and this.' And that changed as we worked on it, because we'd do these shots and then something else would stand out." They would end up redoing five hundred shots in the first three movies, inserting wholly new scenes, new characters, changing the motivations of existing ones: in the 1977 Star Wars Han Solo was seen to shoot an alien down in cold blood; an added sound effect now made it clear that he was returning fire. A quick cleanup had shaded, imperceptibly, into revisionism.

Knoll, like many who now worked at Industrial Light & Magic, was a teenager when the first Star Wars came out—his father worked there as a model maker, and one day in 1978 invited him out there to visit, which was, he says, like entering the Valley of the Kings—so he says he had "mixed feelings about working on the special edition. I kind of felt

like those are a classic product of their time, and all the things that are kind of dated about them, well, that's because of when they were made, and the conditions they were made under. That's fine, you don't go back and remake films from the forties to try and make the sets more believable. They are what they are. They have a stylization that comes from the period they were made." It was a high-tech version of the perfectionist's paradox—the search for perfection unearthing only more imperfections—and something of the same aggravated itch seemed to spread to the film's fans, who, upon the film's release, joined Lucas in his labyrinth. "The scene is ruined! Han isn't the type to only shoot in self-defense. That was a terrible change," wrote one of the added blaster shot. "An utterly pointless change," said another. "George was sloppy," using the mother-knows-best tone in which *Star Wars* fans often speak. In some ways, they *did* know best, for they were the only ones to stay abreast of an endlessly expanding fictional universe that had long since spilled beyond the actual films—into the novelizations, video games, and comics, each turning up new worlds and characters along the way.

For the fans, then, *The Phantom Menace* was always going to be more than just a movie, and would be received with the same scholastic rapture as the Dead Sea Scrolls; while for Lucas, it was an attempt to wrest control of a saga that had long since passed from his hands. "It was pretty clear to a lot of us that [the special editions were] a dry run, a test on a lot of different levels," says Knoll. "One was: George had been away from doing visual effects for a while, and wanted to get familiar with how easy it is to do this kind of shot and how hard it was to do that kind of shot. Get familiar with working with the medium." It is important to remember: Lucas was new to CGI. His company, ILM, had developed it, and his technicians had used it at the behest of other filmmakers, but he himself did not have a drop of CGI in his creative bloodstream. Its effect on his system was therefore rapacious and all-consuming, a little as if Toad of Toad Hall had returned to a car salesroom, after an absence of twenty-two years, and decided to tak the newest Porsche out for a spin. Most accidents involving Porse happen within five minutes of the showroom.

The sheer scale of the production first dawned on the effe at ILM when Lucas initially led everyone through his story

the film—all 3,500 of them, posted up on thirty-five boards, each with ten columns with ten shots to a column. "We'd started hearing things like two hundred shots and everyone started scattering. I said, 'Is this going to continue?'" says Dennis Muren, who along with Knoll and Scott Squires headed up three teams of digital artists, many of them just children when the first *Star Wars* had come out, like Knoll—six hundred all told, more than half of ILM's workforce, using computers whose amassed power was a little less than that used by NASA but more than that used by the Pentagon. In the autumn of 1997, some photographic footage was shot, using real actors—Liam Neeson and Ewan McGregor and Natalie Portman—but this was just raw material, to be shaped and molded at will in the computers. Some scenes of straight dialogue ended up using up to six layers of computer-composited imagery. In one scene, Natalie Portman's best take had been take seven; but child actor Jake Lloyd's was take one; so they simply spliced them together; but Lloyd's mouth still gaped open unappealingly at the end, so they went to take fifteen, in which it was closed, and patched that in; and when Portman looked down to Lloyd, instead of up, they ran those few seconds backward, and when this caused steam to rise in reverse, they flipped the steam back . . . Liam Neeson would, upon release of the film, take the opportunity to declare his retirement from movies. "We are basically puppets," he complained. "I don't think I can live with the inauthenticity of movies anymore."

Lucas, however, was in his element, finally able to attempt the epic vision he insists he missed in *Star Wars*. "I'd wanted to make it much bigger than it was," says Lucas, "much more out there in terms of creatures and aliens, and the environments and all that stuff and I had to really restrict my imagination to a very very thin line that I could make work. . . . I was forced constantly to write something very very small, even though *Star Wars* seems very big, it was an illusion, it's technically very small, and I was always going 'I wanna do this, Oh, I can't do that, I wanna do those, Oh I can't do that.' In those three films there's a lot of frustration in not being able to do the things I wanted to do."

Says Knoll: "George liked to repurpose things, shoot elements and then decide he wanted to make it a wide shot, blow this up and change this and put that character there: 'What if I take this guy from this shot and put him in the back of this scene?' There's a lot of torture of elements that goes on. You go, 'You know, this is just not the right way to do this shot. All right, but this is the way George wants to do it, so I'll go and figure out how to not make it look bad.' You go and try and put something in that's acceptable." Knoll had originally tried to assign different planets to different illustrators, in an attempt to maintain consistency of design, but the plan soon sunk beneath the workload and their employer's mix-and-match instincts: a levitational platform intended for Tatooine instead popped up on Corruscant; some beasts of burden called Kaadu were moved from Naboo to Tatooine. When some illustrators pointed out that the civilization in *The Phantom Menace* looked more advanced than that in *Star Wars*, which it was supposed to precede, Lucas had an answer ready: "George would say, 'Well not when you think about it. Because in the previous trilogy we never see civilization. Everywhere we're taken in *Star Wars, Empire* and *Jedi*, are sort of the boonies,'" says Knoll. "'Tatooine is this far-flung outpost, very remote. You never really see a thriving civilization, so here was this chance to see what mainstream *Star Wars* looks like.' They were very understandable and well-thought-out rationales for why things were the way they were." That's the way Lucas would always respond to any querulous staff, with lofty invocations of the grand design of the saga: you weren't to know this, he would say, but it's important for the third film. Or: you don't understand, but it's part of the stylistic patterning, the musical riff, I've got going in my head.

They worked like this for close to three years, the children of *Star Wars*, from the spring of 1997 to the summer of 1999, with Lucas hovering at their backs, correcting and refining, mixing and matching elements, much like Walt Disney used to do with his illustrators. In a sense, he hadn't returned to moviemaking at all, but waited until moviemaking had come to him in a form more conducive to his shy, synthesizing talents. "I have a sneaking suspicion that if there were a way to make movies without actors, George would do it," Lark Hamill had once remarked. Now Lucas had found the glimmers of a way. As the film neared completion, the usually press-shy director embarked on a full publicity junket, waxing lyrical about the Renaissance, Kierkegaard, Dante, Shakespeare, and telling journalists, "It's really about the downfall of Anakin Skywalker, the young Darth Vader and his descent into evil," he said. "That's the real story. It's always been about the redemption of Anakin Skywalker, it's just that it's always been told from his son's point of view." Although Lucas seemed a little unsure on this point, later saying, "In *Episode IV* where the story is told through the point of view of the droids, this one is the point of view of the Jedi." And again: "This story is told primarily from the Jedi's point of view, but the story that's being told is essentially the story of Queen Amidala." Well, which?

At a rough cut of the film in March, the cracks were beginning to show. The film told so many stories, it was beginning to sink beneath its own weight, and as it finished, everyone sat back in silence.

"It's a little . . . disjointed," admitted Lucas, finally.

"It seems like . . . a lot of short scenes," suggested his producer, Rick McCallum.

"It's bold in terms of jerking people around," said Lucas, quietly, "but I may have gone too far . . . in a few places."

"In a space of about ninety seconds," said Ben Burtt, the film co-editor, "you go from lamenting the death of our hero, to escape, to slightly comedic with Jar Jar, you know, to Anakin returning . . . It's a lot, really . . . in a very short time."

"You know, I've thought about this quite a bit," replied Lucas, "and the tricky part is you can't take any of those pieces out of there now, because each takes you to the next place. You can't jump because you don't know where you are."

Lucas, Burtt, and McCallum retired to the water-cooler outside for further conference, where McCallum tried to put a brave spin on things. "When you think about the first *Star Wars*, sitting there," he said gesturing to the cupboard containing the original film's reels, "it starts out and you don't know what the hell—"

Mention of the first *Star Wars* only seemed to anger Lucas, who cut him off.

"It's a very hard movie to follow and at the same time, I've done it a little more extremely than I've ever done it in the past. It's stylistically designed to be that way, and you can't cut that, but we can diminish the effect of it, we can slow it down a little bit . . ." They agreed to meet the next day and continue to work on it.

□ □ □

The effect on fans was spectacular and divisive. The more scholarly put pen to paper and wrote essays with titles like "Learning to Cope with *The Phantom Menace*," but the real backlash came, appropriately enough, by computer—via the two hundred Web sites devoted to *Star Wars* on the Internet, where apologists for the film, "Gushers," did battle with those who had hated it—"Bashers"—in what became known as the Gusher-Basher Wars. "It was as if Lucas were making two films," wrote one Basher. "One full of sophomoric humor and silliness for the kiddies, and one intense in plot and subterfuge, aimed more at adults." The Gushers responded with what became known as the "eyes of a child gambit," suggesting that the Bashers had simply grown too old for a film that was always intended to be for children: Jar Jar Binks "may seem like cheap comedy relief but he drove the entire third act of the friggin' movie," said one. "As for all the 'yippees,' that's how little kids talk." It was a long and hard fight, which finally reached a stalemate, with the two sides calling a truce and agreeing not to trespass on each other's territory. "I fear there can be no true reconciliation," intoned one, with a glumness worthy of Obi Wan, while another attempted to effect a compromise within her own breast: "People like me, who enjoyed *The Phantom Menace* more on repeated viewings, did so because we began to tune out Jar Jar," she wrote. There is probably a no more heartbreaking note in all the fan literature devoted to *Star Wars*: the plaintive sound of a fan, masking her heartbreak, and returning to see the film, again and again, in the hopes that she may one day grow to love it.

Needless to say, the online scrap about the film—fierce, prolonged, passionate, and not without an element of ironic role-play—was about ten times more engrossing than the film itself, which opens with the Trade Federation invading the planet of Naboo, and then sits tight for an hour and a half while everyone tries to get the necessary motion passed through the Senate that will allow them to retaliate. In the meantime we get a leisurely tour of the galaxy, with the Jedi first visiting an underwater world, then stopping off on Tatooine for what—a few days, weeks?—in order to make friends and take in a pod race. Thrilling this race undoubtedly is, but you couldn't help wondering what Princess Leia might have said if Han Solo and Luke had stopped off to play space pool while en route to rescue her from the Death Star.

And when the Empire engaged the rebels in battle, they didn't wait two hours before they could get clearance to retaliate, they struck right back. But then that was one of the advantages of *Star Wars:* it was, as it said, a war film. After a decade of moral ambiguity and fug, Lucas offered us a straightforward scrap between good and evil, starting with a space battle that leaves the droids scattered on the space winds, before crash-landing on the far-flung planet of Tatooine. "If there's a bright center to the universe, then you're furthest from it," Luke tells the droids, and if the twin suns setting in the background remains the most beautiful sight in the entire series it is possibly because it is the only shot in which Lucas had the courage to convey *boredom*—the honest-to-goodness boredom of every teenager trapped in the boondocks, dreaming of a life elsewhere. You would hesitate to call *Star Wars* an autobiographical film in the way that, say, *Mean Streets* is an autobiographical film, but there was no doubting the honesty of the note of backwoods longing that it sounded—which Lucas had first sounded in *American Graffiti,* but which he now transplanted to outer space, so everyone could join in.

There were always signs that this was going to change. By the time of the second film, Luke was revealed as the son of Darth Vader; his connection to the saga was no longer accidental; it had been seeking him out all along, and the offer of adventure to audiences was subtly rescinded: the Force, previously open to all, was now merely a matter of good breeding. By the time of the third film, it had changed again; Luke was now revealed as not just the son of a lord, but the brother of a princess; the Force was now by royal appointment only. And so the saga became less American, more European and dynastic in tone, more hermetically sealed from outside interference; as Han Solo, always the voice of reason in the series, says, "I'm out of it for a little while, and everyone gets delusions of grandeur." Ford's powers of sarcasm were always the grit in the oyster, and back in 1977 Lucas hadn't yet found a way to expurgate that grit—all the happy accidents that beset any film born of collaborative process. *Star Wars* was, said Lucas, "only 50–60 percent" a realization of his vision for the film, which is why it is as good as it is: he had to fight for it, which is why there is fight in the picture.

"I would say it's about 90 percent of what I wanted it to be," Lucas would say of *The Phantom Menace*, which is why it is the film that it is—a soothing dream of omnipotence, from which all sense of fight has been surgically removed. A mythos that spoils for a fight had been denied one at every turn. "I kind of enjoyed the idea of making the good guys invincible and having the bad guys cowering in fear," says Lucas, which pretty much explains everything. The hard edges of *Star Wars* have been sanded away to make way for creamy art nouveau designs and spindly droids, through which the Jedis' light-sabers scythe like knives through hot butter, while their powers of mind control have been vastly expanded upon. The picture seems to find its mesmerized center in Liam Neeson's soft-voiced croon, as he whispers irresistible instructions to his enemies—a perfect expression of Lucas's own taste for soft-spoken authority, but a million miles away from *Star Wars*, a picture filled with people running into rooms and shouting urgently inexplicable instructions to one another, a commotion that has now been smoothed away for a series of slow shuffles into vast halls, and endless honorific introductions: "The princess, your honor." And there you have the problem with the prequels: films, in every sense, about keeping the peace. It's passive-aggressive sci-fi.

Trouble is brewing, of course, in the shape of little Anakin Skywalker, whom the Jedi find on Tatooine, no longer the back-end of the universe, but a bustling Constantinople of merchants and slave-traders, and who we find out was born to his mother of immaculate conception: the Force, previously open to all, then by royal appointment only, is now exercised by divine right alone. As Liam Neeson says, "There's always a bigger fish." And there you have the film's governing aesthetic—one of helpless ramification, endless expansion—for it teems with the sort of vast halls, Doric columns, and splashy colonnades that have been preoccupying those blessed with limitless imaginations since Coleridge first put to paper. Why is it that whenever we let these geniuses loose—let your imagination roam, my friend!—they always check out the same book on neoclassical architecture from the library? There is one obvious reason for this genuflection before scale, of course: computers, which just happen to be good at all the things—vast, endless, repetitious shapes and forms—with which Lucas used to tag the evil Empire. His switch of allegiances—which at first seemed evidence of an intriguing moral tussle—really boiled down to an echo of the aesthetic tussle that started up once he decided to produce the film digitally. Once he had decided that, he was always going to be on the side of the Empire, and the Empire would always win. *The Phantom Menace, Attack of the Clones*: even the titles of these movies sound like love letters to the computer's powers of mass multiplication, while also confessing to the airy nebulousness they lend movie plots. Was there ever a menace as phantom as the Trade Federation, which forever hovers in the margins of *Episode I*? Seemingly without a planet of their own, but capable of dropping millions of troops from a clear blue sky, they seem both multitudinous and strangely will-o'-the-wisp. It would be a problem that would haunt the prequels: for with the nascent Darth Vader now holding our attention, Lucas could ill afford to let any other bad guy seize center stage, and so would have to rely on a series of disposable creeps—Darth Maul, Count Dooku—all of whom get summoned, then dropped into the pocket of the next, like Russian dolls, and all eventually pointing back to the chief puppeteer, Lucas himself, Oz behind his curtain.

It's one strange performance, all right, with a sweat of performance anxiety that befits a twenty-two years' absence from the fray—all grandiosity and nervous giggles, fart jokes and echoing halls, like an early Disney movie shot by Leni Riefenstahl, *Mickey Goes Nuremberg*—although one thing the film forcefully and instantly dispelled was the idea that Lucas had some grand plan for his saga. The decision to return to Tatooine was, very simply, a catastrophic idea, piling up so much backstory as to push him further away from the first five minutes of *Star Wars,* not closer, and requiring memory wipes for both droids if *Star Wars* is still to make any kind of sense. It's safe to say, I think, that if a prequel requires amnesia for 50 percent of your cast, then it is not really working as a prequel. You could see the fans in the theater, clutching their foreheads with the effort of processing each fresh revelation: "Darth Vader *built* C-3PO?" "Luke is the son of the son of God?" "Everyone on Tatooine *knew?*" It is one of the ironies of Lucas's position that a filmmaker so averse to joining the dots of his plots should find himself beset by a sea of fans who have seen his films thirty-three times. For Lucas had been caught riffing off his own saga with the sort of zooming ineptitude you'd expect of a fan of the film, not its maker. That's where we'd heard that strange giggly, grand tone before: it was the same tone you got in the fan literature that surrounds the films, which may have been why some fans found themselves unable to forgive Lucas for what turned out to be the most shocking revelation of all: he was just a fan, like the rest of us. Oz was mortal.

"I knew when I did the first one [prequel] that I was doing exactly what the fans didn't want me to do," Lucas says, "which was I was making it about a ten-year-old boy and not Darth Vader, and so I knew I would get killed for that, and I knew that the second one was a love story and I knew I was going to get killed for that, it was not in the genre. I was taking huge chances, and doing things that were very uncommercial with a very commercial property. Now everything is market-driven. They do their market research, they do their marketing, they do test screening, all that stuff which Steven and I aren't a part of. We don't have anything to do with that stuff. We don't have to test-screen our movies. We don't have to have fifteen different studio executives telling us how to make a movie." This is true, although the irony is that if *The Phantom Menace* had been produced within the studio system, it would probably have been a whole lot better than it was. In a sense Lucas is right: he had indeed kicked himself free of the whole edifice, the studios, the test screenings, the push-and-pull of the market. When was the last time he had dipped his toe into the water and felt the piranha-like bite of an audience? When he made *More American Graffiti*, and saw that film fail. But *Star Wars* was another kettle of fish altogether, a franchise of such must-see magnitude that the movie would have had to have been in pieces, scattered in reels over the floor, before the fans would have stayed away. How bad could a *Star Wars* movie get away with being and still be a success? *The Phantom Menace* was your answer: *that* bad. If even the heartbroken were returning to the film again and again, you begin to see why the box office tells you nothing. *The Phantom Menace* took in $28.5 million its first week, beating the first-day record set by *Jurassic Park* in 1993—that was the hard core turning up on day one—but by Thursday, the figure dropped sharply to $12.2 million—that was the heart-break kicking in—and by the end of the weekend, its $64.8 million had failed to break the record set by *The Lost World* in 1997. That was the rest of the world queuing up to find out what was going on. Maybe that was the only way disappointment could show up with a film of such supreme anomalousness: it broke one dino record but not another.

It was also the first billion-dollar blockbuster that Hollywood failed to get rich off. Funded entirely by Lucas, who received the bulk of the film's profits, Fox was merely its distributor, receiving a "handling fee" of about 5–7 percent of the film's revenue, with their profits capped at $50 million. The merchandising told the same story, generating only $300 million, and most of that with the action figures—a sure thing. The clothes, mugs, beach towels were much slower, and soon stores around the country reported that they were having to mark down the items by as much as 50 percent: Hasbro saw its stock dip by 30 percent, while Tricon Global Restaurants saw only a minimal sales boost, complaining "our promotional tie-in with *Star Wars* was surprisingly ineffective." "It's a very, very hard thing to do," says Lucas, "and it's not very profitable. The thing that's made the difference for everybody is the ancillary markets in terms of VHS and DVD. That's where the money comes from. Licensing products to sell toys doesn't give you much money in the end. They throw around billions of dollars but the cut for the filmmakers is about 2–3 percent."

The Phantom Menace would end up triggering a complete overhaul of the whole world of film merchandising, as what became known as "post–*Star Wars* disorder" set in. "*Star Wars* started it all, and you come full cycle with *Episode I*," says Warren Cornblum, chief marketing officer for Toys R Us. "As this machine snowballed, and gained momentum, it took on a life of its own. It had a Field of Dreams quality: if we produce it, they will come. And the result was a glut of merchandise being made, and nobody made any money. The manufacturers didn't. The retailers didn't. In the last year or two a whole rethink has been going on. We have to take the same view that filmmakers take, and be much more selective now." In one sense, the failure of the film's merchandising, like the failure of *Godzilla*'s, was heartening news, for it told us that the merchandising of movies—despite being one of the more observable blots on the landscape for critics—was essentially harmless. It was a self-regulating system, and followed the contours of a film's success with remarkable precision: if a film does well, the merchandising does well; if a film does badly, the merchandising does badly. Nobody was ever persuaded by a doll to go see a movie they didn't like.

The theaters were not so lucky. Back in 1977, it had been the theater owners who got rich off *Star Wars*'s success. As Lucas says, "What happened was, the theaters then decided they had all this money, because they got the most of it, they took the money and they built multiplexes with it, they discovered the multiplex, which came in at the same time, and they said let's build lots of theaters in the same building and then we can move the prints around and make more money." By 1999, Lucas had learned his lesson only too well; thanks to the terms imposed on theaters for the rights to show *The Phantom Menace*—terms that one theater, the Loews Cineplex in New York's Union Square, refused—that trickle-down effect had all but been eliminated. Now it ran the other way. Theaters made much more money off independent successes that came out of nowhere than the big studio blockbusters, whose profits were so carefully carved up that, says John Fithian, president of the National Association of American Theater-Owners. "If you ask a theater owner if they want another five *Greek Wedding*s or another five *Star Wars* they'll pick *Greek Wedding*s every time." *The Phantom Menace* was no *Godzilla*, but those twelve-week contracts imposed by Fox did nothing to reverse the theaters' slow slide into insolvency, and in the next two years, America's four biggest theater chains—Loews, Regal, Carmike, and AMC—lost more than $340 million. By March 2000, two hundred screens a month were closing, and half the nation's theater chains were running for bankruptcy cover, with Carmike blaming the "increased cost percentages" demanded by the studios and Loews tracing its problems to "shorter run times." That is to say: the increased cost percentages demanded by the studios for the rights to show their blockbusters, and the shorter run times of those blockbusters once they were locked onto screens. The blockbuster may not have killed Hollywood, but as the century reached its close, it certainly made a fairly good attempt at murdering the theaters.

The films simply weren't sticking around on screens for anywhere near long enough for the theaters to make any money. The pattern would continue in 2000 and reached its nadir in the summer of 2001, which turned out to be the summer the critics had been waiting for and the theaters dreading. "Welcome to the era of the one-week wonder," reported *Variety* in an article entitled "Gone in Sixty Seconds." Here it was: the world's first fully forgettable summer, as immemorable in its way as the summers of 1977, 1984, 1993, and 1996 had been memorable. Even today, people are hard-pressed to remember exactly what came to pass that year, so quickly did it flash past—mention the summer of 2001 to most people and they glaze over into a deep, thoughtful trance—and only the patient work of a team of blockbuster scholars has made the following reconstruction possible. Let the records simply show that a movie called *The Mummy Returns* opened only to see its box office fall by 50 percent in week two; that the same fate befell an entertainment entitled *Pearl Harbor,* that a movie known only as *A.I.* fell by 52 percent, *Rush Hour 2* by 53 percent, *Jurassic Park III* by 56 percent, and *Lara Croft: Tomb Raider* by 57 percent, although the film that takes the prize for being the blockbuster that people put from their minds with the most speed was *Planet of the Apes,* which fell by an astonishing 60 percent. Needless to say, none of these movies caused the studios much sweat, since they all made their money back, and *Planet of the Apes* and *Pearl Harbor* in particular were acclaimed as rousing successes, taking in $359 million and $446 respectively. "We seem to be able to sell almost anything, regardless of quality. It's a little frightening," one studio head was heard to remark. The system had finally achieved a sort of awful, inverted perfection: a summer of wall-to-wall blockbusters, and no hits.

It was going to happen. It was the inevitable price Hollywood paid for eliminating a certain stratum of failure from its system: the successes don't mean nearly so much, either. If *Godzilla* had proven a new species of flop—the Flop That Wasn't—then these movies were all examples of a new breed of hit, The Hit That Isn't. In a way, though, it was just as well that the summer of 2001 proved so spectacularly forgettable, for it was going to be forgotten anyway. Hollywood's ability to administer its own reality check having failed, the reality check came from elsewhere, the last place anyone expected—it came from reality.

TIME LINE

1999

1. *Star Wars: Episode I—The Phantom Menace* (Fox) $923.1
   (46.7%)
2. *The Sixth Sense* (Disney) $672.8 (43.6%)
3. *Toy Story 2* (Disney) $485.8 (50.6%)
4. *The Matrix* (WB) $456.5 (37.6%)
5. *Tarzan* (Disney) $447.1 (38.3%)
6. *The Mummy* (Universal) $413.5 (37.6%)
7. *Notting Hill* (Universal) $363.1 (32.0%)
8. *The World Is Not Enough* (MGM) $353.1 (35.9%)
9. *American Beauty* (Dreamworks) $347.1 (37.5%)
10. *The Spy Who Shagged Me* (New Line) $310.3 (66.4%)

2000

1. *Mission: Impossible II* (Paramount) $565.4 (38.1%)
2. *Gladiator* (Universal) $457.2 (41.1%)
3. *Cast Away* (Fox) $424.5 (55.0%)
4. *What Women Want* (Paramount) $372.3 (49.1%)
5. *Dinosaur* (Disney) $355.1 (38.8%)
6. *How the Grinch Stole Christmas* (Universal) $345.1 (75.3%)
7. *The Perfect Storm* (WB) $326.0 (56.0%)
8. *Meet the Parents* (Universal) $303.7 (54.7%)
9. *X-Men* (Fox) $294.9 (53.3%)
10. *What Lies Beneath* (Fox/Dreamworks) $288.6 (53.8%)

*Figures show worldwide gross, in millions of dollars, followed by the percentage of
that generated in the U.S.

CHAPTER 17

UN-AMERICAN ACTIVITIES

"Block-buster, an aerial bomb capable of
destroying a whole block of buildings."
— *Oxford English Dictionary*

"What a ruin it will make!"
—H. G. Wells, upon catching sight of the
New York skyline

Jerry Bruckheimer took one look at the images on his TV and
thought they looked fake, like CGI. When he was making *Con Air*,
and the screenplay called for a plane to crash into the White
House, the producer had struck it as being too fanciful: "I just didn't
think it could happen. I thought we had missiles and so on that would
shoot the planes down. So we crashed it into a casino instead."

It certainly had the running time of a movie—from the time the
first plane hit to the time the second tower collapsed came to just
under two hours—but which movie? We'd seen American cities so frequently decimated, desiccated, and dry-roasted over the years that
commentators comparing the events of September 11 to a movie—
and that included just about everyone—were spoiled for choice. Those
with long memories harked back to the time New York had been
bombed back into the jungle (in 1952's *Captive Women*), buried
underground (*Beneath the Planet of the Apes*, 1970), and emptied by

atomic poisoning (*The World, the Flesh and the Devil,* 1959). But it was as nothing compared to the speed-rotation punishment the city had taken in the nineties, when New York was alternately smashed to smithereens by an asteroid (*Armageddon*), by a lizard (*Godzilla*), detonated by aliens (*Independence Day*), and engulfed by tidal wave (*Deep Impact*). Within three days of the attack, DVD bootlegs of the event had appeared in China. Bearing the titles *America's Disaster: The Pearl Harbor of the 21st Century* and *Surprise Attack on America,* and spurious credit lines for Tom Hanks, Columbia Pictures, and Jerry Bruckheimer, and rated R for violence, the DVDs intercut images from the World Trade Center attacks with the theme from *Jaws,* and clips from *Godzilla, Pearl Harbor,* and *The Rock*—the images turned back from whence they came, back into the global static of fictive violence.

It wasn't the first time a world power had rehearsed its demise in fiction. *Independence Day* was, in part, a remake of H. G. Wells's *The War of the Worlds,* whose image of London under fire preceded the First World War by sixteen years—part of a wave of pre-war jitters that had swept British pulp novels in the preceding two decades, when, according to historian W. Warren Wagar: "Great wars that devastated civilizations were fought in the skies and on imaginary battlefields dwarfing those of Verdun and Stalingrad. Fascist dictatorships led to a new Dark Age, class and race struggles plunged civilization into Neolithic savagery, terrorists armed with superweapons menaced Global peace. Floods, volcanic eruptions, plagues, epochs of ice, colliding comets, exploding or cooling suns, and alien invaders laid waste to the world." As a roll call of the images of much nineties cinema, it cannot be bettered; the difference being that everyone in Europe knew that the Great War was coming, whereas September 11 arrived out of a clear blue sky.

It made for particularly uncomfortable viewing for those who had made any of those movies. Joe Viskocil—the explosives expert who had detonated the White House for *Independence Day*—also saw the attacks on TV, like everyone else, and thought to himself: "I have done these shots." "I felt guilty about making my work look so good," he says, "and I felt like shit. I really did. I couldn't leave my condominium for two weeks. I went out for food and I couldn't look people in the face. I started thinking maybe I did my job too well, and it might have been the nucleus of an idea for somebody to say, 'Hey, let's crash a plane into the White House.' I thought, 'Oh my God, what have I done?'" He wasn't the only one to entertain such thoughts. For Neal Gabler in *The New York Times,* September 11 didn't just resemble a movie: it *was* a movie, a terror raid on the Hollywood image bank. "American films, thanks largely to videotape, now reach every corner of the world and their images colonize the imaginations of virtually everyone—one reason Muslims hate America," he wrote. "You have to believe at some level it was their rebuff to Hollywood as well as their triumph over it—that they could out-Hollywood Hollywood. This was the terrorists' own real-life disaster movie—bigger than *Independence Day* or *Godzilla* or *Armageddon.*" What Gabler was arguing was essentially a cinematic version of "blowback"—Noam Chomsky's claim that America had, through covert operations in Afghanistan, effectively armed her own enemies and was now reaping what she had sown—and it wasn't without some credence. When Brian Keenan was taken hostage by Hezbollah extremists in 1986 he noted with some puzzlement that they were all dressed as Rambo, with a headband tied and knotted at the side above the ear: "This all-American hero was the stereotype which these young Arab revolutionaries had adopted," he observed. "They had taken on the cult figure of the Great Satan they so despised and who they claimed was responsible for all the evil in the world. Emulating Rambo they would reconquer the world, and simultaneously rid themselves of that inadequacy which they could never admit."

Certainly, the portrait of America's enemies that emerged in the coming months was certainly not your standard-issue mad-mullah-in-a-turban so beloved of Hollywood. Encrypting their directives on their Apple and Toshiba laptops, ordering their flights on Travelocity.com, and circulating their training videos by inserting them into the middle of Hollywood movies, al Qaeda emerged as globalization's bastard brethren—cyber-wraiths in the international static. Even the Taliban—despite their fierce rulings against American culture—were revealed in deep thrall to it, listening to rap music, and even enjoying a vogue for styling their hair after Leonardo DiCaprio in *Titanic.* Later still, it would emerge that the favorite movie of Saddam Hussein's son Uday was *Gladiator*—according to his translator, interviewed in *The Boston*

Globe, Uday was "going mad" to find a bootleg copy of the swords-and-sandals epic three days after it was released in the United States. His father, meanwhile, was more of a Mel Gibson man, favoring the swords, shaggy hair, and blue-woad-streaked Gibson of *Braveheart.* "If I had such a worthy opponent like that man," he was reported as saying, "I could not bring myself to kill him." It isn't too hard to see what they liked about those films, which showed noble warriors rising to defeat a mighty empire. Remember also that Russell Crowe is not just a lowly Gladiator, like Spartacus, but a deposed Roman general, sold into slavery by the emperor. No opponent of empire, he simply wants his fair share. He wants in.

Even more disconcerting, in its own way, was Hollywood's response to the attacks. In October, thirty screenwriters, directors, and producers were invited for a summit at the Institute for Creative Technology, a government-funded think tank set up in 1999 to create training simulations—"virtual battlefields"—for the army, and housed inside a faux futuristic building designed by Herman Zimmerman, the designer of *Star Trek.* The volunteers included *Conan the Barbarian* director John Milius, *Se7en* director David Fincher, and Ron Cobb, the gadget designer for *Star Wars* and *Aliens,* who came up with a heavily shielded personnel carrier with four independent steering wheels. "I think we impressed the military, who probably thought we were all flakes," he said. Milius, meanwhile, sketched a soldier of the future with a Transformer-like weapon that doubled as a vehicle part. "They haven't sent me to Afghanistan," he said, "but I'm waiting." Not since Ian Fleming helped the CIA devise a plan to make Fidel Castro's beard fall out, or the glory days of Ronald Reagan, had there been such a loopy symbiosis between Hollywood's hawks and the American military.

The rest of Hollywood shrank behind its shutters. In the weeks following the attacks, L.A. swung between self-aggrandizing bouts of breast-beating, slight disappointment that nobody had thought to target Los Angeles, and meek avowals toward the new public mood, complicated only by the fact that nobody knew what that mood was—Timorous? Defiant? Vengeful? Somber? Sanguine? Fearful of public censure, Hollywood ticked every box, pushing itself into back-breaking displays of inoffensiveness. The Denzel Washington cop drama, *Training Day,* was pulled on the grounds that it featured a corrupt cop, the Heather Graham romantic comedy, *Sidewalks of New York,* on the grounds that it featured New York and jokes, and the Gwyneth Paltrow comedy, *View from the Top,* on the grounds that it featured flight attendants and jokes. A trailer for *Spider-Man* featuring the Twin Towers was pulled and digitally doctored to exclude the towers; a national TV showing of *Independence Day* was canceled, as were the Emmys, and when the show did finally air, a month later, it did so without host Ellen DeGeneres's monologue, presumably on the grounds that whatever the public mood might turn out to be, wisecracking lesbians were incompatible with it. By far the most prominent Hollywood casualty of the September 11 attacks, though, was Arnold Schwarzenegger, whose terrorist-thumping movie, *Collateral Damage,* was pulled from the schedules, the second time the fate of an Arnie movie had been entwined with that of the World Trade Center—the first being in 1993, when in deference to the unsuccessful attack on the Twin Towers, the producers of *Last Action Hero* had to remove a fake stick of dynamite from a big blowup Arnie doll in Times Square, and substituted instead a police badge. "By last Tuesday afternoon, with firefighters buried beneath the rubble of the World Trade Center, we were thinking, 'Oh my God, how could we possibly mount a publicity campaign?'" said the producers of *Collateral Damage.* The connection between terrorism and movie publicity campaigns remained a little hard to discern, but for Anthony Lane in *The New Yorker,* enough was enough. "It is time to say good riddance to the genre and to [Arnie's] dominance in it," he wrote. "That the destruction of the World Trade Center might spell the end of the blockbuster would be among its more trivial effects, yet it might strike a national nerve."

Even before al Qaeda destroyed the setting for the climax to his movie *Men in Black II,* Barry Sonnenfeld was having a bad summer. For a start he had suffered what he thinks was his first heart attack. He had been in his trailer at the time, while on location in New York, trying to take his mind off the $140 million production sitting outside his door, waiting to get directed. He was meditating. "And while I was meditating I realized I was having a heart attack," he says. "I was rushed to Bellevue Hospital and had all these tests. My dad's cardiologist came and saw me the next day and they did echocardiograms and all that stuff and then she said to one of the producers, 'His heart's in great shape, there's no blockage. It's strong, it's a great heart. However, he is the most stressed out, uptight human being I have ever met in my entire life. You must get him into meditation immediately. He needs help.'"

"No!" yelled his producer. "He was meditating when he *had* the heart attack!"

Sonnenfeld was engaged in one of the more stressful activities to which the human frame can be subjected: attempting to follow up one successful movie about space aliens with another movie, expected to be even more successful, about space aliens. The first time around only he and producer Steven Spielberg had gross participation in the film's profits. This time around, everyone wanted in. Will Smith wanted 20 percent plus $20 million; Tommy Lee Jones wanted 12.5 percent plus $12.5 million, and were it not for Spielberg stepping back from the plate and agreeing to take only 7.5 percent, they would probably still be there today, haggling over points. "It took five years, and then when it all came together, it was like *okayletsgo*," says Sonnenfeld. As is usual, they had a fixed target to hit—they had to get the movie ready in time for July 4th, 2002, when the film would be released on 8,500 screens— and throughout the shoot Sonnenfeld had to fend off a phalanx of nervous Sony executives, asking him questions about every little choice he made: "How are you going to shoot this scene?" they would ask him, and, "What are you going to tell the actors?" Then the World Trade Center had come down, forcing him to reshoot the movie's climax on another, more "generic" rooftop. It was enough to give anyone a heart attack.

"One of the things that worked about *Men in Black* was that it was a surprise," said Sonnenfeld. "What was so relaxing about the first movie was that we weren't a blockbuster, we weren't supposed to be a blockbuster. We were totally under the radar. We weren't *Batman and Robin*, we weren't *The Lost World*. Nobody paid any attention to it: nobody was worried about losing their job if their beloved *Men in Black* doesn't open." By May, Sonnenfeld was to be found in the Cary

Grant Theater, deep in the Sony lot, overseeing the final stages of sound mixing with his two sound re-recording mixers, Kevin O'Connell and Greg Russell. "Greg and Kevin worked on the Jerry Bruckheimer movies, so they're used to big, manly movies," said Sonnenfeld. "*Armageddon* had us living in a caravan for a month," said O'Connell. "We had five weeks to put the whole thing together, which is fine for a movie like *A Beautiful Mind*, but not for a movie like *Armageddon*. It's nothing."

By the end of May the film was almost complete, and was missing only its aliens. They were next door, being tweaked into life on the computer screens at Sony's in-house effects studio, Sony Imageworks. They were originally to have been done at George Lucas's Industrial Light & Magic, but the job spilled over, fell back into Sony's lap, and doing the mopping up was Ken Ralston, who won Oscars for his work on *Forrest Gump* and *Who Framed Roger Rabbit*. An exuberant man whose raccoon eyes nonetheless testify to too many years spent staring at computer screens, Ralston was none too happy about the work. "I'm doing an emergency job and I've tried to do the best thing I can with it, under very constricting circumstances," he said. "I will never do this again. Feeding these monsters takes a lot of work. It's got to a point where the effects community has had to put their foot down and say, 'No, you're killing everybody. You're not getting good work out of this.' You're worthless. You should be put in a hospital for about a month. [The first] *Harry Potter* was murder. Murder. Rob Legato did that at our place. I just watched him having a meltdown while it was going on." Attending the premiere of *Contact*, Ralston found himself in the unusual position of having to leave the theater in order to finish the film. "They'd struck a print that still wasn't done," he says. "I finished it six days before the full release of the movie."

All this was, however, perfectly usual—just another example of "pre-production crunch" in what *Variety* calls Hollywood's "Pre-summer Season of Fear." In the case of *Men in Black II*, the fear was amplified by the back-end deals carved out by all the movie's participants, which meant that the movie, which cost $140 million to make, would only start to earn Sony a profit once it topped $200 million. The film had to break records just to break even. "If this one doesn't break *Men in Black*'s records we're all in deep trouble," said Sonnenfeld. "It's

a no-win situation," he says. "If it does fairly good it makes $200 mil-
lion, everyone goes, 'No okay no yeah that's fine, $200 million is fine,
really . . .' That's no way to make movies." It is, however, how Hollywood makes blockbusters. In the end, the movie opened fine, taking in
$52 million its first weekend, just beating the record of the original
movie; by August it had taken in $189 million, and by the beginning of
September had taken in $215 million worldwide. They had just
squeezed a profit out of the movie. Nobody lost their job. It was Sony's
summer in fact, with *Spider-Man* swinging through a digitally doctored New York—to break all the usual records, while *Men in Black II*,
Harry Potter and the Sorcerer's Stone and *The Lord of the Rings: The Two
Towers* all helped push the year's total box-office take to $8 billion. Jack
Valenti, the head of the Motion Picture Association of America,
declared 2002 "the greatest box office year in film history," just as he
does pretty much every year. The blockbuster had been pronounced
dead, revivified itself, and broke all the usual records, in the space of
one year. America had gone back to the movies.

Perhaps the mistake was to have imagined that terrorism might have
any effect on films, even films about terrorism—maybe particularly
Arnold Schwarzenegger films about terrorism. September 11 found
Hollywood at such a complete right angle to reality, that reality was
always going to float by, dimly waving from the distance. When a
blockbuster like *Spider-Man* did acknowledge what had happened—
via the line in which a crowd of New Yorkers threaten the Green Gob-
lin, "You mess with one of us, you mess with all of us"—the effect was
somehow even spookier, summoning briefly into existence a connection between terrorists and Green Goblins that most of the audience
were happy enough to leave unmade.

"I think it's had a lasting effect but not in any of the obvious ways
we thought immediately after," says *Independence Day*'s producer
Dean Devlin. "I don't think it's going to affect at all what movie we
choose to make. I think it was borne out: the movies that worked
before September 11 worked after, but I think what it's done to the
individuals that actually have to create them is it's taken away some of
our glibness, and especially if you're dealing with mass destruction. I

think you can still do it in a movie but you can no longer ignore the implications of it. Before it was such a fantasy it was so out of the realm of anything that could happen. You were able to do it and be awed by it. Now you can't do it without thinking about the consequences of it, because we've really seen it happen."

"I don't think September 11 is going to create one type of a movie," says Spielberg, "but I think it's going to cause filmmakers to tell more and more personal stories, about isolation, loneliness, and vulnerability. I'm not sure there's going to be a whole spate of movies about 9/11. I certainly hope not. But I think people are going to be looking to tell more stories about the human condition, because America really received its first dose of vulnerability. We were shown we were not invulnerable on September 11." If so, then that day found American movies lost in a soothing dream of invulnerability, although as always with dreams, not without a pointed, perpendicular relation to reality. For in June of 2002, just as President Bush was addressing an audience of graduating cadets at West Point, assuring them "America has no empire to extend or utopia to establish," what were most of them flocking to see that summer? *Attack of the Clones,* the second of George Lucas's *Star Wars* prequels, which had long since switched sides from Luke Skywalker and his merry men to Darth Vader and Supreme Chancellor Palpatine as they struggle to pull a faltering republic into fine imperial shape. The empire strikes back indeed. *Episode II* found Palpatine conspiring in the senate to exaggerate the outside threat to the republic in order to boost his own powers and to build up the republic's war machine, so as to wage war on a series of ever more phantasmal enemies: remind you of anyone? Infinite Justice, Shock and Awe: even the titles of Bush's wars sound like the titles of bad blockbusters.

"I'm a big history buff," says Lucas, "and one of the things that fascinated me was how certain republics, certain democracies, don't get overthrown, which is sort of how we think of it today. They are given up to a tyrant. The people vote the tyrant in and then leave him there. That happened with Caesar, Augustus. It happened with Napoleon, it happened with Hitler. You can see very easily the frailties of a democracy, and how the people ultimately have the psychological need for a father figure just to tell them what to do, and there are a lot of machinations that go on behind the scenes, where the people in power are manipulating the people, like Hitler did. You can actually see there's a lot of similarities going on today."

So now we know: the galactic empire turned out to be not Britain or Germany, but America herself, as she struggled with her role as the world's last remaining superpower. Lucas's gifts as a filmmaker may have atrophied, but his skills as a popular pulse-taker clearly have not, for the prequels' imperial stirrings offer up an uncanny pop-Homeric mirror to America's own. Even their problems with plot seem representative—good guys who are too invulnerable to be interesting and a set of villains too phantasmal to snap into any shape: asymmetrical plotting for the era of asymmetrical warfare. It's hard to escape the conclusion that Bush's America in some sense got, with the prequels, the *Star Wars* movies it deserves. If we had all of us, scattered across the globe, known that this saga, which swept into cinemas on such a democratic breeze, would end in such a flurry of honorifics and dynastic pomp, a lot of us might not have bothered. *That* we could get at home, thank you very much. One needn't get too French about this, of course. There is a big difference between cultural imperialism and the real thing, namely: one is just cultural and one is the real thing. You could argue that America got its entertainments just about right: we got Speer's light-shows without the jackboots, which is by any measure a considerable advance. "The effect, which was both solemn and beautiful, was like being in a cathedral of light," wrote British ambassador Henderson of Speer's Nuremburg show, thus confirming your suspicion, not only that few were immune, but that there was probably no period of world history that calls out for the tender ministrations of Industrial Light and Magic. "After a lapse of twenty-one years, I was struck by the resemblance to a Cecil B. DeMille set," wrote Speer himself from his cell in Spandau prison later. "Designs of such scale naturally indicate a kind of chronic megalomania. . . . Perhaps it was less their size than the way they violated the human scale that made them abnormal. . . ." There are few better accounts of what has gone wrong with American Movies. Whatever happened to that most cherished of American myths, the scrappy underdog who comes from behind to snatch victory from the Goliaths he opposes? Whatever happened to *that* guy? It is a story so hardwired into Hollywood's DNA that it is hard to find a movie that doesn't tap into it. It is the story of *Star Wars* and *Jaws* and *Rocky,* and all those first-generation blockbusters, and yet it finds scant purchase in the frictionless supremacy of today's digital landscape.

"Superheroes didn't go after the shark," says Spielberg of *Jaws.* "Your next-door neighbor went after the shark. A pretentious ichthyologist, a down-on-his-luck police chief who was afraid of water, and an over-the-hill shark slayer who was trying to make a name for himself. It was the proletariat hero that emerged in the summer of '75." By the summer of 1985, a decade later, a different set of heroes had emerged—as ichthyologists made way for cops, archaeologists, fighter pilots, robot assassins, and small ghost-busting start-ups, but still: hardworking men and women with a job to do. Cut another decade to 1996 and things had gotten a little grander still: the usual complement of cops, and a paleobotanist or two, but now mixed in with a herd of presidents and superheroes. Is being a superhero a job? I guess not, for Clark Kent still had to work as a newspaper reporter to earn a living, while Bruce Wayne supported his crime-fighting activities by being a millionaire, but Superman essentially told the story of how the Man of Steel came to transform himself into Clark Kent, and derived much of its drama from his attempt to keep his identity secret. Ten years later, and the writers of *Batman* had no time for such bashful backstory: "You had to wade through twenty years just to get to the first shot of the guy in the costume that we've all come to see," they had said, while the sequels zipped actors into the batsuit so quickly that you barely noticed that Michael Keaton had made way for Val Kilmer, and Kilmer for George Clooney. Now we have the X-Men, who are just the X-Men, twenty-four hours a day. This is their curse. But it is also the movies.

As of the summer of 2003, a very different set of heroes stand amongst us. There's a gladiator and a general or three, some more presidents; there's a great showing of seafarers of various sorts, from fish to pirates, and wizards of all ages, but what do you think the most frequently recurring job title is? You may be surprised to know that the answer is, in fact, God. That's right, the Almighty Lord, or his various incarnations, as realized by Jim Carrey in *Bruce Almighty,* young Anakin Skywalker in the *Star Wars* prequels, and Keanu Reeves, also playing the Second Coming, aka "The One," in *The Matrix* movies, not to mention late-arrival Jim Caviezel, playing the real thing in *The Passion of the Christ*. When it comes to filling theaters these days, it seems that nothing less than full-blown deity will suffice. It's hard to escape the conclusion that today's teenagers have a few identification issues.

Nobody could doubt the heady Mephistophelean rush of the first *Matrix* movie, which was like being promised the world by somebody you didn't quite trust: very exciting. "You feel it. You've felt it your entire life," Morpheus (Laurence Fishburne) whispered to Neo (Keanu Reeves). "You don't know what it is, but it's there like a splinter in your mind. . . . Do you know what it is?" The question of what it was, exactly, inspired more head-scratching amongst Matricians than the glory days of *Alien* and *Blade Runner* scholarship: A Buddhist allegory? Leavened with a smattering of Judeo-Christian teaching, perhaps? What it turned out to be, of course, was the ability to walk up walls in black leather coats, turn masonry into the consistency of meringue with one fist, and to kick your enemy's butt in such beautiful slow motion that you could walk around him three times, pull faces at him and pull down his pants, and still be back in time to administer the final kick up the rear end. That's what *The Matrix* was, and audiences got it instantly. It was the land of milk, honey, and groovier special effects.

The worst news of *The Matrix Reloaded* was that this was not the place where the main thrust of the action would be taking place. We'd set up shop in reality, of all places, one that gave off the distinct air of something tossed off by the Wachowskis during a few seconds of downtime en route to the effects lab—a rather drab affair involving the wearing of handknitted woollen tunics, porridge for dinner, and the high likelihood of being lectured on the finer points of Cartesian philosophy by Laurence Fishburne. Keanu Reeves was still to be let off his leash in the Matrix every now and again, but now with a curious problem on his hands, having been born again in a blaze of light at the end of the first film, namely: how is a digital age deity to most profitably disport himself? As Keanu Reeves flitted around trying to find a foothold in the story, you began to see why the Bible limited God to the odd walk-on part, or burning-bush stunt double. The films quickly unspooled into a series of quite literal deus ex machina standoffs between Reeves and Agent Smith, as Neo kept reloading new skills, and Smith just kept on replicating—caught in a bubble of perfect dramatic stasis, with theoretically no reason why their battle need ever stop. Great news for Warner Brothers, I guess, who after the success of the first film, made a canny attack on any bad word of mouth by shooting both sequals back-to-back and then springing them on us, in global releases, within months of each other, and were duly rewarded with takings of $738 million for *The Matrix Reloaded*—almost twice as much as the first movie—and $423.5 million for *The Matrix Revolutions*. Nearly five hours of reloading and revolution later, however, this Brave New World no longer looked quite so brave or so new. Even that strangely strangled tone in which everybody speaks suddenly seemed awfully familiar, with its echo of the old biblical epics of DeMille, in which American actors abandoned their natural rhythms for a tone suggesting they had just been hit around the head with a small, pointy miracle. As the assorted citizenry of Zion queued up to have their babies anointed by Reeves, now released into full holiness, you couldn't help wondering how it had all come to this, how the early blockbusters of Spielberg and Lucas, so nippy and quick on their feet, so frank in their rebuttal of DeMille's grandiosity, had unspooled into such slack imaginings. After all that: thirty years of blockbuster evolution and it was back to the bloody *Ten Commandments*.

Deliverance was at hand. As always, it came in the most unlikely of forms, and from the unlikeliest of places: a far-off land, tucked away beneath the earth, inhabited by a small race of people, who sent forth a single barefoot emissary, straggly of hair and bulbous of stature, everyone's hopes resting upon his shoulders and his palmful of smelted gold, as he headed off to brave the sulfurous pits of Mordor. No two ways about it: New Zealand was very happy when Peter Jackson won all those Oscars.

TIME LINE

2001

1. *Harry Potter and the Sorcerer's Stone* (WB) $966.7 (32.9%)
2. *The Lord of the Rings: The Fellowship of the Ring* (New Line) $854.9 (36.6%)

3. *Monsters, Inc.* (Disney) $523.5 (48.8%)
4. *Shrek* (Dreamworks) $482.7 (55.5%)
5. *Pearl Harbor* (Disney) $450.5 (44.1%)
6. *Ocean's Eleven* (WB) $446.7 (41.1%)
7. *The Mummy Returns* (Universal) $430.0 (47.0%)
8. *Jurassic Park III* (Universal) $365.9 (49.5%)
9. *Planet of the Apes* (Fox) $359.2 (50.1%)
10. *Hannibal* (M/U) $350.1 (47.2%)

2002

1. *Spider-Man* (Sony) $821.7 (49.1%)
2. *Harry Potter and the Chamber of Secrets* (WB) $779.5 (32.8%)
3. *Star Wars: Episode II—Attack of the Clones* (Fox) $647.8 (47.9%)
4. *The Lord of the Rings: The Two Towers* (New Line) $628.4 (45.1%)
5. *Men in Black II* (Sony) $440.5 (43.2%)
6. *Signs* (Disney) $407.8 (55.9%)
7. *Ice Age* (Fox) $378.4 (46.6%)
8. *Die Another Day* (MGM) $343.2 (45.5%)
9. *Minority Report* (Fox) $342.1 (38.6%)
10. *My Big Fat Greek Wedding* (IFC) $296.9 (77.8%)

2003

1. *The Lord of the Rings: The Return of the King* (New Line) $876.5 (38.5%)
2. *Finding Nemo* (Disney) $844. 3 (40.2%)
3. *The Matrix Reloaded* (WB) $738.0 (38.2%)
4. *Pirates of the Caribbean* (Disney) $654.4 (46.7%)
5. *Bruce Almighty* (Universal) $477.9 (50.8%)
6. *Terminator 3: Rise of the Machines* (Sony) $433.1 (34.7%)
7. *The Matrix Revolutions* (WB) $423.5 (32.8%)
8. *X2: X-Men United* (Fox) $406.4 (52.9%)
9. *The Last Samurai* (WB) $311.6 (33.9%)
10. *Bad Boys II* (Sony) $272.3 (50.9%)

*Figures show worldwide gross, in millions of dollars, followed by the percentage of that generated in the U.S.

CONCLUSION

RETURN OF THE KINGS

"One Ring to rule them all, one Ring to find them,
One Ring to bring them all and in the darkness bind them
In the Land of Mordor where the Shadows lie."

—J. R. R. Tolkien, *The Lord of the Rings*

The moment Spielberg stepped onstage you knew who had won. We all knew who would win anyway, but Spielberg's presence was too piquant an irony: the man who had been shut out in the cold for so long for lavishing his gifts on aliens and spaceships, now a gray-haired grandee of the industry, stepping forward to give the Oscar for Best Film to a fantasy blockbuster. "It's a clean sweep!" announced Spielberg, pulling off the unlikely task of sounding more victorious than the actual victor. Peter Jackson, meanwhile, took to the stage with that shambling, bashful-bison gait of his, and thanked the Academy for "seeing past the trolls and wizards" and rewarding a fantasy film—"the f-word" as he put it. He didn't sound victorious. He sounded the way you'd expect a man who had just spent the last seven years of his life bringing a nine-hour epic to the screen. He sounded *exhausted*.

In many ways, *The Lord of the Rings: The Return of the King* was just the sort of film to strike fear into the heart of the average Oscar-voter, as they performed their annual strip-mining of the year's films for their pockets of prestige. It made $876 million—*Spider-Man* numbers. It had been turned into a lucrative set of plastic toys, like *Star Wars*. It was a sequel, just like *Die Hard 2*. And it was a film with not a shred of historical truth to it, unlike, say *Gandhi* or *Braveheart* or *Titanic,* instead entirely made up from start to finish, full of clearly fictional characters talking obviously made-up languages before plunging into battles that never took place—except in the brain of the man who made it all up. So how had *Lord of the Rings* secured its lock on the Oscars? It helped, of course, that the man in question was English, studied in universities, and dead, which meant that this wasn't some endlessly spilling franchise, but an epic based on three books, with no more where they came from. In a way, the films did amount to a form of historical reenactment, for how thrillingly ancient and foreign it all felt, how gnarled and knotted with Jackson's fidelity, not so much to Tolkien's plots—which he hacked about with due dispatch—but the imaginative climate in which they flourished. You noticed it most on those occasions when his dialogue slipped into the familiar strains of twenty-first-century teen-empowerment—Pippin, atop his tree, crying "Isn't this cool?"—for the one thing *Lord of the Rings* is not is an empowerment manual. The opposite, in fact: it's a fable about disempowerment, the story of Frodo's long journey to destroy the one thing that would turn him into the most powerful warrior in all of Middle-earth—the story, if you like, of Superman's long trudge to the trash heap to turn in his cape. Maybe it took an imagination shaken by firsthand knowledge of the Somme to issue such a stern rebuke to the lures of omnipotence, but when Frodo puts on the ring, the experience is a soul-sucking horror, with none of the glamour of Keanu Reeves's animadversions in wonderland. Too much plugging into *The Matrix,* warns Tolkien, and you, too, could end up with the physique, charm, and table manners of Gollum.

How did Jackson pull it off? The secret is to be found buried in the reams of commentary with which the DVDs came swaddled: you think Frodo's trudge to the tip of Mount Doom was weary-making, try the seventy-two hours—just over three and a half days—of accumulated commentary with which the filmmakers set about reassuring Tolkien fans that all was well in Middle-earth. Just a few hours into it, though, and you hit gold, in the form of this comment from Jackson, so simple you could almost miss it: "I don't like magic." Coming from the director of a film containing two wizards, several fairies, and a small army of elves, all capable of loosing spells at the drop of a hat, this might seem an odd thing to say—even treasonous—but it's true. Survey the trilogy, in all its nine-hour glory, and it's surprising how low the magic-count is. Gandalf uses it in his fight with Saraman, and to summon the large eagle on which he makes his rather stylish getaway, but seeking entry to the Dwarf Caves, a vast stone door remains unmoved by his incantations, and when it comes to battle he must duly take his place, sword in hand, alongside his friends. "Certainty of death—small chance of success—what are we waiting for?" comments Gimli, pointing up one of the chief glories of the films: the return they offered audiences to the pleasures of the unevenly matched battle, with no sudden deus ex machina escapes, no shortcuts, no reloading, or revolutions: just the thrilling prospect of having to hew and hack your way through a rising sea of Orcs.

Maybe it took a New Zealander to tilt the deck of the drama so decisively this way, or maybe just the director of *Heavenly Creatures*. There was much head-scratching over Jackson's seemingly quantum leap from such small art house offerings to $300 million blockbusters, although there shouldn't have been, first because *Heavenly Creatures* displayed such an insider's understanding of the minds of chronic fantasists, and second because, as James Cameron's example first showed, it is precisely those schooled in the hard thrift of low-budget filmmaking that you *do* entrust with $300 million. It's the middle-ranking guys you have to be careful of—the directors used to handling $100 million but think themselves entitled to a little more, who wake up in the morning with a $200 million movie flashing up in their heads, just dying to get out.

Peter Jackson's career path has proved the exemplary one, with Bryan Singer, Guillermo del Toro, Darren Aronofsky, Ang Lee, Sam Raimi, Chris Nolan, all mixing up low-budget indie success with stints at the helm of the big studio blockbusters. Having been commandeered by first the producers in the late eighties, and then the executives in the early nineties, the blockbuster has now been returned to the directors, with whom it first started, as it had to, if it was to be restored to some of its old luster, and regain a little muscle tone. Jackson is currently filming a remake of *King Kong*, for release in the summer of 2005, before which we'll have seen a fourth *Die Hard* and the final prequel of Lucas's *Star Wars* saga, with a fourth *Indiana Jones* also in the works. Quite a year, in other words, with its face-off between the blockbuster's youngest pups and its graying forefathers, let loose from the paddock for one last canter. And when they are done, Spielberg and Lucas will do what they always do: they will fly to Hawaii and build a sandcastle for their movies, to wish them luck—a gesture from another age, almost, a bit of boyish nostalgia for the time when Hollywood hadn't replaced luck with $100-million marketing budgets, and when movies, rather than blockbusters, ruled the earth.

Let's imagine the world other than it is, a world ardently wished for by some: a world in which *Jaws* and *Star Wars* bombed. Imagine that instead of *Jaws*, Spielberg directed *Lucky Lady,* the musical about rum-runners starring Paul Newman he'd had his eye on. It did okay, but it didn't make Spielberg a household name, and afterward, he found it impossible to find any takers for his long-planned movie about UFOs, and so directed *The Bingo Longo Traveling All-Stars and Motor Kings* instead. It's how the rest of his career would pan out, as he alternated small personal movies with occasional attempts to resuscitate the musical. *Star Wars*, meanwhile, came out in 1977 and proved once and for all that science fiction was best left to the cultists. The big Oscar success, a few months earlier, had been *Taxi Driver,* which gleaned Martin Scorsese the first of many statuettes—and whose success marked a decisive triumph for the New Hollywood auteurs: Scorsese, Robert Altman, Arthur Penn, Francis Ford Coppola. They became Hollywood's newest most golden boys, in whose image the industry hastily set about reshaping itself. It got a little tiring for audiences after a while, all those unhappy endings, fractured narratives, and scuzzy exterior shoots—it became a cinematic manner like any other, and some began to wonder what had ever happened to the glory days of the studio system, when Hollywood made movies that didn't begin in the gutter and end in a bloodbath.

Lucas, meanwhile, licked his wounds, and got a job at Disney, which in the early eighties enjoyed quite a renaissance, after the fallout of 1977. Tim Burton, Joe Dante, Robert Zemeckis, Chris Columbus all found safe haven at the House of the Mouse, feeding their energies into remakes of the old Disney features. There were some raised eyebrows from traditionalists when Tim Burton produced his sequel to *Snow White and the Seven Dwarfs,* featuring Snow White in dark cloak and hood, hanging from the rafters of her cottage, while the dwarfs ran riot below; and Ridley Scott's *Peter Pan* remake, now featuring a gang of marauding Replicants in Neverland, was not well received. These were frustrating years for these directors—their taste for special effects, big budgets, and media hype entirely frustrated by the public's taste for cinema-verité footage, shoestring productions, and critical word of mouth. Occasionally one of them would try and make a break for it on the outside, trawling the international tax shelters for the millions they needed to raise money for a "blockbuster" movie, but these remained a minority taste, doing the rounds of the art house circuit, where they were supported by a small, loyal fan base of teenagers, but that was about it. By the mid-nineties, Zemeckis and Gale were *still* writing *Back to the Future,* although by the time Marty McFly hits fifty-five, they may stand a little more of a chance of getting it made. The over-fifties are where it's at these days, demographically speaking. *Titanic* did okay, thanks to Jim Cameron's use of the eighty-seven-year-old Gloria Stuart to play her seventeen-year-old self, although his refusal to properly explore the reasons the ship sank was the occasion of much controversy: there just wasn't enough money to stage the scenes, said Cameron, although critics suspected he was too interested in his characters to give his special effects their due. For now, though, it's back to the usual summer fare: *Driving Miss Daisy II: Drive Harder,* and *On Golden Pond VII: Just Got That Little Bit Older.*

No, it won't wash. The idea that Lucas and Spielberg are responsible for today's annual blockbuster binge credits them with too much and not enough; too much in that it ascribes to two individuals—two movies—quite phenomenal powers of historical course alteration. Too little in that the argument is only ever made by people who don't like their films. But if Peter Biskind's recent history of the American indie film movement proved anything, it is that the hard-and-fast rules by which you could distinguish between an art film and a studio blockbuster in the seventies didn't outlive that decade. What, today, are you to do with the Coen brothers, or Quentin Tarantino or Bryan Singer— genre nuts to a man—or a film like *American Beauty,* which offers a far more entertaining night out than any film about the disintegration of the American family really should. It's certainly ten times more watch-able than Robert Redford's movie on the same subject, *Ordinary People,* back in 1980. That was the real casualty of the blockbuster era, not the art house, which rediscovered the joys of plot and thrived, but Holly-wood's middle class of movies: the *Ordinary People*s and *Kramer vs. Kramer*s and *On Golden Pond*s. They're the films you don't see a lot of these days, and it's hard to weep too much. Any revolution that left it difficult for Robert Redford to make a movie as self-importantly glum as *Ordinary People* can be no bad thing. You have to say, in fact, that on balance, the system we have right now—with films like *Mystic River* and *The Deep End* on the one hand and the *Lord of the Rings* trilogy and *Finding Nemo* and *Pirates of the Caribbean* on the other, with less dab-bling around in the middle—is actually pretty good. It works.

The only other casualty of *Jaws* and *Star Wars,* of course, were movies like *Jaws* and *Star Wars,* and all those other first-generation blockbusters that now feel almost like films from another medium, their artistry an unasked-for bonus, a by-product of the time they were made: that brief window when the blockbuster came into its own but before it became the world's plaything. It's difficult to imagine anyone devoting three years of their life, as Zemeckis and Gale did with *Back to the Future,* to writing any of today's summer block-busters, most of which give the impression of having been knocked off in three minutes, while the special effects of films like *Close Encounters* and *Blade Runner* remain unsurpassed by the pitiless perfection of CGI. It's hard not to feel sorry, in fact, for your average teenage thrill junkie these days, who seems to have gotten the thin end of the lol-lipop. We got *Raiders of the Lost Ark,* they get *The Mummy Returns;* we got *Top Gun,* they get *Armageddon,* we got *Star Wars,* they get the pre-quels. No contest.

The summer is now so packed, and the beaches of popular film-making so well patrolled, that it is difficult, if not completely impossi-ble, for anything like that to happen. They don't seem to mind: the audiences who trot out of *Spider-Man* seem content enough, and doubtless one of them will one day write a book rubbishing this one, pointing out what a bunch of bores we first-generation blockbuster fans are, still banging on about *Raiders of the Lost Ark* after all these years. To be sure, audiences still get movies they love—no world containing the glory that is Pixar is worthy of anybody's despair—but we don't get to *fall* in love in the same way. We don't have time. We have to move so fast, and in synchronized tandem with everyone else on the globe, that it's more like picking someone up at a disco. The closest thing we have to a sleeper hit like *Star Wars* these days is a $75 million extravaganza like *The Matrix,* news of which unfurled on the Internet, which is where that long-hounded enemy of the studios—word of mouth—seems to have found a home for itself and dug in, tenaciously. If there is one single challenge facing the makers of popular cinema these days—the guys who want nothing more than to set the public's pulse racing and dream of happy enslavement to the box office—it is that the box office is no longer the feather-sensitive register of popular approval that it once was. The information filmmakers are getting from audiences is not good, not reliable, not half as reliable as the information Spielberg got when he made *Jaws,* and then, on the back of that film's success, felt emboldened to make *Close Encounters;* and then, on the back of that, overstepped with *1941,* when the sting of failure sent a duly chastened director back to basics with *Raiders,* and then, his confidence back, on to *E.T.* Spielberg's powers of audience rapport are anomalous, of course, but it's difficult to imagine anything like the intimacy of that conversation taking place today. Back then, the only walls separating director from audience were the walls of the lobby, behind which a nervous Spielberg crouched, anxiously awaiting screams and cheers. These days, the walls are tenfold and made of titanium: you have a film's marketing campaign, its global release strategy, its overseas and ancillary revenues, all of them serving to muffle news of a movie's quality, princess-and-pea fashion, and make it ten times more difficult for audiences to make themselves heard. By the time we've all seen that it sucked, it's a hit. The dollar value of our butts in the seats has never been greater, but what it signifies has never meant less.

Spielberg says he can still feel it, though: the heat rising in an audience when they know they're onto something. "You walk into an air-conditioned, freezing theater and in about twenty minutes it gets really hot and people start making noise and having a good time," he says.

"There is nothing greater than hearing that audience, being part of the experience, between that and the smell of popcorn and the feeling that there's a screw loose in the seat you're sitting on. Any time the audience senses that there is something new under the old sun, they're going to be there on Friday night." Can't wait.

ACKNOWLEDGMENTS

A book is a series of conversations passing themselves off as a monologue. This book started life as a conversation with my friend Quentin Curtis, and with my friend, then agent, the peerless Emma Parry; it continued in the form of conversations with my two excellent editors, Andrew Gordon in the U.K. and Amy Scheibe in the U.S.; and it drew on conversations with many filmmakers conducted over the last few years. My thanks in particular go to Steven Spielberg, Ridley Scott, and George Lucas for their time.

I would also like to thank Kevin Curran, Helen Fielding, Chris Weitz, Carlyn Henry, and Mickey Mandelbaum for their hospitality while I was in Los Angeles. Also, Greg Dillon, Chris Edgar, and all my other American friends who talked me through various aspects of growing up in their country. The release of *Star Wars* found me, not in the front row of Mann's Chinese Theater in L.A. knocking back popcorn, but in Cornwall, in the southwest of England, munching on pasties, so thanks are due to my mother for giving me enough pocket money to see the film ten times, and for a bunch of other stuff that escapes me at the moment. The memory of my late, lovely sister—to whom this book is dedicated—was instrumental in whatever slim balance I may have struck between so-called boy's films and girl's films. That distinction, if it exists at all, exists within movies, and moviegoers, not between them. "He's such a girl," she once said of Luke Skywalker, as I shimmied into my apprentice Jedi costume one day. "But Han Solo is . . . *ooh*." At the time, this struck me as unutterably philistine—what film had she been watching? But her words now carry the ring of adamantine truth.

My highest respect goes to Dave Smith, who began it all for me by answering my questions about Conrad and *Apocalypse Now* as I trailed him around the corridors of Varndean Sixth Form College, sometime in the mid-eighties. My failure to follow up on any academic promise I may have shown back then is entirely my own fault, but I received excellent help in my efforts toward comprehensive intellectual retardation from all the old gang at *The Modern Review*—Julie Burchill, Toby Young, Cosmo Landesman—without whose endless late night debates on the relative merits of the *Alien* movies this book would not be as it is. Nor would it be as it is without all the other friends with whom I saw so many of these movies, in particular Gav, with whom I co-digested *Aliens, Batman, Die Hard, Terminator 2,* and *Titanic.* I would also like to thank my grandparents, Joan and Derek, for first teaching me the value of storytelling, and for subbing me when money got tight—the very model of a Hollywood studio. Also the British Film Institute for access to their excellent library and Dana Deree, vice consul at the U.S. embassy in London, for his help after a regrettable deportation incident.

But above all, Courtney, without whose love, support, strength, and understanding I would still be buried deep in the forest under the Overlook, typing out the words "blockbuster, blockbuster, blockbuster" in all sorts of neat and new configurations. Really: Thank you.

SOURCES

Introduction: The Boys of Summer

This chapter is based on the author's interviews with Steven Spielberg, George Lucas, Bob Gale, and Robert Zemeckis conducted in 2000–03. Further information on the childhood of the directors discussed was supplied by the 1973 *American Film Institute Report*, the *Chicago Herald Tribune*, *Inter/view*, the *Los Angeles Times*, *People*, *Time*, the *Toronto Star*, *Mythmaker* by John Baxter, *Skywalking* by Dale Pollock, *Steven Spielberg* by Joseph McBride, *The Movie Brats* by Michael Pye and Linda Miles, and *James Cameron* by Marc Shapiro.

Chapter 1: Panic on the 4th of July

This chapter is based on the author's interviews with Steven Spielberg, David Brown, Richard Zanuck, and Sidney Sheinberg conducted in 2002–03. Additional information on the shooting and release of *Jaws* was supplied by *Cinema Papers*, *Daily Variety*, *Film Comment*, *Newsweek*, *The New Yorker*, *The New York Times*, *Premiere*, *Sight & Sound*, *Take One*, *Time*, *The Washington Post*; *The Jaws Log* by Carl Gottlieb, and *Nigel Andrews on Jaws* by Nigel Andrews. Information on the box office of *Gone With the Wind* was supplied by *Daily Variety* and *Showman* by David Thomson; information on Hollywood in the sixties and seventies was supplied by *American Film*, *The New York Times*, *The Sixties* by Paul Monaco, *Lost Illusions* by David Cook, *The Studio* by John Gregory Dunne, *The Genius of the System* by Thomas Schatz, *The Kid Stays in the Picture* by Robert Evans, and *Disaster Movies* by Stephen Keane.

Chapter 2: Empire State Express

This chapter is based on the author's interviews with George Lucas, Alan Ladd, Dennis Muren, Peter Suschitzky, and Ken Ralston conducted in 2002–03. Additional information on the shooting and release of *Star Wars* was supplied by *American Film*, *Cinefex*, *Cinefantastique*, *Daily Variety*, *Details*, *Film Comment*, the *Los Angeles Times*, *Newsday*, *Newsweek*, *The New York Times*, *The New Yorker*, *Starburst*, *Starlog*, *Time*, *The Washington Post*, *The Making of Star Wars* (ABC), *Omnibus* (BBC), *Mythmaker* by John Baxter, *Easy Riders, Raging Bulls* by Peter Biskind, *A Galaxy Not So Far Away* edited by Glenn Kenny, and *Skywalking* by Dale Pollock. Further information on the early days of cinema was supplied by *American Film*, *American Magazine*, *Daily Variety*, the *Los Angeles Times*, *The Transformation of Cinema, 1907–1915* by Eileen Bowser, *Adventures with D. W. Griffith* by Karl Brown, *The Emergence of Cinema* by Charles Musser, and *D. W. Griffith* by Richard Schickel.

Chapter 3: Halloween for Grown-ups

This chapter is based on the author's interviews with Steven Spielberg, Michael Kahn, Scott Ross, Peter Guber, Lorne Peterson, John Milius, and Joe Viskocil conducted in 2002–03. Additional information on the shooting and release of *Close Encounters of the Third Kind* was provided by *American Film, American Cinematographer, Cinefex, Cinema Papers, Daily Variety, Film Comment, Newsweek, Starlog, Vanity Fair, The Washington Post, Making* Close Encounters, documentary produced by Isaac Mizrahi/Morgan Holly, *Indecent Exposure* by David McClintick, *Truffaut and Me* by Bob Balaban, *Steven Spielberg* by Joseph McBride, *You'll Never Eat Lunch in This Town Again* by Julia Phillips, and *Schrader on Schrader* edited by Kevin Jackson. Further details of the career of Dino de Laurentiis and Peter Guber were supplied by *Newsweek, Time, The Washington Post,* and *Lost Illusions* by David Cook.

Chapter 4: The Education of Ellen Ripley

This chapter is based on the author's interviews with Sigourney Weaver conducted in 1991 and with Ridley Scott, Alan Ladd, and Terry Rawlings conducted in 2002–03. Additional information on the shooting and release of *Alien* was supplied by *American Cinematographer, American Film, Cinefantastique, Daily Variety, Film Comment, Films and Filming,* the *Los Angeles Times, Newsweek, Starlog, Starburst, The Alien Quadrilogy, The Alien Quartet* by David Thomson, *Ridley Scott* by Paul Sammon, and *The Book of Alien* by Paul Scanlon and Michael Gross. Quotations from academic papers on *Alien* are from *Alien Zone* edited by Annette Kuhn. Michael Eisner's comment on Jeffrey Katzenberg is from *Work in Progress* by Michael Eisner and Jack Valenti's quotation is from *A New Pot of Gold* by Stephen Prince.

Chapter 5: First Action Hero

This chapter is based on the author's interviews with George Lucas, Steven Spielberg, Sidney Ganis, Michael Kahn, Ridley Scott, and Alan Ladd conducted in 2002–03. John Baxter's *Mythmaker* was an invaluable source of infomation on the making of *Raiders of the Lost Ark;* additional information was supplied by *American Film, American Cinematographer, Daily Variety,* the *Los Angeles Times, Newsweek,* the *New York Times, Rolling Stone, Saturday Review, Starlog, Time, The Washington Post, Projections 3: Filmmakers on Filmmaking* edited by John Boorman and Walter Donohue, *When Hollywood Had a King* by Connie Bruck, *Work in Progress* by Michael Eisner, and *Steven Spielberg* by Joseph McBride. *Future Noir* by Paul Sammon was an invaluable source of information on *Blade Runner,* with further information supplied by *Cinefex,* the *Los Angeles Times, The New York Times; Ridley Scott* by Paul Sammon. Quotations from academic papers on *Blade Runner* are from *Retrofitting Blade Runner* edited by Judith Kerman.

Chapter 6: Morning in America

This chapter is based on the author's interviews with Steven Spielberg, Scott Ross, Sidney Sheinberg, John Williams, John Lasseter, Robert Zemeckis, Bob Gale, and John Milius conducted in 1998–2003. Additional information on the genesis of *Back to the Future* was supplied by *American Cinematographer, American Film,* the *Chicago Tribune,* the *Los Angeles Times, New York, The New York Times, Newsweek,*

Playboy, Premiere, Time, The Wall Street Journal, and *The Washington Post.* Further information on the shooting and release of *E.T.* was provided by *American Cinematographer, Cinefex, Cinefantastique, Entertainment Weekly,* the *Los Angeles Times, Time, Starburst, Starlog, The Washington Post,* and *Steven Spielberg* by Joseph McBride. Quotations from letters to E.T. are from *Letters to E.T.*

Chapter 7: Time Travelers Inc.

This chapter is based on the author's interviews with Robert Zemeckis, Gale Anne Hurd, Stan Winston, Scott Ross, Bob Gale, Sidney Sheinberg, and Ken Ralston conducted in 2000–03. Additional information on the shooting and release of *The Terminator* was supplied by *American Cinematographer, Cinefex, Daily Variety, Starburst, Starlog, Dreaming Aloud* by Christopher Heard, *James Cameron* by Marc Shapiro, and *True Myths* by Nigel Andrews. Further information on the shooting and release of *Back to the Future* was supplied by *American Cinematographer, American Film,* the *Chicago Tribune,* the *Los Angeles Times, The New York Times, Newsweek, Playboy, Time, The Washington Post, Lucky Man* by Michael J. Fox, and *The Directors: Take Two* by Robert Emery.

Chapter 8: Ripley Redux

This chapter is based on the author's interviews with Sigourney Weaver conducted in 1991, and with Gale Anne Hurd, Peter Lamont, Scott Ross, and Stan Winston conducted in 2002–03. Further information on the making of *Aliens* was supplied by *American Film,* the *Chicago Tribune, Cinefantastique, Cinefex, Daily Variety, Films and Filming,* the *Los Angeles Times, Movieline, Newsweek, People, Starlog, Starburst, Time Out, Time, The Alien Quadrilogy,* interview with James Cameron (documentary Sci-Fi Channel, 1986), *Dreaming Aloud* by Christopher Heard, and *James Cameron* by Marc Shapiro.

Chapter 9: War Zones, High Concepts

This chapter is based on the author's interviews with Jerry Bruckheimer and Peter Guber conducted in 2003. *High Concept* by Charles Fleming was an invaluable source of information on the early career of Don Simpson and the making of *Top Gun;* further information was supplied by *Advertising Age, Adweek,* the *Chicago Tribune,* the *Los Angeles Times, Newsweek, The New York Times, The Washington Post, Hollywood Animal* by Joe Eszterhas, *The Keys to the Kingdom* by Kim Masters, and *The Barry Diller Story* by George Mair. Details on *Top Gun*'s release on video and Hollywood's ancillary revenues are from *A New Pot of Gold* by Stephen Prince. Details on the shooting of *The Witches of Eastwick* were supplied by articles in *The Australian,* the *Los Angeles Times, Newsday, Premiere,* and *The Washington Post.*

Chapter 10: The Long Dark Night

This chapter is based on the author's interviews with Tim Burton in 1999 and with Peter Guber, Dan Romanelli, and Terry Ackland-Snow conducted in 2002–03. Further information on the shooting and release of *Batman* was supplied by *American Cinematographer, Cinefantastique, Daily Variety, The Hollywood Reporter,* the *Los Angeles Times, The New York Times, Newsday, Newsweek, Premiere, Starburst, Starlog, Time, The Washington Post, Inner Views* by David Breskin, *Tim Burton* by Ken

Hanke, *Hit and Run* by Nancy Griffin and Kim Masters, *Burton on Burton* edited by Mark Salisbury, and *A New Pot of Gold* by Stephen Prince.

Chapter 11: Extinction

This chapter is based on the author's interviews with Peter Guber and Sidney Ganis conducted in 2002–03. Nancy Griffin and Kim Masters's reporting for *Premiere* magazine was an invaluable source of information on the making of *Last Action Hero;* further information was supplied by *Daily Variety,* the *Dallas Morning News, Entertainment Weekly, The Hollywood Reporter, The New Yorker, The New York Times,* the *Los Angeles Times, Premiere, True Myths* by Nigel Andrews, *The Directors: Take Two* by Robert Emery, and *You're Only as Good as Your Last One* by Mike Medavoy.

Chapter 12: Planet Hollywood

This chapter is based on the author's interviews with Steven Spielberg, Sid Sheinberg, Dennis Muren, Stan Winston, and Jack Valenti conducted in 2002–03. Information on the shooting and release of *Jurassic Park* was provided by articles in *Adweek, Advertising Age, American Cinematographer, Daily Variety,* the *Dallas Morning News, The Financial Times, The Hollywood Reporter,* the *Los Angeles Times, The New York Times, Premiere, Starburst,* the *Toronto Star, The Washington Post, The Making of Jurassic Park,* documentary directed by John Schultz, *The Making of Jurassic Park* by Don Shay and Jody Duncan, *Steven Spielberg* by John Baxter, and *Steven Spielberg* by Joseph McBride. Information on *Jurassic Park* in France and Hollywood overseas was provided by Agence France Presse, *Le Monde, Le Parisien Libere, Libération, The Times, The Observer, The Guardian, The Economist, Global Hollywood* edited by Toby Miller, and *Jihad vs. McWorld* by Benjamin Barber.

Chapter 13: Oops, Apocalypse!

This chapter is based on the author's interviews with Roland Emmerich, Dean Devlin, Tom Sherak, Joe Viskocil, Volker Engel, and Jan de Bont conducted in 2002–03. Additional information on the making of *Independence Day, Twister,* and the summer of 1996 was supplied by *American Cinematographer, Cinefex,* the *Chicago Tribune, Daily Variety, Entertainment Weekly, The Hollywood Reporter,* the *Los Angeles Times, Newsweek, The New York Times, Premiere, Starburst, Time,* and *The Washington Post.*

Chapter 14: Staring into the Abyss

This chapter is based on the author's interviews with Bill Mechanic, Scott Ross, Rob Legato, and Peter Lamont conducted in 2002–03. *Titanic and the Making of James Cameron* by Paula Parisi was an invaluable resource, and the source of the conversation between Cameron and Crane; additional information was provided by *American Cinematographer, Cinefex, Daily Variety,* the *Daily Telegraph, DGA Magazine, Entertainment Weekly, The Financial Times, The Guardian, The Independent,* the *Los Angeles Times,* the *Montreal Gazette, Newsday, Newsweek, The New York Times, Premiere,* the *Toronto Star, Time, The Washington Post,* Twentieth Century Fox Home Video International interview with James Cameron (documentary 1998), *The Directors: Take Two* by Robert Emery, *Dreaming Aloud* by Christopher Heard, *James Cameron's Titanic* by Ed W. Marsh, and *James Cameron* by Marc Shapiro. The online reception of *Titanic* is described in *Ain't It Cool? Hollywood's Redheaded Stepchild Speaks Out* by Harry Knowles and *Titanic: Anatomy of a Blockbuster,* edited by Kevin Sandler and Gaylyn Studlar.

Chapter 15: Does Size Matter?

This chapter is based on the author's interviews with Barry Sonnenfeld, Ken Ralston, Roland Emmerich, Dean Devlin, Volker Engel, and Rob Fried conducted in 2002–03. Additional information on the making of *Men in Black* and *Godzilla* was supplied by *The Advertiser, American Film, Brandweek,* the *Daily Telegraph* (Sydney), *Daily Variety, Entertainment Weekly, Film Comment, The Hollywood Reporter,* the *Los Angeles Times, The New York Times, Time,* and *The Gross* by Peter Bart.

Chapter 16: The Empire Strikes Back

This chapter is based on the author's interviews with George Lucas, Dennis Muren, John Knoll, Scott Ross, Lorne Peterson, John Fithian, and Warren Cornblum conducted in 2002–03. Additional information on the making and release of *The Phantom Menace* was supplied by *American Cinematographer, Cinefex, Daily Variety, Entertainment Weekly, The Financial Times, The Guardian, The Hollywood Reporter,* the *Los Angeles Times,* the *New York Times, Newsday, Newsweek, The New Yorker, The Making of the Phantom Menace* (documentary, Fox), *Premiere, Time, The Wall Street Journal, Using the Force* by Will Brooker, *The Unauthorised* Star Wars *Compendium,* and *A Galaxy Not So Far Away,* edited by Glenn Kenny.

Chapter 17: Un-American Activities and Conclusion: Return of the Kings

These chapters are based on the author's interviews with Ridley Scott, Martin Scorsese, Dean Devlin, Jerry Bruckheimer, Joe Viskocil, Barry Sonnenfeld, Kevin O'Connell, Greg Russell, Steven Spielberg, and George Lucas conducted in 2002–03. Additional information on New York and disaster movies was provided by *Ecology of Fear* by Mike Davis and *Celluloid Skyline* by James Sanders. Invaluable information on al Qaeda was supplied by *Holy War Inc* by Peter Bergen. Information on *The Matrix* and the *Lord of the Rings* trilogy was supplied by *Daily Variety, Entertainment Weekly, The Hollywood Reporter,* the *Los Angeles Times, The New York Times, The New Yorker, Newsweek, Time,* and *The Washington Post.*

BIBLIOGRAPHY

Amis, Martin. *The Moronic Inferno*. London: Jonathan Cape, 1986.

Andrews, Nigel. *Nigel Andrews on Jaws*. London: Bloomsbury, 1999.

————. *True Myths: The Life And Times of Arnold Schwarzenegger*. London: Birch Lane, 1996.

Arroyo, José, ed. *Action/Spectacle Cinema: A Sight & Sound Reader*. London: BFI, 2000.

Ashfield, Andrew, and Peter Le Bolla, eds. *The Sublime: A Reader in 18th-Century Aesthetic Theory*. Cambridge: Cambridge University Press, 1996.

Bach, Stephen. *Final Cut: Art, Money and Ego in the Making of Heaven's Gate, the Film That Sank United Artists*. New York: Morrow, 1985.

Balaban, Bob. *Spielberg, Truffaut and Me*. London: Titan, 2003.

Barber, Benjamin R. *Jihad vs. McWorld*. New York: Times Books, 1995.

Bart, Peter. *The Gross: The Hits, the Flops: The Summer That Ate Hollywood*. New York: St. Martin's, 2000.

————. *Who Killed Hollywood? And Put the Tarnish on Tinseltown*. New York: Renaissance, 2000.

Bart, Peter, and Peter Guber. *Shoot Out: Surviving Fame and (Mis)Fortune in Hollywood*. New York: Putnam, 2002.

Baxter, John. *Mythmaker: The Life and Work of George Lucas*. New York: Spike, 1999.

————. *Steven Spielberg: The Unauthorized Biography*. New York: HarperCollins, 1997.

Benchley, Peter. *Jaws*. New York: Hyperion, 1989.

Bergen, Peter. *Holy War Inc.: Inside the Secret World of Osama Bin Laden*. New York: Free Press, 2002.

Bettelheim, Bruno. *The Uses of Enchantment: The Meaning and Importance of Fairy Tales*. New York: Knopf, 1976.

Biskind, Peter. *Easy Riders, Raging Bulls*. New York: Simon & Schuster, 1998.

Bowser, Eileen. *The Transformation of Cinema, 1907–1915*. New York: Scribner, 1991.

Breskin, David. *Inner Views: Filmmakers in Conversation*. London: Faber & Faber, 1992.

Brooker, Will. *Using the Force: Creativity, Community and Star Wars Fans*. London: Continuum, 2002.

Brown, Karl. *Adventures with D. W. Griffith*. New York: Farrar, Straus & Giroux, 1973.

Bruck, Connie. *When Hollywood Had a King*. New York: Random House, 2003.

Campbell, Joseph. *The Hero with a Thousand Faces*. New York: Princeton University Press, 2004.

————. *The Power of Myth*. New York: Doubleday, 1988.

Cannadine, David. *Ornamentalism: How the British Saw Their Empire.* Oxford: Oxford University Press, 2001.

Champlin, Charles. *George Lucas: The Creative Impulse.* New York: Abrams, 1997.

Cook, David. *Lost Illusions: American Cinema in the Shadow of Watergate and Vietnam, 1970–1979.* New York: Scribner, 2000.

Davis, Mike. *Ecology of Fear: Los Angeles and the Imagination of Disaster.* New York: Metropolitan, 1998.

Drew, William M. *D. W. Griffiths's Intolerance: Its Genesis and Vision.* New York: McFarland, 1986.

Dunne, John Gregory. *The Studio.* New York: Farrar, Straus & Giroux, 1969.

Eisner, Michael. *Work in Progress.* New York: Random House, 1998.

Emery, Robert J. *The Directors: Take One.* New York: Allworth, 2002.

———. *The Directors: Take Two.* New York: Allworth, 2002.

Essoe, Gabe, and Raymond Lee. *DeMille: The Man and His Pictures.* New York: Barnes, 1970.

Eszterhas, Joe. *Hollywood Animal.* New York: Knopf, 2004.

Evans, Robert. *The Kid Stays in the Picture.* New York: New Millennium, 2004.

Fleming, Charles. *High Concept: Don Simpson and the Hollywood Culture of Indulgence.* New York: Doubleday, 1998.

Fox, Michael J. *Lucky Man.* New York: Hyperion, 2002.

Fried, Richard M. *The Russians Are Coming! Pageantry and Patriotism in Cold War America.* Oxford: Oxford University Press, 1998.

Friedman, Lester D., and Brent Notbohm, eds. *Steven Spielberg: Interviews.* New York: University Press of Mississippi, 2000.

Gabler, Neal. *Life, The Movie: How Entertainment Conquered Reality.* New York: Vintage, 1998.

Galipeau, Steven A. *The Journey of Luke Skywalker: An Analysis of Modern Myth and Symbol.* New York: Open Court, 2001.

Gilbey, Ryan. *It Don't Worry Me.* London: Faber & Faber, 2003.

Gottlieb, Carl. *The Jaws Log.* New York: Newmarket, 2001.

Griffin, Nancy, and Kim Masters. *Hit and Run.* New York: Simon & Schuster, 1996.

Hanke, Ken. *Tim Burton: An Unauthorized Biography of the Filmmaker.* New York: Renaissance, 1999.

Heard, Christopher. *Dreaming Aloud: The Life and Films of James Cameron.* New York: Bantam, 1998.

Hillier, Jim. *The New Hollywood.* New York: Continuum, 1994.

Hinton, David B. *The Films of Leni Riefenstahl.* New York: Rowman & Littlefield, 1991.

Jackson, Kevin, ed. *Schrader on Schrader.* London: Faber & Faber, 1990.

Jenkins, Garry. *Harrison Ford: Imperfect Hero.* New York: Replica, 2000.

Keane, Stephen. *Disaster Movies: The Cinema of Catastrophe.* New York: Wallflower, 2001.

Kenny, Glenn, ed. *A Galaxy Not So Far Away: Writers and Artists on 25 Years of Star Wars.* New York: Owl, 2002.

Kerman, Judith B., ed. *Retrofitting Blade Runner: Issues in Ridley Scott's Blade Runner and Philip K. Dick's Do Androids Dream of Electric Sheep?* New York: Popular, 1991.

Kline, Sally, ed. *George Lucas: Interviews.* New York: University Press of Mississippi, 1999.

Knowles, Harry. *Ain't It Cool? Hollywood's Redheaded Stepchild Speaks Out.* New York: Warner, 2002.

Kuhn, Annette, ed. *Alien Zone: Cultural Theory and Contemporary Science Fiction.* London: Verso, 1996.

Litwak, Mark. *Reel Power: The Struggle for Influence and Success in the New Hollywood.* New York: Morrow, 1986.

Mair, George. *The Barry Diller Story.* New York: Wiley, 1997.

Marsh, Ed W. *James Cameron's Titanic.* New York: HarperCollins, 1997.

Masters, Kim. *The Keys to the Kingdom: The Rise of Michael Eisner and the Fall of Everyone Else.* New York: Morrow, 2000.

McBride, Joseph. *Steven Spielberg: A Biography.* New York: Simon & Schuster, 1997.

McClintick, David. *Indecent Exposure: A True Story of Hollywood and Wall Street.* New York: Random House, 1985.

Medavoy, Mike. *You're Only as Good as Your Last One.* New York: Atria, 2002.

Miller, Mark Crispin, ed. *Seeing Through Movies.* New York: Pantheon, 1990.

Miller, Toby, ed. *Global Hollywood.* London: BFI, 2001.

Monaco, Paul. *The Sixties.* Los Angeles: University of California Press, 2003.

Morris, Edmund. *Dutch: A Memoir of Ronald Reagan.* New York: Modern Library, 1999.

Musser, Charles. *The Emergence of Cinema: The American Screen to 1907.* New York: Scribner, 1991.

Parisi, Paula. *Titanic and the Making of James Cameron.* New York; Newmarket, 1998.

Phillips, Julia. *You'll Never Eat Lunch in This Town Again.* New York: Random House, 1991.

Pollock, Dale. *Skywalking: The Life and Films of George Lucas.* New York: Random House, 1984.

Prince, Stephen. *A New Pot of Gold: Hollywood Under the Electronic Rainbow, 1980–1989.* New York: Scribner, 1999.

Pye, Michael, and Linda Miles. *The Movie Brats.* New York: Holt, Rinehart & Winston, 1984.

Salisbury, Mark, ed. *Burton on Burton.* London: Faber & Faber, 2000.

Sammon, Paul M. *Future Noir: The Making of Blade Runner.* New York: Harper, 1996.

———. *Ridley Scott: The Making of His Movies.* New York: Thunder's Mouth, 1999.

Sanders, James. *Celluloid Skyline: New York and the Movies.* New York: Knopf, 2001.

Sandler, Kevin S. and Gaylyn Studlar, eds. *Titanic: Anatomy of a Blockbuster.* New Brunswick, N.J.: Rutgers University Press, 1999.

Sardar, Ziauddin, and Merryl Wyn Davies. *Why Do People Hate America?* Disinformation Company, 2003.

Scanlon, Paul, and Michael Gross. *The Book of Alien.* London: W. H. Allen, 1979.

Schatz, Thomas. *The Genius of the System: Hollywood Filmmaking in the Studio Era.* New York: Pantheon, 1989.

Schickel, Richard. *D. W. Griffith: An American Life.* New York: Simon & Schuster, 1984.

Seabrook, John. *Nobrow: The Culture of Marketing, the Marketing of Culture.* New York: Knopf, 2000.

Shapiro, Marc. *James Cameron: An Unauthorized Biography of the Filmmaker.* New York: St. Martin's, 2000.

Shay, Don, and Jody Duncan. *The Making of Jurassic Park.* New York: Ballantine, 1993.

Speer, Albert. *Inside the Third Reich.* London: Trafalgar Square, 1969.

Spielberg, Steven, ed. *Letters to E.T.* New York: Putnam, 1983.

Stringer, Julian, ed. *Movie Blockbusters.* London: Routledge, 2003.

Thomson, David. *The Alien Quartet.* London: Bloomsbury, 1999.

———. *The New Biographical Dictionary of Film.* New York: Knopf, 2002.

———. *Showman: The Life of David O. Selznick.* New York: Knopf, 1992.

Vogel, Harold L. *Entertainment Industry Economics: A Guide for Financial Analysis.* Cambridge: Cambridge University Press, 1995.

Woodward, Christopher. *In Ruins.* New York: Random House, 2001.

Wyatt, Justin. *High Concept: Movie and Marketing in Hollywood.* Austin: University of Texas Press, 1994.

Yeffeth, Glenn, ed. *Taking the Red Pill: Science, Philosophy and Religion in the Matrix.* New York: BenBella, 2003.

PICTURE CREDITS

1) British Film Institute; 2) Lucasfilm; 3) Lucasfilm; 4) The Everett Collection;
5) The Everett Collection; 6) British Film Institute; 7) The Everett Collection;
8) The Everett Collection; 9) The Everett Collection; 10) The Everett Collection; 11) British Film Institute; 12) The Everett Collection; 13) The Everett
Collection; 14) The Everett Collection; 15) Getty Images; 16) Corbis; 17) The
Everett Collection; 18) The Everett Collection; 19) The Everett Collection;
20) Getty Images; 21) British Film Institute; 22) The Everett Collection;
23) The Everett Collection.

INDEX

Abyss, The, 196, 218, 250, 253
Academy Awards, 31, 39–40, 171, 241, 299, 305, 307–8, 310
action films, 28, 169–70, 171, 200, 201, 235, 261
    metamorphosis of, 145–48
    see also specific movies
Adams, John, 56–57
Addams Family, The, 265
Adventure Theater, 3
After School, 107
A.I., 291
Ain't It Cool? (Web site), 258–59
Airport, 9, 31, 167
Airport 1975, 32, 167
Airport '77, 31, 67, 167
Alien, 6, 34, 82, 86–95, 96–98, 110, 113, 116, 118, 147, 162, 169, 170
    academic analysis of, 93–95, 96, 119, 304
    early drafts of, 86–88
    filming of, 90–91, 116, 164
    sexual overtones in, 89, 93–94, 95
Alien: Resurrection, 173, 247
Aliens, 97, 145, 147, 150, 159, 162–64, 168–71, 183, 190, 250, 253, 296
    filming of, 164–66
    heavy use of gunplay in, 161, 165–66, 170
Alien^3, 137, 172
Allen, Irwin, 2, 31, 112, 236
Allen, Woody, 55
All the President's Men, 56, 181
Almodóvar, Pedro, 169, 226
al Qaeda, 295, 297
Altman, Robert, 9, 59, 225, 310
Always, 135, 223
Amblin, 137, 219
American Beauty, 311–12
American Graffiti, 45, 48, 51, 285
Amistad, 136
Andrews, Julie, 28, 29
Anna Karenina, 261
Annie Hall, 40, 55
Apocalypse Now, 63, 113, 118, 119

Armageddon, 8, 244, 265, 266, 294, 295, 299, 312
Aronofsky, Darren, 309
art films, 9, 34, 39, 57, 80, 208, 311, 312
    blockbusters as, 172–73
Astérix and Obélix, 57
Atari, 99, 129
At Long Last Love, 35, 50
Attenborough, Richard, 222
"auteurs," 5, 83–84, 179
Awakenings, 53
Azaria, Hank, 271

Bach, Danilo, 175
Bach, Steven, 211
Back to the Future, 6, 12, 34, 122, 151–54, 155–57, 158, 159, 197, 311, 312
    early drafts of, 125–27, 152–53
    filming of, 153–54
Back to the Future Part II, 158–59, 196
Baker, Rick, 127
Balaban, Bob, 73, 75
Balladur, Edouard, 225
Barrymore, Drew, 136
Barwood, Hal, 70
Basic Instinct, 245
Basinger, Kim, 190, 191, 194
Batman, 62, 69, 147, 183, 185–93, 194–98, 202, 242, 303
    critical response to, 189, 191–92, 195, 197, 213
    early drafts and rewrites of, 188–89, 190–91, 195
    filming of, 189–91
    marketing and merchandising of, 186–87, 191–94, 196
Batman and Robin, 259, 298
Batman Forever, 242
Baxter, John, 76–77
Beatles, 11, 35, 39, 71, 86, 125
Beatty, Warren, 132, 199, 200
Beautiful Mind, A, 299
Beetlejuice, 188, 189
Begelman, David, 72, 74
Bellow, Saul, 261

Benchley, Peter, 26, 32, 68, 223
Beneath the Planet of the Apes, 293
Bernstein, Elmer, 123
Bertolucci, Bernardo, 226
Beverly Hills Cop, 34, 150, 175, 176, 179
Biddle, Adrian, 164
Biehn, Michael, 144, 149
Big, 34
Big Momma's House, 263
Big Trouble, 265
Billy Jack, 26
Bingaman, Jeff, 131
Birth of a Nation, The, 29, 62, 85, 132
Biskind, Peter, 9, 10, 14, 35, 58–60, 61, 105, 311
Bisset, Jacqueline, 68
Black, Shane, 204
Black Stallion, The, 128
Blade Runner, 97, 112, 113, 114–21, 130, 304, 312
blockbuster films:
    academic analysis of, 14, 93–96, 118–19, 284, 304
    Academy Awards snubbing of, 39–40, 171, 307
    as "art," 172–73
    costs of, 35, 45, 67, 68, 72, 73, 74, 98, 105, 107, 116, 117, 124–25, 144, 162–63, 164, 201, 204, 205, 208, 209, 236, 240, 250–51, 253–55, 256–57, 262–63, 274, 299, 313
    critics of, *see* critics
    as "death of cinema," 9–11, 13–14, 34, 35, 58–60, 61, 63–64, 112–13, 151, 172, 225–26, 241, 250, 261–63, 311–12
    decline in quality of, 12–15, 155, 181–83, 199–200, 201, 243–44, 262–63, 274, 291, 302, 305, 312–13
    French attitudes toward, 57–58, 215, 224–26, 228
    globalization of, 215, 224–29, 241, 295–96
    "high concepts" and, 174–76, 177, 202
    Hollywood's attitude on, 13–14, 38–39, 98–99, 199–202, 211–12, 247, 250–51, 262, 299–300
    hype surrounding, 37–38, 77, 193–94, 241, 271, 276–77, 311
    marketing and merchandising of, *see* marketing; merchandising
    and metamorphosis of action movies, 145–47
    origin of term, 28
    politics and, 37, 131–33, 240–41
    product placement in, 133, 158–59
    rise of multimedia industry and, 60, 151, 180–82, 262, 274, 289

September 11th, 2001 terrorist attacks
    and, 293–95, 298, 300–301
silent era and, 60–62, 81
special effects in, *see* special effects
test screenings of, 23–26, 29, 50–51, 54–55, 75, 117, 154, 208, 209, 259, 273
theaters hurt by, 274–76, 290–91
word of mouth and, 29, 35, 36, 129–30, 197, 313
see also box office grosses; sequels; *specific films*
Blues Brothers, The, 107
Bogart, Humphrey, 108
Bogdanovich, Peter, 59
Bonfire of the Vanities, The, 201, 206
Bonnie and Clyde, 4, 58, 59
Boozer, Jack, Jr., 120
box office grosses, 7–9, 15, 27, 28–30, 69, 97–98, 273
    all-time lists of, 8–9, 16–19
    calculating of, 242
    drought of 1960s and, 30, 99, 262
    emerging importance of, 211–12, 242
    film quality and, 13–15, 242, 273–74, 288–89, 313
    in 1970s, 8, 9, 27, 30–31, 35, 41–43, 51–52, 64, 65–66, 76, 82–83, 97–98, 99–101
    in 1980s, 8, 83, 111, 112, 117–18, 121, 130, 138, 150–51, 158, 160, 180, 184, 196, 197–98
    in 1990s, 8, 210, 214, 224, 227, 229–30, 242–43, 246, 247, 248, 259, 263, 264, 272–73, 274, 277, 288–89, 292
    overseas, 214, 224, 227, 228, 229–30, 248, 263, 272, 274, 277, 313
    of sequels, 167
    in 2000s, 8, 291, 292, 300, 305–6, 307
    year-by-year lists of, 41–43, 64, 100–101, 138, 160, 184, 198, 214, 229–30, 248, 263, 277, 292, 305–6
Brando, Marlon, 98, 112–13
Braveheart, 296, 308
Brazil, 118, 190
Bride of Frankenstein, 168
Bridges, Jeff, 67
Bridge Too Far, A, 67
Broderick, Matthew, 271, 272
Bronson, Charles, 67
Brown, David, 23, 24, 27, 36–37, 70, 105
Brown, Karl, 62
Bruce Almighty, 303
Bruckheimer, Jerry, 174–75, 176, 177–78, 179, 182, 201, 202, 293, 294, 299
Buchanan, Pat, 131
Bugsy, 199, 203

Bullitt, 108
Bullock, Sandra, 242, 243
Burbank, Calif., 187–88
Burger King, 206, 207
Burton, Tim, 183, 217, 269, 310–11
  Batman and, 187, 188–91, 193, 195,
    198
Burtt, Ben, 283
Buscemi, Steve, 244
Bush, Dick, 164
Bush, George H. W., 131, 170
Bush, George W., 301, 302

CAA, 216–17
Cahiers du Cinéma (Truffaut), 84
California Raisins, 158, 193
Calley, John, 269
Call to Glory, 177
Cameron, James, 8, 12, 45, 85, 113, 137,
    143, 144, 147, 161–62, 171, 196, 218,
    248, 265–66, 269, 309
  Aliens and, 145, 162–66, 168, 169–70,
    250, 253
  childhood of, 4–5, 6, 249
  explosive temper of, 141, 148–50, 164,
    165, 249, 252–53, 254, 257–58
  Terminator and, 141–43, 144, 145, 147,
    148–50, 161, 169, 204, 250, 261
  themes in films of, 162, 169, 170
  Titanic and, 249–50, 251, 252–55, 256,
    257–58, 260–62, 311
Cameron, Mike, 5
Campbell, Joseph, 47, 93
Canby, Vincent, 146
Cannes Film Festival, 86, 257
Cannonball Run, The, 110
Canton, Mark, 202, 203, 204, 205, 206, 208,
    269
Cape Fear, 247
Capra, Frank, 195
Captive Women, 293
Carcopino, Jerome, 7
Carmike Theaters, 275, 290
Carpenter, John, 124
Carradine, Keith, 86
Carrey, Jim, 303
Carter, Jimmy, 132
Cartwright, Veronica, 90–91, 92
Cary Grant Theater, 298–99
Casablanca (film company), 186
Cash, Jim, 176–77, 266
Cassavetes, John, 33
Castle, William, 6
Castro, Fidel, 296
Caviezel, Jim, 304
CGI (computer-generated imaging), 12,
    62, 293, 312
  in *Jurassic Park,* 217–19, 220–21
  in *Phantom Menace,* 280–82, 286–87
  see also special effects
Cher, 183
Chernin, Peter, 249–50, 253, 258
Chinatown, 58
Chomsky, Noam, 295
Christian, Roger, 90
Cicero, Marcus Tullius, 7
Cimino, Michael, 211
Citizen Kane, 118
Cleopatra, 30
Clerks, 92–93
Clinton, Bill, 240
Clinton, George, 75
Clooney, George, 303
Close Encounters of the Third Kind, 70–71,
    72–76, 77–81, 82, 84, 99, 113, 127,
    129, 132, 134, 135, 181–82, 222, 228,
    236, 271, 312, 313
  filming of, 72–74
  marketing and merchandising of,
    74–75, 77
Cobb, Ron, 89, 296
Cobra, 180
Coca-Cola, 57, 127, 158, 248
Cocker, Joe, 176
Cocks, Jay, 58
Coen brothers, 269, 311
Cohen, Rob, 70
Collateral Damage, 297
Collins, Jackie, 182
Color Purple, The, 135, 136, 182, 223
Columbia, 30, 68, 71–72, 75, 76, 99, 127,
    128, 151, 181, 201, 202–3, 204,
    209–10, 217, 227, 268, 294
Columbia Tristar, 269
Columbus, Chris, 127, 310
Commentary, 35
Con Air, 266, 293
Conan the Barbarian, 144, 145, 296
Connery, Sean, 83, 110
Connick, Harry, Jr., 243
Conrad, Joseph, 86, 93
Contact, 299
Continental Divide, 107
Coppola, Francis Ford, 58, 59, 128, 168,
    171–72, 310
Corey, Harold, 61
Corman, Roger, 143–44
Cornblum, Warren, 289
Coward, Noël, 261
Cracknell, Derek, 189–90
Crane, Simon, 252–53
Creed, Barbara, 95
Crichton, Michael, 206, 216–17, 219,
    222–23

critics, 7, 9–11, 14, 35, 75, 83, 120, 134, 136,
       145–46, 151, 154, 155, 171, 180, 181,
       213, 241, 244, 270, 272, 273, 290,
       291, 311
    on *Batman,* 189, 191–92, 195, 197, 213
    on *Last Action Hero,* 210–11, 213
    of silent era, 60–63
    on *Star Wars,* 53, 56, 58–59, 63
    on *Titanic,* 261–62
Crowe, Russell, 296
Cruise, Tom, 147, 178, 180, 201, 266
Curtis, Tony, 94
Cusack, John, 266

Daley, Richard, 4
Daly, John, 142, 149–50
Damnation Alley (*Survival Alley*), 44
Dance, Charles, 208
Dances with Wolves, 227
Dangerous Days, 114
Dante, Joe, 127, 150, 187, 217, 310
Daviau, Allen, 129
Days of Thunder, 201
Day the Earth Stood Still, The, 236
Dean, James, 188
Death Wish, 67, 189, 195
de Bont, Jan, 227, 244–45, 246, 247–48,
       263, 269
Deeley, Michael, 114, 116, 117
Deep, The, 67, 68–69, 182
Deep End, The, 312
Deep Impact, 294
Deer Hunter, The, 56
De Laurentiis, Dino, 67, 68, 113
del Toro, Guillermo, 309
DeMille, Cecil B., 1, 29, 68, 200, 250, 265,
       302, 305
Demme, Jonathan, 144
De Palma, Brian, 50, 169
Depardieu, Gérard, 225
Deschanel, Caleb, 252
Devlin, Dean, 234–36, 237–38, 239–40,
       241, 267–68, 269, 270, 272, 273, 276,
       300–301
DiCaprio, Leonardo, 252, 254, 260, 295
Dick Tracy, 200, 201
Die Hard, 12, 34, 113, 145–46, 147, 166–67,
       204, 245
Die Hard 2: Die Harder, 159, 167, 210, 307
Die Hard: With a Vengeance, 245–46
Digital Domain, 137, 162, 255–56
Diller, Barry, 106, 112, 175
Dillon, Melinda, 78, 81
Dirty Harry, 146, 147
Disney, 8, 36, 126, 128, 188, 199–200, 201,
       202, 242, 259, 310
Disney, Walt, 8, 123, 282

Doctor Dolittle, 30, 99
Doctor Zhivago, 259
Dole, Bob, 240–41
Dole, Elizabeth, 240
Donner, Richard, 217
Douglas, Michael, 151
Dreamworks, 267
Dreiser, Theodore, 261
Dreyfuss, Richard, 32–33, 38, 39, 67, 79, 97,
       113, 134, 221, 243
Drive, He Said, 71
Driver, The, 87, 146
Dr. No, 83
Duel, 70, 80
Duel in the Sun, 29
Duellists, The, 86, 90, 116
Dune, 114, 150
Dykstra, John, 49

Earthquake, 32, 246
Eastwood, Clint, 98, 123, 148, 155
Easy Rider, 59–60, 71, 144
Easy Riders, Raging Bulls (Biskind), 9, 58–59
Eaton, William, 60
Eisner, Michael, 28, 98, 100, 104, 105–6,
       175–76, 177, 179, 181, 200, 228
Elliott, Ted, 268
Emerson, Ralph Waldo, 157
Emmerich, Roland, 227, 233–36, 237, 239–40,
       245, 247, 267, 269, 270, 272, 273
Empire of the Sun, 136, 223
Empire State Express, 61, 64, 130
Engel, Volker, 235, 236, 241
Engelhard, Steven, 187
Entertainment Merchandising, Inc., 75
Epps, Jack, 176–77, 266
E.T. the Extra-Terrestrial, 40, 78, 79, 80, 122,
       128–31, 132–36, 154, 221, 223, 228,
       259, 313
    box office grosses of, 17, 18, 130, 138,
       158, 197, 224
    critical response to, 134
    as cultural phenomenon, 130–31, 133,
       134
    early drafts of, 128–29
    marketing and merchandising of,
       129–30, 133–34, 135
Evans, Robert, 30–31
Evening's Entertainment, An, 62
Exorcist, The, 8, 9, 27, 59, 74
Exorcist II: The Heretic, 67

Fancher, Hampton, 112, 114, 115
Farber, Stephen, 35
Farrelly brothers, 263
Fiddler on the Roof, 28
Field of Dreams, 198

Field of Honor, A, 123
Fields, Verna, 24
Fierstein, Harvey, 243
Fincher, David, 137, 172, 296
Finding Nemo, 155, 312
Fire Down Below, 203
First Blood, 147
Fishburne, Laurence, 304
Fisher, Carrie, 51, 65, 93
Fithian, John, 275, 290
Five Easy Pieces, 63, 71, 112–13
Flanagan, William, 75
Flashdance, 157, 176, 179
Fleming, Ian, 296
Fleming, Victor, 29
Fog, The, 124
Fonda, Peter, 60
Forbidden Planet, 78, 86
Force 10 From Navarone, 110
Ford, Harrison, 50, 54, 58, 65, 110, 112, 128,
    129, 285
    in *Blade Runner,* 112, 116–17, 119,
      120–21
    as *Indiana Jones,* 102, 110, 111, 113
Ford, John, 121
Forrest Gump, 8, 40, 122, 299
48 Hours, 146, 176
For Your Eyes Only, 110
Fox, Michael J., 153–54
France, attitudes on blockbusters of, 57–58,
    215, 224–26, 228
Frankfurt, Stephen, 98
Freeman, Paul, 102
French Connection, The, 34, 59, 108, 146, 265
Friday the 13th, 183
Fried, Rob, 268, 269, 275
Friedkin, William, 9–10, 59
Friedman, Robert, 257
From Mao to Mozart, 132
Fugitive, The, 247
Furst, Anton, 187, 190, 192, 202

Gable, Clark, 29, 227
Gabler, Neal, 295
Gafner, Rabbi Zvi, 224
Galaxy Not So Far Away, A (Lethem), 10
Gale, Bob, 6, 106, 123–27, 152–53, 154, 157,
    158, 159, 311, 312
Gandhi, 40, 308
Ganis, Sid, 112, 202–3, 206, 208, 209, 210
Garbo, Greta, 129, 205
Garr, Teri, 78
GATT, 215, 225–26
Gerbrandt, Larry, 247
Gere, Richard, 178
Germinal, 224, 226
Geronimo, 268

Ghost, 201, 259
Ghostbusters, 34, 150, 169, 265, 266
Ghost Riders in the Sky, 263
Gibson, Mel, 168, 296
Giger, Hans Rudi, 89
Gilbert, Earl, 73
Giler, David, 86, 87, 90, 144–45, 162, 163,
    164, 165
Girl and Her Trust, The, 61
Gish, Lillian, 81
Gladiator, 295
Glover, Danny, 168
Godard, Jean-Luc, 124
Godfather, The, 6, 9, 26, 27, 30–31, 37,
    58–59, 63, 99, 118, 171–72
Godfather films, 168, 171–72
Godzilla (1998), 15, 267–71, 272–74, 275,
    290, 291, 294, 295
    marketing and merchandising of, 264,
      266, 267–68, 269–71, 272, 289
Godzilla films, 5, 95, 188
Goldberg, Whoopi, 183
Goldblum, Jeff, 241, 243, 244, 272
Goldman, William, 205
Gone With the Wind, 8, 28–29, 30, 37, 56,
    104–5, 200, 261, 262
Goodyear, Charles, 156
Goonies, The, 127, 155
Gossett, Louis, Jr., 178
Gottlieb, Carl, 32
Graham, Heather, 297
Grease, 9, 100
Great Balls of Fire!, 196
Great Britain, 57, 272
Great Escape, The, 123
Greatest Show on Earth, The, 1
Great Expectations, 259
Gremlins, 127, 150
Griffith, D. W., 29, 61–62, 68, 81, 132, 250,
    252
Grisham, John, 242
Grodin, Charles, 67
Grossman, Sam, 75
Guber, Lynda, 202
Guber, Peter, 68–69, 181–83, 185–86, 187,
    188, 189, 191, 196, 198, 202, 203,
    204, 206–7, 208, 211, 268, 269
Guinness, Alec, 65
Gulf + Western, 105

Haber, Kate, 116
Hackford, Taylor, 176, 178
Hackman, Gene, 4, 31
Hamill, Mark, 65, 112, 282
Hamm, Sam, 187, 190
Hanks, Tom, 294
Hannah, Daryl, 119

Hanover Street, 110
Harlin, Paul, 227
Harris, Richard, 67
Harry Potter and the Sorcerer's Stone, 299, 300
Hasbro, 277, 278–79, 289
Hauer, Rutger, 119
Havana, 199, 201
Hawks, Howard, 34, 84, 146, 162
Heavenly Creatures, 309
Heaven's Gate, 107, 211, 251
Heaven's Gate, Final Cut (Bach), 211
Heavy Metal (comic book), 114
Hecht's Metro Center, 193
Heir to the Empire (Zahn), 278
Hello, Dolly!, 30, 46, 99
Henderson, British ambassador, 302
Henn, Carrie, 165
Henriksen, Lance, 165
Herbert, Frank, 114
Herbie, 48
Hero with a Thousand Faces, The (Campbell), 47
Hershey, Barbara, 112
Hershey's, 133
Heston, Charlton, 32
"high concepts," 174–76, 177, 202
Hill, Walter, 87–88, 90, 144, 145, 146, 162
Hirsch, Judd, 243
Hirschfield, Alan, 72
Hitchcock, Alfred, 34, 84, 120, 247
Hoffman, Philip Seymour, 244
Hollywood, 8, 15, 28, 45, 56, 126, 146, 151,
     154, 181, 182, 197, 212, 235, 261,
     266, 291
   attitudes on blockbusters in, 13–14,
       38–39, 98–99, 199–202, 211–12, 247,
       250–51, 262, 299–300
   "auteurs" of, 5, 83–84, 179
   globalization of, 215, 224–29, 241,
       295–96
   response to September 11th by, 293–95,
       296–97, 298, 300–301
   silent era of, 60–62, 81
   studio system in, 104–5, 310
   see also blockbuster films; *specific films
       and filmmakers*
Hollywood Reporter, 210
Holm, Ian, 96
Home Alone, 227
Honey, I Shrunk the Kids, 137, 196
Honky Tonk Freeway, 34, 107
Hook, 135, 203, 221, 223
Hooper, Tobe, 92
Hope, Bob, 37
Hopper, Dennis, 59, 60, 245
horror films, 168, 183, 188
House on Haunted Hill, 6

Howard the Duck, 136, 137
Hudson Hawk, 100, 210
Hulk, The (comic book), 5
Humanoids from the Deep, 144
Hunt, Helen, 269
Hurd, Gale Anne, 143–44, 150, 161,
     162–64, 166
Hurt, John, 90–91, 92, 93–94
Hussein, Saddam, 170, 295–96
Hussein, Uday, 295–96
Huyck, Willard "Bill," 12, 48, 50, 106
"hype," 35, 37–38, 77, 193–94, 241, 271,
     276–77, 311

I'll Do Anything, 268
Independence Day, 8, 233–35, 236, 239–44,
     245, 246, 265, 269, 271–72, 294, 295,
     297, 300
   marketing of, 234, 239, 267–68, 270
   special effects on, 236–37, 239–40, 241,
       294
independent films, 14, 63, 241, 250–51, 263
Indiana Jones: *Raiders of the Lost Ark,* 11,
     40, 61, 79, 83, 102–3, 107, 109–12,
     113, 120–21, 128, 130, 135, 220, 221,
     266, 312, 313
   brainstorming for, 108–9
   marketing of, 111–12
   radical development deal for, 103–4,
       105–6
Indiana Jones and the Last Crusade, 13,
     102–3, 168
Indiana Jones and the Temple of Doom, 80,
     102, 150, 167, 196
Indiana Jones films, 6, 34, 102–3, 130, 147,
     159, 203, 309–10
Industrial Light & Magic (ILM), 45–47,
     49–50, 51, 84, 85, 137, 217–19,
     220–21, 279, 280–82, 299, 302
Inside The Deep (Guber), 68–69
Institute for Creative Technology, 296
Internet, 258–59, 284, 313
Intolerance, 62, 68, 81
Invasion of the Body Snatchers, 103
Ishtar, 110
It Happened One Night, 227
It Started in Naples, 227
It! The Terror Beyond Space, 86–87
I Wanna Hold Your Hand (film), 125

Jackson, Peter, 305, 307, 308–9
James, Henry, 261
Japan, 118, 133, 219, 224, 272
Jaws, 16, 32–41, 55, 58, 59, 63, 70, 72, 79,
     80, 93, 105, 106, 130, 135, 138, 143,
     195, 197, 215, 218–19, 221–22, 223,
     228, 239, 271, 294, 303

Academy Awards snubbing of, 39–40
box office grosses of, 9, 18, 27, 51, 99
critical response to, 35
as cultural phenomenon, 27–28, 35–39,
    131
lack of stars used in, 32, 97, 110, 112
marketing and merchandising of, 23,
    26–27, 32, 35–36, 44, 69, 74, 238
as "revolutionary" blockbuster, 12,
    33–35, 36–37, 64, 238, 243, 310, 312,
    313
rip-offs of, 67–69, 127, 144, 154, 175
test screenings of, 23–26, 39, 75,
    122–23, 313
Jaws 2, 67, 159
Jazz Singer, The, 213
Jobs, Steve, 137
Johnstone, Joe, 137
Jones, Tommy Lee, 265, 298
Jumanji, 137
Jurassic Park, 6, 7, 8, 58, 68, 76, 79, 206, 210,
    213, 215, 216–25, 227, 241, 242, 244,
    267
    as digital effects revolution, 213,
        217–19, 220–21
    early drafts and pacing of, 217, 221–23
    GATT free trade talks and, 225–26, 228
    marketing and merchandising of,
        219–20, 223–24
Jurassic Park: The Lost World, 7, 241, 247,
    267, 289, 298
Jurassic Park III, 291

Kael, Pauline, 127, 154
Kahn, Michael, 73, 109, 220–21
Kamar, 133
Kasdan, Lawrence, 57, 108
Katz, Gloria, 48, 49, 50, 106
Katzenberg, Jeffrey, 98, 175, 177
    memo written by, 199–201, 203
Kaufman, Philip, 103
Kavenagh, James, 82, 94–95
Kazanjian, Howard, 107, 108
Keaton, Buster, 111
Keaton, Diane, 132
Keaton, Michael, 185, 189, 303
Keenan, Brian, 295
Keitel, Harvey, 86
Kennedy, Kathy, 133
Kenner, 10, 66, 219, 278
Kenny, Chris, 190
Kilmer, Val, 178, 303
Kingdom Come, 71
King Kong (1977), 67
King Kong (2005), 309
King of Marvin Gardens, The, 71
Knoll, John, 279–80, 281–82

Knowles, Harry, 258–59
Koepp, David, 217, 219–20, 221
Kolb, William M., 119
Koszarski, Richard, 26
Kramer vs. Kramer, 28, 312
Kubrick, Stanley, 5, 96
Kurtz, Gary, 46, 85

Ladd, Alan, Jr., 45, 46, 50, 51–52, 55, 66, 86,
    90, 91–93, 115, 116–17
Lakewood Theater, Calif., 23–26
Lamont, Peter, 165, 251–52, 253
Landau, Jon, 253, 255
Lane, Anthony, 271, 297
Lang, Fritz, 247
Lang, Jacques, 225, 226
Lara Croft: Tomb Raider, 291
Lasseter, John, 137
Last Action Hero, 15, 110, 199, 204–10, 223,
    227, 251, 268
    critical response to, 210–11, 213
    early drafts and rewrites of, 204–6, 212
    marketing and merchandising of,
        206–8, 210, 213, 297
Last Days of the Raj, The, 87
Last Movie, The, 9
Last Picture Show, The, 9, 71
Lawrence, Martin, 259
Lee, Ang, 173, 309
Leff, Adam, 204
Legato, Rob, 299
Leigh, Vivien, 29
Le Parisien Libéré, 225
Lethal Weapon, 146
Lethal Weapon 3, 210, 245
Lethal Weapon 4, 168
Lethem, Jonathan, 10
Levin, Bob, 266–67, 269
Lewis, Huey, 155
Libération, 225
Lloyd, Christopher, 156
Lloyd, Jake, 281
Loews Cineplex, 290
London, England, 88, 157
Lonedale Operator, The, 61
Longbeach, Calif., 208, 209
    Jaws test screenings in, 23–26
Look Who's Talking, 197
Lord of the Rings, The (Tolkien), 307
Lord of the Rings: Return of the King, 8,
    307–9
Lord of the Rings: The Two Towers, 300
Lord of the Rings trilogy, 307, 308–9, 312
Los Angeles Times, 35, 192, 225, 257–58, 261
Lost World, The, 2
Lost World, The: Jurassic Park 7, 241, 247,
    267, 289, 298

Love Bug, The, 48
Lovejoy, Roy, 189–90
Love Story, 9, 30, 37, 99, 259
Lucas, George, 12, 56, 59, 76, 84–85, 123,
    137–38, 171, 220, 228, 229, 235, 258,
    271, 290, 299, 301–2, 305, 309
  childhood of, 2–3, 5, 6, 47, 54, 76
  cinema revolutionized by, 9–10, 11, 12,
    15–16, 45, 57, 58–59, 63–64, 83–84,
    144, 172, 310, 311
  early work of, 47–48
  Phantom Menace and, 8, 78, 275, 277,
    279, 280–83, 285–88, 289
  Raiders of the Lost Ark and, 11, 83,
    103–4, 105–6, 107, 108–9, 112
  as special effects and digital pioneer,
    46–47, 48, 51, 85, 136–37, 144, 218,
    286–87
  Spielberg's style vs., 3, 83–84, 85, 109, 111
  Star Wars and, 44–45, 46–47, 48–50,
    51–52, 57, 62–64, 65, 66, 82–83, 85,
    93, 103, 132, 136, 280, 281, 282, 283,
    285
Lucas, Marcia, 50, 51, 52
Lucasfilm, 84, 136–37, 276, 277, 278–79
Lucky Lady, 35, 70, 310
Lundgren, Dolph, 235

McBride, Joseph, 76
McCallum, Rick, 283
McCartney, Paul, 39, 75
McCloud (TV series), 123
MacDonald, Peter, 190
McDonald's, 9, 57, 65, 71, 219, 224
McGillis, Kelly, 179
McGregor, Ewan, 281
McKeown, Charles, 190
McTiernan, John, 204–6, 208, 210
McVeigh, Timothy, 233
Mad Max films, 155, 168
Magical Mystery Tour, 71
Magnificent Ambersons, The, 118
Mancuso, Frank, 100, 201–2
Mankiewicz, Tom, 187, 188
Mann's Chinese Theater, 45
Man of Iron, 132
marketing, 6–7, 13, 29, 37–38, 44, 63,
    68–69, 98, 150, 151, 193–94, 196,
    201, 203, 219, 237–38, 250, 266–67,
    274, 288, 310, 313
  backlash to, 211, 213, 241
  of *Batman,* 186–87, 191–94
  of *Close Encounters,* 74–75, 77
  of *E.T.,* 129–30
  of *Godzilla,* 266, 267–68, 269–71, 272
  of *Independence Day,* 234, 239, 241,
    267–68, 270

  of *Jaws,* 23, 26–27, 32, 35–36
  of *Jurassic Park,* 219
  of *Last Action Hero,* 204, 206–8, 209,
    210
  of *Phantom Menace,* 275, 276–77,
    282–83
  of *Raiders of the Lost Ark,* 111–12
  see also merchandising
Martin, Dean, 31
Martin, Hy, 26
Marvel Comics, 5, 6
Marvin, Lee, 148
Mathison, Melissa, 128–29, 131, 136
Matrix, The, 119, 304, 308, 313
Matrix Reloaded, The, 7–8, 173, 304, 305
Matrix Revolutions, The, 305
Matrix trilogy, 96, 303, 304–5
Matsushita, 206, 215
Mattel, 206
Mean Streets, 58, 285
Mechanic, Bill, 247, 250, 253, 254, 255,
    256–57, 262, 263
Medavoy, Mike, 141, 203
Me Myself and Irene, 263
Men in Black, 7, 264, 265–66, 267, 298
Men in Black II, 297–300
merchandising, 6–7, 11–12, 13, 29, 36, 40,
    74–75, 78, 99, 151, 180, 196, 241,
    262, 270–71, 307
  of *Batman,* 186–87, 192–93, 196
  of *Close Encounters,* 74–75
  of *E.T.,* 133–34, 135
  failures of, 264, 289–90
  of *Godzilla,* 264, 270–71, 289
  of *Jaws,* 36, 40
  of *Jurassic Park,* 219–20, 223–24
  of *Last Action Hero,* 206–7
  of *Phantom Menace,* 276–77, 289–90
  of *Star Wars,* 6, 10–11, 12, 66, 78, 133,
    135, 186, 277, 278–79, 280, 289, 307
  see also marketing
MGM, 30, 99, 104–5
Milius, John, 83, 124, 296
Miller, George, 182–83
Miramax, 63, 242, 250
Mission: Impossible, 169, 238
Mitchum, Robert, 148
Mitterrand, François, 225
Moon 44, 235
Moore, Roger, 110
More American Graffiti, 288
"motion control," 47
Motion Picture Association of America
    (MPAA), 100, 150, 225, 300
Movie Brats, The (Pye and Myles), 35
MTV, 57, 118, 196, 206
Mummy Returns, The, 291, 312

Murdoch, Rupert, 253, 258, 263
Muren, Dennis, 217–18, 221, 281
musicals, 30, 46, 262
    see also specific musicals
My Big Fat Greek Wedding, 290
Myles, Linda, 35
Mystic River, 312

NASA, 207, 209, 281
Nashville, 35, 63
National Association of Theater Owners,
    275, 290
Neeson, Liam, 281, 286
Newman, Paul, 70, 310
New Option, The, 266
Newsweek, 35, 39, 45, 255, 268
Newton, Judith, 95
New World, 143–44
New Yorker, 155, 271, 297
New York Times, 27–28, 35, 62, 69, 145–46,
    151, 207, 215, 225, 261, 278, 295
Nicholson, Jack, 60, 112, 183, 189, 191, 195,
    199, 203
nickelodeons, 61
Night Skies, 127–28
9 to 5, 98, 99
1941, 106, 107, 109, 111, 124–25, 221, 265, 313
Nixon, Richard, 132
Noah's Ark Principle, The, 235
Nolan, Chris, 309
Nolte, Nick, 68
Nothing to Lose, 259

O'Bannon, Dan, 86
O'Connell, Kevin, 299
Officer and a Gentleman, An, 34, 175–76,
    178, 179–80, 181
Olivier, Laurence, 94, 113
One Flew Over the Cuckoo's Nest, 40
1.42:08, 48
Orca, 67
Ordinary People, 40, 312
Orion, 144, 150, 203
Oscars, see Academy Awards
Other Side of Midnight, The, 45, 67
Outland, 110

Pacino, Al, 112, 168
Pack, The, 67
Paint Your Wagon, 30
Pale Rider, 155
Paltrow, Gwyneth, 297
Paramount, 28, 31, 67, 86, 99–100, 105, 106,
    111–12, 153, 175, 177, 180–81, 200,
    201–3, 250, 257, 258
Parton, Dolly, 98, 99
Passion of the Christ, The, 304

Patton, 132
Paxton, Bill, 269
Pearl Harbor, 8, 15, 291, 294
Peckinpah, Sam, 146
Pee-wee's Big Adventure, 188
Penn, Arthur, 9, 58, 310
Penn, Zak, 204
Peoples, David, 115
Pepsi, 158, 196, 248, 276
Peters, Kristine, 202
Peters, Jon, 75, 182–83, 185–86, 187, 188, 189,
    190–92, 193, 195, 196, 197, 198, 202
Peterson, Lorne, 46
Pfeiffer, Michelle, 183
Phillips, Julia, 17, 64, 73–74
Phillips, Michael, 71, 72
Pinocchio, 8, 73, 75
Pinwood Studios, 190
Piranha, 127
Piranha Part Two: The Spawning, 143, 144
Pirates of the Caribbean, 312
Pitt, Lou, 142, 204
Pixar, 85, 136, 137, 312
Planet of the Apes, 291
Pliny the Elder, 7
Pocahontas, 242
Poetic Justice, 268
Pollack, Sydney, 225
Pollock, Dale, 76
Pollock, Tom, 104
Porky's, 152
Porky's II: The Next Day, 152
Porky's Revenge, 152
Portman, Natalie, 281
Poseidon Adventure, The, 31, 33, 99
Premiere, 207, 250
Pretty Woman, 201, 227, 259
Price, Frank, 128, 201
Price, Vincent, 4
Princess Bride, The, 205
product placement, 158–59
Proser, Chip, 174–75, 177
Puig, Manuel, 257, 258
Pullman, Bill, 240, 243
Puzo, Mario, 98, 171–72
Pye, Michael, 35

Rabwin, Marcella, 29
Radio Flyer, 203
Radioland Murders, 136
Radnitz, Robert, 151
Ragtime, 132
Raimi, Sam, 309
Raise the Titanic, 34
Ralston, Ken, 47, 51, 299
Rambo films, 132, 159, 166, 227, 295
Rambo First Blood, 147

Rambo: First Blood Part II, 144, 145, 147, 149, 190
Rather, Dan, 131
Rawlings, Terry, 92
Ray, Nicholas, 195
Reagan, Ronald, 37, 122, 131–33, 134, 152, 240, 296
Rebel Without a Cause, 188
Redford, Robert, 199, 312
Reds, 132
Redstone, Sumner, 257
Reebok, 206
Reese's Pieces, 40, 133, 158
Reeves, Keanu, 94, 213, 245, 246, 303, 304, 305, 308
Reitman, Ivan, 187
Remar, James, 164
Reynolds, Burt, 53, 110
Rickman, Alan, 146
Right Stuff, The, 110
Rising Sun (Crichton), 219–20
RKO Pictures, 29
Robbins, Matthew, 70
Robe, The, 30
RoboCop, 146, 147, 167
Rock, The, 233, 294
Rocky, 167
Rocky III, 167
Roffman, Howard, 278
Rogers, Will, 194
Rolling Stone, 130
Rolling Stones, 86, 118
Romancing the Stone, 151
Romanelli, Dan, 186–87, 192
Room with a View, A, 180
Rose, Billy, 194
Rosemary's Baby, 98
Ross, Scott, 85, 137, 145, 161–62, 251, 255–56
Rossio, Terry, 268
Roth, Joe, 247
Rudin, Scott, 264, 265
Run DMC, 196
Rush Hour 2, 291
Russell, Greg, 299
Russia, 57, 157, 224

Safe Place, A, 71
Salkind, Ilya, 98
Sanchini, Rae, 255
Sarandon, Susan, 183
Saturday Night Fever, 99, 176
Sayles, John, 127
Scheider, Roy, 24, 25, 32, 159, 271
Schindler's List, 80, 135, 136, 216, 220, 221, 241
Schlesinger, John, 107

Schmitt, Jack, 131
Schneider, Bert, 71
Schneider, Harold, 253
Schrader, Paul, 65, 71, 151
Schwarzenegger, Arnold, 94, 131, 170, 203, 213, 227, 235, 260, 297, 300
    in *Last Action Hero,* 199, 204, 205–6, 207–8, 209
    in *Terminator* films, 113, 141–42, 144, 145, 148–49, 204
Science Fiction Studies, 82, 94, 95
Scorsese, Martin, 9, 34, 58, 59, 80, 144, 171, 310
Scott, Ridley, 86, 171, 311
    Alien and, 86, 88–89, 90–92, 93, 94, 96–97, 113, 116, 162, 164, 169, 170, 172
    Blade Runner and, 97, 112, 113–17, 119–20
Scream 2, 242
Screen Actors Guild, 256
Se7en, 119, 296
Sega, 219
Selznick, David, 28–29, 34, 200
Sennett, Mack, 111
September 11th, 2001 terrorist attacks, 300–301
sequels, 13, 66, 67, 97–98, 106, 130, 144, 186, 217, 223, 250, 262, 303, 307
    box office grosses of, 167
    1980s influx of, 159, 196
    rules of making, 159, 167–69
    see also specific sequels
Serpico, 112
Shaw, Robert, 68, 123
Shaw, Run Run, 116
Sheinberg, Sidney, 37–38, 106, 154, 158, 197, 216
Shepperton Studios, England, 89, 164
Sherak, Tom, 196, 237–38, 239, 242, 275–76
Shrek, 268
Sidewalks of New York, 297
Siege, The, 276
Siegel, Don, 146
Sight and Sound, 120
silent era, 60–62, 81
Silva, Sebastian, 257
Simpson, Don, 174–78, 179–80, 181, 182, 201, 202
Singer, Bryan, 263, 309, 311
Singin' in the Rain, 261
Skaaren, Warren, 177, 190
Skerritt, Tom, 90–91, 178
Skywalker Ranch, 106, 258
Small Soldiers, 267
Smith, Kevin, 92
Smith, Will, 213, 243, 244, 265, 266, 298

Snyder, David, 115
Sonnenfeld, Barry, 264–65, 266, 297–300
Son of Kong, 168
Sontag, Susan, 7
Sony, 97, 202, 203, 206, 207, 212, 215, 266–67, 268, 269, 270, 274, 275, 298, 299
Sony Imageworks, 299
Sorcerer, 9, 10, 45, 67
Sorcerer's Apprentice, 77
Sorrow and the Pity, The, 55
Sound of Music, The, 12, 28, 29, 30, 46
Spartacus, 94, 144
special effects, 4, 12, 44, 63–64, 74, 79, 98, 113, 144, 156, 159, 235, 246, 249, 299, 304, 311, 312
in *Independence Day,* 236–37, 239–40, 241, 294
in *Jurassic Park,* 213, 217–19, 220–21
in *Phantom Menace,* 280–82, 286–87
in *Star Wars,* 45–47, 49–51, 58, 62, 84, 279
in *Titanic,* 251, 254, 255–56, 257
Speed, 245–46, 269
Speed 2: Cruise Control, 247–48, 257, 262
Speer, Albert, 57, 302
Spider-Man (comic book), 5, 6
Spider-Man (film), 7–8, 297, 300, 307, 312
Spielberg, Steven, 8, 50, 56, 65, 106–7, 137, 138–39, 147, 171, 182, 215, 226, 235, 236, 246, 264, 267, 270, 271, 279, 288, 301, 305, 307, 313
childhood of, 1–2, 3, 5, 6, 30, 76, 77, 188
cinema revolutionized by, 9, 11, 12, 15–16, 34–35, 45, 58–59, 63–64, 83–84, 172, 243, 246, 310, 311, 313
Close Encounters and, 70–71, 72, 73–74, 75, 76, 77–81, 82–83, 106, 129, 135, 271, 313
E.T. and, 78, 79, 80, 127–30, 132–36, 149, 158, 197, 221, 223, 313
as executive producer, 125, 126, 127, 152, 153, 154–55, 246, 265, 298
Jaws and, 23–28, 32–34, 35, 36, 38, 39, 40–41, 67, 70–71, 72, 80, 106, 112, 122–23, 130, 135, 195, 215, 216, 221–22, 223, 303, 310, 313
Jurassic Park and, 76, 79, 206, 213, 215, 216–17, 218, 219, 220, 221–22, 223–24, 228
Lucas's style vs., 3, 83–84, 85, 109, 111
Raiders of the Lost Ark and, 11, 79, 83, 103–4, 105–6, 107, 108–9, 111–12, 128, 129, 135, 220, 221, 313
themes in films of, 78–79, 80, 134–36, 224
on today's blockbusters, 12–13, 216, 241, 250–51, 274

Zemeckis and, 122–23, 124–26, 152, 153
Squires, Scott, 281
Stallone, Sylvester, 167, 180
Stanfill, Dennis, 46, 65, 66
Stanton, Harry Dean, 96, 162
Starbeast, 86–87
Stargate, 234, 236
Star Is Born, A, 10, 75, 182
Starlog, 52, 259
Star Trek, 98, 296
Star Wars, 9, 12, 40, 44–60, 62–64, 84, 89, 92–93, 99, 110, 112, 113, 116, 132, 136, 149, 151, 174, 175, 218–19, 228, 236, 238, 275, 281, 282, 283, 285, 286, 287, 290, 296, 303, 310, 312, 313
box office grosses of, 9, 17, 18, 51–52, 65–66, 82–83, 97
critical response to, 53, 56, 58–59, 63
as "death of cinema," 9–11, 58–60, 61, 63–64, 112–13, 311–12
early drafts of, 48–49
influence of, 85–86, 138, 144, 235, 245
massive appeal of, 10, 52–58, 66, 74, 85
merchandising of, 6, 10–11, 12, 66, 74, 78, 133, 135, 186, 278–79, 280, 307
prequels to, 279, 286, 287, 288, 301, 302, 303, 309, 312
release of, 9–10, 51–52, 82–83
screenings of, 50–51, 54–55
special editions of, 279–80
special effects of, 45–47, 49–51, 58, 62, 84, 237, 279
struggles in making of, 44–47, 48–51
use of "junk" in, 53–54, 78, 103
see also Lucas, George
Star Wars: Episode I—The Phantom Menace, 8, 78, 275–77, 280–84, 285–90
digital effects of, 280–82, 286–87
fans backlash to, 284, 287–88
marketing and merchandising of, 275, 276–77, 282–83, 289–90
Star Wars: Episode II—Attack of the Clones, 287, 301
Star Wars: *Return of the Jedi,* 167, 278, 282, 285
Star Wars: *The Empire Strikes Back,* 12, 52, 84, 167, 282, 285
Steel, Dawn, 175
Stepford Wives, The, 35
Stewart, Douglas Day, 176
Sting, The, 9
Stoltz, Eric, 153, 154
Streisand, Barbra, 75, 182
Striking Distance, 268
Stuart, Gloria, 311

Sugarland Express, The, 38, 74
Superman, 34, 98, 99, 147, 167, 187, 188, 303
Survival Alley (Damnation Alley), 44
Suschitzky, Peter, 52
Sweet Tooth, 204, 205

Taking of Pelham One Two Three, The, 146
Taliban, 295
Tandem, 115, 116, 117
Tanen, Ned, 104, 125
Tarantino, Quentin, 171, 311
Tavernier, Bertrand, 225
Taxi Driver, 310
Ten Commandments, The, 29, 305
Terminator, The, 6, 12, 34, 61, 113, 141–44, 157, 161, 168, 169, 203, 204, 237, 250, 260, 261
    early drafts of, 142–43
    filming of, 148–50
    lack of marketing for, 150
Terminator 2, 149, 170, 205, 215, 218, 227, 237
test screenings, 29, 51, 75, 117, 154, 208, 209, 259, 273, 288
    of *Jaws,* 23–26, 75, 313
    of *Star Wars,* 50–51, 54–55
Texas Chainsaw Massacre, The, 92
Thank God It's Friday, 182
theaters, modern blockbusters as hurting, 274–76, 290–91
There's Something About Mary, 263
This Is Spinal Tap, 151, 252
Thomson, David, 7, 28, 151
Time, 30–31, 58, 130, 151, 197, 255, 268
Time Machine, The (Wells), 141, 157–58
Time to Kill, A, 242–43
Time Warner, 228
Tingler, The, 4, 6
Tippett, Phil, 217, 218
Titanic, 8, 40, 62, 247, 249–50, 251–62, 295, 308, 311
    costs of, 250–51, 253–55, 256–57
    critical response to, 261–62
    filming of, 251–56, 257–58
    special effects of, 251, 254, 255–56, 257
Tolkien, J. R. R., 307, 308
Tootsie, 34
Top Gun, 12, 157, 174–75, 177–81, 190, 201, 266, 312
    early drafts of, 176–77
Total Recall, 203, 227
Toubon, Jacques, 225
Towering Inferno, The, 9, 31–32, 99, 166–67, 236
Toy Story, 137
"trailer wars," 267–68

Training Day, 296–97
Trainor, Mary Ellen, 126
Treasure of the Sierra Madre, The, 108
Tricon Global Restaurants, 277, 289
Trip, The, 60
TriStar, 268
Truffaut, François, 70, 78, 84
Trumbell, Douglas, 74, 76
Turan, Kenneth, 261
Twentieth Century Fox, 30, 44, 45, 46, 50, 65–66, 67, 83, 86, 87, 89, 90, 98, 99, 150, 151, 162–63, 196, 200, 217, 233–35, 236, 237, 239, 240, 247, 249–50, 253, 255, 258, 259, 262, 275, 276, 289, 290
Twister, 8, 233, 238, 244, 245, 246–47
2000 A.D. (comic book), 10
2001: A Space Odyssey, 5, 44, 92
2010, 150
Two Jakes, The, 199, 201

Une femme ou deux, 163
United Artists, 30, 67
United Nations, 130, 133, 226, 233
Universal, 26, 27, 30, 32, 36, 37, 39, 44, 67, 70, 83, 99, 104, 105, 106, 123, 125, 127, 130, 133, 134, 153, 154, 201, 202, 206, 215, 216, 217, 219, 220, 227
Universal Soldier, 235
Updike, John, 261
Used Cars, 125, 151
Uslan, Michael, 69, 185–86
Usual Suspects, The, 263

Valenti, Jack, 100, 150, 225, 300
Van Damme, Jean-Claude, 235
Van Nuys, Calif., 45–47
Van Sant, Gus, 225
Variety, 26, 27, 28, 72, 97, 99, 155, 181, 197, 200, 210, 213, 226, 251, 255, 272, 276, 291, 299
Venice Film Festival, 225
Ventura, Michael, 134
Verhoeven, Paul, 227, 235, 245, 247
Verne, Jules, 84
Vertigo, 120
Viacom, 105
video industry, 60, 119, 180–82, 203, 207, 274, 289
View from the Top, 297
Viskocil, Joe "Boom Boom," 84, 237, 294–95

Wachowski brothers, 96, 156, 304
Wagar, W. Warren, 294
Wall Street Journal, 27, 130, 192
Walsh, M. Emmet, 115

Wanger, Walter, 226–27
Wargames, 132
Warner, Frank, 79
Warner, Jack, 105
Warner Brothers, 26, 30, 67, 99, 114, 116,
        186, 187, 189, 191, 192, 197, 201,
        202, 217, 234, 238, 242, 305
War of the Worlds, The (Wells), 294
Washington, Denzel, 296–97
Wasserman, Lew, 26, 39, 104, 105
Waterworld, 15, 68, 274
Weaver, Sigourney, 82, 89–90, 91, 96, 97,
        113, 163, 164, 165, 166, 169, 170,
        171
Wells, Frank, 187
Wells, H. G., 141, 157–58, 293, 294
Wells, Jeff, 209
Wenders, Wim, 226, 235
Wexler, Haskell, 48
Wharton, Edith, 261
White Buffalo, The, 67
White Dog, 175
Who Framed Roger Rabbit, 122, 299
Wilder, Billy, 215, 247
Wild Wild West, 15, 274
Williams, John, 11, 47, 65, 75, 98, 99
Williams, Steve, 218
Willis, Bruce, 113, 146, 159, 245–46
Willow, 48, 136, 137
Wilson, Woodrow, 132
Winger, Debra, 176
Winslet, Kate, 252, 254, 257–58, 260
Winston, Stan, 217

Witches of Eastwick, The, 183
Woo, John, 169
Woods, Cary, 268, 269
Woollcott, Alexander, 62
Working Girl, 157
World, the Flesh and the Devil, The, 294
World Trade Center, 233, 294, 297, 298
        see also September 11th, 2001 terrorist
        attacks

X-Men, 263, 303
X-Men (comic book), 5, 6

Yost, Graham, 245
Young Einstein, 196
Young Sherlock Holmes, 127, 217

Zabriskie Point, 34
Zahn, Timothy, 278
Zaillian, Steven, 216
Zanuck, Darryl, 105, 200
Zanuck, Richard, 12, 23, 24, 26, 27, 37, 70,
        105
Zelazny, Roger, 44
Zemeckis, Robert, 106, 122–27, 151, 157,
        310
        Back to the Future and, 125–27, 151–53,
        154, 156, 157, 158, 159, 311, 312
        childhood of, 4, 6
        Spielberg and, 122–23, 124–26, 152
Zimmerman, Herman, 296
Zsigmond, Vilmos, 72–73

ABOUT THE AUTHOR

TOM SHONE was born in Horsham, England, in 1967. From 1994 to 1999 he was the film critic of the London *Sunday Times,* and has since written for a number of publications, including *The New Yorker, The New York Times,* the London *Daily Telegraph,* and *Vogue.* He currently lives in Brooklyn, New York. This is his first book.